The Visitor's Guide to the Birds of the Central National Parks

UNITED STATES AND CANADA

Roland H. Wauer

ILLUSTRATIONS BY MIMI HOPPE WOLF

John Muir Publications
Santa Fe, New Mexico

John Muir Publications, P.O. Box 613, Santa Fe, New Mexico

© 1994 by Roland H. Wauer
Cover © by John Muir Publications
All rights reserved. Published 1994.

Printed in the United States of America

First edition. First printing August 1994.

Library of Congress Cataloging-in-Publication Data
Wauer, Roland H.
  The visitor's guide to the birds of the central national parks :
  United States and Canada / by Roland H. Wauer
      p.   cm.
Includes bibliographical references and index.
ISBN 1-56261-140-2 : $15.95
    1. Bird watching—United States—Guidebooks. 2. Bird watching—
  Canada—Guidebooks. 3. National parks and reserves—United
  States—Guidebooks. 4. National parks and reserves—Canada—
  Guidebooks. 5. Birds—United States. 6. Birds—Canada. I. title.
QL682.W38 1994
598'.0723473—dc20   94-912
                                               CIP

Design: Ken Wilson
Illustrations: Mimi Hoppe Wolf
Typeface: Minion
Typography: Marcie Pottern
Printer: Malloy Lithographing, Inc.

Distributed to the book trade by
W. W. Norton & Company, Inc.
New York, New York

Cover photo: Cedar waxwing, Photo Researchers, Inc.

Contents

Great Plains

Southern

Foreword

It is with much pleasure that I write this foreword to *The Visitor's Guide to the Birds of the Central National Parks: United States and Canada*. The Humane Society of the United States (HSUS) is proud to provide, through this important book, an expanded opportunity for wildlife appreciation to those who visit our national parks.

The HSUS has been known widely for its proactive advocacy-oriented programs to protect animals. We have championed the cause of companion animals, urging those who acquire pets to treat them with consideration and care. We have worked to eliminate the suffering of animals used in laboratories and have aggressively advanced the use of alternatives. We have challenged the all too prevalent inhumane rearing of farm animals and successfully helped promote reforms within the industry, while at the same time urging a reduction and replacement of meat and other farm products in one's diet.

Our wildlife programs have been equally forceful and proactive. Among them are the elimination of commercial killing of fur seals on Alaska's Pribilof Islands and the slaughter of the world's great whales, halting the sale of elephant ivory, protecting from destruction animals that would have been destined for fur fashions, and saving millions of animals from brutal elimination under predator control programs.

The HSUS, an organization of more than a million and a half constituents, is equally committed to promoting an appreciation and enjoyment of wild animals and wild places. This book opens the doors to that appreciation in a unique and authoritative way. Ro Wauer, drawing amply on his lifelong interest in and love for animals, walks each visitor through the national park units of the central states and provinces with the skill and accomplished grace of a dedicated birder and naturalist. Firsthand, the reader is drawn into the habitat and environment of each park and its bird life. Through these pages, the reader feels the interrelations and interaction of the animals and plants and the enjoyment of a lifetime spent in studying the intricacies of nature.

For my family, this book, with its invitation to sight a particular bird and then move quickly on to discover another, is far more important than a field guide. This book encourages the reader to know a park and understand its animal life in a way that all concerned citizens must if essential qualities of our parks are to be preserved for future generations.

Finally, the HSUS is pleased and gratified to have a book of this quality that actively encourages wildlife enjoyment and environmental appreciation. To protect wildlife, people need to understand wild creatures more thoroughly and to appreciate the subtleties of their interaction with the environment that sustains them. This book provides the knowledge and information that can make these values truly available to each reader.

Ro Wauer has done a magnificent job of integrating his own special interest in wildlife and his personal commitment to environmental quality into a readable text that will make park exploration an exciting and unique experience. I wish you many delightful visits.

April 15, 1994
Washington, D.C.

John A. Hoyt
Chief Executive
The Humane Society of the United States
President, Humane Society International

Preface

The national parks of the United States and Canada possess the best examples of the continent's natural heritage, complete with the grandest scenery and most stable plant and animal communities still in existence. In a large sense, North America's national parks represent a microcosm of our last remaining wildlands.

The Visitor's Guide to the Birds of the Central National Parks: United States and Canada describes the bird life in each national park in the central states and provinces. This book is intended to introduce the park visitor to the most common and obvious birds and to the fascinating world of bird identification and behavior. In addition, the book can be used as a reference to the park and its bird life during a park visit, as well as a valuable tool in preparing for that visit.

Birds of the Central National Parks is not intended to be used as a field guide or a book on bird identification per se. Several excellent field guides, which are already available, can be used as companion volumes to this book. Nor is this book intended to help the birder find the rarities or out-of-the-way specialties. Its purpose is to help the park visitor better appreciate the park and its bird life. If, in making new acquaintances, the park visitor should become interested in birds and more concerned about their well-being, all the better.

Thirty-one national parks are included in this book, from Canada's Elk Island and Prince Albert national parks, numerous parks surrounding the Great Lakes, south to Amistad and Padre Island in Texas, and Jean Lafitte in Louisiana. The 31 parks are grouped into four geographic or biotic regions: the Northern

Forest, Eastern Deciduous Forest, Great Plains, and Southern. The four categories provide continuity in discussion of the parks and the biotic communities they contain, as well as a perspective for planning a trip.

Each chapter begins with a personalized experience that might occur to anyone visiting the park. At Voyageurs, for example, the reader is introduced to that park through a morning canoe trip. Each chapter then continues with a description of the park, including its plant and animal communities, visitor facilities, interpretive activities, and addresses and telephone numbers for additional information. The chapter then returns to the bird life, describing common birds within several of the area's most popular and accessible places to visit. Each chapter ends with a summary of the park's bird life and a list of a few key species.

A visit to any of the national parks should begin with a stop at the visitor center or information station to obtain a park brochure and activity sheet. These will contain basic information about roads and trails, accommodations, campgrounds, picnic sites, hiking routes, interpretive activities, descriptions of the park's key resources, and so on. The numerous sites mentioned in the book can best be located by using the area map found in the park brochure.

Common bird names used throughout the book, including a comprehensive checklist at the end of the book, are taken from the most recent checklist of birds published by the 1994 American Ornithologists' Union (AOU) and used in all the up-to-date field guides. In the case of plants, because common plant names vary so much from one part of the country to another, a list of all common plant names used, along with their scientific names, is included following the bird checklist.

A bibliography includes all references used by the author in writing this book, in hopes that the reader will utilize the references for continued study of bird life.

—Roland H. Wauer

Acknowledgments

This book would not have been possible without the kind assistance of dozens of employees of the U.S. and Canadian national park systems: superintendents, rangers, naturalists, resource specialists, and others. I especially want to thank the following individuals: Anne Quintard at Agate Fossil Beds; Elizabeth Armijo, Larry Barnett, Deborah Nordeen, and Superintendent Robert Reyes at Amistad; Betsy Bartelt, Kayci Cook, Neil Hauk, Bob and Susan Mackreth, Michael Marion, Nancy Peterson, and Julie Van Stappen at Apostle Islands; Valarie Naylor and Joe Zarki at Badlands; Dave Baker and Mary Reed at Big Thicket; Jennifer Barratt and Marc Wiercinski at Bruce Peninsula; John Apel, Superintendent Jack Linahan, Rhonda Terry, and Doug Wilson at Buffalo River; Chris Czazasty and Randy Fehr at Chickasaw; Diane Chelfant, Paul Motts, and Garry Williamson at Cuyahoga Valley; Miki Hassel, George San Miguel, and Richard Smith at Devils Tower; Ken Green and Dennis Madsen at Elk Island; Maureen Briggs, Superintendent Dean Einwalter, John Myrured, and Rick Yates at Grand Portage; Florence Miller, Leon Perault, Vicki Sahanatien, and Jacques Saquet at Grasslands; Earl Adams, Mark Blaeuer, Superintendent Roger Giddings, and Mary Smith at Hot Springs; Jack Arnold, Ken Brock, Eddie Childers, Bob Daum, Ralph Grundel, Randy Knutson, Noel Pavlovic, and Bill Supernaugh at Indiana Dunes; Paul Gerrish, Terry Lindsay, Candy Peterson, and Rolf Peterson at Isle Royale; David Muth, Percy Prestenbach, and K. M. Schoenberger at Jean Lafitte; Michael Gossett and Cindy Von Halle at Ozark Riverways;

Paul Eubank and John Lujan at Padre Island; Michelle Baldwin, Gregg Bruff, Brian Kenner, and Walter Loope at Pictured Rocks; Tom Hince, Mike Malone, Laurel McIvor, and Jennifer Tiessen at Point Pelee; Michael Fitzsimmons and Bill Garner at Prince Albert; Robin Heron, Doug Tate, and Craig Zimmerman at Pukaskwa; Celes Davar, Koren Kines, and Diana McIntyre at Riding Mountain; Robert Manasek at Scotts Bluff; Neal Bullington, Max Holden, Bev and Clair Postmus, and Frank Spitzer at Sleeping Bear Dunes; Superintendent Pete Hart and Bruce Kaye at Theodore Roosevelt; Carol Borneman, Mac Brock, and Bob Whistler at Voyageurs; Denise Dowling, Larry Hays, Thomas Kopp, Mike and Mary Laycock, Ed Rossi, and Superintendent Jimmy Taylor at Wind Cave.

I also want to thank Jan Hartke and President John Hoyt of the Humane Society of the United States (HSUS) and Earthkind. The monetary assistance provided by HSUS made possible the travel and research required for this book. Their contributions are most appreciated.

This project was the idea of my friend Bob Cahn, who provided encouragement throughout. Pat Cahn also lent her editorial expertise in the initial development of ideas and review of early chapters.

A few additional folks were involved with the production of this book. Artist Mimi Hoppe Wolf's wonderful pen-and-ink sketches have greatly enhanced many of the highlighted bird species. Bill Coville produced the maps. And I am indebted to the entire staff at John Muir Publications for their cooperation and professionalism; editor Elizabeth Wolf has been particularly helpful and extremely easy to work with.

Last, but certainly not least, I thank my wife, Betty, who supported this project with editorial advice and assistance as my "travel slave" throughout the 15,200 miles we traveled in preparation of this book.

1

Birds—What They Are and How to Find Them

The bond between birds and man is older than recorded history. Birds have always been an integral part of human culture, a symbol of the affinity between mankind and the rest of the natural world, in religion, in folklore, in magic, in art—from early cave paintings to the albatross that haunted Coleridge's Ancient Mariner. Scientists today recognize them as sure indicators of the health of the environment. And as modern field guides make identification easier, millions of laymen watch them just for the joy of it.

—Paul Brooks

How often I have wished I could fly. To soar high over the mountains and valleys. To explore secluded places that are impossible to reach any other way. To escape this earthbound existence with the ease of a bird. These were among my secret desires as a youngster. How I envied the hawks and the swallows and even the tiny hummingbirds. They were the masters of my universe.

Only birds and bats, of all the warm-blooded creatures, can fly for more than a few yards. Only birds possess the combination of feathers, powerful wings, hollow bones, a remarkable respiratory system, and a large, strong heart. They are truly magnificent flying machines. The power of a wing beat, due to the marvelous flight feathers, allows a bird to cruise at speeds of 20 to 40 miles (32-64 km) per hour while flying nonstop across the Gulf of Mexico or the Arctic tundra. The tiny hummingbird has been clocked at 50 miles (80 km) per hour. And the powerful peregrine falcon is thought to stoop at speeds in excess of 200 miles (322 km) per hour.

A blue-winged teal banded in Quebec, Canada, was killed by a hunter less than four weeks later in Guayana, South America, more than 2,500 miles (4,023 km) distance. A Manx shearwater, taken from its burrow on Skokholm Island, Wales, and carried by airplane to Boston, Massachusetts, returned to its burrow on the 13th day, having flown 3,000 miles (4,828 km) across the Atlantic Ocean. And a lesser yellowlegs banded in Massachusetts was captured six days later 1,900 miles (3,058 km) away on Martinique, in the Lesser Antilles. That bird had averaged 317 miles (510 km) per day.

Migrating birds usually fly below 3,000 feet (914 m) elevation, but observers at 14,000 feet (4,267 m) in the Himalayas reported storks and cranes flying so high overhead, at an estimated 20,000 feet (6,096 m) elevation, they could barely be seen through binoculars.

Other marvelous features of birds are their bill shapes and sizes. Anyone who has watched birds for any time at all cannot help but notice the diversity of feeding methods. Hummingbirds, for example, have long, thin bills that they utilize to probe into flowers to feed on nectar, sometimes deep inside tubular flowers. Their bills are especially adapted to this type of feeding. Many shorebirds, such as dowitchers and common snipes, also have long bills, but they are much heavier for probing for food in mud. The long-billed curlew's bill can reach into deep burrows to extract its prey.

The many insect feeders have dainty bills for capturing tiny insects. Vireos and warblers are gleaners that forage on trees and shrubs, picking insects off leaves and bark. A careful examination of feeding warblers will further suggest the size of their preferred food on the basis of their bill size. Flycatcher and swallow bills are wider to enhance their ability to capture flies in midair. Woodpecker bills are specialized so they are able to drill into insect-infested trees and shrubs to retrieve the larvae there.

Finch bills are short and stout, most useful for cracking seeds or crushing armored insects. Crossbills are able to extract seeds from conifer cones. And grosbeaks are able to feed on much larger fruit, actually stripping away the husk from fleshy seeds. Many birds feed on fruit when it is abundant in late summer and on insects at other times of the year.

And then there are the predators with their variety of bill shapes and sizes. Raptors possess short, stout bills with a specialized hook for tearing apart prey. Wading birds possess large, heavy bills for capturing prey. And diving birds have bills that are hooked for catching fish and serrated on the edges for a better grip.

Feet are another fascinating feature of anatomy helpful to understanding a bird's requirements. Webbed feet suggest adaptation to water for swimming, and flattened toes help birds walk on soft mud. Tiny, flexible toes suggest an ability to perch on small twigs and branches. And large, powerful feet with sharp talons are required to capture and grip prey.

There are about 9,600 kinds of birds in the world; about 900 of those are found in North America. And every one has slightly different characteristics that permit it to utilize a slightly different niche (the combination of its needs) from any other species. Whenever two or more species have the same needs, in all likelihood only one will survive.

A bird is a very specialized creature, indeed, but its bill and feet are usually less obvious than its plumage, the sum total of its feathers. A bird's plumage is unquestionably its most obvious and usually most attractive characteristic. This is especially true for the more colorful and contrasting birds, such as warblers, hummingbirds, some waterfowl, and some finches. Birds are the most colorful of all vertebrates.

Feathers reveal every color in the rainbow. The colors we see are the product of pigments and the reflection and refraction of light due to feather structure. The concentration of pigments produces intensities of color, as in the vivid red of a male vermilion flycatcher and the diluted red of a female northern cardinal. The total lack of pigment production results in white plumage. Many colors we see are due to light that may be reflected or absorbed by feathers. The bright blues of Steller's jays or bluebirds are due to a particular arrangement of cells in the feather, which produces iridescence. A dull velvet color is the reversal of iridescence.

Of all the aesthetically pleasing characteristics of birds, birdsong may be the most enduring. Louis Halle wrote, "As music is the purest form of expression, so it seems to me that the singing of birds is the purest form for the expression of natural beauty and goodness in the larger sense, the least susceptible of explanation on ulterior practical grounds."

But birds possess additional values that are sometimes ignored, perhaps because they are often taken for granted. For instance, certain birds are extremely adept at catching and consuming large quantities of insects, many of which are considered pests. These include obnoxious insects, as well as those that are a serious threat to food crops.

Human beings have utilized birds from earliest history. Birds were worshiped by many early civilizations. Cormorants were ringed for catching fish. Pigeons carried our messages. Songbirds were taken into mines and brightened our homes with their wonderful songs. In literature, Samuel Coleridge has immortalized the albatross, Percy Shelley the lark, and Edgar Allan Poe the raven. The concept and development of manned flight was derived from observations of birds. Every state and province has an official bird, many of which highlight flags and seals. Most Canadian coins and paper money display common bird species. And the most powerful country in the world utilizes a bird as its symbol: America's bald eagle is one of the most visible symbols in the United States.

Birds truly are an intricate part of the human ecosystem, an important link to nature. Birds, more than any other creatures, are obvious and omnipresent companions to the human community.

Birding for Fun

There comes a time when those of us with a natural curiosity and appreciation for the outdoors want to know the names of the various creatures we see around us. The spark to identify birds may be kindled by some exceptional happening or a special sighting. Watching a family of gray jays at a campground as they actively investigate you and your food supply or suddenly being mobbed by a flock of cliff swallows at a nest site is likely to foster interest in those species and what they are about.

But identifying those birds can be somewhat difficult unless you know where to begin. Although the average park visitor usually can identify more birds than he or she might first assume, further identification requires some basics, just like any other endeavor. The basics include two essential pieces of equipment: a field guide and a pair of binoculars.

There are several very good field guides that utilize the bird identification technique developed by Roger Tory Peterson. Peterson's field guides and those published by the National Geographic Society and Golden Press utilize bird paintings. These guides are preferred over those with photographs, because the paintings highlight key features that only occasionally are obvious in photographs.

Binoculars are absolutely essential for identifying, watching, and enjoying most birds. Binoculars vary in power, illumination, and field of vision, as well as price. The most popular birding binocular is an 8x35 glass. "8x" is the power of magnification; "8x" magnifies a bird eight times, "7x" magnifies a bird seven times, and so on. "35" is the diameter of the objective lens in millimeters and is used to illustrate illumination. Illumination (brightness) can be determined by dividing the magnification into the size of the optical lens; a 7x50 binocular produces a brighter image than a 8x35 binocular by 7.1 to 4.4. Although the 50mm binocular provides a brighter image than the 35mm and is better in dim light, it usually is too heavy for a full day in the field. Also, binoculars 9x and above are often too powerful for beginners who are not yet comfortable with holding binoculars perfectly still. Pocket-sized, lightweight binoculars (those with a small objective lens) are good for occasional use, but continuous use can cause eyestrain. Select binoculars that are best suited for you.

Field of vision, determined by the binocular design, usually is also marked in degrees (angle visible out of 360 degrees) or feet (width visible out of 1,000 ft. or 305 m). The 7.3 degree field of vision (out of 360 degrees) for my wife's 9x35 Discoverer binoculars and the 395 feet of vision (out of 1,000 ft.) for my old 9x35 Burton binoculars, will remain the same no matter what the distance of the bird being observed.

In addition, central-focus binoculars are a must. Minimum focusing distance is important, as well, for focusing on a bird that may be as close as 12 to 15 feet (4-6 m). Binoculars range widely in price, but the moderately priced ones usually work just as well as the most expensive, which may be more water resistant, less inclined to fog, and armored for rough use.

Using binoculars usually requires some experimentation, but the skill is easy to learn. First make sure that the right ocular is set at "0" for 20/20 vision. Then while looking directly at an object, bring the binoculars into position without changing your position or looking elsewhere, and use the center wheel to focus on the object. A few tries will produce immediate success.

The next step is to get acquainted with your field guide. Start with leafing through the entire guide and locating the first page of tyrant flycatchers, just beyond woodpeckers. Flycatchers and all the birds illustrated beyond are perching birds (songbirds). All the non-perching birds (seabirds, waders, waterfowl, raptors, shorebirds, gulls and terns, grouse, hummingbirds, woodpeckers, etc.) are located within the first portion of the book.

Next read the introductory section, especially the discussion about field marks. You will find a drawing of a typical bird showing basic field marks. Look these over so that you have a good idea of where the bird's crown, eye line, eye ring, chin, upper and lower mandibles, flank, upper tail and under tail coverts, wrist, wing bar, and so on, occur. Be ready to refer to this illustration for help when necessary.

Now that you have discovered the value of a field guide, it is time to start identifying real birds. You should have an idea of what features to look for. The following suggestions provide an identification strategy of sorts:

1. Size. It is a good idea to relate bird size to those species you already know. For instance, consider five categories: sparrow-size, robin-size, pigeon-size, duck-size, and heron-size. With a few exceptions, such as the common raven, any bird the size of a duck or larger is a nonperching bird and will be found in the first half of the field guide. By thinking size, you immediately know where to start your search. Also, one can often pick out odd-sized birds in a flock for further attention or to recognize different species that might be foraging together. For example, a tiny bird within a party of warblers will more than likely be a chickadee, kinglet, or brown creeper.

2. Shape and behavior. Does your bird possess any outstanding features? Is it a wader with long legs and an upright posture? Possibly a heron. Is it walking along the shoreline? Possibly a shorebird. Is it swimming on a lake or river? Probably a waterfowl or gull. Is it soaring high in the sky? Possibly a turkey vulture or hawk. Is it perched on a wire or tree limb? Certainly a perching bird. Is it a perching bird eating seeds at a feeder? Probably a sparrow or finch. If it is smaller

than a sparrow, is creeping up a tree trunk, and is all brown, it is sure to be a brown creeper.

3. Color and pattern. Obvious plumage is an immediate give-away. Cardinals, crows, robins, yellow warblers, and red-winged and yellow-headed blackbirds are the first to come to mind. Their bold and obvious color or pattern, or both, stand out like a sore thumb. But many of their neighbors will require more study. Do the all-white underparts extend onto the back, or does your bird have only white wing bars? Does its white neck extend only to the lower mandible or onto the face? Does its reddish color extend onto the back, or is it limited to the tail and wings? Do the yellow underparts include the throat and belly or only the chest? Answering these questions will eventually become second nature to you.

Field Techniques
Bird-finding techniques are often personal ones, and you will discover your own methods. For example, I like to move very slowly through a particular habitat, trying to discover all of the birds within that immediate area. I find that part of birding most enjoyable and challenging. Other birders prefer to move faster, stopping only to watch birds that become obvious. This method is based on the concept that they will find more birds by covering more ground. That is definitely the reason for visiting as many habitats as possible, but I believe that the largest number of species can be found by slowly moving through each habitat, making yourself part of the scene, both physically and mentally.

There are definite clues to bird finding that you can use to your advantage. First are bird sounds. During the breeding season, bird-song is the best indicator of a bird's presence and location. Songbirds often sing throughout the day. They almost always sing at dawn and dusk, but a few species sing only at dawn. The more serious birders get out at dawn to experience the dawn chorus while other birders are still asleep. The majority of the birds, however, can usually be found throughout the day.

Rustling leaves in the underbrush can be another valuable clue. Leaf rustling can be caused by numerous creatures, but when the leaves seem to be thrown back as if being cleared away for finding food underneath, the rustler is likely to be a thrasher, fox sparrow, or rufous-sided towhee.

Songbirds tend to ignore intruders who are quiet and move slowly, unless they get too close to a nest or fledgling. You can get surprisingly close to songbirds by moving slowly. Also, wearing dull-colored clothing helps you to blend into the environment, usually permitting closer viewing.

Some of the nonperching birds will permit a slow, cautious approach, but wading birds, ducks, and raptors are not as trusting. You will need to observe these birds from a distance, and you may want to use a spotting scope for these observations. Or you may be able to use a blind, sometimes installed at bird-viewing sites.

During the nonbreeding season, birds often occur in flocks or parties. Flocks of waterfowl or blackbirds can number in the hundreds or thousands and be readily visible from a considerable distance. But a party of songbirds moving through the forest will require quiet study for identifying all the members. It is possible to wander through the woods for some time before discovering a party of birds that may include a dozen or more species. Migrant songbirds usually travel in parties that can include hundreds of individuals of two or three dozen species. If you find such a party, remain still and let the party continue its feeding activities without disturbing it.

In cases when a bird party is just beyond good viewing distance, you can sometimes attract a few of the closer individuals by "spishing"—making low, scratchy sounds with your teeth together and mouth slightly open—a few times; attracting the closer individuals often entices the whole flock to move in your direction. However, I find that spishing within a bird party tends to frighten some species off or to move the party along faster than it might otherwise go.

At times, a bird party is concentrated at a choice feeding site, such as flowering or fruiting trees and shrubs. So long as they are not frightened or unduly agitated by noises or movement, they may remain and continue feeding for some time, once they overcome their initial concern for your presence. Also, their activities will tend to attract other birds, allowing you to see a broad spectrum of birds at one spot.

Generally, birding along a forest edge, often along the edge of a parking lot, can produce excellent results in the early morning. Bird parties prefer sunny areas at that time of day, to take advantage of greater insect activity. Within two or three hours, however, feeding birds tend to move into the cooler vegetation, especially on hot, sunny days.

Birds may then need to be enticed into the open; many species respond well to some sounds. Spishing often works very well. Squeaking sounds made with your lips against the back of your hand or finger may work at other times. Birds are naturally curious and will often come to investigate. At other times, spishing or squeaking seems to frighten birds away. And some species will be attracted once, but will be difficult to fool twice. So always be prepared to focus your binoculars on the bird immediately when it pops up from a shrub or out of a thicket.

As mentioned above, the best way to find a large number of birds is to visit a variety of bird habitats. All birds occur in preferred habitats, especially during their nesting season. But they tend to frequent a broader range of sites in migration and in winter. Learn where species can most likely be expected. For instance, boreal chickadees occur only in northern coniferous forests; this species cannot be found at Padre Island National Seashore. And one cannot expect to find a roadrunner in the boreal forest. A new birder should learn to take advantage of the range map and habitat description for each species that are included in the field guides. It can save time and considerable embarrassment.

Birding by song is often left to the experienced birder, but many novices are as well equipped to utilize birdsongs as many of the experts. For anyone with an ear for melody, many records, tapes, and CDs are available to help you learn the birdsongs. During spring and summer, there is no better method of identification. When tiny passerines are singing from the upper canopy of the forest, finding and observing those individuals can be most difficult. But their songs are an instant method of recognition that does not involve eye and neck strain from staring into the high canopy for hours on end. And observing rails can also be trying, if not outright dangerous. Fortunately, rails and other marsh birds sing their own unique songs that can usually be easily identified.

Much of the knowledge required to make quick bird identifications must come from field experience. An excellent shortcut is spending time with an experienced birder who is willing to share his or her knowledge. That person can pass on tidbits of information that otherwise might take years to acquire. Most national parks have staff naturalists who give bird talks and walks during the visitor season. This kind of assistance can be extremely worthwhile for bird finding and identification.

Birding Ethics

As with any other activity, there are certain rules of the game. Birding should be fun and fulfilling. It can be a challenge equal to any other outdoor endeavor, but it should never become so all-consuming as to threaten the bird's health and habitat. Any time we are in the field, we must realize that we are only visitors to that habitat on which a number of birds depend for their existence. We must not interfere with their way of life. Disturbing nests and nestlings, for whatever reason, cannot be tolerated. Tree whacking, to entice woodpeckers and owls to peek outside, is not acceptable.

Most national parks are adequately posted, but sometimes just plain thoughtlessness can lead to severe impacts on the environment. These acts range from shortcutting to actually driving over a tundra or meadow. Respect closures in the park; they are there for very good reasons. The survival of nesting swans or peregrines may depend upon it.

The hobby of birding can be a most enjoyable pastime. It costs very little and can require little or no special training. It can be pursued alone or in a group and at any time of the day or night. And there is nowhere on earth where birds are not the most obvious part of the natural environment.

Early naturalist Frank Chapman, in his *Handbook of Birds of Eastern North America*, summarized the enjoyment of birds better than anyone else. Chapman wrote that birds "not only make life upon the globe possible, but they may add immeasurably to our enjoyment of it. Where in all animate nature shall we find so marvelous a combination of beauty of form and color, of grace and power of motion, of musical ability and intelligence, to delight our eyes, charm our ears, and appeal to our imagination."

2

Parks as Islands

Without our national parks, we lose more than just beauty.
— Robert Redford

The last viable peregrine falcon populations anywhere in North America south of Alaska were those remaining in national parks in the Rocky Mountains, Colorado Plateau, and West Texas. The discovery that populations of this and several other high-level predators were being decimated by DDT and other chlorinated hydrocarbons, and the eventual banning of DDT use in the United States and Canada in 1972, came too late to save the eastern peregrines. The last active aerie in the Appalachian Mountains was at Great Smoky Mountains National Park. The entire population of that subspecies became extinct in three decades. Fewer than thirty pairs were known in the United States by 1975. Peregrines in Big Bend, Black Canyon, Dinosaur, Grand Canyon, Mesa Verde, and Zion, however, were isolated and numerous enough to ensure the survival of an adequate breeding population.

These examples demonstrate the value of national parks as natural refuges. The western parks provided the last strongholds for peregrine populations to withstand human-induced pollutants. In most cases, those peregrines fed primarily on resident bird life that had not been subjected to DDT elsewhere. But the Great Smoky Mountains population relied on prey that had acquired DDT from adjacent farmlands or during migration. The eastern peregrines disappeared forever.

During the 1980s, when peregrine restoration programs were being implemented, park sites in the Great Smoky Mountains and at

Isle Royale, Bighorn Canyon, Capitol Reef, and Dinosaur were among the first selected. Nearly 2,500 peregrines were released in the West, according to James Enderson, leader of the Western Peregrine Recovery Team. By 1990, peregrines once again began to frequent their old haunts and even nested at several areas. The finding of 58 active aeries at Grand Canyon in 1989 suggests that peregrine populations have recovered sufficiently to consider delisting the species. The locations of current populations further highlight the importance of national parks to species' recovery.

In spite of an apparent peregrine "fix," many other bird populations continue to decline. The most serious losses are occurring in Neotropical species, long-distance migrants that nest in the United States and Canada and winter to the south in the Greater Antilles, Mexico, Central America, and to a lesser extent in northern South America. According to U.S. Fish and Wildlife Service Breeding Bird Survey data, 44 of 72 Neotropical species declined from 1978 to 1987. These include almost all the warblers; five vireos; five flycatchers; and various thrushes, buntings, orioles, tanagers, cuckoos, and grosbeaks; and the blue-gray gnatcatcher.

The reasons for the declines are varied. Neotropical migrants are less adaptable than most resident species. They have a shorter nesting season, with only enough time to produce one brood before they must depart on their southward journeys. Long-distance migrants tend to arrive on their breeding grounds later and to depart earlier. They also produce smaller clutches than the full-time residents. And most of the Neotropical species place their nests in the open, either on the ground or on shrubs or trees. Their nests, therefore, are more susceptible to predators and brood parasitism by cowbirds than those of the full-time residents, many of which are cavity-nesters (woodpeckers, chickadees, titmice, wrens, and bluebirds). If a racoon, skunk, or fox destroys the nest of a full-time resident, the bird can start over, but one episode of predation or parasitism can cancel an entire breeding season for a Neotropical bird.

Breeding bird studies in the fragmented environment of Rock Creek Park, Washington, D.C., from 1947 through 1978, revealed that six Neotropical species (yellow-billed cuckoo, yellow-throated vireo, and parula, black-and-white, hooded, and Kentucky warblers) could no longer be found to nest. And several other species, including Acadian flycatcher, wood thrush, red-eyed vireo, ovenbird, and scarlet tanager, had declined by 50 percent.

Conversely, at Great Smoky Mountains National Park, with its 494,000 acres (200,000 ha) of mature forest, breeding bird censuses conducted in the late 1940s, and repeated in 1982 and 1983, "revealed no evidence of a widespread decline in Neotropical migrants within the large, relatively unfragmented forest" of the park, according to the National Fish and Wildlife Foundation.

These divergent examples, peregrines in Big Bend, Grand Canyon, and other western parks, and Neotropical breeders in the Great Smoky Mountains, demonstrate the value of large natural parks as preserves for the perpetuation of wildlife resources.

Threats to the Parks

North America's national parks are not immune, however, to the abundant environmental threats. Every park has experienced impacts that threaten its ecological integrity. Although its exterior shell may appear unchanged, and the average visitor may find the scenery looks pretty much the same from year to year, a number of strands in the park's fragile ecological web have been damaged.

During their early years, most of the natural parks had sufficient buffers to insulate their hearts from development and pollution outside their borders. But with continued population growth and increased adjacent land uses, the parks' buffer zones dwindled. Many parks are bordered by farmlands that are maintained by chemicals, forests that are clear-cut, and increasing numbers of industrial centers, malls, and housing developments. Widespread air pollution reaches great distances and affects even the most remote parkscapes.

Long-term monitoring of air quality values in several of the midwestern parks reveals that prevailing winds, especially in summer, carry pollutants from far-away urban and industrial areas. Plant and animal communities all over the globe are linked by the air that is moved around by weather patterns. In a sense, our world is like a large room that shares the same recirculated air. This circulation has created pollution in over one-third of the national parks. Even at isolated and pristine Isle Royale, windborne chemicals have turned up in inland lakes. Birth defects in aquatic birds and cancerous tumors in fish have been linked to the toxins.

Inside the parks, roadways, trails, campgrounds, and other facilities, permit greater human use of the resources. But they often are poorly sited and designed, so they increase fragmentation and stress resources already threatened by external disturbances. Habitat degradation within the parks by improper management can have serious consequences for the park's bird life. Any fragmentation reduces the integrity of the unit, lowering its value for wild species. New sites increase access to the forest interior for predators that feed on birds and their eggs; parasitic cowbirds that lay their eggs in other species' nests; exotic house sparrows, European starlings, and other invaders that compete for nesting space and food; and exotic plants that can drastically change the habitat.

A number of recent studies suggest that cowbird parasitism can affect songbirds even in large forest tracts and may be the major cause of the decline of many Neotropical migrants. Researchers have concluded that cowbirds "will commute up to seven kilometers [4.35 mi] from feeding areas to search for nests to parasitize." John Terborgh reports in the May 1992 issue of *Scientific American* that "A seven-kilometer [4.35-mi] radius describes a circle of 150 square kilometers [58 sq mi], equal to 15,000 hectares [37,065 acres]. It is disturbing to think a forest that might offer at its center a haven from cowbird parasitism would have to be at least that size."

Cuts into the forest interior also increase populations of other open-area birds, such as American crows, jays, magpies, and grackles, which prey on other birds and their eggs and hatchlings.

Once a park's natural ecosystem has been damaged by fragmentation and pollution, all the resources become more susceptible to impacts from natural disasters, such as hurricanes, floods, fires, and diseases. These catastrophes can seriously affect small-bird populations that already have been reduced by pollution, predators, parasites, and competitors.

Wildland Fires and Their Effect on Bird Life

Environmental changes are part of every natural system, but a healthy bird population is better able to withstand those changes. Wildland fires, which occur in most forest, shrub, and grassland communities, are one example. Indeed, many plants and animals are fire dependent. Some pinecones must burn to open, drop their seeds, and regenerate. Woodpeckers frequent freshly burned sites to feed on various wood-boring beetles that are attracted to weakened trees. Many raptors are attracted to prairie fires to feed off the displaced rodents and insects.

Wildland fires have received considerable scrutiny by the public and government officials since the highly visible Yellowstone National Park fire of 1988. Almost 1 million acres (404,694 ha) of Yellowstone's parklands were affected by that burn. Although park officials readily point out the negative effects of fire, largely in areas where the fuel loads built up in excess over too many years without burning, they also are eager to discuss the benefits of fire to the Yellowstone ecosystem. Fire is a natural part of the ecosystem. Old-age forests do not have the diversity of wildlife that occurs in mixed-aged forests created by fires. Fire opens the forest so that new vegetation, such as grasses, aspens, and a variety of shrubs that had been overcome by the old-age forest, can contribute to the mix of habitats. Terry Rich's article, "Forests, fire, and the future," in *Birder's World*, includes a good summary of the Yellowstone fire and its effects on the park's bird life.

My own research at Bandelier National Monument indicates that the 1977 La Mesa Fire initiated a series of changes that continue 15 years later. All three of my study sites revealed increased numbers of bird species and populations following the fire. Significant population increases occurred almost immediately in woodpeckers, with minor increases in all the other insect feeders, such as violet-green swallows, nuthatches, and warblers. Seed feeders like sparrows, juncos, and finches initially declined in varying degrees, but soon increased with the newly available grass seed. Once woodpeckers became established, other cavity-nesters like ash-throated flycatchers, violet-green swallows, mountain chickadees, nuthatches, and bluebirds increased to take advantage of vacated nest holes. Predators also increased with the additional prey base and more open character of the landscape. A few lowland species, such as mourning doves, ash-throated flycatchers, Say's phoebes, scrub jays, and rufous-sided towhees, moved in to utilize the open and warmer terrain. Snag-fall provided increased habitat for house wrens. Although the initial influx of downy, hairy, and three-toed woodpeckers and northern flickers tapered off by the fifth year, Lewis' woodpeckers moved into some of the vacated nest holes. And vireos, Virginia's warblers, black-headed grosbeaks, towhees, and dark-eyed juncos were soon able to take advantage of the young aspens and oak thickets.

The Future

Although extinction is part of the natural process, the rate of extinction has never been as swift as it is at present. The IUCN (International Union for the Conservation of Nature and Natural Resources) predicts that by the year 2000 the world will have lost 20 percent of all extant species.

The greatest losses are occurring within the tropical forests, where many of our songbirds spend their winters. The Council of Environmental Quality's *Global 2000 Report to the President* stated: "Between half a million and 2 million species—15 to 20 percent of all species on earth—could be extinguished by 2000, mainly because of loss of habitat but also in part because of pollution. Extinction of species on this scale is without precedent in human history. . . . One-half to two-thirds of the extinctions projected to occur by 2000 will result from the clearing or degradation of tropical forests."

In North America, at least 480 kinds of plants and animals have become extinct since Europeans first arrived. Seven species have disappeared since 1973, when the U.S. Congress enacted the Endangered Species Act. Canada established a Committee on the Status of Endangered Wildlife in Canada in 1977. More than 600 species have since been listed as threatened or endangered. Endangered species are those in danger of becoming extinct; threatened species are those on the verge of becoming endangered. Howard Youth of the Worldwatch Institute reports that worldwide "about 1,000 bird species—more than 11 percent—are at risk of extinction, while about 70 percent, or 6,300 species, are in decline."

Today, the concept of threatened and endangered species is an accepted part of our world. Significant decisions are based on whether a species is "listed" or not. And many of our "T and E" species have become household terms. Who has not heard of the plight of the peregrine falcon, humpback whale, and snail darter?

The shortcoming of the Endangered Species Act is that it addresses individual species instead of communities of plants and animals. Attempts to restore species do not always give adequate attention to the natural processes on which they depend. And at a time of inadequate funding and moral support, only the more charismatic species receive attention.

An Endangered Ecosystem Act would have much greater success in saving species by giving adequate protection to large tracts of intact landscape (at least 58 sq mi or 150 sq km) that contain several threatened and endangered species. These larger areas are the essence of the national parks.

The bottom line is that our North American birds are losing their breeding grounds, winter habitats, and many of the stopover places in between.

What Is Being Done in the Parks?

Much has been written about the threats to park resources. The U.S. National Park Service itself has been in the forefront of expressing concern about those threats. A major State of the Parks initiative was undertaken in 1980 and 1981 to identify the threats and to establish a program for preventing additional threats and mitigating current impacts. Parts of that strategy continue to the present, but other portions were eliminated, reduced, or ignored due to in-house bureaucracy or insufficient funding.

In Canada, the National Parks Act was amended in 1988 to require the Minister of the Environment to report to the Parliament on the State of the Parks every two years. In response, Canada's Green Plan was developed and includes the goal of setting aside 12 percent of Canada's total lands and waters as protected space. The Green Plan includes targets and specific actions, including five new national parks by 1996, and completion of the Canadian Parks System by the year 2000.

In addition, many of the national parks in the central states and provinces, from Elk Island and Prince Albert in Saskatchewan, the numerous Great Lakes parks, south to Amistad and Padre Island in Texas, and Jean Lafitte in Louisiana, are involved with bird-oriented research, monitoring, and restoration activities.

Examples of park research include the long-term effects of fire on red-cockaded woodpeckers at Big Thicket, bald eagle ecology at Apostle Islands, peregrine falcon migration at Padre Island, long-eared owl ecology at Badlands, and Swainson's warbler ecology at Ozark Riverways.

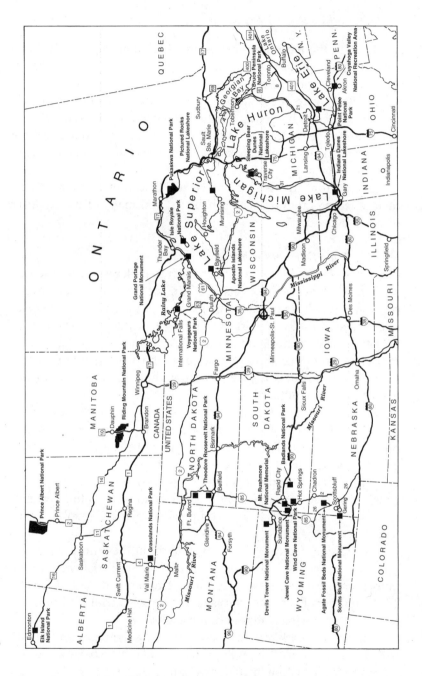

Central National Parks, United States and Canada, upper portion

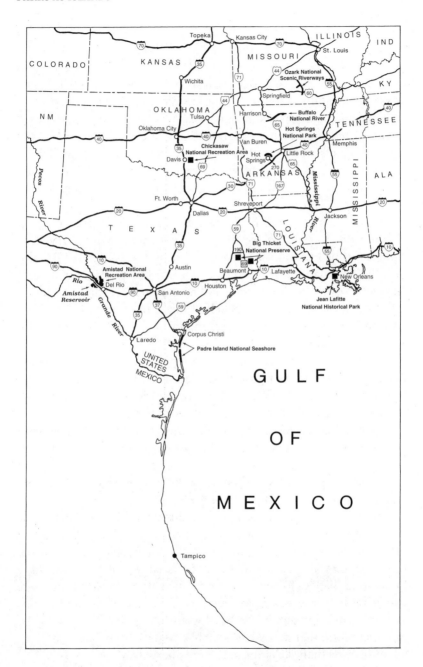

Central National Parks, United States and Canada, lower portion

Projects include an abundance of Christmas Bird Counts, numerous breeding bird surveys, and several monitoring programs involving threatened or endangered species. Examples are bald eagles at Voyageurs and Isle Royale, peregrine falcons at Isle Royale, ospreys at Voyageurs, and raptors in general at Apostle Islands and Pictured Rocks. Other monitoring programs include colonial water birds at Apostle Islands and Padre Island, heron rookeries at Indiana Dunes and Voyageurs, gulls and terns at Bruce Peninsula and Isle Royale, sharp-tailed and sage grouse at Grasslands, and red-cockaded woodpeckers at Big Thicket.

In addition, the U.S. National Park Service and Canada's Parks Canada are participating in the Neotropical Migratory Bird Conservation Program, as coordinated by the National Fish and Wildlife Foundation. The primary focus of this program will be to "integrate research, monitoring, and management (including ecological restoration activities) on behalf of migratory nongame birds" for "the conservation of Neotropical migratory birds" (National Fish and Wildlife Foundation 1990).

Many of the national parks also are participating in "Partners in Flight," a consortium of government agencies and private organizations. This is an international program to identify and conserve species of birds and their habitats that are in peril.

Early emphasis has been placed on the development of a network of parks and protected areas in the Western Hemisphere that are linked by Neotropical migratory birds. Migratory bird watch programs have begun in more than 30 parks as another way to develop linkages among pertinent park units.

Yet in spite of the parks' mandates for unaltered ecosystems, the dual charge of "protection and enjoyment" has too often been interpreted to mean that parks are primarily for people instead of the resources they contain. And so even the largest of the parks have undergone changes to benefit the human visitor, while creating more chinks in the parks' ecological integrity. These incremental bites may seem insignificant separately, but together they have eaten into the essential fabric that keeps parks viable. Many of our national parks are little more than skeletons of their former selves.

Today's national parks more and more are becoming islands within a great sea of disturbance. They can be equated with sea islands, with few connections to continental sources for species renewal. The longer an island is isolated, the less its flora and fauna have in common with other communities, and the greater likelihood of species loss.

The Value of National Parks

How important are national parks for the perpetuation of our North American bird life? Except for a few of the largest and most remote public forests and refuges and an insignificant scattering of private preserves, only the national parks are dedicated to the preservation of complete ecosystems. Most other managed areas are primarily dedicated either to the perpetuation of one or a few species, or to the area's multiple use values. The perpetuation of unaltered ecosystems is too often given secondary importance.

In spite of changes, the national parks still represent some of the finest of our natural environments. Many units contain some of the least disturbed habitats in North America. And each park increases in value with every passing day.

The national parks contain far more than tracts of natural landscape, scenic beauty, and places of inspiration. The parks literally serve as biological baselines for the continent, where gene pools of diversity can be found that have disappeared almost everywhere else. The national parks contain our last remaining outdoor laboratories in which we can learn about the past in order to prepare for the future. They represent the last reasonably intact examples of what North America was like before our resources were exploited for the benefit of a few.

A survey of the national parks quickly reveals that the park systems of the United States and Canada are far from complete. Many of North America's major biotic communities have been left unprotected. Both the United States and Canada have recognized this shortcoming, have taken steps to identify the needs, and are trying to complete the systems.

In addition, only a few of the parks and reserves are large enough to represent entire ecosystems. Few parks contain a complete spectrum of natural processes that shape the ecosystem, so that the nutrient, hydrologic, fire, and other natural cycles are allowed to function unfettered by human constraints.

The key to long-term perpetuation of native species is the complete protection of intact ecosystems. They must be fully protected from all degrading activities, including grazing, timber cutting, mining, all forms of pollution, fragmentation by overdevelopment or overprotection (such as fire roads), and various forms of recreation incompatible with the purpose of the park.

C. F. Brockman expressed the greatest value of the parks when he wrote:

"The national parks are charged with the obligation of preserving superlative natural regions, including wilderness areas, for the benefit of posterity. Attentiveness to the pleasure and comfort of the people is essential, but it cannot mean catering to absolutely unlimited numbers unless the second function is to destroy the first. In a theatre, when the seats in the house have been sold out and the available standing room also has been preempted, the management does not jeopardize the main event by allowing still more onlookers to crowd upon the stage and impede the unfolding of the drama."

NORTHERN FOREST

The North Country is a siren. Who can resist her song of intricate and rich counterpoint—the soaring harmonies of bird melodies against the accompaniment of lapping waters, roaring cataracts, the soft, sad overtones of pine boughs.

—Grace Lee Nute

3

Elk Island National Park, Alberta

R ed-necked grebes had built their floating nests all along the shallow shoreline of Tawayik Lake. I counted 14 active nests within a
stone's throw of the viewing platform. Several other nests were visible beyond. All but one of the nearer nests were occupied by an
adult grebe; the other contained two bluish white eggs. And farther
up the shore I discovered a tiny, stripe-headed youngster, truly an
early bird, accompanied by one of its parents. All in all, there must
have been three dozen red-necked grebes visible at the near end of
the lake.

Each nest was built of pieces of reeds, cattails, and bottom
grasses piled around one or two anchoring plants and held together
with mud. The nest platform floated on the surface, sticking up 4 or
5 inches (10-13 cm), permitting fluctuations in water level. It was
impossible to determine which parent was incubating; male and
female red-necks look essentially alike. But seen through binoculars
from less than 100 feet (30 m) distance, their reddish necks, whitish
throats and cheeks, and yellowish bills were obvious.

Red-necked grebes are medium-sized grebes, compared with the
larger Clark's and westerns and the smaller eared, horned, pied-
billed, and least grebes. They are one of seven species in North
America and 21 species worldwide. Red-necks also are among the
most unusual of grebes; they truly possess a dual personality. They
spend their summers on inland, freshwater habitats from the Great
Lakes to Alaska, usually nesting in small colonies. But they winter at
sea along both coasts, where they normally are solitary. In winter,

they are usually quiet, but on their breeding grounds, they more than make up for their months of silence. Then, they are extremely boisterous, both night and day, making sounds that range from loonlike wailings, whinnying, and groans to loud chatterings.

Grebes generally are fish eaters that chase down and capture their prey underwater. While nesting, however, red-necks prefer aquatic insects and other invertebrates. They start their chicks on a diet of insect larvae, but within a couple of weeks they switch to small fish and feathers. The feathers apparently provide padding against the sharp bones and also help to slow down digestion, so that the bones can dissolve rather than pass through the youngsters' intestines.

Red-necked grebes possess another fascinating adaptation, transporting their young on their backs, often tucked under a wing to keep them secure. There are even sightings of birds diving underwater with chicks riding piggyback. The youngsters hang on with their bills clamped onto their parents' feathers. Reports of birds being transported aerially are doubtful.

Because of the red-necked grebe's abundance and high profile within the park, it was selected as the official symbol for the Friends of Elk Island Society. Red-necked grebes and Elk Island are truly synonymous.

Red-necked grebe

The Park Environment
Elk Island National Park, established in 1930, includes 75 square miles (196 sq km) of Alberta's Beaver Hills, which rise 100 to 200 feet (30 to 60 m) above the surrounding plains. The park represents the "aspen parkland" natural region that lies between Canada's boreal forests and vast prairie. Because of the region's abundant lakes, ponds, and sloughs, the topography is locally described as "knob and kettle" landscape.

About 20 percent of the park's landscape in comprised of 250 lakes, ponds, and sloughs, that usually are surrounded by dense mats of cattails and sedges. Beavers dam the streams and change the configurations of the waterways; bison dominate the drier sites. The aspen parkland communities cover the higher ground and form a mosaic of aspen forest. Pockets of balsam poplar, white spruce, and paper birch; shrub lands; sedge meadows; and grasslands are interspersed throughout. The forest understory is often dominated by beaked hazelnut, wild roses, wolf-willow, chokecherry, and saskatoon.

Parks Canada operates two information facilities in the park, an information center at the South Gate and an interpretive center featuring a theater and displays at Astotin Lake. A few publications, including bird field guides and a checklist, are available at the Astotin Lake Recreation Area. A campground and snack bar can also be found there.

Summer interpretive activities include theater programs, evening presentations, and some special tours. And in addition, there are more than 60 miles (100 km) of trails, several of which include interpretive exhibits.

Additional information can be obtained from the Superintendent, Elk Island National Park, R.R. # 1, Site 4, Fort Saskatchewan, Alta. T8L 2N7; (403) 992-6380.

Bird Life
Water birds dominate the park's bird life. The abundant **ring-billed gulls**, for instance, can occur almost anywhere. Although an occasional Franklin's gull, with black head, red bill, and white-tipped wings, and California gull, with yellow bill with a red spot, occur in summer, and a few others appear in migration, ring-bills are by far the most numerous of the park's gulls. Ring-bills are easily identified

by the black ring on their otherwise all-yellow bill. They are especially abundant at Astotin Lake Recreation Area, where they serve as
natural vacuum cleaners, picking up after picnickers. However, Elk
Island's ring-billed gulls are summer visitors only, representing nonbreeding populations in summer and moving south for the winter.

Two terns, like small buoyant gulls, are also present in summer:
common and black terns. The common tern can be identified by its
gray back, black cap, bright red legs, and bright red bill with a black
tip. Watch for this bird over Astotin Lake. The **black tern** looks very
different; it has an all-black body with grayish wings. It is most common on Tawayik Lake, but visits all the other lakes in the region.

Black terns nest on submerged vegetation in marshes and on
shorelines throughout the prairies, and they are particularly abundant at Elk Island. Unlike other fish-eating terns, breeding black
terns feed primarily on insects, which they catch in the air or skim
off the surface of the water. It is not unusual to see a courting black
tern trying to attract a mate with a bill full of insects.

Twenty-nine ducks and geese have been reported for Elk Island,
and there are few places anywhere in North America where one can
observe ducks more easily. Everyone of the park's lakes, ponds, and
sloughs contains a population of ducks in summer. And their diversity, even within the smallest ponds, can be amazingly high. Puddle
ducks and divers occur together, nesting reasonably close and feeding
together without any apparent habitat partitioning. Mallards, blue-
winged and green-winged teal, redheads, lesser scaup, and common
goldeneyes occur side by side.

One of the park's most abundant ducks is the **mallard**, a reasonably large duck with a yellowish bill. The male features a glossy green
head, white collar, and chestnut chest. The female is drab, but, like
the drake, has a blue speculum bordered with white, best seen in
flight. Mallards also are summer residents only, arriving in mid-April
and departing for warmer climes by mid-November. They nest in
pond-side vegetation, where both sexes build the nest. However, one
week after the start of incubation, the drake deserts the family and
joins bachelor flocks, where he molts and prepares for the fall migration. He will also change mates the following year.

Mallards are one of the "tipping" or "dabbling" ducks, not "diving" ducks that feed on shoots and seeds of sedges, willows, and such

on the bottom of shallow ponds. Tipping ducks simply tip down to feed, leaving their rear end sticking straight up. They also forage on seeds in fields and along the shore. The mallard is probably the best known duck in North America.

I spent almost an hour scoping the north end of Tawayik Lake for water birds one day in mid-June. Although the mallard was most numerous, I also found substantial numbers of other species: Green-winged teal males had green and chestnut heads and green wing speculums; male blue-winged teal were obvious by a large, white crescent patch in front of each eye. Northern shoveler males had all-green heads, white chests, and chestnut sides, and both sexes had large, spatulate bills. American wigeon males showed white foreheads and caps and buff chests, while male ring-necked ducks had dark heads and chests and a white band on their dark bills. Lesser scaup males had glossy purple heads and light-colored bills.

A few other ducks were found in lesser numbers: gadwall males were the plainly marked ducks with solid black rumps; male red-heads featured reddish heads, black chests, and whitish bodies. Common goldeneyes appeared to have swollen heads with golden eyes, and buffleheads were small ducks with white-and-black heads. Ruddy duck males showed deep chestnut bodies with black-and-white heads, bluish bills, and stout, upturned tails; and hooded merganser males possessed crested, black-and-white heads.

The only songbird as obvious as the ducks that day was the **red-winged blackbird**. The males, with coal black body and bright red wing patches, and females with heavily striped body and just a touch of red on the wings, were visible everywhere along the shoreline. And their loud, gurgling "konk-la-reee" songs and abundant "chack" calls were almost obnoxious. I watched males and females carrying nesting materials into the cattails, where they apparently were building nests. Red-wings weave nests from various grasses onto the cattails and other wetland vegetation. Although pairs stay together during nesting, they join huge blackbird flocks by late summer or fall, and overwinter to the south, where they roost in marshes and feed in grain fields and other seedy localities.

All of the **trumpeter swans** seen were found on Astotin Lake, two along the west shore and three from the Lakeview Trail on the east side. These were beautiful, long-necked, snow white birds with solid black bills. They also showed flesh-colored "grin stripes" at the base of their bills. Trumpeters are wonderfully statuesque with a wingspan of 6 to 8 feet (1.8-2.4 m) and the body size of a turkey. The trumpeter was named for its voice, something like the sound of a French horn. Frank Bellrose, in *Ducks, Geese & Swans of North America*, described its call as a "high-pitched, often quavering oo-oo-oo, accentuated in the middle. It is reminiscent of a flock of snow geese calling, but is more melodious."

The trumpeter swan is the world's largest waterfowl. It once nested from western Alaska to Indiana, but by the early 1930s, filling of wetlands for development and shooting of birds for food and feathers had greatly reduced their range and documented their population to fewer than one hundred outside of Alaska. Elk Island's birds are the result of a reintroduction program funded by Parks Canada, Alberta Parks and Recreation Foundation, Canadian Wildlife Service, and the Friends of Elk Island Society. The program's purpose is to restore the trumpeter to the park as a free-flying migratory breeding bird and to diversify migration and wintering opportunities. The program has so far proved highly successful.

Trumpeter swans

White pelicans and double-crested cormorants also are seen on Astotin Lake. Both of these large water birds have taken up summer residency only recently, according to park warden Dennis Madsen. Seen only since 1989, as many as 225 white pelicans can now be found on the lake. The cormorants have "been observed in the park on Astotin since 1981, and established a nesting colony in 1991 . . . 72 observed in 1993," according to Madsen.

Waterfowl, as well as land birds, were abundant along the 2-mile (3.3 km) Lakeview Trail one June morning. The calls of ring-billed gulls along the lakeshore dominated the bird sounds. From the parking area, songs and calls of American crows, blue jays, red-eyed vireos, yellow warblers, and Baltimore orioles also were obvious. The loudest were the **Baltimore orioles**, singing a rich, somewhat disjointed series of clear, flutelike notes, sometimes described as a musical, but irregular, series of "hew-li" and other notes. Male Baltimore orioles are beautiful birds with all-black hood and upper back, black-and-white wings, and bright orange everywhere else. Females are mostly yellowish with blackish backs and wings. This bird is undoubtedly one of the best known birds in North America; illustrations are used to decorate items from plates to coasters to calenders.

A merlin suddenly appeared overhead, carrying a small bird in its talons. The merlin is a small falcon that summers in the park, and one of the most dashing and secretive raptors in the bird world; its presence suggests a rather stable community. Pete Dunne and colleagues, in *Hawks in Flight*, described merlins as "highly aggressive, pugnacious raptors with little tolerance for other birds of prey. They go out of their way to harass a bird that crosses into their territory or occupies their space." For more about this little falcon, see chapter 6 on Voyageurs.

The various ponds along the trail contained a variety of ducks, several with youngsters in tow. Most paddled away to the far side of the pond or hid amid the vegetation or behind the beaver lodges as I passed. But others, especially some of the males that seemed more restless, took flight.

The willows and other shrubs about the ponds housed a variety of songbirds; the most numerous were the little **yellow warblers**. Males had chestnut streaks on their bright yellow breasts, while the females showed a slightly duller yellow. They sang a loud, lively, and cheerful song, a rapid and musical "wee wee wee witita weet." I spished on one occasion and a pair immediately responded, coming to a nearby willow and chipping loudly at me, apparently for interfering with their chores. Their black eyes contrasted with their bright yellow plumage.

Then a low-pitched "chirry chirry chirry chorry chorry" song exploded less than a dozen feet to my left. I froze, so as not to frighten the little songster partly visible amid the heavy undergrowth. Within seconds a male mourning warbler appeared; its gray hood and blackish chest, no eyering, bright yellow underparts, and yellow-gray back were in full view. It remained only a few seconds, then dropped back into the protection of the shrubbery. It sang once again, "chirry chirry chirry chorry chorry," and then it was gone. A beautiful bird on a bright spring morning!

I found several other songbirds along the Lakeshore Trail during the morning. Least flycatchers called their sharp "che-BEK" from the aspen groves, and house wrens sang their bubbling melodies from a number of thickets. Ruby-crowned kinglets and red-breasted nuthatches were restricted to the white spruce in the drier coves. Warbling vireos sang harsh rambling songs, while the numerous "witchity witchity witchity" songs were those of common yellowthroats. Lincoln's sparrows chipped at me from the shoreline shrubbery, and I heard the buzzing songs of clay-colored sparrows in open, brushy areas on several occasions. A bright yellow-and-black American goldfinch male sang its rapid trills and twitters from a willow on the edge of the lake.

I also encountered a number of **brown-headed cowbirds** that morning; drab birds that exploit other bird species by laying eggs in smaller birds' nests. Cowbirds have been found to parasitize more than two hundred species. In spite of their obnoxious and special habit, I couldn't help but think how they fit in at Elk Island. Cowbirds evolved on the prairie with bison, feeding on ticks and insects disturbed by the roving herds. It is still known as "tick-bird" in many locations. What better place to observe these social parasites than in the company of Elk Island's own bison?

I also walked the 1.6-mile (2.5-km) Amisk Wuche (the Indian name for the Beaver Hills) Trail that loops through an assortment of rich habitats—aspen, birch and spruce stands—and crosses wetlands on floating boardwalks. The route offered all the songbirds found on the Lakeshore Trail, plus a few additions: yellow-rumped warbler, ovenbird, rose-breasted grosbeak, white-throated sparrow, and purple finch.

Ovenbirds were heard on several occasions singing a shorter version of their "teacher" song, which is common in the southeastern forests. The Elk Island songs were reduced to "teach teach teach TEACH TEACH TEACH," becoming louder with each note. It took me several minutes to get a good look at one of these ground-loving warblers. I was able to attract one closer by making sharp chip sounds; it flew to an open tree limb at about eye level that was only partially hidden from view. Its whitish underparts with black breast stripes, olive back, white eye rings, and orange crown stripe bordered with brown were clearly evident through binoculars. It seemed curious, looking in my direction and walking along the limb. It then put its head back and sang again: "teach teach teach teach TEACH TEACH TEACH."

The songs of **white-throated sparrows** were most numerous along the trail, and I had superb looks at several of these large sparrows. Their snow white throat, black-and-white crown, and small yellow patch in front of each eye were obvious. Their songs were most appropriate for this park: "ah sweet Can-a-da Can-a-da." For more about this sparrow, see chapter 8 on Isle Royale.

White-throated sparrows and many of the other songbirds spend only a few weeks at Elk Island, just enough time to establish territories, court, nest, and raise families before they head south for the winter. Their lives are hectic during the short summers. And their migrations take a heavy toll. Although some of Elk Island's migrants winter north of the tropics, most are Neotropical migrants that reside longer in the tropics in Mexico, the West Indies, Central America, or South America than they do in Canada. If we are to continue to enjoy our North American songbirds, we must protect their summer and winter homes alike.

In winter, only a handful of the hardier species are left behind. Winter bird populations are monitored annually during the Christmas period, and those statistics become part of the continent-wide Christmas Bird Count. For example, in 1991, 27 counters tallied 2,835 individuals of 37 species at Elk Island. The dozen most common species, in descending order of abundance, included black-capped chickadee, common redpoll, black-billed magpie, house sparrow, evening grosbeak, white-winged crossbill, rock dove, pine grosbeak, blue jay, snow bunting, downy woodpecker, and hairy woodpecker.

In summary, the 1987 Elk Island National Park bird checklist includes 229 species; 122 of those are listed as permanent or summer residents and, therefore, considered to nest. Of the 122 species, 33 are water birds (grebes, waders, waterfowl, rails, and shorebirds), 9 are hawks and owls, and 9 are warblers.

Birds of Special Interest

Red-necked grebe. These long-necked, red-necked birds are abundant at Tawayik Lake in summer; they build floating nests along the shore.

Trumpeter swan. This is the large, snow white bird with a coal black bill and a long, graceful neck.

Mallard. Males are easily distinguished by their glossy green head, white collar, and chestnut breast; females are drab in comparison but, like the drakes, possess blue speculums bordered with white.

Ring-billed gull. The park's most common gull, it is best identified by the black ring on its otherwise yellow bill.

Black tern. This is the small, gull-like bird with a gray back, black cap, bright red legs, and red bill with a black tip.

Yellow warbler. Males are overall bright yellow with chestnut streaks on the chest; females are duller versions without the chest stripes.

Ovenbird. This little warbler is distinguished by its orange head stripe and song: "teach teach teach TEACH TEACH TEACH," each note louder than the last.

White-throated sparrow. A common sparrow with a white throat, black-and-white crown, and tiny spot of yellow in front of each eye; it sings a lovely song: "ah sweet Can-a-da Can-a-da."

Red-winged blackbird. Abundant at all the wetland areas, males possess an all-black body with bright red wing patches.

Baltimore oriole. Males have an all-black hood and upper back and black-and-white wings. They are bright orange elsewhere. Females are mostly yellowish with a blackish back and wings.

4

Prince Albert National Park, Saskatchewan

"A h-sweet Can-a-da Can-a-da" greeted me at the entrance to the Amiskowan Trail. "Ah-sweet Can-a-da Can-a-da," sang a white-throated sparrow from the willow thicket. Its song resounded through the forest, providing a most appropriate welcome to one of Prince Albert's short trails. My soft spishing noise immediately attracted the little songster into a nearby alder, where it called an emphatic "clink" at me for my intrusion. Even without binoculars I could clearly see its snow white throat, boldly striped black-and-white head, with a bright yellow dot between the bill and each eye, and gray-brown underparts.

White-throats are one of the park's most common songbirds, residing in all the brushy habitats. I assumed that this individual had a nest nearby, well concealed under a bush or clump of grass and consisting of fine grasses, moss, and strips of bark. It "clinked" at me again.

A thin, higher-pitched "tsip" drew my attention to a smaller bird just beyond the sparrow. It, too, had been attracted by my spishing and appeared highly agitated; it "tsipped" loudly and constantly. This was a Tennessee warbler with several little moths held tightly in its very thin bill. It apparently was feeding nestlings, and my intrusion had interfered with its busy schedule. It was a rather dull female with little color; its principal markings were whitish eye lines above its very black eyes. Then suddenly the male appeared, also agitated and "tsipping" loudly. Its bill, too was full of insects: moths and at least one green caterpillar.

Through binoculars, I could see its subtle beauty: a gorgeous blue-gray crown and nape and a deep, olive-green back. But most obvious were its snow white underparts, which extended up to its blue-gray crown except for the blue-gray stripe that ran from its bill through its eye. For several seconds, I admired this lovely little warbler as it nervously "tsipped" and fluttered about. Then, knowing that I was keeping its nestlings from their breakfast, I moved on. But a few seconds later, one of the Tennessee warblers sang a rapid song of several high-pitched notes. Paul Lehman, in *The Audubon Society Master Guide to Birding*, described this song as "a fairly loud, staccato 'sidit-sidit-sidit-sidit-siditi-swit-swit-swit-swit-swit-swit-sit-sit-sit-sit-sit-sit' increasing in speed toward end."

A third song echoed through the forest, the explosive "ateach ateach ateach teach TEACH TEACH TEACH" song of an **ovenbird**, each note louder than the last. It took me several minutes to find this little songster in spite of its constant singing. It wasn't until it flew to a new perch that I pinpointed its location. Ovenbirds blend into their environment remarkably well; its striped breast and dull olive-green back made it next to impossible to locate. Finally, through binoculars, I was able to see its bold white eye rings and russet head stripe.

It was perched about 30 feet (9 m) above the ground on the bare limb from which it had sung its distinct song. I watched it walk back and forth along the limb and bob up and down several times. Then, as I was watching, it sang again: "ateach ateach ateach teach TEACH TEACH TEACH."

The Park Environment

A roadside interpretive sign near the Height-of-Land Overlook provides an excellent perspective on the park: "For centuries these hills have echoed the sounds of wildness—the howl of the wolf, the scream of the eagle, and the wind. To the horizon and beyond lies this National Park where the sounds of wildness will always be heard. Listen."

Prince Albert contains a subtle, but remarkable, beauty: rolling hills and ridges clad in dark green conifers and patches of white-barked aspens and birch, hundreds of lakes and waterways edged with sedges and thickets of alders and willows, scattered bogs, and grasslands in the southwest. White and black spruce are the most characteristic trees, although tamarack occurs throughout, and jack pine and balsam fir are common in the east and central areas.

Aspen groves, with an understory of willows, saskatoon, prickly rose, beaked hazelnut, and alders, are most common in the southern portion of the park. Conifers are predominant in the north, where white spruce is most common in the uplands and well-drained lowlands, and patches of jack pine grow on gravel ridges and low, sandy lands. The undergrowth consists of prickly rose, speckled alder, and swamp birch in the spruce forest, and velvetleaf blueberry, prickly rose, mountain alder, Labrador tea, high bush cranberry, and willows in the pine stands.

Deciduous vegetation, including dense thickets of smooth willow and green alder, dominates the edges of the forest and many of the roadways. Other common woody plants found along the edges include wolf-berry, thin-leaved snowberry, wild rose, shrubby cinquefoil, red osier dogwood, high-bush cranberry, chokecherry, pincherry, and saskatoon.

The 957,533-acre (389,508-ha) Prince Albert National Park is located near the geographic center of Saskatchewan, 56 miles (90 k) north of Prince Albert. Elevations range from 1,500 feet to 2,600 feet (457-792 m), with a mean elevation of 1,800 feet (549 m). Services such as food, lodging, camping, and gas are concentrated at Waskesiu, on the eastern edge of the park. Hiking, backpacking, fishing, canoeing, boating, and golf are available. The park's administration building, information center, and a nature center operated by Friends of Prince Albert National Park are all in Waskesiu. The information center has an information desk and a few handouts. The nature center contains an auditorium for orientation programs, several exhibits, and a sales area; bird field guides, a checklist, and a booklet by Suzanne Henry, *Bird-Watching in Prince Albert National Park*, are available.

A wide range of interpretive activities are offered by Parks Canada from late June through August. These include nightly programs, daily nature walks, and other activities such as a junior naturalist program and special movies and musicals. In addition, two trails—Boundary Bog and Mud Creek—are self-guiding. A schedule of interpretive activities is available for the asking.

Additional information can be obtained from the Superintendent, Prince Albert National Park, Box 100, Waskesiu Lake, Sask. SOJ 2YO; (306) 663-5213.

Bird Life

The Amiskowan Trail, named after a Cree Indian word for "home of beaver," cuts through the mixed forest of broadleafs and conifers to the lakeshore and a lookout platform. Additional forest birds encountered along the trail included a yellow-bellied sapsucker, several black-capped chickadees, a Swainson's thrush, a pair of red-eyed vireos, a black-and-white and several yellow-rumped warblers, and pine siskins. An evening grosbeak called as it passed overhead.

I walked to the viewing platform and slowly scoped the calm waters of Amiskowan Lake. The most obvious birds were a pair of **common loons**, so close that I could easily see their black-and-white back, forest green head, heavy black bill, and streaked neck with a broad green band—very striking birds. I had heard them singing as I approached the lake, crying loud yodeling calls that seemed to permeate the very soul of the place. I remembered what Louis Halle had once written: "The wildness of the loon . . . is not dependent on antiquity. It is the wildness uncontaminated by human associations."

These loons seemed apropos in this setting. For me, few creatures so represent the northern wilds as does the common loon. I am told that loons will not nest on polluted lakes, but frequent only those bodies of water uncontaminated by human beings. During my five-day exploration of Prince Albert, I found more common loons, sometimes two or three pairs at a time, than anywhere else I have visited.

Common loons are incredible birds for many reasons, not the least of which is their wonderful song. They are among the first birds to arrive in spring, harbingers of spring. As soon as water opens on lakes they appear, arriving from their wintering grounds at sea. Singing immediately begins in earnest and continues unabated day and night until nesting is well underway. Then, there is a hiatus, except at dawn and dusk, until the adults are accompanied by fledged young, when the chorus commences once again. Only when the lakes freeze and the birds move to open water at sea are they silent. For more information about the common loon, see chapter 6 on Voyageurs.

Also present near the platform was a family of common goldeneyes, an adult female with ten fledglings swimming and diving a hundred feet (30 m) from one of the loons. The tiny ducklings, with black caps and white cheeks, floated alongside the female like corks. Suddenly, without any apparent reason, the loon made a wild charge at the adult goldeneye. It was a crazy chase, with the hen flapping and paddling out of harm's way, and the ducklings either chasing after her or diving underwater. She made a wide circle back to her youngsters, trying to herd them toward the grassy shore, while the loon continued to charge her and the ducklings. It lasted less than 20 seconds and was then over, with none of the goldeneyes injured. But they left the area to the dominating loon, who raised up almost completely out of the water and flapped its wings. It then settled down again to guard its apparent territory. It, too, must have had a nest nearby.

Ring-necked ducks were the most numerous waterfowl on the lake. They were widely spaced out along the shore, remaining considerable distances from any of the loons. Ring-necks sit upright in the water, showing a black head, back, and wings that contrast with their snow white flanks, and a dark gray bill ringed with a white band just behind the black tip. Their name is confusing; they do not have a ringed neck. Females are dark gray-brown with a ringed bill. Like goldeneyes, ring-necks are diving ducks that find food by diving completely underwater. But unlike goldeneyes, ring-necks feed on

Ring-necked duck

aquatic vegetation and associated invertebrates, while goldeneyes feed primarily on animal life with some aquatic vegetation. Also, the two ducks utilize very different nest sites. Ring-necks nest on dry, grassy areas along the water's edge, while goldeneyes are cavity-nesters, utilizing holes in nearby trees. Getting the nestlings out of the cavity, onto the ground, and into the lake is left to the coaxing female; males go off in bachelor flocks soon after hatching occurs.

Mallards, with the male's bright green head, ringed neck, and chestnut breast, were also numerous about the lake or flying over. Smaller numbers of green-winged and blue-winged teal and buffle-heads were visible from the viewing platform, as well. Tree and barn swallows were "flycatching" over the lake surface. And the dark brown, hairy creatures that swam across the lake were beavers, the architects of the park's lakes and ponds.

The loudest of the songbirds along the shore were the male **red-winged blackbirds**, with their coal black body and bright red wing patches (epaulets). An occasional female, with dull, striped plumage, was evident as well. The males flew from shrub to shrub, calling loud "konk-a-reee" notes from each post. Occasionally, one made a long circle flight over the marshy area or up to the top of an adjacent spruce to sing.

The "witchity witchity witchity" songs of common yellowthroats were evident as well. A lone great blue heron and a belted kingfisher flew across the lake, en route, no doubt, to better fishing grounds elsewhere. A sora called whinny notes from the grassy shoreline across the lake. A lone brown-headed cowbird flew over, calling squeaky whistle notes. Then I heard the faint call of an alder fly-catcher down the shore; I listened intently, trying to decipher notes that sounded like "cheeur" or "peeu," with emphasis on the last sylla-ble. Kenn Kaufman, in *Advanced Birding*, wrote that alder flycatcher songs are "harsh and burry, often described as a three-syllabled 'fee-bee-oh,' but actually sounds like a two-syllabled 'ree-beep'; a faint third syllable, as in 'rrree-beea,' may or may not be audible. At times the song is shortened to an ascending 'rrreep!' "

Four species of sparrows were evident from the platform. White-throats were singing from the willows along the shoreline. Their "ah-sweet Can-a-da Can-a-da" rang out loud and clear. The chipping sparrow's dull, extended buzzes, all on one pitch, were commonplace. Two or three of these little reddish-capped birds appeared nearby. Also, the clay-colored sparrows' more excited buzz songs, in either one, two, or three buzzing renditions, were heard on several occasions. A pair of these brown-cheeked sparrows were apparently feeding young in a nest at the base of a nearby willow, judging from the number of trips they made there with food. And the loud "weet-weet-weet-weet-weet" songs of swamp sparrows were also commonplace. They stayed farther from the platform, but I was able to get a good look at one bird that had just captured a juicy caterpillar and was about to carry it to waiting nestlings. Its reddish wings, back, and crown and gray eyebrows were most evident.

Strange mewing calls along the edge of the forest attracted my attention, and I turned just as a pair of **gray jays** sailed into the top of a tall spruce tree. I located them with my binoculars just as three younger birds, calling high-pitched "chew" sounds, joined the adults. They all sat near the top of the tree, now perfectly silent, apparently content that they had my attention. I could see the younger birds' grayish bills, in contrast to the black bills of the two adults. The young birds' plumage was darker, too, without the whitish head and throat of the adults. Then, for no apparent reason, they sailed away along the shoreline, as silent as ghosts. I could not help but wonder if these jays, locally called "whiskey jacks," were searching for picnickers to harass. Whatever they were up to, gray jays are excellent indicators of the boreal forest influence in the Prince Albert ecosystem.

The vegetation along the Narrows Road varies from conifers to aspens to mixed forest to roadside thickets of deciduous trees and shrubs. Park naturalist Bill Garner had told me that this habitat is one of the best birding areas in the park, so I spent most of one early June morning on this route. At one especially active spot spot along the road, just beyond the Trippes Beach pull-off, I identified two dozen songbirds.

I had stopped at Trippes Beach to search Lake Waskesiu for pelicans and gulls. From the beach where a female common merganser paddled away (she probably had a nest hidden in some cavity on the shore or in a tree), I found about 55 American white pelicans across the bay in the lee of a little island. Just beyond were about 35 double-crested cormorants, sitting on a shallow bank to the right of the island. Birds of both species were coming and going; it seemed like a good place to rest and meet their neighbors. These birds, along with gulls and terns, nest annually on isolated Lavallee Lake in the northwest corner of the park. Approximately ten thousand white pelicans make the 3,100-mile (5,000-km) journey from the Gulf of Mexico to Lavallee Lake each year. This ancestral breeding ground is the second largest colony in Canada. Although listed as endangered for many years, white pelicans were eventually de-listed in Canada, "the first bird species to recover successfully," according to Henry in *Bird-Watching in Prince Albert National Park*.

Gulls are also common visitors to the Waskesiu townsite beach. Several Franklin's, a few ring-billed and California, and a couple of herring gulls frequented a little spit that juts into the lake near the dock.

I walked down the Narrows Road beyond the Trippes Beach parking area. Red-eyed vireos and yellow-rumped warblers were most obvious, their distinct songs emanating from the adjacent vegetation. An American redstart was singing from a willow thicket. I spished, and a male with yellow-orange and black plumage came to investigate. I also attracted a brightly marked male **yellow-rumped warbler**. Its white, black, and yellow plumage, with four yellow patches on its cap, sides, and rump, were visible. Its snow white throat identified it as a member of the eastern race of yellow-rumps. Once known as the "myrtle" warbler, this bird and the western "Audubon's" warbler, which sports a yellow throat, were lumped into one species and renamed yellow-rumped warbler. Its song is a musical trill, "'tuwee-tuwee-tuwee or *tyew-tyew-tyew*,' often changing to higher or lower pitch near the end," according to Kenn Kaufman in *The Audubon Society Master Guide to Birding*.

I found a pocket of songbirds 200 to 300 yards (183-274 m) beyond Trippes Beach in a mixed association of willows, alders, aspens, and spruce. A least flycatcher sang sharp "che-bec" calls from the thicket. Ovenbirds, black-capped chickadees, hermit and Swainson's thrushes, and black-and-white warblers sang from the forest, and common yellowthroats and white-throated sparrows among the thickets. I stopped to appreciate the lovely song of the hermit thrush which contained a series of flutelike phrases on different pitches with short pauses between them. The first notes were the longest and lowest. John Terres provides the best description I found found for this song: "opens with clear flutelike note, followed by ethereal, bell-like tones, ascending and descending in no fixed order, rising until reach dizzying vocal heights and notes fade away in silvery tinkle."

I was attracted to the rather swinging, but short, "wee-o wee-o wee-che" song of a magnolia warbler. I found this little bird gleaning insects from spruce boughs. Its bright yellow underparts were heavily streaked with black, which formed a larger spot on its bib, and I also could see its tail distinctly marked with a broad white band. Then, higher up to the right was another, darker warbler. I spished slightly to entice it into the open, and suddenly I was enveloped in warblers. Four black-throated greens, a Blackburnian, a black-and-white, and a magnolia were all in front of me, chipping excitedly over my presence. I remained perfectly still, and within 5 or 10 seconds they resumed feeding in reasonably open view.

I was most interested in the black-throated greens and the Blackburnian. The black-throated greens included two adults and two fledglings that were begging for handouts from their brightly marked parents. The male was truly spectacular, with its coal black throat and breast, canary yellow face, except for black eyes and a greenish black stripe through the eye, and blackish wings with two white wing bars. And when one sang, I was mesmerized. Arthur Bent describes its song as a "dreamy, attractive lisping or buzzing ... with series of 'zree' notes; one song likened to 'trees, trees, murmuring trees.'"

The Blackburnian warbler was named for Ashton Blackburn of Scotland, who was first to collect a specimen according to Edward Gruson in *Words for Birds*. This male sported a black and bright orange head and throat, black back with white streaks, and streaked flanks. Its head pattern was most spectacular: deep orange throat, yellow-orange crown patch and eyebrows, and coal black cap and streaks to the bill and surrounding the eyes. Its song was similar to those of the black-throated green and black-and-white warblers, but even lispier. Wayne Peterson, in *The Audubon Society Master Guide to Birding*, interpreted its song as "very thin and wiry, consisting of 2 or 3 parts. Variations are 'sip sip sip titi tzeeee,' last note very high and ascending; also 'zillup zillup zillup zizizizizi.'"

Treebeard Trail, near the end of the Narrows Road, was even more exciting. The .7-mile (1.2-km) loop trail passes through one of the park's few stands of old-growth forest, a habitat that has been seriously depleted by timber cutters throughout the province. Less than 5 percent of the park consists of old-growth forest; Parks Canada should be complimented for preserving such treasures. Here are 170-year-old mature white spruce that tower over mosses, ferns, and a diversity of herbs and shrubs. It was the only place in the park where I encountered winter wrens and bay-breasted warblers.

The **winter wrens** sang their very rapid, rambling songs from the mossy carpet and among the dense spruce foliage. Florence Bailey, in Chapman's *Handbook of Birds of Eastern North America*, wrote that its song is "full of trills, runs, and grace notes, it is a tinkling, rippling roundelay." It is not an easy bird to find, however, even when it is singing so soundly. First of all, the winter wren is a tiny, reddish bird that blends perfectly into its environment. Even when it is sitting on an open limb and shaking all over with enthusiasm for its song, it can be wonderfully concealed. But with persistence, one can find its dark reddish-brown body, slightly paler below and with dusky barring. Its very short tail helps to pin down its identity.

Winter wren nests are hidden in cavities in rotted stumps and logs or in roots and debris. Males also build one to four "dummy" nests to fool predators. Each consists of a mass of mosses, grasses, twigs, feathers, hair, and the like. Their diet is primarily insects and spiders that they find by poking into every conceivable crack and crevice in their territory.

Conversely, the **bay-breasted warbler** is a bird of tall mature spruce trees, usually foraging at mid-level and persistently searching each bough for insects. The bay-breast is a rather large warbler that, according to Arthur Bent, in *Life Histories of North American Wood Warblers*, early-day ornithologist William Bartram called "little chocolate-breasted titmouse" because of its color and behavior. Males possess a lovely chestnut breast, sides, and cap, black cheeks, distinct buff neck patch, buff underparts, blackish wings with two bold white wing bars, and a striped back. They are lovely birds; however, females lack the chestnut and black colors. Its song is a "seetzy seetzy seetzy see" that Frank Chapman called "liquid and inarticulate."

Other songbirds found along the Treebeard Trail that morning included boreal and black-capped chickadees; red-breasted nuthatches; brown creepers; ruby-crowned kinglets; American robins; veeries; Swainson's and hermit thrushes; cedar waxwings; solitary and red-eyed vireos; Tennessee, magnolia, yellow-rumped, black-throated green, black-and-white, and mourning warblers; purple finches; and pine siskins.

Most of these songbirds are Neotropical migrants that spend summers in Canada and winters in the tropics in Mexico, Central America, South America, or the West Indies. Their survival depends upon the protection given them and their essential nesting habitats, such as the old-growth forest, as well as the tropical forests where they winter.

Highway 263, south of Waskesiu, is locally known as the "Scenic Drive" because of its overviews, trails, and side roads. Betty and I drove this route one rainy afternoon, stopping at various sites as we progressed southward. A broad-winged hawk soared across the ridge at Height-Of-Land; a pair of Canada geese with a single gosling were discovered near the far shore at Namekus Lake; we surprised a cow moose at Trappers Lake; and we stopped at Spruce River to bird that wetland area.

I added only one species to my growing bird list, a winnowing common snipe that circled high overhead. We watched it with fascination as it made several circles; every 10 to 15 seconds it dipped slightly to gain speed and spread its outer tail feathers so that the rushing air vibrated the distended feathers, producing a hollow whistle. Like the loon's wild songs, the winnowing of a common snipe is its unique territorial signature.

Senior park warden Michael Fitzsimmons told me, "The best place to find a spruce grouse is Boundary Bog." So, late evening found me on this 1.2-mile (2-km) loop route, where I spent two hours slowly walking the trail. Boreal chickadees, Swainson's thrushes, brown creepers, Tennessee and yellow-rumped warblers, ovenbirds, chipping sparrows, and dark-eyed juncos were all evident. The stunted spruce and tamarack forest that surrounds the "Eye of the Bog" also produced a number of swamp and Lincoln's sparrows, a lone olive-sided flycatcher that called loud "quick, three beers" at me from the tip of the tallest spruce tree, and a pair of rusty blackbirds that called "pt-keee" over and over as I passed by. But no spruce grouse.

Knowing that the time of year for spruce grouse to display had long since passed, I realized that my best chance at finding this bird would be very early in the morning. I might discover a tardy display if I could get there before any other visitor disturbed the birds. Daylight comes early at Prince Albert in spring, so I was on the trail for the second time at 4:30 a.m. All the birds I had found the previous evening were present. And common loons called as they flew overhead.

Suddenly, a distant wolf howl echoed across the bog. Another, then five more long, drawn-out howls. It was like discovering some prehistoric creature still alive. Then there was silence; I think even the songbirds paused to salute this marvelous mammal. Interestingly enough, I was standing atop Rendezvous Ridge. According to the nature trail brochure, "By late June and early July, when the young wolf pups have grown into a platoon of clumsy two-month-old juveniles, the wolf pack leaves the den and relocates to a rendezvous site. This site, usually located on a well-drained ridge, such as the rim of the bog, becomes the temporary headquarters of the pack." I could find no evidence of wolves visiting the site, but the distant howl has become an indelible memory.

I had not progressed more than 100 feet (30 m) farther when I was suddenly almost eye to eye with a male **spruce grouse**, frozen in place on a bare limb of a jack pine. We stared at one another, and I slowly lifted my binoculars into position so I could study it better. What a remarkable bird! My first impression was of how its coal black breast and throat contrasted with its bright red eye combs. As I watched, it slowly spread its black tail so that the brown tips were obvious. Then it slowly turned so that its black rump feathers, tipped with white, looked like protruding spears. It still did not fly, but drooped its wings slightly and shook them, showing a dazzling pattern of blacks and browns that had partially covered its black-and-white belly. I continued to gawk at this wonderful bird.

It then fluttered to the bare ground, sounding like a much larger bird. And when I took a few steps closer, it flew back up to the same limb and repeated the stretching and fanning behavior. It stayed for another minute or so, then flew back to the ground and sauntered off into the forest.

Spruce grouse

I had experienced a territorial male still ready to defend its territory against an intruder. I wondered if it would have attacked me if I had been more aggressive. Whatever the case, my early morning visit to Boundary Bog had paid off handsomely. Not only had I enjoyed a view of a spruce grouse that I previously had only dreamed of, but I also had entered another dimension of wildness with the wolf howls.

In retrospect, I would like to return to Prince Albert someday to experience its winter wilderness. Wolves are more evident at that time of year, although the bird life reaches a low ebb. Annual Christmas Bird Counts produce only a fraction of the species present in spring, summer, and fall. In 1992, counters tallied 53 individuals of 13 species. These included, in descending order of abundance, black-capped chickadee, black-billed magpie, gray jay, boreal chickadee, white-breasted nuthatch, and six species tied with one apiece: ruffed grouse; downy, hairy, and pileated woodpeckers; common raven; and red-breasted nuthatch.

In summary, the park's bird checklist includes 231 species, of which 154 are known or assumed to breed. Of those, 39 are water birds (loon, grebes, cormorant, waterfowl, rails, shorebirds, gulls, and terns), 18 are hawks and owls, and 20 are warblers.

Birds of Special Interest
Common loon. This large, black-and-white water bird occurs on all the park lakes and is often seen flying overhead; its loud and wild calls are memorable.

Ring-necked duck. One of the park's most common ducks, the male possesses a blackish head, breast, and back, and a gray bill with a white band near the black tip.

Spruce grouse. The most likely place to find this large black, brown, and white grouse with bright red eye combs is Boundary Bog.

Gray jay. Locally known as "whiskey jack," it is a gray, black, and white jay that has learned to beg food from backcountry campers.

Winter wren. This tiny, reddish bird with a short tail requires old-growth forest habitat; look for it on the Treebeard Trail.

Tennessee warbler. Common in the mixed forest habitats, it sings a rapid, three-part song: "sidit-sidit-sidit-swit-swit-sit-sit-sit-sit-sit-sit."

Yellow-rumped warbler. This common little warbler with black, white, and yellow plumage is best identified by its bright yellow rump.

Bay-breasted warbler. Look for it in tall spruce trees on the Treebeard Trail; males have a chestnut cap, throat, and sides, black face, and cream ear patch.

Ovenbird. This little forest bird is best identified by its distinct song, a loud "ateach ateach teach teach TEACH TEACH TEACH," each note louder than the last.

White-throated sparrow. It usually is detected first by its "ah sweet Can-a-da Can-a-da" song; adults have a white throat, black-and-white head pattern, and a yellow dot in front of each eye.

Red-winged blackbird. This wetland species is best recognized by the male's all-black body with bright red epaulets; it sings a loud "konk-a-reee" song.

5

Riding Mountain National Park, Manitoba

Ominnik Marsh is located at the edge of Wasagaming townsite and within walking distance of the many motels and campground. A floating boardwalk provides ready access into the heart of the wetlands. Two dozen or more birds can easily be sighted on a morning visit to Ominnik, and a sharp-eyed observer can possibly locate twice that number.

American robins and a red-eyed vireo greeted me at the brushy entrance to the marsh. One American robin sat in the open near the top of a willow, its brick red breast gleaming brightly in the morning light. Its loud song, "cheer-up, cheer, cheer cheer-up," was most welcome. Conversely, the red-eyed vireo stayed hidden amid the taller aspen foliage. But the song that it sang over and over again was just as lively: "cheery-o-wit, cheree, sissy-a-wit, tee-oo." Another interpretation is "you-see-it, you-know-it, do you hear me? do you believe it?" Red-eyes rarely come to lower, open vegetation; it takes persistence to find one. But patience will eventually reveal a bird of subtle beauty, with olive-green upperparts, whitish underparts, and a distinct head pattern of bold white eyebrows, red eyes, and a gray crown bordered with black.

Ominnik Marsh begins just beyond the border of trees and, at first, is crowded with small alders and willows. Swamp sparrows were the first marsh birds I encountered. Their rapid, even-pitched, but melodic "weet-weet-weet-weet-weet" songs echoed across the wetland. I slowly swept the low-growing vegetation with my binoculars, searching for one of these little songsters. There, at the top of a low alder, was one of the reddish sparrows. I could see its chestnut crown, shoulders, wings, and tail, gray face, and whitish throat. As if on cue, it put its head back and sang again, "weet-weet-weet-weet-weet."

I was suddenly attracted to a **red-winged blackbird** male that flew across my view and settled on a nearby shrub. Its coal black body, except for bright red epaulets, made identification easy. Then it sang a loud, almost obnoxious "konk-a-reee," with a grating "reee." Red-wings were common throughout the marsh, singing their loud songs or giving harsh "chack" calls. I watched one male fly out from its cattail perch 30 or 40 feet (9-12 m) in the air then glide back with wings out to display its bright red epaulets, singing and "chacking" all the while. I also discovered a red-wing nest fastened to a cattail, a foot or so above the surface of the water. A female, with heavily striped plumage, carried a large, fat worm to the nest; apparently it was feeding young. Although these birds consume considerable amounts of seeds as adults, flocking together on farmlands and wetlands to the south, they feed their young only nutritious insects.

Red-winged blackbird

"Witchity witchity witchity," sang a common yellowthroat from near the boardwalk. I spished ever so slightly, and immediately a little yellow throated male, with a bold black mask, popped into view. I admired its aggressive stance and bright plumage. Then a marsh wren sang a rapid melody among the cattails beyond. A sora gave a long whinny from the far cattails. From the taller willows beyond, an alder flycatcher called "rree-beea." And a least flycatcher called an emphatic "che-BEC" at the outer edge of the marsh. It is rare to find these two *Empidonax* flycatchers so close together.

There were several flybys during my two-hour walk: ring-billed gulls were most numerous; two common loons called wild yodels in flight; a great blue heron lumbered by; tree and barn swallows searched the sky for insects; two American white pelicans passed overhead; American crows were constantly calling beyond the marsh; a number of pine siskins flew by; brown-headed cowbirds called squeaky whistle-notes in passing, and several other cowbirds, like tiny vultures, sat on conifers along the edge of the marsh; and numerous ducks passed overhead.

The open water at the far end of the marsh contained a variety of water birds. Mallards already were escorting partly grown young; the male's bright green head was obvious. Ring-necked ducks were most numerous. Their upright stance, slightly peaked, blackish head, chest and back, and grayish bill with distinct white band helped to identify these lovely ducks; females are brownish versions of the more colorful males. Pairs of blue-winged teal and lesser scaup, three immature buffleheads, a common goldeneye and a redhead were present, as well. At the far edge of the pond was a beaver, the pond's architect, cutting a wedge through the water en route to its lodge near the far outlet.

A red-necked grebe swam around the little island near the viewing platform. I searched the shore for a nest without success. This large grebe constructs its floating nest of fresh and decayed reeds anchored along the shore or in the water. Its reddish neck and white throat were obvious. For more about this fascinating bird, see chapter 3 on Elk Island.

The far end of the trail climbed to a platform on the ridge where I could look back across the marsh. The trail then skirted the edge of the marsh, passing through thickets of aspen, willow, and alder, and looped back to the start. American redstarts, chestnut-sided warblers, and white-throated sparrows dominated the thickets, singing their lively songs as a fitting farewell to a most rewarding morning walk.

The Park Environment

Riding Mountain was named for the traditional practice of riding horseback from the local communities into the uplands. This upland, locally known as a mountain, rises about 1,500 feet (457 m) above the surrounding farmlands. It is part of an ancient escarpment that was thrust upward along with the Rocky Mountains some 85 million years ago. It was later bulldozed by Pleistocene glaciers that carried much of the mountain into South Dakota. Huge Lake Agassiz, which drains northeast into Hudson Bay, was formed by the retreating glaciers. The ice also left behind rich soils that today support huge grain farms.

Today's vegetation is primarily a mixed forest environment of northern conifers and broadleaf trees and shrubs of eastern affinity. Communities of aspen, balsam poplar, white birch, white spruce, and balsam fir occur on the well-drained uplands; jack pine and white spruce in drier areas; and black spruce and larch in low, wet areas. American elm, green ash, Manitoba maple, and bur oak are scattered throughout. The understory contain alders, beaked hazel, round-leaved hawthorn, aspen saplings, prickly rose, twinning honeysuckle, wild gooseberry, sasparilla, mosses, lichens, and liverworts. Speckled alder, willows, snowberry, saskatoon, and red-fruited chokecherry occur in mixed white spruce communities. Prickly rose, beaked willow, and few-flowered snowberry are common under jack pine and black and white spruce communities. And on the eastern escarpment the dominant understory consists of beaked hazel, nanny berry, saskatoon, prickly rose, and few-flowered snowberry.

The park's visitor center is in the village of Wasagaming, on the southern shore of Clear Lake. This center contains an information desk, exhibits, and an auditorium for audiovisual orientation programs. A separate book shop operated by Riding Mountain Park Plus People, Inc. carries bird field guides and a park checklist, as well as the little book *Birder's Guide to Southwestern Manitoba*, by Calvin Cuthbert and colleagues, which includes a section on the park.

Interpretive activities run from late June through the first of September, and include nature walks, evening talks, and a variety of special programs such as the Education Services for Schools. Dramatic evening programs are presented at the Community Center and feature relevant park issues. The park maintains several self-guiding trails, including Ominnik Marsh at Wasagaming and Boreal Island along the north entrance road. Riding Mountain Park Plus People, Inc. sponsors environmental studies that include sessions on wildflowers, large predators, water quality, and wilderness survival. Details are available from Parks Plus People, Box 9, Wasagaming, MB ROJ 2HO.

Additional park information is available from the Super-intendent, Riding Mountain National Park, Wasagaming, Man. ROJ 2HO; (204) 848-2811.

Bird Life
Several of the songbirds found on the Ominnik Marsh Trail were concentrated along the aspen-dominated ridge near the end of the trail, between the elevated platform and parking area. The short, emphatic songs of chestnut-sided warblers and slurred songs of American redstarts were most numerous. I stopped below the canopy to get a better look at a **chestnut-sided warbler** that was vigorously singing just above the trail. Peter Vickery's interpretation of its song in *The Audubon Society Master Guide to Birding*, "so pleased, so pleased to meet cha," with the accent on the last two syllables, seemed most appropriate. I could see the little songster through the leaves: a male with deep chestnut sides and flanks; white underparts, cheeks, and neck; black face and eyebrows; and an orange-yellow crown. A remarkably lovely bird. I could not help but wonder where in Central America this bird would spend its winters. Chestnut-sides are Neotropical migrants whose survival depends as much on a stable winter home in the tropics as it does on a protected summer home where, in a few short weeks, it must select and defend a territory, nest, and raise a family.

My chestnut-sided warbler began to move away, so I spished rather loudly to get its attention. Almost immediately I was innundated with several other songbirds. White-throated sparrows seemed to close in around me, calling loud "clinks." A northern waterthrush came out of the undergrowth to look me over, calling a sharp, metallic "chink." A pair of yellow-rumped warblers came within a dozen feet (3.7 m) of me. A male Nashville warbler, carrying a little green caterpillar, stopped by for a quick look before going to feed nestlings. And at least four American redstarts chipped at me from the surrounding foliage.

Other songbirds detected in the same or adjacent thickets included singing house wrens and red-eyed vireos, a black-and-white warbler, and a rose-breasted grosbeak. Also found were downy woodpeckers, northern flickers, black-capped chickadees, cedar waxwings, gray catbirds, common grackles, purple finches, and American goldfinches.

Later, when reviewing the "wildlife notebook" of sightings in the visitor center, I discovered that a great gray owl had been seen along Highway 19 a few days earlier. I also found records of a "jackalope" and "aliens," which I had grave doubts about. But chief park interpreter Celes Davar verified the owl sighting, telling me that this species is seen regularly in the 1980 burn, an area rich in voles and mice, between Lake Katherine and Whirlpool Lake.

I spent much of the following morning birding that old burn site, but did not find a great gray owl. However, the new growth of alder and aspen did produce an amazing number of **mourning warblers**. This secretive little bird is usually detected first by its energetic song, usually written as "chirry chirry chirry chorry chorry." It is difficult to see well because it is extremely active and stays in dense undergrowth. But persistence prevailed, and a close-up view revealed an incredibly lovely bird. In the right light, its slate gray hood turns a radiant bluish-gray color that is highlighted by its black bib and olive-green back. Its name comes from the black bib that, according to early ornithologists, suggested it is in mourning.

Other birds found in the old burn from along the roadway included common mergansers; common goldeneyes; hairy and pileated woodpeckers; northern flickers; western wood-pewees; barn swallows; gray jays; black-capped chickadees; house wrens; American robins; red-eyed vireos; orange-crowned, Nashville, and yellow-rumped warblers; and chipping, white-throated, and Lincoln's sparrows.

I was initially surprised to find **common goldeneyes** flying about the fire-killed trees. Then I realized that such an environment, consisting of acres of snags, provides excellent habitat for these cavity-nesters. Fire is an important part of the park's ecology, producing new habitat for a number of creatures. Goldeneyes utilize tree cavities, open or enclosed, lined with wood fragments and feathers, in which they lay about nine eggs. Soon after incubation begins, male goldeneyes desert their expected families and go off in bachelor flocks to isolated lakes and ponds. Incubation, feeding the nestlings, enticing the youngsters from the nest to the ground, and leading them to a safe pond are the tasks of the females.

Great gray owls also utilize burned stumps for nesting, as well as abandoned stick nests of hawks and eagles. But male great grays remain with their mates throughout incubation, actually bringing food to the incubating female. In *The Birder's Handbook*, Paul Ehrlich and colleagues report that the female "broods chicks nearly continuously for 14 days. Young return to roost in nest well after departure and remain with parents for up to several months post-fledging; fly at 60-65 days."

Great gray owl

The great gray owl, Manitoba's official provincial bird, is not only our largest North American owl, but also one of the few owls that are active during daylight hours. And the fact that they frequent clearings, often perching on snags where they permit a reasonably close approach, makes them an extremely popular owl wherever they occur. Great grays are easily recognized by their size (24-33 in or 61-84 cm), overall gray color, lack of ear tufts, and large facial disks that surround their bright yellow eyes. Also, when viewing this owl straight on, notice the white "bow tie" on the throat.

But it is the great gray owl's "muffled booming" voice that is most memorable. Julio De La Torre, in *Owls: Their Life and Behavior*, describes their song as "a lazy series of 6-12 evenly spaced, very deep pulsing hoots—WHVOOP-WHVOOP-WHVOOP-WHVOOP-WHVOOP-WHO-HOO-HU, like the opening beats of ruffed grouse drum roll, magnified; next-to-last note briefer, sometimes slightly stressed, last note clipped, audible only at close range."

I continued my drive on Highway 19 to the east entrance and beyond to the farming village of McCreary, where I followed the Aggazi Ski Hill Road back into the park to the Oak Ridge Trail. The *Birder's Guide to Southwestern Manitoba* suggests this 2.5-mile (4-km) loop trail, in a mixed forest of deciduous vegetation and balsam fir, as a good place to find golden-winged warblers. I found several along the far side of the loop during my hike, as well as several other birds of interest: red-tailed hawk; yellow-bellied sapsucker; tree swallow; common raven; Swainson's and hermit thrushes; veery; chestnut-sided, yellow-rumped, black-throated green, Blackburnian, and black-and-white warblers; and purple finch. At one point along the trail I was hearing all three thrushes at once. It was exquisite!

The Swainson's thrush, a common species throughout the park, was most vociferous. Its song consisted of a series of ascending, flutelike phrases, like "wip-poor-wil-wil-eez-zee-zee." Veeries sang a downward-spiraling series of flutelike phrases: "whree-u, whree-u, whree-u, whree-u." And hermit thrushes sang an even lovelier song that included a wonderful mixture of high and low notes, all with a quality of rich flute and bell tones. Listening to these glorious renditions was better than hearing any choir in the world's greatest cathedral.

The Oak Ridge Trail loops past a high bluff above Scott Creek, where alders form thickets below the eroded bank. I stood at an overlook enjoying the view, when a **red-tailed hawk** suddenly flew to the top of a tall spruce, screaming at me for invading its territory. A well-marked bird with a brick red tail, it probably was nesting nearby, but I could not spot the nest from my location. It continued its vocal abuse, a loud "kree-e-e-e," until I moved on. Red-tails are listed as "common" on the park's bird checklist, although nesting birds may be less obvious than they are later in the year. Most red-tail sightings are of birds soaring on the thermals that rise over the slopes. This beautiful hawk often soars for hours.

Movement attracted my attention to the thicket below. But it took me several seconds to identify the little yellowish bird as a male Canada warbler, with bold white eye rings, black markings below the eyes, and black necklace against its bright yellow breast. One of the easiest warblers to identify in the field, this Neotropical migrant winters in South America.

Of all the park's excellent birding trails, none was as productive as the 2.5-mile (4-km) Bead Lakes Trail. This loop route skirts a series of little lakes, passing through a variety of rich forest habitats. Chipping sparrows, red-eyed vireos, American robins, and white-throated sparrows greeted me at the parking area. And I had not gone more than 200 feet (61 m) when a Cooper's hawk began a vocal barrage. I apparently was too close to its nest, although I could not locate it amid the thick canopy. The female dived at me several times, calling loud, raspy, and continuous "cac" notes. I assumed the male was sitting tight on the nest. After a minimal search I moved on; this raptor is threatened throughout most of its range and did not need to be unduly disturbed. It is important to remember that, when hiking, we are only visitors to the homes of wildlife, and must respect their privacy.

Warblers were common throughout the Bead Lakes Trail. I found mourning warblers and common yellowthroats in the undergrowth. From the higher foliage, American redstarts, chestnut-sided, yellow-rumped, black-throated green, and black-and-white warblers, and ovenbirds sang their songs. In spruce stands, I found red-breasted nuthatches, brown creepers, house wrens, and ruby-crowned kinglets. Other songbirds along the trail included alder flycatchers, gray and blue jays, Swainson's and hermit thrushes, solitary and Philadelphia vireos, rose-breasted grosbeaks, purple finches, and American goldfinches.

The lakes provided a very different habitat, where I found a few water birds: red-necked grebes, a family of mallards, green-winged and blue-winged teal, American wigeon, ring-necked ducks, common goldeneyes, buffleheads, killdeers, and spotted sandpipers. Red-necked grebes had built at least two nests on little mud islands. One nest contained a single, large, creamy egg with dark streaks. I wondered how such an exposed nest could survive with the abundance of nearby predators.

A pair of Franklin's gulls were also present, calling shrill "kuk kuk kuk" calls. One was sitting on the shore, while the other flew back and forth nearby. Since this species nests in colonies of up to twenty thousand individuals, I doubted if these two were nesting alone.

A high-pitched whistle attracted my attention skyward. An osprey was slowly circling over the far end of the lake. Its long wings with black patches at the wrists and black-and-white head were obvious. Then another, even larger bird appeared, an adult **bald eagle**. I was surprised to find these two species so close together. But both are fish eaters and were undoubtedly fishing the Bead Lakes. It was interesting to see the size difference between these two large raptors. The eagle was at least half again larger than the osprey. An osprey's wingspread is 54 to 72 inches (137-183 cm) while a bald eagle's is 78 to 90 inches (198-229 cm). Through binoculars, I watched the eagle soar in tight circles. Its snow white head and tail were conspicuous, contrasting with its dark body. Both birds gradually circled over the ridge and out of sight.

I searched the far shoreline for a large stick nest, but found none. These two raptors are also alike in nest building; they construct stick nests at the top of trees, usually along lakes, and utilize the same nests for many years. Bald eagle nests have been measured at 8 feet (2.4 m) across and 12 feet (3.7 m) deep, the largest nests built by a single pair of birds.

All the other areas visited in Riding Mountain National Park produced a few additional bird species. On the Boreal Island Trail, I found singing Cape May and bay-breasted warblers amid the spruce stands. At Whirlpool Lake Campground, I found a black-backed woodpecker searching a black spruce for insects. This area is dominated by boreal forest that supports a number of boreal bird species.

Some of the best examples include northern goshawk, spruce grouse, northern three-toed woodpecker, gray jay, and boreal chickadee. As I walked the Gorge Creek Trail, a pileated woodpecker called loud "wuk-wuk-wuk" notes from the adjacent forest. In Grasshopper Valley, I detected a winnowing common snipe over a rather extensive wetland. At the Audy Lake Junction, a merlin flew across the roadway so close that I could clearly see its streaked breast and barred tail. And at Audy Lake I watched 55 to 60 black terns milling back and forth like swallows as they pursued flying insects just above the surface of the lake.

I also found that wherever one goes in Riding Mountain National Park, it is impossible to escape the music of the **common loons**. Their wonderfully wild songs can be heard everywhere. They make morning and evening flights considerable distances from their nesting sites and often sing in flight. This yodel song was phonetically described by Ralph Palmer in *Handbook of North American Birds, Vol. 1*, as "a-a-whoo-quee-quee-whe oooo-quee repeated up to 5 or 6 times, the pitch rising on the whoo and undulating on the rest."

Visitor planning specialist Koren Kines told me that the common loon is her favorite park bird, adding, "It symbolizes spring and the new season." It is one of the earliest birds to return in spring; as soon as open water is available the loons appear as if by magic. For more information on this wonderful bird, see chapter 6 on Voyageurs.

Bird populations at Riding Mountain in winter are only a fraction of what they are in spring, summer, and fall. The best indicator of the winter population is the Christmas Bird Count taken annually in the park. In 1991, 19 counters tallied 2,060 individuals of 26 species. The dozen most numerous birds, in descending order of abundance, included evening grosbeak, black-capped chickadee, common raven, white-winged crossbill, common redpoll, blue jay, pine grosbeak, red-breasted nuthatch, gray jay, boreal chickadee, white-breasted nuthatch, and downy woodpecker.

In summary, the park checklist of birds includes 260 species, of which 182 are known to nest. Of those 182 species, 38 are water birds (loon, grebes, waders, waterfowl, rails, shorebirds, gulls, and terns), 18 are hawks and owls, and 20 are warblers.

Birds of Special Interest

Common loon. This large, common water bird is best known for its wonderful, wild songs, both on the water and in flight.

Common goldeneye. It is best identified by its bright golden eyes; females have deep brown heads and white necks, and males possess a deep green head with a large, round, white spot behind the bill.

Bald eagle. This large raptor can occur anywhere over the park; adults possess a solid white head and tail that contrasts with their dark brown plumage.

Red-tailed hawk. Watch for this broad-tailed raptor, with a red tail, soaring over the ridges.

Great gray owl. This huge, all-gray owl, without ear tufts, frequents openings in the forest and prefers old burns with an abundance of rodents.

Red-eyed vireo. One of the park's most abundant summer residents, it is best located by its loud, constant song with many short whistle notes.

Chestnut-sided warbler. This is a colorful little songbird of the mixed forest; males are distinguished by chestnut sides, white underparts and cheeks, and an orange-yellow crown.

Mourning warbler. Watch for this secretive bird in low thickets; it has an all-gray head, black bib, and bright yellow underparts.

Swamp sparrow. This common marsh bird with reddish wings and crown sings a rapid "weet-weet-weet-weet-weet" song.

Red-winged blackbird. Common at wetlands, males are coal black with bright red shoulder patches; females are heavily striped.

6

Voyageurs National Park, Minnesota

The canoe glided across the glasslike inlet with hardly a trace. I was on silent wings. Sigurd Olson, local woodsman, wilderness guide, and renowned author, wrote in *Songs of the North*: "The movement of a canoe is like a reed in the wind. Silence is part of it, and the sounds of lapping water, bird songs, and wind in the trees. It is part of the medium through which it floats, the sky, the water, the shores."

Water birds flew ahead of us, moving out of our way or, perhaps, leading us away from hidden nests or fledglings along the shore. Mallards, common mergansers, and common goldeneyes were most numerous. One female merganser, distinguished by her white breast, reddish head, and white squares on the trailing edges of her wings, circled back over us uttering loud grunting noises. Mergansers and goldeneyes are cavity-nesters, utilizing holes in trees and brushy places, and later bringing their fledglings to lakes and ponds. I searched the shore for youngsters without success; she undoubtedly had hidden them as we approached.

Overhead, a herring gull passed by en route to some secret gull meeting place. A larger American white pelican, with all-white body except for black wing tips, soared by. And farther away, an osprey, evident by its long, narrow wings bent back at the black wrists and its black-and-white head, lifted off the water. Through binoculars, I could see that the osprey's flight was more labored than usual, as a surprisingly large fish hung from its talons. I watched as it continued on, no doubt to a huge stick nest and waiting nestlings in an isolated pine or spruce tree.

The yodel of a **common loon** sounded ahead of us. A moment later the assumed perpetrator charged from the grassy shoreline and paddled across the water, wings beating furiously to get airborne. It circled back so that we had a superb look at its black-and-white plumage. Most likely, it, too, had a nest along the shore. If it had been loafing or fishing when disturbed, it probably would have dived and swum underwater a safe distance before emerging.

Common loon

Loons are able to remain underwater for up to 3 minutes and have been recorded at depths of 600 feet (183 m). The loon's long, streamlined body and powerful legs placed at the rear of the body are designed for swimming underwater. They actually are able to swim down and swallow their prey, including fish and other aquatic creatures. Larger prey is brought to the surface to mutilate first. Diet varies with locality, but consists primarily of fish (as much as 80%), with smaller amounts of crustaceans and vegetable matter.

But in spite of its fascinating biology, it is the loon's wonderful songs that are most memorable. Its various cries, ranging from sorrowful wails to wild demoniac "laughter," have given rise to the expression "crazy as a loon," and are not easily forgotten by anyone who experiences the northern lakes. The loon is an integral part of the Voyageurs mystique, one part of the wildness of the northern lakes.

The Park Environment

Voyageurs is first and foremost a water park. Of its 218,054 acres (88,245 ha), 38 percent is water and, except for a tiny piece of land at Rainy Lake and a somewhat larger area at Ash River, all the rest is surrounded by water. The heart of the park is the Kabetogama Peninsula, bordered on the north and northeast by Rainy and Namakan lakes (the U.S.-Canada border runs down the center), Black Bay on the northwest, and Kabetogama Lake on the south and southwest. The park is named for the legendary voyageurs, men who canoed the area's waterways while trapping beaver and other furbearers during the late eighteenth and early nineteenth centuries.

Olson wrote that the region "is the most magnificent and beautiful lake and river country on the continent, possibly in the world, nowhere is there such a combination of smooth glaciated and lichen-covered rocks, red and white pines, bogs, forests in such fantastic and glorious profusion." The park brochure further states: "Within its boundaries more than 30 lakes—some huge, some small—fill glacier-carved rock basins. Between these lakes and adjacent rocky knobs and ridges extend bogs, marshes, and beaver ponds. These waters play a major role in your experience in the park."

As might be expected, fishing, boating, and canoeing are extremely popular; 150 primitive boat-in campsites are scattered throughout the park. Most travel is done by water. Suggested canoe trips range from day trips to a 75-mile (121-km) route.

All of the park's forests have been considerably altered by logging and unnatural fires. Loggers cut the entire Kabetogama Peninsula, with the exception of a few private holdings, on at least two occasions before the park was authorized in 1971. Today's forest is only a shadow of its former greatness.

Approximately 70 percent of the vegetation is of boreal affinity, dominated by jack pine, black and white spruce, aspen, and paper birch, with an understory of leatherleaf, Labrador tea, ferns, club mosses, and lichens. Mixed forest communities occur along the lake shores and on rocky ridges and appear more extensive than they truly are. These communities are often dominated by stands of red and white pines, although white elm, red and silver maples, and green ash are common as well. Dense stands of black spruce, and occasionally white cedar and ash, occur in boggy areas. The undergrowth generally consists of hazelnut, red-osier dogwood, elderberry, swamp birch, alder, and sumac.

The National Park Service operates three visitor centers in the park: at Rainy Lake, 12 miles (19 km) east of International Falls; at Kabetogama Lake, in the southeastern corner of the park; and at Ash River, along the southern boundary. Each visitor center has an information desk, exhibits, and a sales outlet where bird field guides and a checklist are available. The Rainy Lake Visitor Center has an auditorium for orientation programs and other activities.

Interpretive programs range from guided walks and cruises to stargazing and environmental puppet shows. Schedules are available at each visitor center. The self-guided Oberholtzer Nature Trail begins at the Rainy Lake Visitor Center. In addition, Voyageurs National Park Boat Tours, Inc. offers a variety of cruises that originate at the Rainy Lake and Kabetogama Lake visitor centers from mid-May through August. For further information, write Voyageurs National Park Boat Tours, Inc., Route 8, Box 303, J2, International Falls, MN 56649.

Additional park information can be obtained from the Superintendent, Voyageurs National Park, 3131 Highway 53, International Falls, MN 56649-8904; (218) 283-9821.

Bird Life

Our small group of travelers landed on the rocky shore, pulled our canoes out of the water, and followed the winding trail through the forest toward the beaver pond. Songbirds called from the surrounding vegetation. The variable songs of song sparrows and the "ah-sweet Can-a-da Can-a-da" songs of white-throated sparrows were most numerous near the shore. Red-eyed vireos sang constant whistle notes from the aspen and birch canopy. Yellow-rumped warblers sang a musical trill from the forest. A chestnut-sided warbler joined the chorus with its "swee swee swee, I'll switch you," song. And the slurred song of an American redstart was also evident.

Several other songbirds were detected along the trail. Veeries serenaded us from the forest with their flutelike "vee-ur, veer, veer" notes, like a descending spiral. Ovenbirds sang a loud "teach teach teach teach teach" song, each note higher and louder than the last. I then detected the high, thin notes of a black-and-white warbler, was singing in a white pine tree almost directly above me. I spished ever so slightly, and immediately a male black-and-white flew to an adjacent perch to investigate. It was distinctly marked with a black throat and many black stripes against its otherwise all-white plumage. It probably had a nest nearby, as it called loud "tick" notes at me as long as I stayed in its territory.

The trail crossed a hill and dropped to the edge of a rather extensive wetland. We had reached the beaver pond, where a huge lodge, about 5 feet (1.5 m) high, sat in the middle. Several dozen dead snags, a few as tall as 25 feet (7.6 m), rose out of the pond like pale ghosts. Along the sides of the pond were mud and stick dams built by beavers to control runoff. Dams in the original stream channel and subsequent runoffs had gradually increased the size of the pond to its present dimensions. The incoming stream was undoubtedly also dammed and backed up for a considerable distance. The live trees around the pond were primarily conifers, since beavers eat the cambium layers of broadleafs, such as aspen, poplar, and willow.

Three mallards flew off the pond when we approached, and I could see their blue wing speculums edged with white. Scoping the far edge of the pond, I found a pair of ring-necked ducks and a lone blue-winged teal male. A **great blue heron**, poised and ready to strike at some passing prey, stood on the far shore. I wondered where this bird had nested, and why it had selected this particular pond. It was an adult, apparently a breeding bird; the black head plumes had not yet worn away. Suddenly, it struck down into the water so fast that I was barely sure of the movement, but then it miraculously held a frog in its long, heavy, yellow bill. A second later the frog was swallowed.

There are nine great blue heron nesting colonies in or adjacent to the park, according to park biologist Lee Grimm. All are associated with beaver ponds or small isolated islands. They are monitored annually by the National Park Service; the 1993 count tallied 430 breeding pairs and 742 estimated young.

Several tree swallows, brightly marked adults and duller immatures, were circling the ancient snags. One suddenly perched at the entrance of a hole a few feet below the top; the nest had apparently been used recently, and the young probably still roosted there overnight. I could not help but connect the beavers and swallows, for so much of the changing scene is orchestrated by beavers, one of nature's most prodigious architects.

When streams are ponded by beavers, many of the flooded trees are not able to adapt and eventually die. As those trees weaken they are usually attacked by a host of bark beetles that eat their way into the trees, lay eggs, and depart. The beetles and their larvae make choice woodpecker foods, and so the trees are soon excavated by woodpeckers. Hairy and downy woodpeckers, as well as northern flickers, may construct nest holes in the trees, which they use for a single season only. The following year, the vacated nests and other holes provide wonderful sites for swallows and other cavity-nesting songbirds, including great crested flycatchers, black-capped chickadees, red-breasted and white-breasted nuthatches, and house and winter wrens.

If the holes become large enough, or if a snag breaks apart in the wind, leaving a depression at the top, wood ducks, common goldeneyes, and common mergansers may take advantage of these nesting sites.

Beaver pond ecology does not stop there. Numerous other birds take advantage of the changing habitat. The flooded stream behind the pond often becomes a tangle of willows, alders, and cattails, which attract puddle ducks like mallards and teal, as well as soras; common snipes; spotted sandpipers; marsh wrens; common yellowthroats; swamp, song, and white-throated sparrows; and red-winged blackbirds.

The presence of all these birds and other pond-loving creatures, such as fish, frogs, and turtles, attracts predators. Beaver ponds and their environs are some of the best places to find herons, bitterns, hawks, owls, and kingfishers.

A **belted kingfisher** landed on top of a snag while I was watching the circling swallows. It was a female with a rusty belly; males possess only a blue chest band across their white underparts. Both sexes have blue upperparts, a shaggy crest, and a large heavy bill. They hunt by flying across a pond or hovering in midair, 35 to 50 feet (10.6-15 m) above the water, searching for fish or other food. Once they find prey, they dive bill first at an exceedingly steep angle. They hit the water with a tremendous force that usually carries them completely underwater. A few seconds later they emerge, usually with prey held tightly in their bill, and fly off to a perch to eat. There they will beat the prey against the limb before swallowing it whole, usually head first. See chapter 27 on Chickasaw for information about the kingfisher's unusual nesting behavior.

A more accessible beaver pond lies along the Ash River entrance road, where the mud banks have actually elevated the pond above the adjacent roadway. Betty and I stopped there one early morning. Green frogs were making hollow plunk notes, like plucked banjo strings. There we found most of the same pond birds found earlier. However, the adjacent broadleaf woodland below the pond, which had received years of good irrigation, contained a number of birds that I had not found elsewhere. I was initially attracted to the parula warbler's buzzy song, which ascends to end with an abrupt and lower note. Parulas are a typical eastern hardwood forest species, and during a 30-minute search of this habitat I found several other eastern forest birds: great crested flycatcher; red-eyed and warbling vireos; Nashville, yellow, and chestnut-sided warblers; American redstart; Baltimore oriole; rose-breasted grosbeak; and American goldfinch.

The **rose-breasted grosbeak** male was truly outstanding. Its rose red breast contrasted with its coal black head and white belly. A duller female, with striped underparts and bold white eyebrows, was also present. The female called loud "chink" notes, but the male sang a liquid caroling song, not unlike a robin's song, but more rapid and continuous. In *Handbook of Birds of Eastern North America*, Frank Chapman described the grosbeak's song as one of "exquisite purity...his song tells of all the gladness of a May morning; I have heard few happier strains of bird-music."

At Ash Bay, I hiked the Blind Ash Bay Trail, which crosses a rocky ridge and loops back to the bay. Habitat along the trail is a good blend of mixed forest with plenty of conifers and northern ground cover. Common birds included northern flickers; blue jays; red-breasted nuthatches; veeries; red-eyed vireos; Nashville, chestnut-sided, yellow-rumped, Blackburnian, and black-and-white warblers; ovenbirds; and chipping and white-throated sparrows. Smaller numbers of least flycatchers; black-capped chickadees; house wrens; Swainson's thrushes; orange-crowned, black-throated green, and Canada warblers; dark-eyed juncos; red crossbills; and evening grosbeaks were also recorded.

I was watching a particularly brightly marked Blackburnian warbler that was singing its lisping "sip sip sip titi tzeee" song from near
the top of a spruce tree, when it suddenly gave a higher pitched
"zeeet" and dived for cover. A **merlin** male passed so close that I am
sure it would have taken the warbler if it had not been distracted by
my presence. I had only a two-second glance, but its striped underparts, barred tail, and slate gray back were forever etched into my
memory.

Merlins are little forest falcons that prey primarily on songbirds.
Their method of attack is extremely swift flight, in contrast to the
stooping of their larger peregrine falcon cousins. John Ehrlich and
colleagues noted: "Male arrives on breeding ground before female,
usually returning to same area each year. Male does all of hunting
from courtship through incubation, occasionally through nesting
period. Yearlings, especially males, occasionally serve as helpers in
territorial defense, feeding of female, etc. Females take heavier prey
than do males; seasonal changes in diet correspond to prey availability."

Merlins were the topic of a Master's Thesis that Thomas
Doolittle undertook in the park from 1988 through 1990. Doolittle
located 50 nesting territories and reported that the "density for all
years for active nests was calibrated at a pair/49.8 sq km [19.2 sq mi]

Merlin

or for every 94 km [58 m] of shoreline." This is the highest density of merlins ever reported. Doolittle found that the mean distance between nests was 6.4 miles (10.3 km), but the three closest active nests were as little as 1.6, 1.2, and .7 mile (2.6, 1.9, and .75 km) apart. Later, at Apostle Islands, Doolittle told me he had calculated that each nesting pair takes about 650 songbirds per season; the most common prey species are cedar waxwings and yellow-rumped warblers, two species that spend much time "flycatching" in the open.

I also visited with Lee Grimm about park raptors, and learned that the park's **bald eagle** population was doing very well, after suffering great losses before DDT was banned in the United States and Canada in 1972. Lee told me he had found 32 nesting pairs of bald eagles in 1993; 28 pairs hatched young, and 43 chicks were banded with a special blue band to identify them as Voyageur birds wherever they may be.

Ospreys, however, are not doing as well. Lee explained that the park population included 24 pairs in 1985 and 1986, but he has since recorded a steady decline, corresponding to the increase in bald eagles. He believes that competition for nest sites with the larger, more aggressive eagle is threatening the osprey.

American white pelicans have also increased steadily since the DDT ban; this is another species at the top of the food chain. They have established foraging areas in the shallow bays on Rainy and Kabetogama lakes and are often found feeding and resting with double-crested cormorants. All of Voyageurs' white pelicans appear to be products of the Lake of the Woods colony, but this species is expected to start a new breeding colony on Rainy Lake or elsewhere in the park.

White pelicans are one of the park's most charismatic species. Their great size and wonderful soaring ability are most impressive, and watching a flock of fishing pelicans is a real treat. They do not dive on prey like their marine cousins, the brown pelicans, but fish from the surface by literally scooping up prey. I watched a family group of five pelicans swimming abreast, when suddenly they formed a semicircle facing the shore and, with great amounts of splashing and wing movement, herded fish ahead of them to shallower water. There they scooped them into their great gular sacs. I never saw any of the fish, but when one pelican tipped its head back,

I knew it had already forced the water (as much as 3 gallons) out of its distended pouch and was swallowing its catch. I was reminded of a well-known limerick that begins:

A wonderful bird is the pelican,
His bill will hold more than his belican.

One early July morning I found four pelicans, two double-crested cormorants, and several herring and ring-billed gulls perched on the rocky spit across from the end of the Oberholtzer Nature Trail. Farther out on Black Bay, white pelicans sat like huge corks on a checkerboard. Closer to shore were several common loons, each "in startling black and white, with its necklace of silver and jet and five-foot spread of wings," as described by Olson.

The foreground was filled with marsh, the domain of the red-winged blackbird, common yellowthroat, swamp sparrow, and American bittern. Most obvious were the two dozen or more **red-winged blackbirds** that called loud "konk-a-reee" songs from the cattails or chased one another wildly over the wetland. The males' coal black plumage and bright red epaulets glimmered in the morning sunlight. Females are duller versions of the males, with heavily striped underparts. Both sexes were feeding young, making numerous trips to feeding sites and returning with insects in their bills. Many were finding food on the adjacent conifers.

The forest habitat along the nature trail also produced a variety of birds. American crow calls were heard continually. The most obvious forest birds included black-capped chickadees, with their black cap and bib, offset by snow white cheeks, and their "chick-a-dee-dee-dee" songs; veeries, with their spirally descending "whree-u, whree-u, whree, veer, veer" songs; red-eyed vireos singing a long series of short whistles, chestnut-sided warbler males sporting contrasting chestnut sides, white neck, black throat and eyebrows, and orange-yellow crown; black-and-white warblers; ovenbirds; American red-starts, with the male's black, orange-red, and white plumage; and song and white-throated sparrows.

Song sparrows were most abundant along the start of the trail, singing songs that usually began with clear "sweet sweet sweet" notes, followed by a jumble of notes and a trill of varying lengths. This species was the subject of a 1943 study of birdsongs by ornithologist Margaret Nice, who discovered that an Ohio song sparrow sang a total of 2,305 songs during a single day in May. Its reputation for being a remarkable songster is well deserved. In fact, the bird's scientific name is *melodia*, Greek for melody or melodious song. For more about this research, see chapter 16 on Cuyahoga Valley.

Voyageurs's song sparrows possess light brown plumage with darker streaks; the heavy streaks on their whitish breasts form a black stickpin. When flying from one singing post to another, they pump their rather long tails up and down, as if to get cranked up for their next series of songs.

Smaller numbers of yellow-bellied sapsuckers, least flycatchers, blue jays, red-breasted nuthatches, and Nashville and magnolia warblers were found along the trail. Along the edges, including the visitor center parking area, were a few yellow-shafted northern flickers, black-and-white eastern kingbirds, all-yellow (except for the male's chestnut breast stripes) yellow warblers, larger all-black common grackles, and bright yellow-and-black American goldfinches.

Many of the park's breeding songbirds are Neotropical migrants that spend their winters far to the south in Mexico, Central America, South America, or the West Indies. For instance, yellow warblers winter in Mexico and Central America; chestnut-sided warblers winter in Central America from Nicaragua to Panama; many of the black-and-white warblers frequent mangrove forests in the West Indies; and the abundant red-eyed vireos migrate all the way to South America. The long-term survival of these birds depends on finding viable, healthy habitats at all times of the year.

Winter at Voyageurs is very different from the short summer; bird populations are at a minimum. The best indicators of the avian winter populations are the Christmas Bird Counts. Two counts were undertaken in the early 1970s. In 1973, three counters tallied 733 individuals of 25 species on the International Falls count. The dozen most numerous species, in descending order of abundance, included evening grosbeak, common redpoll, house sparrow, common raven, pine grosbeak, European starling, rock dove, the black-capped chickadee and white-winged crossbill were tied, red crossbill, pine siskin, and snow bunting.

In summary, the park's 1986 bird checklist included 240 species, of which 82 are listed as nesting. Of those 82 species, 18 are water birds, 7 are hawks and owls, and 9 are warblers. I located an additional 4 warblers and 2 sparrows, all feeding young.

Birds of Special Interest
Common loon. This large, charismatic bird can be found on all the park's water areas; it is best known for its wonderful songs which epitomize the northern lakes.

Great blue heron. Its long legs and neck, heavy yellow bill, 6-foot (1.2 m) wingspan, and blue-and-white plumage make identification easy.

American white pelican. Watch for these large all-white birds, except for black wing tips, soaring overhead or fishing the park's many lakes.

Bald eagle. The adult is distinguished by its snow white head and tail, which contrast with its otherwise dark plumage.

Merlin. This is the speedy little forest falcon with a dark back, streaked underparts, and barred tail.

Belted kingfisher. It is readily identified by its all-blue back, white underparts crossed by a broad blue chestband, and large bill; females have a rusty belly.

Red-eyed vireo. This common songbird of the mixed forest sings loud and continuous short whistle phrases with no particular melody.

Red-winged blackbird. Among the park's most abundant marsh birds, male red-wings are coal black with bright red epaulets and sing loud "konk-a-reee" songs.

Rose-breasted grosbeak. The male possesses a rose red throat that contrasts with its coal black head and white belly.

Song sparrow. This abundant little songbird prefers edges of wetlands and brushy areas; it is best identified by its variable songs, striped underparts, and dark stickpin.

7

Grand Portage National Monument, Minnesota

Mount Rose rises approximately 300 feet (91 m) above the lakeshore, providing a majestic backdrop to the historic Grand Portage Stockade. A half-mile-long (.8-km) self-guided trail ascends the southern slope, switchbacking through the mixed forest and offering several views of Lake Superior, the fur trading post, and adjacent hills. From the summit, one can trace the historic portage route used by the Northwest Company voyageurs in bringing their furs to Grand Portage, considered the most profitable fur company on the Great Lakes.

As I gazed out over the Grand Portage, I wondered if any of those hardy trappers had wandered up Mount Rose to the summit. Mount Rose undoubtedly looked somewhat bare then, having supplied much of the timber for the stockade and for firewood. But 200 years later, Mount Rose probably looks much as it did prior to settlement. And now the bird life is more like what existed when Simon McTavish and his partners started their fur trading company in 1784.

During my walk to the summit, I recorded more than three dozen bird species. An amazing number, considering the small area. And most exciting, 11 of those species were warblers. Four of the warblers were surprisingly abundant, evident by their constant singing and activity along the entire trail. The loudest was undoubtedly the **ovenbird**, with its distinct "teach teach teach teach TEACH TEACH" song, each note louder than the last. This little forest bird can usually be found stalking insects and other invertebrates in the undergrowth or on the ground. When disturbed, it utters low-

Oven bird

pitched "check" notes and may even come out of the dense cover to investigate. Its olive back, white underparts with heavy black streaks, bold white eye ring, and russet crown stripe help to identify this lovely creature.

Its name is derived from its roofed nest, built of grasses, leaves, and moss on the forest floor, resembling a miniature Dutch oven. The ovenbird is also known as "wood wagtail" for its strange bobbing motion in walking over the forest floor or on a tree branch. In Jamaica, wintering ovenbirds are called "land-hickup."

The **American redstart** exhibits a very different behavior, usually foraging among the outer foliage of trees and shrubs and flitting here and there after prey, rather than stalking it as the ovenbird does. The male's bicolored plumage with coal black hood, back, tail, and wings, and bold orange-red patches on its sides, wings, and tail gives it a dashing countenance; females are gray-olive with yellow patches. Redstarts often flash their tail and wings while foraging, a trait that tends to startle insects for capture. And their song is also distinct. Peter Vickery, in *The Audubon Society Master Guide to Birding*, describes it best: "Song is usually shrill, strident, not especially tuneful, and slow enough to hear each note. Most frequent song has 5 or 6 rapid notes with last 2 syllables strongly accented; 'zee-zee-zee-zawaah' (down-slurred), 'zee-zee-zee-zee-zweee' (up-slurred)."

Magnolia warblers were also common along the trail, most evident by their rising "wee-o wee-o wee-chy" songs. I attracted several of these colorful songsters into view with quiet spishing. Males were especially vivid with their bright yellow underparts with heavy black streaks, black back and and face, white eyebrows, gray crown, and square white patches on their brownish gray tail.

Several black-throated green warblers were seen and heard along the trail, as well. Like their cousins, black-throated greens possess a distinct song, a husky "zee zee zee zoo zee" rendition that can be heard at a surprising distance. As expected from its name, this little warbler sports a coal black throat and chest, yellow face with a greenish stripe through the eye, and yellow-green upperparts.

All four of these warblers, indeed as the majority of the songbirds along the Mount Rose Trail, are Neotropical migrants, which nest in the United States and Canada, but spend their winters in the tropics. All four migrate to southern Mexico, Central America, or the West Indies after nesting, expecting to find intact and viable wintering grounds. If their winter habitats have been cut and burned, as they increasingly are, their survival is tenuous at best.

The Park Environment
The 710-acre (283-ha) Grand Portage National Monument is divided into two principal parts: the historic fur trading post, with reconstructed stockade, Great Hall, kitchen, warehouse, and gate house, and the Grand Portage Route itself. The Grand Portage Route, an 8.5-mile-long (14-km), up to 600-feet-wide (183-m) corridor, runs between the site of Ft. Charlotte on the Pigeon River, east to the Grand Portage Fur Trade Headquarters on the shore of Lake Superior. The Grand Portage corridor bisects the reservation of the Grand Portage Band of the Minnesota Chippewa Tribe.

Although the terrain is rugged, it varies in elevation only from 602 feet (183 m) on the lakeshore to 1,250 feet (381 m) near Ft. Charlotte. Most of the landscape is covered with mixed forest dominated by various conifers, including jack, white, and red pine, white spruce, white cedar, and balsam fir. Aspen, paper birch, and red and mountain maples are widely intermixed, and aspen and birch dominate disturbed areas. Additional areas of white cedar occur in the lowlands and on rocky ridges; black spruce and tamarack occur in wetlands; and heart-shaped birch, with an understory of ninebark, thimbleberry, and juneberry, dominates the lakeshore.

A ranger station is located near the Grand Portage Stockade, although park headquarters is in the town of Grand Marais. The stockade contains historic furnishings and fur trade exhibits, and interpretive programs and demonstrations are offered there. A sales outlet for publications and crafts exists in the Great Hall. The Mount Rose Trail is self-guiding.

Additional information can be obtained from the Superintendent, Grand Portage National Monument, P.O. Box 668, Grand Marais, MN 55604; (218) 387-2788.

Bird Life

Other common warblers along the Mount Rose Trail that July morning included yellow-rumped, black-and-white, and Canada. Smaller numbers of Tennessee, Nashville, parula, chestnut-sided, Blackburnian, pine, and mourning warblers were detected. **Yellow-rumped warblers** responded to my spishing, sometimes coming into the foliage just above my head. One particularly well-marked male chipped loudly at me, apparently highly disturbed by my presence. I was able to get a close look at this little black, yellow, and white bird from about 12 feet (3.7 m). Its four yellow spots, on its sides, crown, and rump, contrasted with its snow white throat and black chest, sides, and cheeks. A duller female suddenly appeared with a fat, green larva held tightly in its thin bill. As nervous as they both were, I was sure that they had nestlings nearby.

Another surprise was to discover that Mount Rose supported four thrushes, and at least two of the four species were singing simultaneously at various times during my visit. Most numerous, it seemed, were **Swainson's thrushes**, evident by their upward-rolling series of fluteline phrases, like "whip-poor-will-a-will-e-zee-zee-zee." One bird carrying food managed, even with a full bill, to call mellow "pink" notes at me. It remained in the shadows, and all I could see was its brown back, lighter underparts with a buff breast and darker spots, and buff eye rings and cheeks.

Veery songs were identified by their descending spiral characteristic, a breezy "whree-u, whree-u, whree, veer, veer." But hermit thrush songs were the most outstanding. Arthur Bent, in *Life Histories of North American Thrushes, Kinglets, and Their Allies*, provides the best description: "open with clear flutelike note, followed by ethereal, bell-like tones, ascending and descending in no fixed order, rising until reach dizzying vocal heights and notes fade away in silvery tinkle." And American robins sang their familiar caroling songs, usually described as "cheerily-cheery-cheerily-cheery."

Other songbirds along the trail included yellow-bellied and least flycatchers; black-capped chickadees; golden-crowned kinglets; brown creepers; cedar waxwings; solitary, Philadelphia, and red-eyed vireos; and chipping and white-throated sparrows. A dozen or more evening grosbeaks and a lone pine siskin flew overhead, and a merlin called in the distance.

Of these latter species, the **red-eyed vireo** was most numerous. I detected a dozen or more along the trail; on one occasion a family of five or six were flying back and forth amid white birch trees. The fledglings were still begging for handouts, while the adults attempted to keep their distance. This large vireo is best identified by its bold white eyebrows, gray crown bordered with black, and red eyes. It is otherwise pale below and olive-green above. But what makes this bird most noticeable is its loud, continual song, consisting of numerous short, robin-like whistles, each with a slightly rising inflection, without a melody. Red-eyed vireos, common summer residents in every forest habitat in the park, are one of our last songbirds to discontinue its singing in late summer.

The Grand Portage (historic) Compound and adjacent lake and shoreline provided several other bird sightings during my visit. Most obvious were the abundant **herring gulls** that were perched on the buildings, flying overhead, or incessantly calling "kleew kleew." There is no better representative of Lake Superior than this large white-and-gray gull. Adults are distinguished by a snow white head, throat, and underparts, pale gray mantle, and black wing tips with two white spots. Through binoculars, their yellowish eyes and eye rings and the orange spot on their large yellow bill are also evident. These gulls do not attain adult plumage until their fourth year.

Common loons, common mergansers, and common goldeneyes were found along the rocky shore and in the adjacent bay. The loons stayed some distance out, but an occasional wild, lonesome yodel resounded over the compound and forest. The two common goldeneyes were females, with a brown, rounded head and golden eyes.

There were at least two dozen **common mergansers** present.

Most of these "fish-ducks" were youngsters, yet already the size of the adults, and apparently being trained to fend for themselves. Betty and I watched one flock of two adults and eight youngsters for a considerable time. They were swimming at a good speed offshore, and every few minutes all would dive, like synchronized swimmers, remain underwater for 10 to 20 seconds, then bob up, again in synchrony, and look around at each other for approval. Since none appeared with a fish, I assumed that this was a diving and underwater swim exercise. The adult male was most colorful, possessing a bright green head, red bill, and white throat and sides. The female and all the youngsters had a reddish head, whitish throat, and grayish body.

Only a few birds were found in the Grand Portage Compound itself. Herring gulls and several barn swallows, with long forked tails and reddish throats, soared back and forth overhead. Numerous American crows flew here and there, calling loud "caw" notes en route; a pair of eastern phoebes were "flycatching" from the stockade posts. Yellow warblers sang their cheery "tseet tseet tseet, sitta sitta see" songs from the adjacent vegetation; song sparrows sang their varied songs; and the "ah sweet, Can-a-da, Can-a-da" song of white-throated sparrows echoed across the compound.

I also walked a few miles on the Portage Trail, beginning along Old Highway 61 and going northwest to Beaver Pond Swamp. Birds recorded in the forest along the way were much the same species I had found on Mount Rose, with a few exceptions: winter wrens sang rapid tinkling songs that continued on and on; a parula warbler sang a buzzing, ascending song that ended with an abrupt lower note; a pair of mourning warblers were discovered carrying food for nestlings; downy woodpeckers and northern flickers called from the forest; red-breasted nuthatches called nasal "yank" calls, like toy horns; and a Cooper's hawk passed over the trail and retreated into the forest.

The Beaver Pond Swamp contained a whole different group of birds, with the exception of the abundant **song sparrow**. This little long-tailed sparrow had also been common along the edge of the Grand Portage Compound, singing its varied song from high posts as well as the adjacent shrubbery. It is distinguished by its heavily streaked plumage, including its lighter underparts, on which the dark streaks come together to form a "stickpin" in the center of its breast. Its song usually begins with three "sweet" notes, followed by a jumble of notes, and ending with an extended trill. See chapter 16 on Cuyahoga Valley for more about this bird's singing ability.

A great blue heron flew away at my approach; its long neck and legs and blue-and-white plumage were obvious. Several common grackles gathered in the surrounding trees, protesting my arrival. Swamp sparrows sang loud and rapid "weet weet weet weet weet" songs from the low shrubbery. One individual came to my spishing, and I was able to see its reddish wings and crown, and plain, unstreaked underparts. And marsh wrens sang rapid, reedy songs from among the cattails. But the most abundant marsh bird was the **common yellowthroat**. Its "witchity witchity witchity" songs were audible from the start, but it was not until I spished up the swamp sparrow that its numbers became so obvious. A dozen or more called loud "catch" notes at me from various hiding places, and several males came out for a closer look at the disturbance. Each possessed a bright yellow throat and chest, coal black mask, grayish forehead, and olive-brown back—a beautiful little warbler.

Park ranger John Myrruel had told me that this swamp also contained nesting American bitterns, soras, and yellow rails, but I detected none of these marsh birds. My afternoon arrival undoubtedly precluded my chance of finding these elusive species.

In the late fall and winter, bird life is only a fraction of what it is in spring and summer at Grand Portage. Only a handful of the hardier species remain; they are joined by a few more northern species that stay for the winter. Maureen Briggs told me that the fall migration can produce some fascinating birds. During late September to mid-October, flocks of Lapland longspurs and snow buntings appear and feed on grassy areas. Owls, especially snowy and great gray owls, and northern hawk-owls, arrive about Halloween; in 1992, she found three snowy owls perched on the roof at park headquarters. Bald eagles pass through during October and November, and sea ducks, including oldsquaws, harlequin ducks, and scoters, arrive in November to spend the winter.

October can produce some real surprises. Maureen told me that the worst blizzard on record occurred in October 1991, and soon afterward three very out-of-range species were discovered: purple sandpiper, Anna's hummingbird, and fieldfare.

Some fall migrants stay for the winter and are recorded during the occasional Christmas Bird Counts at Grand Marais. In 1985 (most recent count reported), counters tallied 2,532 individuals of 40 species. The dozen most numerous birds, in descending order of abundance, included pine siskin, black-capped chickadee, white-winged crossbill, evening grosbeak, mallard, red-breasted nuthatch, herring gull, cedar waxwing, downy woodpecker, common raven, common goldeneye, and common redpoll.

Birds of Special Interest
Common merganser. In summer, family groups gather along the adjacent bay; adult males possess a green head and white breast, and females have a reddish head and white throat.

Herring gull. This abundant gull has an all-white head and underparts, gray mantle, and yellow bill with a red spot on the lower mandible.

Barn swallow. Watch for this long-tailed swallow with a reddish brown throat about the Grand Portage Compound.

Swainson's thrush. Common in the forest, it is best detected by its lovely song, an upward-rolling series of flutelike notes.

Red-eyed vireo. This hardwood forest songbird usually stays in the canopy; it sings an extensive song with many short single and double notes and no particular melody.

Yellow-rumped warbler. Common throughout the park, it sports a white throat and four yellow spots on its sides, crown, and rump.

Ovenbird. This forest warbler spends much time in the undergrowth; it sings a loud "teach teach teach teach TEACH TEACH" song, each note louder than the previous one.

American redstart. Watch for this warbler along the forest edges; males are identified by their black plumage with orange-red patches on the sides, wings, and tail.

Common yellowthroat. Males sport a bright yellow throat, heavy black mask, and whitish forehead; they sing "witchity witchity witchity" songs.

Song sparrow. One of the park's most common birds, it is heavily streaked, with a dark central breast spot, and has varied songs that begin with "sweet sweet sweet" and end with a trill.

8

Isle Royale National Park, Michigan

Rock Harbor, located near the eastern end of Isle Royale, provides access to secluded coves, scenic overlooks, rocky shores, and northern forest habitats. All of these areas support a variety of birds. Most obvious are the abundant herring gulls, American black ducks, and common mergansers, while the vocally active, but less obvious, winter wrens and white-throated and song sparrows are abundant as well.

Herring gulls were commonplace from the start of my midsummer visit, soaring over the cold waters of Lake Superior and greeting each new arrival to Rock Harbor with loud "keeyow" calls. They also were common along the park's inland lakes, streams, and trails. It seemed that everytime I stopped along a trail, a herring gull would appear overhead to check my whereabouts. Once in Tobin Harbor, I found a herring gull trying to kill a large fish by whacking it with its massive bill and beating it against a rock. Then a second herring gull swooped down, grabbed the fish and began to drag it away. The theft created a great gull squabble that included considerable wing flailing and screaming, which I was sure was audible up and down the harbor. The second gull eventually flew away with the fish, with the original claimant in hot pursuit.

Herring gulls are unquestionably the dominant bird at Isle Royale, filling a number of roles, from predator, scavenger, and camp robber to passive observer and overseer. Paul Gerrish, a friend who worked at the park for 12 years, told me that cooking outdoors

Herring gull

required one's full attention, or a herring gull would surely steal dinner. Watching fishermen cook their catch at the Rock Harbor Marina
at the end of the day, I noticed they spent an inordinate amount of
time protecting their meals from these bold and aggressive gulls.

Except for an occasional ring-billed gull, a smaller gull with an
obvious ringed bill, herring gulls are the park's only resident gull.
Their all-white head and underparts, yellow bill with a red spot on
the lower mandible, and black wings with white spots near the tips
make identification easy. And their loud calls, "keeyow, kyow-kyow-
kyow," are unique. It seems incongruous that such a spectacular bird
should possess such an obnoxious call.

Of all the common land bird species at Rock Harbor, the **winter
wren** may be the most complete antithesis of the herring gull. This
tiny forest bird is seldom seen because of its love for the shadowy
undergrowth. However, it is impossible to be out of range of its continual singing, which sounds like distant silver bells tinkling in the
forest. Its song is so constant that the hiker may take it for granted.

But the song of the winter wren should never be ignored. Arthur
Bent, in *Life Histories of North American Nuthatches, Wrens,
Thrashers, and Their Allies*, described its song as a rising and falling
series of high-pitched notes, like a silver thread of music lasting
about 7 seconds and containing 108 to 113 separate notes. To me, its
song represents the northern forests better than that of any other
songbird. And yet, up close, the winter wren is little more than an

ounce or two of reddish brown feathers on a stubby tail and a heart containing all outdoors. If you are fortunate enough to watch it sing amid its hallowed sylvan halls, you will discover that it sings with great energy, head thrown back, bill open, shaking with excitement. For additional details about this songster, see chapter 4 on Prince Albert.

The most obvious forest bird at Rock Harbor is probably the **white-throated sparrow.** Its loud "ah sweet Can-a-da, Can-a-da" song often dominates the compound. Although some folks interpret its song as "old Sam Peabody, Peabody," this bird is too close to Canada not to sing the Canadian version. And I discovered that Isle Royale's white-throats sing an extended version of the Canada song, often tacking on one, two, or even three more "Can-a-da" phrases.

Up close, the white-throated sparrow is a lovely creature with a bold black-and-white head pattern, including a snow white throat, and a bright yellow spot in front of each eye. During early summer, adults spend all their daylight hours singing, nest building, and rearing young. By mid-July, when the young are fledged, flocks of a few to several families can usually be found together. They then can easily be attracted by spishing; they will often gather around the perpetrator with loud "chink" calls. Immature birds lack the contrasting head pattern, but still show a yellow spot in front of each eye.

Even in late summer, adults still sing during the early mornings and evenings. The songs of white-throated sparrows are usually the last a camper hears at bedtime and the first birdsong at dawn.

White-throated sparrow

The Park Environment
Nobody goes to Isle Royale except to experience this great wilderness park. Most park visitors are devoted to nature, either as lovers of wild, inaccessible places or as wilderness enthusiasts eager to explore the abundant land and water trails. Isle Royale National Park contains plenty of both.

To describe Isle Royale as an "island" is not totally correct. The park comprises about four hundred islands and rock outcrops that cover about 210 square miles (81 sq km) or a total of 571,790 acres (231,400 ha) of land and water. The main island is 45 miles (72 km) long and up to 8.5 miles (13.6 km) wide and rises to 1,394 feet (425 m) at the summit of Mount Desor. Lake Superior is 602 feet (183 m) above sea level. Although Isle Royale National Park is part of the state of Michigan, it is closest to Ontario, Canada (13 mi or 21 km); it is 18 miles (29 km) from Minnesota and 56 miles (90 km) from Michigan.

The entire archipelago, which runs southwest to northeast, is the result of the erosion of faulted and uplifted lava flows accentuated by glacial erosion. The ancient glacial gouges are today's bays, lakes, and lowlands, and Greenstone Ridge forms a prominent backbone.

Vegetation covers almost all the terrain; even bare rock is blanketed by lichens that create soil to support higher plant life. Rocky south slopes are dominated by grasses and common juniper, with scattered stands of jack pine. Of the park's five forest types, the white spruce-balsam fir-white birch community, considered to be climax forest, is most widespread. This environment has an understory of saplings, mountain ash, mountain maple, willows, red-osier dogwood, mountain alder, and cranberries. Typical breeding birds include the gray jay, Swainson's thrush, black-capped chickadee, golden-crowned kinglet, red-breasted nuthatch, and a number of warblers.

About a quarter of the island—the 100-year-old burns—is covered with a community of aspens, white birch, and conifers, while the more recent burn (1936) is dominated by aspens and white birch. The understory of these communities normally contains saplings, mountain ash, mountain maple, beaked hazelnut, yellow birch, and honeysuckle. Typical breeding birds include the red-eyed vireo, chestnut-sided warbler, ovenbird, and American redstart. Mature forests of sugar maple and yellow birch persist on less than 10 percent of the landscape, and bog forests of black spruce, white cedar, and white fir exist in scattered patches. The entire Isle Royale system embodies ecological change that affects all the flora and fauna. Much can be explained by the classic theories for island biogeography, including the fact that islands support only a fraction of the plants and animals found on the mainland. Many species never reach the islands, and those that do must be replenished with a constant gene flow; when additional mainland genes do not arrive, species may drop out altogether. Therefore, common mainland forms not present on Isle Royale are as interesting as those that are.

Napier Shelton, in *The Life of Isle Royale,* provided some ecological insight when he wrote: "Perhaps the small size of the mammal cast heightens our interest in it; certainly it focuses the action of the play." Missing are bear, deer, raccoon, skunk, porcupine, cottontail, chipmunk, and various rodents common on the mainland. Lynx, coyote, pine marten, and woodland caribou were resident at one time, but are no longer present. Moose and wolves, absent prior to the 1900s, are now the dominant species. Ruffed and spruce grouse, mainland residents, have never been recorded on the island, and sharp-tailed grouse, fairly common at one time, seem to have disappeared.

Candy Peterson, wife and research companion of wolf biologist Rolf Peterson (they have lived on Isle Royale for 23 summers), explained that the absence of some songbirds "allows one to appreciate those that do spend their summers here even more."

And the park brochure helps put the ecological scene into perspective:

The island's uniqueness lies in its complex, yet simple, system in which moose are dependent upon both wolves and beaver-wolves to control their numbers, and beaver to provide dams and in turn the aquatic vegetation upon which the moose feed. The beaver also serve as a summer food for the wolf, and the beaver ponds eventually become meadows that support a variety of smaller animals. The red fox eats the hare who, if left unchecked, would destroy the forest that supports the moose that supports the wolf. In such a system, a dynamic equilibrium is struck in which each species has an important role.

Because of Isle Royale's wilderness character and ecological importance, the park was given special recognition as a Biosphere Reserve under the auspices of UNESCO (United Nations Education, Scientific, and Cultural Organization). Ninety-nine percent of the park is legally designated wilderness.

The National Park Service operates two visitor centers, at Rock Harbor and Windigo, which have an information desk and back-country permit operation, orientation programs, exhibits, and a sales outlet. Bird field guides and the little booklet, *Wildlife of Isle Royale*, with a checklist, are available. Park interpreters provide activities at Rock Harbor and Windigo, as well as Daisy Farm and McCargoe Cove campgrounds, during the summer season. These include nature walks and evening programs; further details are available at ranger stations and on park bulletin boards.

Access to Isle Royale is commercially available only by water and air from Houghton and Copper Harbor, Michigan, and Grand Portage, Minnesota. Lodging is available only at Rock Harbor, although primitive camping, some in enclosed shelters, is available throughout. Travel on the island is limited to boats (private or rental) and 165 miles (266 km) of trails.

Additional information can be obtained from the Superintendent, Isle Royale National Park, Houghton, MI 49931; (906) 482-0984.

Bird Life

My dawn wake-up call was supplied by a **song sparrow** singing loud, rambling songs on the porch rail just outside my window. Each rendition began with "sweet sweet sweet," followed by various notes and ending with trills of different lengths. As I lay there listening to that incredible song, I remembered that ornithologist Margaret Nice had reported that an Ohio song sparrow sang a total of 2,305 songs during a single day in May. I did not bother to count this bird's songs, but I did peek outside just as it dived off the porch into the shrubbery.

During my visit, I found song sparrows common along the shorelines, at the edges of wetlands, and at all the sites of human habitation. They seemed to have a special liking for developments, in spite of being shy and elusive. They also responded to spishing and squeaking sounds, often coming within a few feet and allowing close-up views. They are dark brown, heavily streaked birds with a dark spot on their whitish breast.

In the harbor, a family of **American black ducks** patrolled the shore, searching for natural foods and scraps left by boaters. They seemed to have adopted a lone Canada goose that joined them on their forays; the goose remained for a couple of days then disappeared. Both male and female black ducks look much like the closely related female mallard, but possess purplish wing speculums bordered with black instead of white like mallards. Their loud "quack" calls, however, are identical to those of a mallard. Frank Bellrose, in *Ducks, Geese & Swans of North America*, states that, with good visibility, "the contrast between the lighter brown head and the brown-black body of the black duck is noticeable." He also points out, "the white underwings of the black duck flash in vivid contrast to the brown-black body" in flight.

The other water bird often found in the harbor was the **common merganser**. It, too, was shepherding fledglings. But this duck was much more elusive, staying at a considerable distance from human activity. However, early in the mornings, before the dining hall opened for breakfast, I found a female and five youngsters along the shore pecking at insects and whatever else they could find. The female sported a reddish head with feathers that stuck out behind, forming a sort of double crest. The fledglings possessed whitish cheeks and a thin yellowish bill.

Several days later in upper Tobin Harbor I found a female common merganser with a pod of 14 youngsters. Since this species normally produces a clutch of eight eggs, I imagined that this female was tending fledglings from a second female along with her own, or that her clutch had included eggs that had been "dumped" into her nest by other females. This cavity-nester, which utilizes trees and ground sites, is well-known for depositing eggs in other nests. Male common mergansers, with bright green head and white breast and sides, desert their mates during incubation and go to isolated ponds in bachelor flocks. Completing the incubation, enticing the chicks out of the nest to the ground, leading them to the safety of a lake or pond, and teaching them the fundamentals of fishing are left solely to the females.

The larger **double-crested cormorant** is now a common visitor to the inner harbor area and one of the most abundant species seen around the island. Its all-black plumage, except for the adult's bright yellow throat is readily apparent. The cormorant requires a running start and considerable effort to get airborne, and it flies with an outstretched neck and fast wing beats. On several occasions, a few to two dozen individuals were observed flying overhead in some semblance of a V-formation. But for all its apparent awkwardness out of the water, this bird is able to swim down fish prey underwater.

Cormorants at Isle Royale, like so many other species, are much more abundant than they were 20 years ago. A 1988 survey of the park's colonial water birds produced 2,286 nests in 72 colonies, according to ornithologist Christian Martin. Candy Peterson told me that the increased population may be related to the recovery of Lake Superior herring, and Rolf added that cormorant recovery throughout the Great Lakes may represent a general recovery from earlier effects of DDT.

No discussion of water birds would be complete without the **common loon**, undoubtedly the park's most charismatic species. Without its presence on almost every one of the park's abundant lakes, harbors, and bays, Isle Royale would lose much of its North Woods character. Loons add so much to the park's wildness that it would seem sterile without their wonderful songs and stately appearance. Author George Harrison wrote: "If perchance you have never had the good fortune to hear the mournful cry of the common loon, you have missed the full enjoyment of the wilderness. Like the howl of a timber wolf, the bugling of a bull elk, and the singing of a humpback whale, the mournful cry of the loon is unique" (Klein 1989).

Common loons are amazing birds for a number of reasons, but mostly because of their four types of calls: The tremolo, most familiar, is often referred to as "loon laughter" and is used to signal alarm, annoyance, or greeting; the wail or the "long call," usually with a rise and fall, is used to contact a mate. The undulating yodel is given only by the male and usually repeated several times. It is considered a territorial song or response to another male, and the hoot is used for communications, to signal a loon's whereabouts to its mate and other family members. For more about this fascinating species, see chapter 6 on Voyageurs.

Some other forest birds commonly found at Rock Harbor, and along the adjacent Scoville Point Trail, include the northern flicker, black-capped chickadee, red-breasted nuthatch, brown creeper, golden-crowned kinglet, Swainson's thrush, cedar waxwing, red-eyed vireo, Nashville warbler, and ovenbird.

One day I accompanied Candy Peterson and Terry Lindsay, the park's chief of interpretation, on the Daisy Farm Loop hike. We birded our way through the varied habitats, covering the 5.5-mile (8.8-km) route in an easy going 6 hours. I recorded a total of 45 bird species, several moose, including a cow with twin calves, numerous red squirrels, an inquisitive red fox, and one red-bellied snake. And just beyond the Mount Ojibway Tower, Candy discovered a fresh wolf track on the trail; she had visited the same area two days earlier without finding fresh tracks. It was exciting to know that such a creature was nearby; knowledge of its presence increased my appreciation of the wilderness.

The Daisy Farm Loop Trail contains a smorgasbord of bird habitats, ranging from clearings like Daisy Farm Campground and the open ridge to mixed and hardwood forests, conifer stands, and wetlands. Warblers were of special interest to me because of their lovely songs, their colorful plumage, and also, perhaps, their rather distinct habitat preferences. For example, Nashville and chestnut-sided warblers and American redstarts were most common at the edges of clearings and in second-growth hardwoods. Magnolia, yellow-rumped, black-throated green, and black-and-white warblers were in the more evenly mixed forests. Mourning warblers were found in the dense growth aspen and birch saplings. Blackburnian warblers sang from mature conifers. Ovenbirds frequented mixed forests with a relatively dry understory; a Canada warbler was found in dense deciduous cover; and common yellowthroats were in wet brushy areas.

Of all these warblers, the Nashville, chestnut-sided, magnolia, yellow-rumped, and black-throated green warblers and ovenbirds were most obvious. In most cases, we first detected the birds by their distinct songs, which we identified by using mnemonic devices. Knowing their habitat preferences and their songs, we were able to make species identifications. For example, the "see-it, see-it, see-it" and trill emanating from the edge of hardwoods belonged to a Nashville warbler; chestnut-sides sang songs that could be interpreted as "so pleased, so pleased, so pleased to meet cha." The short, rising "wee-o, wee-o, wee-chy" among the dense hardwoods was that of a magnolia warbler. Yellow-rumps sang a musical trill, "tuwee-tuwee-tuwee," and black-throated greens sang husky "zee zee zee zoo zee" notes from mixed forest areas. Ovenbirds sang loud, dramatic, "teach teach teach teach TEACH TEACH" songs, each note louder than the previous one, probably the easiest of all warbler songs to remember.

Chestnut-sided warblers and American redstarts may be two of the most numerous warblers in the park, because of their affinity for second-growth deciduous woodlands, which are prevalent about clearings and along Greenstone Ridge. **Chestnut-sided warblers** are gorgeous songbirds with chestnut sides, white cheek patches that extend onto the neck, black face and eyebrows, and golden yellow crown. They are surprisingly tame for warblers, often fluttering close enough to allow examination without binoculars.

American redstarts are also flashy warblers, but with a completely different color pattern. Male redstarts are all-black, except for orange-red patches on their sides, wings, and tail. Females possess the same pattern, but with duller plumage and yellow patches. Their

American redstart

typical behavior of flashing their contrasting wings and tail to startle insects reminds one of a butterfly. On its wintering grounds in Latin America it is called *candelita* or "little torch." This brightly marked warbler also has a lovely song. Ornithologist Allen Cruickshank, in Griscom and Sprunt's *The Warblers of America*, described it as "a rather thin, sibilant unexciting 'see see see see see see' (rising inflection at end), 'tsee tsee tsee tsee tsee-o' (ending in downward slur) or 'chewee chewee chewee.' Many birds alternate between two favorite songs, some indulge in unique individual renditions."

Other birds found along the Daisy Farm Loop included an American kestrel; a yellow-bellied sapsucker; downy, hairy, and pileated woodpeckers; an alder flycatcher; blue jays; black-capped chickadees; red-breasted nuthatches; brown creepers; winter wrens; golden-crowned kinglets; Swainson's and hermit thrushes; American robins; cedar waxwings; solitary and red-eyed vireos; and chipping and white-throated sparrows. At clearings, we found a lone ruby-throated hummingbird, eastern kingbirds, American crows, song and swamp sparrows, red-winged blackbirds, and common grackles. And overhead we detected a broad-winged hawk, common ravens, eastern bluebirds, and evening grosbeaks.

The flutelike songs of thrushes were especially appealing. Most numerous were **Swainson's thrushes** singing their upward-rolling melody, "wip-poor-wil-wil-eez-zee-zee," over and over. Although I never got a good look at one of these dwellers of the shadowy forest, their wonderful music was sufficient. Few songbirds possess such subtle colors; the olive-brown back, whitish breast with heavy spots, and buff eye ring and cheeks blend perfectly into the undergrowth.

We heard our first hermit thrush song, like a distant magic flute, as we began our climb onto Greenstone Ridge. Its song is even lovelier than that of the more common Swainson's thrush. Frank Chapman, in *Handbook of Birds of Eastern North America*, described its song as remarkable for its "purity and sweetness of tone and exquisite modulation." This thrush introduces each phrase with a single clear note on a different pitch. For more than 15 minutes it serenaded us along our route, each series of notes lovelier than the last. It, too, wears subtle forest colors, olive-brown back and whitish underparts with heavy, dark spots. But the hermit thrush, unlike the Swainson's, shows reddish color on its rump and tail.

Beyond Daisy Farm and across Moskey Basin, a huge **bald eagle** nest is perched at the top of a large aspen tree. Most years, at least since DDT was banned in the United States and Canada, the residsent eagles have produced a pair of fledglings. The nest continues to grow with the annual addition of sticks and debris. By July, the young of the year can sometimes be seen soaring up and down Moskey Bay. Although they lack the pure white head and tail of the adults, their large body size and 90-inch (229-cm) wingspan are unmistakable.

Ospreys also utilize tree top nests and can be mistaken for bald eagles. But the smaller, much lighter-colored ospreys fly with bent wings that have black patches at the wrists; eagles fly with their all-dark wings held straight out. Both species fish the bay waters; a bald eagle skims the water and grabs its prey, while an osprey dives from a height of 30 to 40 feet (9-12 m) directly into the water, becoming completely submerged, before it flaps its way back into the air. Both birds then carry their prey to a favorite perch to consume it.

The park's most common raptor, however, is the broad-winged hawk of the hardwood and mixed forests. Most often detected by its high-pitched, plaintive whistle, the broad-wing is a relatively small hawk, about crow-size, with broad wings, reddish barring on its underparts, and a conspicuous black-and-white banded tail. The larger red-tailed hawks are also present in summer and are distinguished by their dull to brick red tail.

Two smaller and fairly common raptors are the American kestrel and the merlin, both falcons with pointed wings and rapid wing beats. Male kestrels possess a reddish back and tail, bluish wings, and double sideburns on each cheek. This little raptor prefers clearings, often perching in the open on snags where it can survey the ground for mice and insects. Candy Peterson told me that a pair has lived near the Ojibway Tower for many summers. Conversely, merlins are forest birds that seldom perch in the open. Bulkier falcons with a dark crown and heavily streaked underparts, merlins prey on song-birds. I located one just behind the Rock Harbor Visitor Center. For further details about this little predator, see chapter 6 on Voyageurs.

Of all Isle Royale's raptors, the endangered peregrine falcon receives the greatest attention. This large, slaty backed falcon with single, heavy black sideburns was totally eliminated from the Great

Lakes during the 1950s, primarily the result of DDT use throughout its range. However, since that deadly pesticide was banned in the United States and Canada in 1972, the species has begun a steady recovery. Aided by numerous restoration programs, including the release of 51 birds on Isle Royale from 1987 through 1991, peregrines are expected to eventually return to their ancestral cliff sites to nest. Visitors will then again experience this amazing creature, which can dive at more than 200 miles (321 km) per hour. One more piece of the ecological puzzle will be returned. For information about peregrines during migration, see chapter 29 on Padre Island.

Peregrines and most of the summer birds leave the park in fall and migrate south. Many are Neotropical migrants that travel all the way to southern Mexico, the West Indies, Central America, and even northern South America. There they must find habitats to support them until they return to their nesting grounds the following spring. The decline of some North American songbirds is undoubtedly related to the destruction of wintering habitats; if that trend continues we will find fewer and fewer birds to enjoy in our northern forests.

Winter populations of birds on Isle Royale are only a fraction of what they are in summer. Only a few of the hardier species remain, and even fewer species from father north come south and stay. Examples of full-time residents include the northern goshawk, great horned owl, the woodpeckers, gray jay, common raven, black-capped chickadee, and red-breasted nuthatch. Northern visitors include the gyrfalcon, snowy owl, boreal chickadee, and several northern finches: the snow bunting, crossbills, purple finch, common redpoll, pine siskin, American goldfinch, and evening grosbeak.

In summary, the Isle Royale bird checklist includes 208 species, of which 128 are either permanent or summer residents and assumedly nest. Of those 128 species, 20 are water birds (loon, grebe, cormorant, waders, waterfowl, rail, shorebirds, and gulls), 14 are hawks and owls, and 21 are warblers.

Birds of Special Interest
Common loon. Most evident by its unique songs, the loon is a reasonably large water bird with a solid black head, heavy bill, banded neck, and black-and-white checkered back.

Double-crested cormorant. This water bird is all-black except for its yellow throat patch. It is common around the island and requires a long running start when taking off.

American black duck. The park's most common harbor duck, it has a sooty brown body, paler head and neck, and purple speculum.

Common merganser. Males possess a glossy green head and white breast and sides, and females have a reddish brown, crested head; both have a thin reddish bill and red feet.

Bald eagle. The adult's snow white head and tail, which contrast with its dark brown body and wings, are unmistakable.

Herring gull. This is the common gull with an all-white hood and underparts, gray mantle, and large yellow bill with a red spot on the lower mandible.

Gray jay. Often present at campsites, where it can be noisy and obnoxious or silent and observant, it can be recognized by its all-gray appearance, with a darker back and cap and whitish throat and forehead.

Winter wren. More often heard than seen, this tiny forest songster sings a continual song like tinkling silver bells.

Swainson's thrush. This thrush sings a flutelike song that consists of an ascending series of notes, "wip-por-wil-wil-eez-zee-zee."

Chestnut-sided warbler. Males possess chestnut sides, white patches on their cheeks and neck, black eyebrows, and golden-yellow crown.

Yellow-rumped warbler. This common forest bird has an all-white throat and four yellow patches on its sides, crown, and rump.

American redstart. Males sport all-black plumage, except for orange-red side, wing, and tail patches; females are duller with yellow patches.

Song sparrow. This heavily striped, long-tailed bird sings numerous songs; each begins with "sweet sweet sweet" and ends with an extended trill.

White-throated sparrow. It is distinguished by its black-and-white head pattern and distinct song, "ah sweet Can-a-da Can-a-da."

9

Pukaskwa National Park, Ontario

Hattie Cove Campground and vicinity is a very birdy place. Two dozen or more species reside in the campground and sing their wonderful songs to one and all. The most obvious of these songbirds, notable for its early-morning wake-up calls, is the white-throated sparrow. Its slow and purposeful renditions of "ah sweet Can-a-da, Can-a-da" permeate the morning stillness. Typical calls are loud, sharp "pink" notes, often given when disturbed. It sometimes sings only one "Can-a-da," but at other times extends the song to three, four, or even five "Can-a-da" phrases. And by mid-July, when the youngsters are out trying to imitate their parents, white-throat songs can range from the norm to the ridiculous.

White-throated sparrows are readily identified by their snow white throat, black-and-white striped head, and bright yellow dot in front of each eye. Common throughout the park, white-throats utilize a wide range of habitats from the deep forests to brushy edges and wetlands. They are common nesting birds from eastern British Columbia to Newfoundland. They leave their breeding grounds in fall and migrate south into the United States and northeastern Mexico for the winter; often they are feeder birds, taking advantage of handouts wherever possible. But with the first spring days at Pukaskwa, they are right back at Hattie Cove, singing their "ah-sweet Can-a-da, Can-a-da" songs.

The Park Environment

Pukaskwa National Park (pronounced puck-a-saw), on the northern shore of Lake Superior, has been described as the "wild shore of an inland sea." The park, however, includes more than shoreline; it embraces 464,063 acres (187,804 ha) of Canadian Shield wilderness, comprised of dissected uplands with terraces and steep-sided valleys, fast-flowing rivers, and waterfalls.

The rugged terrain is mostly covered with boreal forest that is dominated by black spruce, jack pine, and white birch, with lesser amounts of balsam fir, aspen, white spruce, mountain ash, tamarack, and white cedar. Prominent understory species include mountain maple, red-osier dogwood, blueberry, common juniper, speckled alder, bush honeysuckle, Labrador tea, and squashberry. In the southern portion of the park are communities of red and sugar maples, yellow birch, and white and red pines, which are considered transition forests between the boreal and the Great Lakes-St. Lawrence Forest regions.

More than 95 percent of Pukaskwa is inaccessible by roads and trails. This area supports several packs of timber wolves and one of the southernmost herds of woodland caribou. These large ungulates normally stay along the coastline; they utilize the adjacent islands for calving, and the lake provides escape routes from the predatory wolves.

Three principal rivers—White, Willow, and Pukaskwa—provide access through the interior to the coast. Coastal sites are accessible by water and the Coastal Hiking Trail, which runs from Hattie Cove for 36.5 miles (58.7 km) to North Swallow River. Registration is required for travel into the backcountry.

The Hattie Cove area, in the park's northwestern panhandle, contains administrative facilities and the only visitor facilities. The visitor center has an information desk and sales outlet where Friends of Pukaskwa sell gifts and publications, including bird field guides. A free bird checklist is also available. The Hattie Cove Visitor Center is the heart of the park's interpretive activities. Programs include naturalist-guided walks and evening programs; schedules are posted at park bulletin boards and are available at the entrance station and visitor center. Also, the park maintains four self-guided trails: Halfway Lake Trail, Southern Headland, and Beach Trail at Hattie Cove, and the first 19 miles (30 km) of the Coastal Hiking Trail.

Additional information can be obtained from the Superintendent, Pukaskwa National Park, Highway 627, Hattie Cove, Heron Bay, Ont. POT 1RO; (807) 229-0801.

Bird Life

A summer morning stroll through the Hattie Cove Campground can produce a good assortment of birds. After the numerous white-throated sparrow songs, the lovely flutelike songs of the **Swainson's thrush** are next in abundance. It seems strange that such an elusive bird, a lover of the shadowy forest, should be so numerous in the campground. But its ascending notes, "wip-poor-wil-a-will-e-zee-zee-zee," resound from various directions at once. Sometimes it adds an extra "a-will." Arthur Bent, in *Life Histories of North American Thrushes, Kinglets, and Their Allies,* included a description of its song by ornithologist Aretas Saunders: "There is a somewhat windy quality about it, as though the bird was saying 'whao-whayo-whiyo-wheye-wheeya.' Each phrase is slightly different in arrangement or pitch from the others, but the difference is less apparent than in other thrushes." Bent also reported that ornithologist Stewart Edward White found Michigan thrushes to sing "on an average of nine and a half times a minute with extreme regularity." White calculated that each of his study birds sang 4,360 songs per day.

The Swainson's thrush was earlier called "olive-backed thrush," due to the pervasive color of its upperparts. Its underparts are a soft fawn with blackish spots, and its face and eye rings are washed with buff, which forms bold spectacles. But this thrush is rarely seen well; it is a forest species that prefers the shadowy undergrowth, where it

Swainson's thrush

gleans insects from vegetation or, occasionally, chases them on the ground. Paul Ehrlich and colleagues, in *The Birder's Handbook*, reported it to be the "least terrestrial of the eastern 'ground-dwelling' thrushes." In late summer and fall, especially during migration, it relies heavily on berries.

I located several other common campground residents. The melodic trills of dark-eyed juncos were heard often; these little slate gray birds show noticeable white edges on their otherwise all-dark tails. Golden-crowned kinglets sang high-pitched "see see see see" notes from the conifers. Red-breasted nuthatches called nasal "nyak" notes, like toy horns, from the taller spruce and fir trees. The "chick-a-dee-dee-dee" songs of black-capped chickadees were heard throughout. Yellow-rumped warblers spent considerable time singing and "flycatching" from the various trees; I had good looks at several of these yellow, black, and white songsters. Male American redstarts, with their coal black body and orange-red patches on their sides, wings, and tail, were common. But the most colorful warbler was the little magnolia warbler, distinguished by its bright yellow underparts with bold black streaks on its breast, black face, white eyebrows, and white tail patches. It also sings a short and easily recognized song, a rising "wee-o wee-o wee-chy." And the constant tinkling songs from the dense undergrowth were those of the reddish winter wrens.

Winter wrens are mystery birds that are continually heard, but seldom seen. Their wonderful songs seem to go on without end, filling the air with the sound of miniature silver bells. Bent reported that 7-second songs possess 108 to 113 separate notes. Most sightings of these tiny songsters are serendipitous; one may suddenly appear at a campsite or while sitting in the woods. They are constantly searching for insects and spiders, creeping in and out of every nook and cranny. They nest in dark places under roots and trees, or even in deserted cabins, and the male usually builds one to four dummy nests to fool predators. But it is their tinkling bell songs that are most memorable.

Other less common species found about the campground included downy woodpeckers, northern flickers, ruby-crowned kinglets, cedar waxwings, red-eyed vireos, black-throated green and Blackburnian warblers, ovenbirds, and song sparrows.

Halfway Lake Trail, along the edge of the campground, passes through a variety of habitats on its mile-long (1.6-km) circle. Halfway Lake was named for its location halfway between the Pic River and Hattie Cove, along the traditional trail that linked these sites, according to park interpreter Doug Tate.

The thickets of alder, willow, birch, and fir near the outlet were most productive. An especially bright male **American redstart** attracted my attention with its lovely song and characteristic behavior. It was "flycatching" by swooping down and up with much wing flashing and tail spreading, looking like a fat black-and-red butterfly. Every few minutes it would stop on an open limb, put its head back, and sing a thin but rollicking song, "chewee chewee chewee."

Red-eyed vireos were common, as well, singing their continual whistle notes from the canopy. Alder flycatchers; black-capped chickadees; winter wrens; Swainson's thrushes; Nashville, magnolia, and yellow-rumped warblers; white-throated sparrows; and dark-eyed juncos were also present.

Beyond the hardwood thicket, the trail climbed a little rise and passed through a mixed forest that was busy with bird activity. A pair of black-and-white warblers were carrying food to a nest hidden near or on the ground. A family of red-breasted nuthatches were gleaning the fir and spruce boughs for insects. An ovenbird sang its loud "teach teach teach teach TEACH TEACH" song. A Blackburnian warbler sang a thin "sip sip sip titi tzeeee" song in the distance.

Suddenly, almost directly above me, a **black-throated green warbler** began singing its distinct five-syllabled song, a husky "zoo zee zoo zoo zee." It took me several minutes to find this little bird, which continued to sing every few seconds. It was a brightly marked male with an all-black throat and chest, yellow face, and blackish wings with two white wing bars. Viewed from below, its black markings formed a large, inverted V that highlighted its all-white belly. It is a gorgeous bird, and one that was surprisingly common throughout the park. In fact, Tate told me that local ornithologists believe the breeding population of black-throated green warblers along Lake Superior's north shore may be the highest concentration anywhere.

I strolled out on the Halfway Lake Trail boardwalk, which extends over the shallow end of the lake. A male red-winged blackbird called "konk-a-ree" from across the little bay, but common yellowthroats and swamp sparrows dominated the surrounding shrub-bery. The yellowthroats sang "witchity witchity witchity" songs, and I was able to attract one male closer by spishing; its bright yellow throat contrasted with its heavy black mask. The more visible **swamp sparrows** required no coaxing; they sat on willow and alder shrubs singing loud and penetrating "weet-weet-weet-weet-weet" songs. Unlike most swamp sparrow songs, which are even-pitched, the song of the Halfway Lake swamp sparrows descended slightly and was more musical. Aretas Saunders points out in Bent's *Life Histories of North American Cardinals, Grosbeaks, Buntings, Towhees, Finches, Sparrows, and Allies*, that much of the swamp sparrow's song can only be heard close-up: "Some songs are double; that is, notes are sung on two pitches at once, the higher notes being slow and sweet in quality, and the lower notes faster and somewhat guttural. There are generally three notes on the lower part to one of the upper. The two notes are harmonious and usually about a third apart in pitch." Perhaps that explains the different songs.

The swamp sparrow is a lovely bird with a deep red crown and reddish shoulders and wings, although these features can only be seen in good light. The remainder of the bird is plain: all gray underparts, cheeks and collar, a dark line behind the eyes, and a striped back.

Hattie Cove, just behind the campground, supports a pair of **common loons** that make their unique music all spring, and most of the summer and fall. Usually, the loons' lonesome tremolos, yodels, and wails carry into the campground to entertain campers. Their songs are important ingredients in a North Woods experience. See chapter 8 on Isle Royale for details about their vocalizations. The Hattie Cove loons often come within easy viewing distance of the visitor center.

The loon is a large water bird that appears all black-and-white at first sighting, but in the right light its head often seems dull green, sometimes velvet green. Its back is a checkerboard pattern of black and white, and underparts are snow white. A loon in flight shows its white underparts with dark trailing edges on the wings; it flies in a strange position with neck and head lower than the shoulders. But its wonderful songs are most memorable. Park visitors should never leave without experiencing a common loon in its natural environment.

A few other water birds are likely to be encountered in Hattie
Cove during the summer months: herring gulls are regular visitors
but more numerous on the outer bays; ring-billed gulls are only
occasional visitors. American black ducks can usually be found along
the shore and identified by their blackish brown plumage, lighter
head, and purple speculums bordered with black. Mallards can be
expected in the cove, and red-breasted mergansers are present in
summer. Watch also for ring-necked ducks and common goldeneyes.

Another day I walked the Coastal Hiking Trail to White River. It
was a wonderful experience. The trail skirts Hattie Cove, passes
through several moss-covered hollows, crosses forested ridges, skirts
the shore of Playter Harbour, and winds through a diversity of hardwood and conifer forest communities. I found all of the common
birds that occur at Hattie Cove, plus a few additions.

At the start of the trail near the visitor center, I could see a moose
at the far end of Hattie Cove, but it had disappeared into the forest
by the time I reached that area. I checked the abundant snags there
for a great gray owl, but to no avail. Tate had told me that a great
gray had lingered here one winter, roosting on snags when it was not
hunting. The only birds I found were numerous common yellowthroats and swamp sparrows, a great blue heron, and several cedar
waxwings.

Farther along the forest trail, **ruffed grouse** were surprisingly
common in early morning; I saw none on my return trip. They
seemed to prefer the hardwood hollows and cautiously walked ahead
of me up the trail rather than flying. They reminded me of bantam
roosters with their jerky movements and low "quit" sounds. On two
occasions, males puffed out their black neck ruffs and fanned their
gray-brown tails with a blackish terminal band. They were exquisite
creatures.

Unfortunately, it was too late in the season to experience this
bird's drumming behavior. This occurs in late spring, when courting
males display for their ladies; the drumming sound is "produced by
the cupped wings of the male grouse striking the air as he flaps them
forward and upward," according to Ehrlich and colleagues. The
"drumming serves for both territorial defense and mate attraction
and is easily detectable as much as a quarter of a mile away." Male
ruffed grouse are promiscuous. Tate told me that ruffed grouse drum

again in September and October, a behavior that may be a response to the amount of daylight, which is similar to that of spring, and may serve to establish territory.

Spruce grouse also occur along this trail, utilizing drier ridges dominated by jack pine. Males sport bright red eye combs, black feathers on their throat, neck, and chest, and a black tail edged with buff. Like the ruffed grouse, the spruce grouse performs elaborate displays in spring, beating wings rapidly together and flying several feet in the air. See chapter 4 on Prince Albert for more information on this grouse.

I discovered a lone **spotted sandpiper** along the grassy shoreline of Playter Harbour; I imagined that it had a nest in the vicinity. It was heavily spotted, walked with jerky motions, and teetered back and forth. This little shorebird is one of the few species (less than 1% of all birds) in which the female is dominant and mates with more than one male (polyandry). The females arrive on the nesting grounds before the males, select territories, and fight each other for preferred mates. This system is apparently successful for spotted sandpipers, considered the most widespread sandpiper in North America.

The bird of the day, however, was the **black-backed woodpecker**. I found a family of at least four of these northern woodpeckers searching for insects on old spruce trees. I was reminded that this species feeds primarily on wood-boring beetles and ants; Ehrlich and colleagues reported that they may consume up to 13,500 insects annually. They also eat fruit, mast, and cambium. Seen through binoculars, the male's yellow crown patch was obvious. I also could clearly see the bird's solid black back, whitish underparts with barred sides, and the bold white line that runs from its forehead, below the eyes, to its nape. Although this species is a relatively uncommon woodpecker, I was surprised how tame it was; the female allowed me to approach within about 25 feet (7.6 m), and then she only moved to the opposite side of the tree. In New Mexico, I have located this bird from a quarter-mile (.4 km) away by walking toward the drumming sound. It usually will remain in the same tree for a considerable period of time.

Other birds that I found along the Coastal Hiking Trail, but did not detect elsewhere, included an osprey; belted kingfisher; yellow-bellied flycatcher; a family of boreal chickadees; gray and blue jays; wood thrush; solitary and Philadelphia vireos; Tennessee, bay-breasted, and Canada warblers; and purple finch.

A pair of **Canada warblers** literally attacked me, striking my pant legs, flying around in a circle, and flopping along the trail to get my attention. They undoubtedly had a nest close-by; the female carried a fat green caterpillar. They called sharp "chik" notes all the while. It was not until I moved down the trail that they calmed down enough to allow me a good look. Even then they were animated and nervous, and the male continued to castigate me. The Canada warbler is one of my favorite birds, with contrasting yellow, black, and gray plumage. Most obvious are its canary yellow underparts, which are crossed by solid black lines on the breast to form a necklace. It also has bold yellowish eye rings that are set against black facial markings. And in the right light, its gray back becomes a lovely shade of bluish gray.

Canada warbler

Frank Chapman, in *The Warblers of North America*, includes the following description of the Canada warbler by G. H. Thayer: The Canadian is a sprightly, wide-awake, fly-snapping Warbler, vivid in movement and in song; clearly marked and brightly colored. In actions it is like the Wilson's, a sort of mongrel between *Dendroica*, an American Redstart, and a true Flycatcher. It darts after flying insects like one of the Tyrannidae [flycatcher family], and its bill may sometimes be heard to 'click' when it seizes something; it has much of the Redstart's insistent nervousness of motion, but it is a less airy 'flitter'; and, finally, it glides and gleans among leaves and twigs like a true gleaning Warbler.

The Canada warbler and most of its neighbors spend only a few weeks on their breeding grounds before they must leave for their winter homes. These are Neotropical migrants that nest in the northern forests and migrate to southern Mexico, the West Indies, Central America, and northern South America in late summer and fall. The Canada warbler travels all the way to South America, where it must find adequate habitat to supply shelter and food until it can migrate all the way back to Pukaskwa to nest. The long-term survival of Canada warblers and other Neotropical migrants depends on viable, healthy environments at both ends of their journeys.

Pukaskwa's bird population in winter is only a fraction of what exists in spring, summer, and fall. Only a few of the hardier species, along with some individuals from father north that come to the park for the winter, are present. The best sampling of the winter populations is the annual Christmas Bird Count, undertaken within a 15-mile diameter area during a single day of the holidays.

A local Christmas count is done at nearby Marathon and provides a good perspective on species in the park. In 1991, two counters tallied 523 individuals of 18 species. The dozen most numerous species, in descending order of abundance, included common raven, herring gull, pine grosbeak, black-capped chickadee, European starling, redpolls (common and hoary redpolls combined), American crow, downy woodpecker, hairy woodpecker, blue jay, and gray jay and evening grosbeak (tied).

In summary, the park's checklist of birds, based on a 1978 survey by Skeel and Bondrup-Nielsen, includes 222 species, of which 136 are considered to nest. Of those 136 species, 24 are water birds (loon, grebes, cormorant, waders, waterfowl, rails, shorebirds, gulls, and terns), 13 are hawks and owls, and 21 are warblers.

Birds of Special Interest

Common loon. Its loud, melancholy songs can be heard throughout the summer; a pair can usually be seen from the Hattie Cove Visitor Center.

Ruffed grouse. This gray-brown grouse of the hardwood forest is reasonably common; it displays in early spring, when its drumming can be heard for a considerable distance.

Spotted sandpiper. Watch for this teetering, spot-breasted shorebird along the grassy shoreline; it utters a loud series of "weet" notes when aroused.

Black-backed woodpecker. This is the park's only all-black-backed woodpecker; it prefers spruce-fir communities.

Winter wren. More often heard than seen, it sings continual songs, like tinkling silver bells, from the undergrowth.

Swainson's thrush. This thrush is surprisingly common throughout the park; it sings a flutelike song "wip-poor-wil-a-will-e-zee-zee."

Black-throated green warbler. A common forest warbler with a black throat and yellow face, it is usually detected first by its husky song, "zoo zee zoo zoo zee."

American redstart. Males possess coal black plumage with orange-red patches on their sides, wings, and tail; females are duller versions with yellow patches.

Canada warbler. Watch for this bright yellow-and-black warbler among hardwood thickets; males possess canary yellow underparts, black necklace, and yellowish eye rings.

White-throated sparrow. This is the common bird that sings loud "ah sweet Can-a-da Can-a-da" songs throughout the day and occasionally at night, as well.

Swamp sparrow. Look for this little sparrow with a reddish crown and shoulders in the park wetlands; it sings a rapid series of "weet" notes.

10

Bruce Peninsula National Park, Ontario

From Cyprus Lake Campground, I followed Horse Lake Trail toward Georgian Bay early one morning. Horse Lake was like a sheet of blue glass. Various grasses and sedges crowded the shore, and farther out, two black rocks protruded above the surface like beached whales. Each contained one white bird that apparently had roosted there overnight. The closer and larger of the two was a ring-billed gull, one of the park's most common summer residents. Through binoculars I could see its yellow bill with a black ring near the tip, white head and underparts, grayish back, and black wing tips with tiny white spots. It seemed content to remain there until something more exciting than a hiker came along.

The smaller rock contained a Caspian tern, distinguished by its surprisingly large, coral red bill, black cap, and white-and-gray body. It, too, seemed content, although it called one loud "kowk" at me as I passed by. Both species nest in island colonies on nearby Georgian Bay.

On the other hand, the forest birds along the trail were already foraging for meals: chasing insects, gleaning the foliage for insects, seeds, and fruit, or searching the forest floor for tidbits. Among the most vocal was a winter wren singing its rapid bubbling notes from the shadowy undergrowth. Chipping sparrows sang extended trills, while several American robins caroled their cheerful songs. A red-eyed vireo sang an extended series of whistle notes without any particular melody; a yellow-rumped warbler offered a drawling series of "tuwee-tuwee-tuwee" notes; and an ovenbird called a loud "teach

teach teach TEACH TEACH" song. Then, almost directly above my head, I detected the husky, but melodic, notes of a **black-throated green warbler.**

It was a brightly marked male with a coal black throat, upper breast, and sides, like an inverted V, bright yellow face with blackish cheeks, and olive-green back. As I watched, it put its head back and sang: "zee zee zee zoo zee," a very typical song. Frank Chapman, in *Handbook of Birds of Eastern North America*, described the black-throated green's song as sounding "like the droning of bees; it seems to voice the restfulness of a midsummer day."

Black-throated green warbler

During several days of birding Bruce Peninsula, no other song-bird was as abundant as this forest warbler. While several of the other warblers had completed nesting by my mid-July visit, black-throated greens were still busy feeding nestlings or fledglings. This Neotropical migrant does not arrive on its nesting grounds until mid-May, leaving only about 10 to 12 weeks before it must depart for its wintering grounds far to the south in Mexico, Central America, northern South America, or the Greater Antilles.

Territory selection and defense undoubtedly begin as soon as it arrives; that is usually when singing is most profuse. Nests constructed of conifer leaves, grass, and moss (bound with plant down and spider webbing) are usually placed on horizontal branches of conifers from a few inches to 40 feet (12 m) off the ground. Hair, feathers, and fur are used for lining. Nest construction requires several days. Incubation of the four or five eggs normally takes another 12 days, and it takes an additional eight to ten days before the young are fledged. The entire process, including the selection of territory and nest site, requires 20 to 37 days, leaving barely enough time to prepare for a southbound journey of at least 2,400 miles (3,862 km).

The Park Environment
The 38,054-acre (15,400-ha) Bruce Peninsula National Park lies at the northern tip of Ontario's Bruce Peninsula, also the northern end of the ancient Niagara Escarpment. The national park was only established in 1987, so about half of the area is still in private ownership and, therefore, unavailable to the public. The park's largest intact area lies along the eastern side of the peninsula between Cameron and Cyprus lakes and George, Lower Andrew, Upper Andrew, and Moore lakes; the Cyprus Lake and Emmett Lake roads provide access. In addition, the extensive Bruce Trail follows the Georgian Bay shoreline for the entire length of the park. Scattered park lands also lie along the western side of the peninsula. The largest and most accessible of these is the Singing Sands Beach area, adjacent to the Federation of Ontario Naturalists Nature Preserve.

Vegetation throughout the park is largely second-growth forest with extensive areas of northern white cedar, paper birch, balsam poplar, balsam fir, and white spruce. Drier sites include jack and white pine. Understory plants vary with the soil and moisture, but saplings, ferns, creeping and common junipers, willows, dogwoods, wild sasparilla, chokecherry, and other shrubs are common. Hardwood communities of beech and sugar maples with scattered aspens and paper birch, bogs, and other wetlands are also scattered throughout.

The park visitor center, a temporary structure with an information desk and exhibits, is in the village of Tobermory. Most of the park's interpretive activities are based around Cyprus Lake

Campground and include naturalist-guided hikes and evening programs. Guided trips to Flowerpot Island, part of adjacent Fathom Five National Marine Park, are provided from Tobermory. Schedules of interpretive activities are posted.

Additional information can be obtained from the Superintendent, Bruce Peninsula National Park, Box 189, Tobermory, Ont. NOH 2RO; (519) 596-2233.

Bird Life

Horse Lake Trail is only .6 mile (1 km) from the Head of Trails (trailhead) to its junction with the Bruce Trail. From that point I followed the Bruce Trail northwest to Halfway Rock Point, which provides a commanding view of the lakeshore. Numerous **double-crested cormorants**, all-black except for the adults' bright yellow throat, with a long neck and bill, were swimming just off shore. As I reached the top of the point, several cormorants took flight, running along the surface with much flapping of wings before they were airborne. Cormorants appear awkward in takeoff and flight, but underwater is another matter. They are pursuit swimmers that dive forward from a floating position and swim down their prey. They can reach a depth of 100 feet (30 m) and capture prey with their hooked bill. Once they catch a fish, they usually come to the surface to swallow it whole. However, cormorants must come out of the water often to dry. Unlike most water birds, they do not have enough oil glands to keep their plumage properly waterproofed. They often are found standing spread-eagle while drying their feathers.

Another large water bird was fishing nearby, diving and surfacing numerous times while I watched the cormorants. It suddenly took flight with a long takeoff like that of the cormorants, but instead of following the cormorants down the shore, it flew directly into a ledge or cavity in the cliff about 500 feet (152 m) beyond my observation site. This was a common merganser female that I assumed had a nest there. During the half hour that I was on the Point, it flew in and out of the cliff site four times. This "fish-duck" is well known for nesting on cliffs and other cavities, from nest boxes to natural tree holes to deserted chimneys.

I also observed numerous ring-billed gulls, a few of the larger herring gulls, with a yellow bill with a red spot on the lower mandible, and a pair of Caspian terns flying up and down the lake. In scoping the shoreline I discovered a couple dozen gulls perched on the rocks farther down the shore. Park biologist Mark Wiercinski later told me that all these birds, as well as cormorants and a few black-crowned night-herons, nest on Devil Island and other isolated islands in Georgian Bay. Wiercinski also has found four herring gull nests on cliffs, rare in southern Ontario.

Common ravens also nest on the cliffs; Mark has found six nests. He explained that the Bruce Peninsula ravens represent a southern extension of this boreal species in Canada. The common raven is larger than the closely related American crow and can best be identified by its broad wings, wedge-shaped tail (not rounded like that of a crow), craggy head, and large heavy bill. Ravens hunt Highway 6 in the early morning for overnight casualties.

Cliff swallows also are cliff nesters; a dozen or so were flying over Halfway Rock Point, calling nasal "nyew" notes and chasing insects. Through binoculars, I could see their whitish underparts with a dark rufous throat and buff rump patch. Barn swallows were present as well; they are easily distinguished from the cliff swallows by their long, forked tail, compared with the cliff swallow's square tail.

The lush greenery adjacent to the point held a number of songbirds. A family of **black-capped chickadees** were most evident. The young birds called high squeaky sounds as they chased their parents about begging for handouts. The adults sang a clear "fee-bee-ee" song, although they also sing "chick-a-dee-dee-dee" on occasion. The adults and fully grown youngsters were difficult to tell apart; they all possessed a coal black cap and throat, white cheeks, and blackish wings with white edges on their coverts. There were at least eight youngsters, and I could not help but wonder how this cavity-nester could manage so many babies in a tiny space like a deserted downy woodpecker nest.

Other songbirds within hearing distance of my perch included golden-crowned kinglets with their high-pitched "tzee tzee" notes; more red-eyed vireos and black-throated green warblers; black-and-white warblers singing six to eight high-pitched "wee-see" notes; and a pair of American redstarts. In *The Audubon Society Master Guide to Birding*, Peter Vickery describes the redstart's song as "5 or 6 rapid notes with last 2 syllables strongly accented: 'zee-zee-zee-zawaah' (down-slurred), 'zee-zee-zee-zee-zwee' (up-slurred)." The male was a gorgeous creature with all-black plumage, except for orange-red patches on its sides, wings, and tail; its lady was a duller version with yellow patches.

En route back to Cyprus Lake Campground, I followed the Georgian Bay Trail along the west side of Horse Lake, stopping at a boardwalk overlook about half way around. The Caspian tern had been replaced by a smaller common tern on one rock, and two ring-billed gulls sat side by side on the larger rock. I watched as two more common terns approached along the far side of the lake. Suddenly, the lone common tern flew up and charged the two oncoming terns, which immediately turned back. There was a great commotion and considerable screaming, like drawn-out "kee-ar" notes, from all three terns. But the one individual managed to chase off the newcomers. I wondered if it had also chased off the Caspian tern that had roosted there overnight. It shortly returned to its rock, like the proverbial king of the hill, or, in this case, an already staked-out feeding territory. I could not help but admire its assertiveness. Through binoculars, I could see its bright red bill with a black tip, black cap, snow white underparts, and dark gray back. It, too, is a colonial nester on the outer islands.

The yodel of a common loon then attracted my attention, and I watched a loon approach and fly over the lake toward some loon rendezvous farther down the peninsula. It seemed awkward in flight, with its neck and head hanging lower than its shoulders and its legs stretched out behind. This charismatic bird nests on a few of the park's more isolated lakes in summer, but its loud music is its most memorable quality. The northern lakes would lose their wilderness character without the wild laughter of the common loon.

The southern fringe of Horse Lake contained an extensive area of grasses, sedges, willows, alders, and related vegetation. **Song sparrows** were most abundant, undoubtedly the dominant species in this habitat. All their songs began with three "sweet" notes, followed by a varied middle melody and ending with a trill. These little birds, with a long floppy tail, are heavily striped; their chest stripes form a central stickpin. See chapter 16 on Cuyahoga Valley for more about this bird's singing ability.

Other wetland birds I detected that morning included of swamp sparrows, which sang rapid "weet weet weet weet weet" songs; common yellowthroats with their "witchity witchity witchity" songs; and a few **red-winged blackbirds**. The males, black except for bright red wing patches (epaulets), called loud "tee-ay" notes. Their normal territorial song is an expressive "konk-a-reee," with much emphasis on the "reee." The females and youngsters are distinguished by their heavily striped plumage. Red-wing pairs nest in marshy areas during the summer, but gather in huge flocks by early fall. They feed in weedy fields during the winter, usually far to the south. But whenever possible they roost overnight in cattail swamps.

Other birds found on my Horse Lake loop route included a pair of belted kingfishers; numerous downy woodpeckers and northern flickers; a pileated woodpecker was calling "wuk-wuk-wuk" in the distance; eastern wood-pewees with their sorrowful "pee-weee" songs; a few great crested and least flycatchers; several blue jays; red-breasted nuthatches; American robins; veeries; a lone solitary vireo; and several rose-breasted grosbeaks.

The **blue jays** were most attracting, with their blue-and-white plumage and crest. A blue jay family near the Head of Trails included at least four youngsters that trailed after their parents, begging for food with squeaky "jay jay jay" notes. In spite of this bird's reputation as a campground pest and raider of other birds' nests, I can not help but admire its ability to adapt to new situations. It is one of the first birds to invade developed sites in the forest, where it soon begins to take advantage of other species. Like its cousin, the American crow, the blue jay can survive on a highly diverse diet that can include everything from insects to seeds, as well as snails, fish, frogs, mice, bats, and small birds and their eggs. See chapter 26 on Hot Springs for more about this adaptable species.

Another morning I birded an old logging road that parallels the Cyprus Lake Road, which begins directly across Highway 6 from the Dorcas Bay Road. This route passes through some very good hardwood forest habitat. Most of the species I recorded that morning duplicated those I had found around Horse Lake. But it was the only place in the park where I found white-throated sparrows, much to my surprise. Wiercinski told me that this normally common sparrow had not shown up that spring, and he did not know why. This sparrow sings a loud "ah sweet Can-a-da, Can-a-da" song, an important ingredient in the flavor of the northern forests.

Wiercinski has established several breeding bird forest monitoring plots along this roadway. In 1993, he recorded 29 species nesting here: yellow-bellied sapsucker; downy, hairy, and pileated woodpeckers; eastern wood-pewee; least and great crested flycatchers; black-capped chickadee; winter wren; veery; Swainson's and hermit thrushes; American robin; solitary, yellow-throated, and red-eyed vireos; Nashville, yellow, magnolia, black-throated blue, black-throated green, black-and-white, and mourning warblers; American redstart; common yellowthroat; scarlet tanager; rose-breasted grosbeak; brown-headed cowbird; and Baltimore oriole.

The largest and most impressive-looking of all these birds is unquestionably the **pileated woodpecker**, a Woody Woodpecker look-alike. According to *Webster's Ninth New Collegiate Dictionary*, both "pie-le" and "pill-e" pronunciations are correct. This wonderful woodpecker, with a black body, bright red crest, and bold white lines that extend from its white cheeks down its neck, is heard more often than seen. Its loud "kuk, kuk, kuk, kuk, kuk" calls resound through the forest. Observers may glimpse more than a large flying bird with contrasting black-and-white underwing linings. The lucky hiker who sees this woodpecker up close cannot help but notice, beyond its large size, its very heavy bill. This tool is used to rip into larvae-infested trees and carpenter ant nests for food.

Pileated woodpeckers require big trees and large acreage. They have disappeared from many parts of their former range due to timber cutting and fragmentation of their habitat. They utilize year-round territories and may mate for life. Nest cavities are constructed in dead trees usually 28 to 35 feet (9-11 m) above the ground.

Dorcas Bay and the adjacent nature preserve (within the park boundary) are also worth visiting. The shallow bay and mud flats provide good feeding areas for waterfowl and shorebirds. In July, Canada geese and killdeers were most numerous. The six or seven **killdeers** called loud "kill-dee" notes as I approached and flew off up the shore. Few birds are as clearly marked as the killdeer, with distinct double black bands on its otherwise all-white underparts, and its white, black, and brown head. In flight, it also shows orange color on its rump. This is a bird of the lakesides, meadows, and wet fields.

It preys mostly on insects and other invertebrates, which it finds by sight and chases down on foot.

Another common shorebird that nests in the park is the elusive **American woodcock**. Wiercinski told me that, to his knowledge, Bruce Peninsula boasts the highest population of these birds. During the several days I spent in the park, I did not find one. However, it is more likely to be encountered in spring. These chunky, robin-sized shorebirds are among the earliest to commence courtship. Woodcocks prefer dense woods and are crepuscular in nature, going about their territorial activities at dawn and dusk. They select open grassy places in which to court. The woodcock's incredible sky dance was described by Frank Chapman, in *Handbook of Birds of Eastern North America*:

> He begins on the ground with a formal, periodic "peent, peent" an incongruous preparation for the wild rush that follows. It is repeated several times before he springs from the ground, and on whistling wings sweeps out on the first loop of a spiral which may take him 300 feet [91 m] above the ground. Faster and faster he goes, louder and shriller sounds his wing-song; then after a moment's pause, with darting, headlong flight, he pitches in zigzags to the earth, uttering as he falls a clear, twittering whistle (actually produced by the wings). He generally returns to near the place from which he rose, and the "peent" is at once resumed as a preliminary to another round in the sky.

American woodcock

Nesting usually occurs in moist woods or boggy streamsides. Then the woodcock is difficult to find, due to its nocturnal feeding habits. However, it often feeds in small congregations in clearings and brushy areas, where it may eat more than its weight in earthworms (up to 55) daily. It pokes its long bill deep into the mud and uses the tips of its flexible mandibles like tweezers to feel for and extract earthworms, which it swallows whole. The following morning, a careful search may uncover some of the probe holes left by the woodcock's nightly feeding.

I found two beautiful warblers along the nature reserve trail: black-throated blue and Blackburnian. My first clue to the presence of a black-throated blue was its distinct song: a short, lazy "zwee-a zwee-a zweee." It took me several minutes to find the perpetrator hidden among the foliage of a white cedar. Male black-throated blues are worth the time and effort necessary to find them, however. At first glance it can appear all-black, except for its white belly and a tiny square, white wing patch. But in good light, its crown, back, and shoulders appear to be covered with a spectacular deep blue shawl, and its face, throat, wings, and tail are almost leaden black.

The Blackburnian warbler male possesses a contrasting orange, black, and white plumage. Its head is most striking, with a brilliant orange throat, crown patch, and eyebrows, and a black cap, bold eye rings, and extensions behind the eyes. Its back and wings are also black, with white streaks on the back and a large white wing bar. Its song is also very distinct, a thin and wiry melody usually described as "sip sip sip titi tzeee."

The bird find of the day was a family of **ruffed grouse**. I discovered these birds at the beginning of the Backlands Trail, which branches off the main reserve trail. There were at least four youngsters and one or two adults. I encountered an adult female first, walking down the trail ahead of me. When I stopped to study it through binoculars, it clucked like a rooster and walked nervously into the shadowy forest. However, I could clearly see its mottled back and partly spread tail with a dark terminal band. A slightly smaller grouse appeared alongside it, but rather than following the adult it suddenly took off, flying with a roar of its wings into the adjacent forest. Almost immediately three or more similar-sized grouse flushed to my left, probably not more than 10 feet (3 m) away, and whirled out of sight.

Other birds detected in the reserve included downy woodpeckers; northern flickers; great crested flycatchers; black-capped chickadees; American robins; yellow-rumped, black-throated green, pine, and black-and-white warblers; American redstarts; chipping sparrows; purple and house finches; and American goldfinches.

I visited a few additional localities during my stay in the park. The open cattail marsh along Highway 6, just north of the Dorcas Bay Road, produced two least bitterns, three soras, and several willow flycatchers one early morning. And the dozen or more cedar waxwings flying about the adjacent clumps of conifer and birch trees suggested a nesting colony of this common species. Betty and I also spent an afternoon in the Emmett and Bartley lakes area; the marsh along the Log Dump Road was most impressive. A dozen or more great blue herons flew up from the marsh or sat like statues on high snags. This area supports breeding olive-sided flycatchers and rusty blackbirds, and, according to Wiercinski, sandhill cranes also nest here.

Fields and grasslands exist in scattered areas of the park. Although birders might pass over these habitats for the more impressive forest habitat, they support a rich assortment of bird species. Some of the park's more common field and grassland birds not already mentioned include the ruby-throated hummingbird, eastern kingbird, purple martin, house wren, eastern bluebird, gray catbird, brown thrasher, European starling, yellow warbler, indigo bunting, field sparrow, and eastern meadowlark.

Most of the park's breeding birds leave for the winter; many of these are Neotropical migrants that spend their winters far to the south in the tropics. The remaining population is only a fraction of what it is in spring, summer, and fall. The park's winter birds are censused annually as part of the continentwide Christmas Bird Count. In 1992, 1,461 individuals of 47 species were tallied on the Bruce Peninsula National Park count. Of those 47 species, the dozen most numerous birds, in descending order of abundance, included black-capped chickadee, herring gull, common raven, pine siskin, common goldeneye, house sparrow, Bohemian waxwing, golden-crowned kinglet, red-breasted nuthatch, blue jay and northern cardinal (tied), and rock dove.

In summary, the park's checklist of birds (for Grey-Bruce) include 304 species, of which 141 are considered (by Wiercinski) as nesting. Of those 141 species, 24 are water birds (loon, grebe, cormorant, waders, waterfowl, rails, and shorebirds), 13 are hawks and owls, and 18 are warblers.

Birds of Special Interest
Double-crested cormorant. Watch for this all-black bird offshore; it feeds on fish that it catches underwater.

Ruffed grouse. This is a shy, chicken-sized forest bird with a broad tail that shows a dark terminal band.

Killdeer. It prefers wet areas and is characterized by its loud "kill-dee" call and double black bands across its white throat.

American woodcock. This chunky shorebird with a long, heavy bill performs a spectacular courtship display in spring.

Ring-billed gull. One of the park's most common summer residents, adults are easily recognized by their yellow bill with a black ring.

Caspian tern. This large tern possesses a black cap and heavy, coral red bill; its distinct calls is a low, harsh "kowk."

Pileated woodpecker. This is the Woody Woodpecker look-alike of the mature forest habitat; it is a very large black woodpecker with a bright red crest.

Blue jay. Everyone knows this crested, blue-and-white bird of the forest and fields; one of its best-known calls is a scratchy "jay jay jay."

Black-capped chickadee. This is the little forest bird with a black cap and throat, white cheeks, and "chick-a-dee-dee-dee" or "fee-bee-ee" songs.

Black-throated green warbler. The park's most common warbler, it sports a coal black throat, yellow face, and olive-green back. It sings a distinctive song: a husky "zee zee zee zoo zee."

Song sparrow. Watch for this long-tailed little bird along the edge of wetlands; it is heavily streaked and has a black stickpin.

Red-winged blackbird. The male of this wetland species has all-black plumage, except for bright red wing patches; the adult female is heavily streaked with faint reddish patches on its head and shoulders.

EASTERN DECIDUOUS FOREST

Nature is part of our humanity, and without some aware-ness and experience of that divine mystery, man ceases to be man.

—Henry Beston

11

Apostle Islands National Lakeshore, Wisconsin

My visit to Sand Island, which included a 2-mile (3.2-km) walk from the dock to the lighthouse, produced a surprising diversity of birds, more than two dozen species. The clearing at the ranger station was filled with singing birds. American redstarts were most vociferous. I located one brightly marked male singing from a white birch. Its coal black plumage, with orange-red patches on its sides, wings, and tail, gleamed in the morning light. And its strident song, a shrill, unmusical series of rapid notes that have been described as down-slurred "zee-zee-zee-zawaa" and "zee-zee-zee-zee-zweee" with a rising inflection, rang across the clearing time and again. It seemed fully intent on dominating the morning songfest.

A chestnut-sided warbler sang a different song that contained six to eight ascending "chev" notes, followed by a sharp, distinct "wis-you." The male had deep chestnut sides, white patches on its cheeks that extended onto the neck, heavy black eyebrows, and a yellow-orange crown. The female, a duller version of the male, held a fat, green worm tightly in its bill. The pair undoubtedly had a nest nearby, probably in the dense undergrowth.

American crow, blue jay, and American robin calls and songs were audible beyond the clearing. An ovenbird's loud "teach teach teach TEACH TEACH" song, each note louder than the previous one, echoed from the forest. The constant whistle notes of a red-eyed vireo were evident, as well. A distant veery sang a series of spirally descending "wheeu" notes. A pair of cedar waxwings flew over, calling high-pitched notes. And down the shoreline came the "ah-sweet" and "ah-sweet Can-a-da, Can-a-da" songs of white-throated sparrows.

Suddenly, a little brownish bird flew across my path into the adjacent alder thicket. I spished quietly, and immediately a **song sparrow** charged out to investigate. It sat in the open, chipping loud, hollow "chimp" notes; it undoubtedly was highly agitated by my presence. It pumped its rather long tail up and down, posturing as if it were about to dive for cover. I was able to examine it carefully through my binoculars. It was heavily streaked throughout; the dark streaks on its whitish breast formed a bold, black stickpin. I also could see its grayish eyebrows and black stripes bordering its whitish throat.

Apparently, it decided that I was not a threat, because it seemed to calm down. Then, as if to reclaim its territory, it put its head back and sang a rambling, but beautiful, song consisting of three clear notes, "sweet sweet sweet," followed by a buzzy "tow-weee," then a trill. A second song sparrow, 40 to 50 feet (12-15 m) to my left, seemed to respond with a somewhat different song, "sweet sweet sweet che-che-che-che-che." I was reminded that Henry David Thoreau had once interpreted this sparrow's song as "maids! maids! maids! hang up your teakettle-ettle-ettle." And in 1943, ornithologist Margaret Nice discovered that an Ohio song sparrow sang a total of 2,305 songs during a single day in May. This bird's scientific name, *melodia*, Greek for melody or melodious song, is well deserved.

The Park Environment
Apostle Islands National Lakeshore comprises 21 islands that range in size from tiny Gull Island (3 acres or 1.2 ha) to Stockton Island, the largest at 10,053 acres (4,068 ha). The farthest island, Outer Island, is 14.4 miles (23 km) from the mainland or 21 miles (34 km) from Bayfield. An 11-mile (17.7-km) strip of land at the top of Bayfield Peninsula is also included in the park.

The islands are accessible only by water. The Apostle Islands Cruise Service (fee) offers a variety of trips from Bayfield and Little Sand Bay docks. A water taxi, which carries up to six passengers, is also available. Campers can make arrangements for drop-off and pickup. Private boats are also welcome.

All visitors are encouraged to stop first at the Headquarters Visitor Center, located in Bayfield in the old county courthouse, or at the Little Sand Bay Visitor Center, 13 miles (21 km) north of Bayfield. Both centers have an information desk, an orientation program, exhibits, and a sales outlet. Bird field guides and a checklist, as well as the little book *Birds of the Apostle Islands*, by Stanley Temple and James Harris (which includes an annotated list of all the birds recorded in the park) are available.

Park interpretive activities vary throughout the summer season. From late June to late August, interpreters accompany cruise boats or meet them on island docks to provide guided walks on Sand and Rasberry islands on Mondays, Wednesdays, and Fridays; on Stockton Island on Tuesdays, Thursdays, Saturdays, and Sundays; and daily at Manitou Island. Walks and evening talks are provided regularly at Little Sand Bay and on Stockton Island. Lectures are offered at the Headquarters Visitor Center every Wednesday evening. A schedule of activities appears in the park's newspaper, *Around the Archipelago*, available at the visitor centers.

The dominant vegetation on the islands is northern hardwood forest, consisting of sugar maple, yellow birch, hemlock, balsam fir, and white cedar, with an understory of saplings. Canada yew is abundant on islands where white-tailed deer have never occurred. Aspen and white birch communities occupy areas previously disturbed by logging and associated fires. Smaller areas of boreal forest, dunes, and pine savannah are also present. Scattered beaver ponds and bogs exist on a few of the larger islands; cattails, alders, and willows, and spaghnum moss, leatherleaf, and Labrador tea dominate these two habitats, repectively.

Additional information can be obtained from the Superintendent, Apostle Islands National Lakeshore, Route 1, Box 4, Bayfield, WI 54814; (715) 779-3397.

Bird Life

Almost immediately after I stepped into the forest, a Nashville warbler sang a two-part song, "see-it see-it see-it, ti-ti-ti-ti-ti," the second half on a lower pitch than the first. As with the song sparrow, my spishing immediately attracted it closer, where I could see its grayish head, bold white eye rings, and yellow underparts.

A larger, two-toned bird moved in the alders beyond, flying out of sight. I continued down the trail, part of which was an elevated boardwalk, moving slowly so that I might find the larger bird. The forest was dominated by constant vireo and warbler songs. Suddenly a cuckoo flew across the trail, landing in a thicket of alders at eye level. I inched forward to get a better view. It was a **black-billed cuckoo**, with a reddish eye ring, brown upperparts, white underparts, and all-black bill.

Cuckoos are fascinating birds that include 127 species worldwide, but only seven North American forms, including the greater roadrunner of the American Southwest. Old World cuckoos are brood parasites that lay their eggs in the nests of other birds. New World cuckoos, however, build their own nests and rear their young. Black-bills usually nest in dense thickets. Their abundance and nesting success often correspond to tent caterpillar outbreaks.

The high-pitched song of a black-and-white warbler awakened me from my trance, and I discovered a brightly marked male barely 10 feet (3 m) above my head. I watched it creep around the trunk of a white spruce, probing every crack that it encountered. Every now and then it sang its distinct song, a thin, unhurried series of six to eight "wee-see" couplets, with emphasis on "wee."

I recorded a number of other birdsongs along the trail: the extended song, like tinkling bells, of winter wrens; the "chick-a-dee-dee-dee" of black-capped chickadees and the more nasal "tseek-a-day-day" of boreal chickadees; the husky songs of black-throated green warblers; and distant whistle notes of a scarlet tanager and rose-breasted grosbeak.

In spots where the vegetation allowed views of the lake, I could see the heavily eroded cliffs, which provide nesting sites for cliff swallows. Several of these square-tailed swallows were flying overhead in their search for insects. I noticed two water birds in the lake: a distant common loon and a nearby family of **red-breasted mergansers**. The merganser family consisted of eight half-sized youngsters and a hen. They all looked much alike: brownish back with a single white wing bar edged in black, reddish head with a feathered crest, white throat, and a narrow, orangish bill. The absent drake possesses a forest green head, white collar, reddish breast, and black-and-white back. I assumed that this merganser family was a product of a cavity nest on the cliffs. The species is known to nest in cavities in trees and cliffs, and even under piles of driftwood. They feed on fish either by diving underwater and pursuing their prey or by submerging only their head. Their bill is serrated to aid in capturing and holding their slippery catch.

Several huge white pines were growing along the far end of the trail, and I stopped to admire one especially large tree; my arms went only partway around its great, solid trunk. Then the nasal call, like a toy horn, of a red-breasted nuthatch echoed down. It took me several seconds to locate the perpetrator, which was searching for insects on the higher branches.

Suddenly, I saw a **merlin** pass overhead and out of sight. Its striped body and banded tail were visible for only a second. I later asked park biologist Tom Doolittle if it was possibly nesting nearby. Tom said he knew of only two or three active merlin nests in the national lakeshore and none on Sand Island. "More likely," he said, "that individual was only hunting on Sand Island." He explained that a pair take and consume about 650 songbirds each nesting season, so they must cover a large area. Apostle Islands' merlins feed primarily on local passerines. See chapter 6 on Voyageurs for additional details about this little falcon.

As I approached the clearing at the lighthouse, I detected a vigorous, but short, song emanating from the dense alders that surrounded the clearing. The song included three swinging and ascending "sweee" notes, followed by two lower "chu cho" phrases. I got reasonably close to the songster, but was still unable to get a good look. Despite my low spishing sounds, the mourning warbler remained in the thicket, but I did glimpse its grayish blue hood, wide black bib, and yellow underparts. It continued to sing all the while, but I did not realize until later that this bird was singing a different song from its typical "chirry chirry chirry chorry chorry" rendition. One indication, perhaps, of the area's unique biogeographic position in the world of North American songbirds.

The Sand Island Lighthouse stood like a giant rock in the grassy clearing. Nancy Peterson, summer volunteer, greeted me, and during our conversation we watched a number of **double-crested cormorants** pass by on their way west. These adult cormorants were undoubtedly returning to their nests with food. They soon would be feeding their nestlings by regurgitating fish, which they had captured during their morning fishing trip, into the gullets of the young cormorants. These large water birds possess all-black plumage with a bare, yellowish throat patch. Their name comes from the French *cormaran*, which means "sea crow," a most appropriate title. "Double-crested" refers to the double tufts on the crown.

Nancy also told me about the chimney swifts that dive into her chimney every evening at dusk. I had heard several of these plain little birds with swept-back wings chippering over the forest from the trail. Chimney swifts also nest in hollows of the large yellow birches.

Suddenly we saw a pair of **bald eagles** soaring over the lighthouse and then moving off toward Lighthouse Bay. Their snow white head and tail, which contrast with their dark brown body, were truly spectacular. For several minutes they were so close that I could see their bright yellow bill and feet. It's no wonder this species was adopted as our national emblem, yet this bird faced sure extinction from pesticides before one of the chief culprits—DDT—was banned in the United States and Canada in 1972. Since then it has made a steady recovery throughout most of its range. However, Apostle Islands' eagles produce fewer young than mainland birds. Of four active nests

Bald eagle

in 1992, located on York, North Twin, Devil's, and Michigan islands, only two fledged young. And in 1993, only three nesting pairs were located; each of the three pairs fledged one youngster. Ongoing research indicates that low productivity probably is due to a combination of factors: elevated levels of PCBs (possibly from feeding on ring-billed gulls that obtain much of their food from dumps outside the region), lower food availability, lower temperatures, and higher wind velocity.

The more common **herring gull** is one of the park's most prominent birds, especially at docks and other places of human use. For instance, they often crowd the Little Sand Bay Dock and Fishery Pier like vultures. But this gull is a full-time resident and an opportunistic scavenger and predator; it feeds on whatever is available, from garbage and dead fish to birds and their eggs.

Herring gulls are large gulls with a snow white head, neck, and underparts, a pale gray mantle, black wing tips with two white patches, pinkish legs, and a bright yellow bill with an orange spot on the lower mandible. The smaller ring-billed gull possesses yellow feet and a bill with a solid black ring. Herring gulls nest along the rocky shoreline on several islands, but are most numerous on Gull and Eagle islands. These two islands support over 800 nests, approximately 85 percent of all herring gull nests in western Lake Superior.

The National Park Service, in conjunction with the Wisconsin Department of Natural Resources, monitors the park's colonial nesting birds regularly. Apostle Islands' resource management specialist Julie Van Stappen told me that double-crested cormorant nesting populations have increased from seven nests in 1978 to more than 725 nests in 1993. This increase is undoubtedly due to a decline in pesticide use, protection from humans, and an increase in lake herring.

Migratory birds have also been surveyed in recent years with some amazing results. According to the 1990 Migratory Bird Survey report by Van Stappen and Doolittle, 13,983 birds of 141 species were counted during 29 hours of spring surveys on Outer Island; migratory flow averaged 383 birds per hour. "Bird composition was strongly dominated by passerines (80%). The raptor component was dominated by broad-winged hawks," according to the report. In fall, the Outer Island survey tallied 140,912 birds of 107 species during 55 hours of observation; migratory flow averaged 2,541 birds per hour. "Bird composition was dominated by passerines (98%). The majority of raptors were falcons—105 merlins and 66 peregrine falcons." Migrant shorebirds were more numerous on Long Island; southbound movement begins in July and continues through October.

Breeding bird surveys conducted in 1990, 1991, 1992, and 1993 on seven islands and the mainland, have recorded a total of 118 species. In 1993, surveyors located 93 bird species. The ten most abundant breeders, in order of abundance, were ovenbird, red-eyed vireo, black-throated green warbler, American redstart, veery, red-winged blackbird, American crow, song sparrow, blue jay, and Nashville warbler. Stockton Island produced the largest number (439) and species (51).

Stockton Island offers the greatest habitat diversity, with the 3.8-mile (6-km) Tombolo Loop Trail the most productive bird-finding area in the park. According to the park's Stockton Island information handout, "towering pines, old and new bogs, a lagoon, beach ridges and Julian Bay Beach" occur along the route. The second-growth hardwood stand at the start of the trail is a good place to watch for least flycatchers, evident by their distinct "che-bec" calls; Swainson's thrushes, with their fluteline songs; and red-eyed vireos, which sing continuous whistle notes from the upper canopy. Also parula warblers, whose distinct song sounds like an ascending trill that ends with a sharp lower note; yellow-rumped warblers, with their variable, slow "tuwee-tuwee-tuwee" songs; magnolia warblers, with their rising "wee-o wee-o wee-chy" song; and Blackburnian warblers, identified by their thin, wiry "sip sip sip titi tzeee" songs.

The **Swainson's thrush** sings one of the most outstanding songs heard in the park. Wayne Peterson, in *The Audubon Society Master Guide to Birding*, describes it as an "upward-rolling series of flutelike phrases, like 'poor-wil-wil-eez-zee-zee.' " And Frank Chapman, in *Handbook of Birds of Eastern North America*, quotes a description by J. Dwight, Jr.: "The effect of its loud and beautiful song is much enhanced by the evening hush in which it is most often heard. It lacks the leisurely sweetness of the Hermit Thrush's outpourings, nor is there pause, but in lower key and with greater energy it bubbles on rapidly to a close, rather than fading out with the soft melody of its renowned rival."

This thrush often sings from the top of a high conifer in the early morning and evening; at these times, in good light, it can be observed. Otherwise, its subtle beauty can hardly be deciphered in the shadowy undergrowth. But in the right light its uniform olive-brown upperparts, buff spectacles, and buff breast with dark spotting can appear almost brilliant. For additional information about this lovely forest thrush, see chapter 9 on Pukaskwa.

Savannah sparrows frequent the grassy habitat along the beach. Chipping sparrows sing their extensive trills, all on the same key, from the trees and shrubs. And pine warblers sing a more melodic trill from the adjacent pines. This little yellowish warbler rarely leaves the security of the pines and usually is located foraging for insects on the outer boughs.

The Stockton Island bog is one of the park's most interesting habitats, supporting several birds that rarely occur elsewhere. A pair of sandhill cranes nest there annually, although, for some unknown reason, they never produce any youngsters. Chief park interpreter Kayci Cook explained that these cranes are "unsuccessful but die-hard nesters. They should consider adopting."

The sedge-filled edges of the bog support a population of sedge wrens, short-tailed wrens with a streaked back and crown, white eyebrows, and buff underparts. Listen, too, for the "rree-BEEA" songs of alder flycatchers. And watch the low shrubbery for common song sparrows, less numerous Lincoln's sparrows, and the yellow-and-black **common yellowthroat**. Yellowthroats are often detected first by their loud "witchity witchity witchity" songs. Spishing will usually attract one of these warblers close enough to reveal its coal black mask, whitish forehead, and bright yellow underparts. I found this songbird in almost all of the park's brushy habitats. Some ornithologists believe that this is our most abundant warbler.

But none of the bog residents is as yellow as the little yellow warbler; even the underside of its tail is yellow. Exceptions include its black eyes and the male's chestnut breast streaks. Its most common song is a lively and cheery "tseet-tseet-tseet sitta-sitta-sitta," but it is known to sing 18 songs, three distinct types with six variations of each. For me, yellow warblers are among the easiest birds to attract close-up. Spishing or squeaking with lips against the back of the hand will usually bring one or more males to investigate.

Another wetland bird is the **red-winged blackbird**. Males are most obvious because of their coal black plumage and bright red wing patches (epaulets); females are duller versions with heavily streaked plumage. Males spend much of their time posturing and defending their breeding territories, sometimes wildly chasing other males that come too close to their nest sites. They usually sit on posts singing loud "konk-a-ree" songs and calling hoarse "chack" notes at passing competitors.

The dead trees in the bog contain natural cavities and vacated woodpecker nests that are utilized by nesting tree swallows and eastern bluebirds. Eastern kingbirds often perch at the top of these snags, which provide excellent lookouts from which to capture passing insects. And great blue herons, mallards, red-breasted and common mergansers, and spotted sandpipers are also bog residents.

The **spotted sandpiper** frequents the edge of the wetlands, sometimes flying up with quick, stiff wing-beats and calling loud "weet weet" notes. Nesting spotties utilize dry ground along the shore, laying eggs in scrapes. But the most unusual characteristic of these sandpipers is polyandry; a female is likely to mate with more than one male, and even defends her mates against other females. The males share nest building, incubation, and feeding of the young. This behavior appears to be extremely successful for this sandpiper; it is the most widespread shorebird in North America. Breeding birds possess a heavily spotted breast, but they lose their spots by early fall.

Beyond the bog is a mixed-conifer community that contains a high diversity of breeding birds. Watch here for golden-crowned kinglets, red-breasted nuthatches, veeries, Swainson's thrushes, and numerous warblers: black-and-white, Cape May, yellow-rumped, black-throated green, Blackburnian, and (rarely) Wilson's. The black-throated green warbler sings a very distinct song, a husky "zee zee zee zoo zee" ditty. Ludlow Griscom and Alexander Sprunt, Jr., in *The Warblers of America*, wrote that its song "is as distinct as any warbler delivery can be, and easily learned. It has a drowsy quality which is appealing and, to some, musical as well. The notes vary from about five to eight, the last ascending, and the bird sings frequently. Mrs. Nice (1932) has counted 466 utterances in an hour." For more details about this lovely warbler, see chapter 10 on Bruce Peninsula.

Most of Apostle Islands' breeding birds leave by early fall and do not return until the following May or June. Stanley Temple and James Harris report, "only about 12 of the over 100 species of birds found on the islands during the summer stay there year-round." Most of those nonpermanent residents are Neotropical migrants that travel to the tropics for the winter. The common Nashville and chestnut-sided warblers spend their winters in Central America; many black-and-white warblers overwinter in mangrove swamps in the West Indies; and the abundant red-eyed vireo and lovely mourning and Canada warblers go to South America.

Winter bird populations consist of only a handful of the "hardiest of the northern forest birds that can withstand the rigors of winter," according to Temple and Harris. "Ravens, woodpeckers, nuthatches, chickadees, and northern finches are the most conspicuous of the winter residents and visitors that include the following species": common goldeneye; bald eagle; herring gull; great horned and barred owls; downy, hairy, black-backed, and pileated woodpeckers; gray and blue jays; common raven; black-capped chickadee; white-breasted and red-breasted nuthatches; northern shrike; pine and evening grosbeaks; red and white-winged crossbills; common redpoll; and pine siskin.

In summary, the park's checklist of birds includes 240 species, of which approximately 118 are known to nest. Of those 118 species, 10 are water birds (loon, cormorant, waterfowl, crane, shorebirds, and gull), 15 are hawks and owls, and 23 are warblers. Three species—glaucous and Iceland gulls and snowy owl—have been reported only in winter.

Birds of Special Interest
Double-crested cormorant. This large water bird is all-black, except for a bare, yellow throat. It may be seen flying or sitting upright on a post over the water.

Red-breasted merganser. Watch for this "fish-duck" along the islands; males sport a forest green head, while females and young possess a reddish brown head.

Bald eagle. The adult's pure white head and tail, contrasting with its dark brown plumage, make identification easy.

Merlin. Watch for this little falcon over the forest; it has pointed wings, striped underparts, and a barred tail.

Herring gull. This large white, gray, and black gull is frequently seen along the shore, over the islands, or soaring high overhead.

Spotted sandpiper. Watch for this little shorebird, with a heavily spotted breast, at any water area; its teetering behavior helps with identification.

Black-billed cuckoo. This secretive bird is distinguished by its two-tone plumage, brown above and white below, and its long tail and red eye rings.

Swainson's thrush. It is best known for its lovely, flutelike songs, upward-rolling "wip-poor-wil-wil-eez-zee-zee" notes.

Chestnut-sided warbler. This colorful little warbler is common at the edge of clearings; males possess chestnut sides, white cheeks and belly, and a yellow-orange crown.

American redstart. A mixed-forest warbler, the male is easily identified by its coal black plumage with orange-red (yellow in female) patches on its sides, wings, and tail.

Song sparrow. This is the long-tailed, brownish sparrow of thickets and wetlands that has heavy, dark stripes and a central stickpin; it sings a variable song that starts with three clear "sweet" notes.

12

Pictured Rocks National Lakeshore, Michigan

Few birds are so animated as the little common yellowthroat. This one seemed to be bubbling over with anxiety at my presence. Its loud and distinct chip notes had begun as soon as I had entered its territory. I was sure that a nest was hidden in the base of the alder thicket that it guarded. I had first been attracted by its loud "witchity witchity witchity" songs as I walked along the Sand Point Marsh Trail boardwalk, but as I approached it had suddenly changed from passive vocalist to spirited aggressor.

Common yellowthroat

My lively common yellowthroat was a brightly marked male with a lemon yellow throat and breast and a coal black mask that covered its eyes and cheeks, extending onto the sides of its neck. Its black mask was offset by a gray forehead. The rest of the bird was olive-brown to buff. Then the female appeared, a duller version of the male without the black mask. She carried a fat green larva in her bill and seemed almost as anxious as her mate for me to leave.

I slowly retreated from the nest site, stopping about 40 feet (12 m) away but keeping an eye on the larva-carrying female. Within seconds she dropped into the thicket and disappeared. The high-pitched chips of anxious nestlings greeted her arrival.

Yellowthroats were not the only marsh birds along the trail that early July morning. The abundant songs of song sparrows were audible throughout. These heavily streaked sparrows, with a black stick-pin in the center of their chest and a noticeably long tail, are renowned for their constant singing. Each song begins with three short, clear "sweet" notes, followed by a variety of notes and usually ending with an extended trill.

The swamp sparrow's three to eight rapid "weet" notes, all on the same pitch, were less noticeable. This sparrow looks different from the closely related song sparrow; it has a pale, unspotted breast and reddish shoulders and crown. It also is more secretive than the song sparrow, seldom leaving the concealment of the marsh grasses and underbrush. Song sparrows often sing from open posts and may allow a reasonably close approach.

The third sparrow I found around the marsh that early morning was the slightly larger white-throated sparrow, a most distinguished bird with a black-and-white head pattern. Adults also sport a snow white throat and a large yellow spot in front of each eye. But their most charming feature is their song, a loud "old-Sam Pea-bod-y, Pea-bod-y," or "ah-sweet Can-a-da, Can-a-da." Distant songs may sound like high-pitched "sweee" notes.

At one point along the trail I spished up a whole family of white-throats. They gathered around me in the shrubbery with many loud "chink" calls. Two or three climbed out of the cranberry shrubs for a closer look. There were at least seven, including five juveniles with grayish throats and indistinct head stripes. Although they generally remained shy, they seemed in no hurry to go about their business.

Suddenly, a male red-winged blackbird sang its loud "konk-a-reee" song from the top of a low tamarack tree. Its coal black plumage gleamed in the morning light. It sang several more times, then flew upward at a steep angle for about 50 to 60 feet (15-18 m) before gliding to another tree on the far edge of the marsh. While descending, it spread its wings to highlight its showy epaulets, no doubt a territorial display. A remarkably beautiful bird, in spite of being one of our most common species.

The Park Environment

Pictured Rocks National Lakeshore parallels the southeastern shore of Lake Superior for about 40 miles (64 km) between Munising and Grand Marais, Michigan. The widest point of the strip is only 5 miles (8 km). The western portion of the shoreline features 200 foot (61 m) high sandstone cliffs streaked with multicolored stains that create fascinating patterns, like paintings, thus the name "Pictured Rocks." The northern end of the shoreline is dominated by steep sand dunes that rise to more than 300 feet (91 m) above the cold lake waters. Among and behind these primary features are broad beaches, inland lakes and ponds, marshes, streams and waterfalls, and a variety of forest communities.

Approximately 80 percent of the forested landscape is deciduous forest, or upland northern hardwoods, which is dominated by beech and sugar maple and lesser numbers of red maple, yellow birch, hemlock, and white pine. Common understory plants include saplings and partridgeberry, red elderberry, and American yew. The best examples of this habitat occur behind Sand Point, at Miners Basin, at the Chapel Lake area, and near Sable Falls, according to botanist Robert Read.

Pine woods and barrens, which make up about 10 percent of the park, occur on coarse outwash and coastal sands and are dominated by red, white, and jack pines, with successional stands of paper birch and aspen. Common understory shrubs include saplings, evergreen bearberry, beaked hazelnut, bush honeysuckle, redberry wintergreen, black huckleberry, blackberry, and blueberries. Scattered wet forest or wetland habitats, also about 10 percent of the park, are dominated by black and white spruce, white cedar, and larch. Bogs, usually filled-in lakes, have a spaghnum base and a variety of ericaceous shrubs, including leatherleaf, bog rosemary, bog laurel, and cranberries, and are edged with alders and willows.

Visitor centers are located at both ends of the park. The Grand Sable Visitor Center near Grand Marais, the Munising Falls Interpretive Center, as well as the visitor information center in Munising, a joint National Park Service-U.S. Forest Service operation, all have an information desk and exhibits. The Grand Sable Visitor Center and the visitor information center also have a sales outlet where bird field guides and a checklist are available.

Park interpretive activities include ranger-guided walks and evening camp fire programs at various locations. Consult schedules and the free *Lakeshore Observer*. Two self-guided interpretive trails are available: the .5-mile (.8-km) Sand Point Marsh Trail across the highway from the Sand Point swim beach parking area and the 2-mile (3.2-km) White Birch Trail at the east end of the Twelvemile Beach Campground.

Additional information can be obtained from the Superintendent, Pictured Rocks National Lakeshore, P.O. Box 40, Munising, MI 49862; (906) 387-3700.

Bird Life

Sand Point Marsh is largely the result of beaver activity. Beaver dams have been built along the waterway, and a beaver lodge is visible from the boardwalk at the far side of one pond. The day I visited the marsh, mallards and wood ducks were swimming on the far shoreline, and a **great blue heron** was fishing the edge. It looked like a statue, frozen in place, waiting for passing prey. Through binoculars, I could see its long legs and neck, bluish back, and extremely heavy, yellowish bill. Then, suddenly, it struck down into the water with its lethal bill, so fast that I would not have noticed if I had not been watching closely. It came back up with a green frog in its bill. It seemed to examine its catch for just a second before swallowing it whole. It walked a few steps on its stiltlike legs and then adopted a statue pose to wait for its next prey.

Many more birds were active amid the taller vegetation along the edge of the marsh. At least two **American redstarts** sang strident notes, which Peter Vickery, in *The Audubon Society Master Guide to Birding*, described as "5 or 6 rapid notes with last 2 syllables strongly accented: 'zee-zee-zee-zawaah' (down-slurred), 'zee-see-see-see-zwee' (up-slurred)." I located one of the perpetrators near the top of a willow. It was a gorgeous warbler, with all-black, almost velvety plumage, except for orange-red patches on its flanks, wings, and tail, and whitish belly. Females are duller versions with yellow instead of orange-red patches.

American redstarts may be our most abundant songbird. Breeding birds range from southeast Alaska to Labrador, south into the northern Rocky Mountain states and deep into the Southeast to Alabama and Georgia. Apparently, it is an extremely adaptable songbird, nesting in a wide variety of broadleaf habitats. Paul Ehrlich and colleagues report that two pairs once shared a "common nest with 7 eggs which females took turns incubating."

I detected two *Empidonax* flycatchers along the boardwalk: The "che-bec" songs of least flycatchers emanated from the adjacent conifers, and at least one alder flycatcher called "rree-BEEA" from the alders. These look-alike flycatchers are best identified by their distinct songs. I also located a male chestnut-sided warbler and admired its contrasting plumage: deep chestnut sides, white cheeks and underparts, black wings and eyebrows, and yellow-orange crown. While I was watching, it put its head back and sang a lovely ditty that has been interpreted as "so pleased, so pleased, so pleased to meet cha."

The flutelike song of a **wood thrush** resounded from the forest beyond. I stopped to listen to its exquisite music, consisting primarily of three syllables, "ee-o-lay." It paused briefly after each "ee-o-lay," and each delivery resulted in a new rendition, sometimes ending with a tinkling sound. I recalled Frank Chapman's comments, in *Handbook of Birds of Eastern North America*, that the wood thrush's "calm, restful song rings through the woods like a hymn of praise rising pure and clear from a thankful heart. It is a message of hope and good cheer in the morning, a benediction at the close of day." Most appropriate.

I found this thrush throughout the park, but its presence was usually detected only by aural clues. This is a deep forest bird that haunts the shadowy undergrowth, rarely coming into the open. During early mornings, however, it may feed on open trails, where the hiker may be fortunate in finding one. It is a large thrush, almost

American robin size, with cinnamon-rufous upperparts and white underparts with bold black spots.

Another deep-forest bird audible from the Sand Point Marsh Trail was the **winter wren**, evident by its extremely rapid song like distant tinkling bells, which seemed to go on and on. Arthur Bent, in *Life Histories of North American Nuthatches, Wrens, Thrashers, and Their Allies*, pointed out that a 7-second refrain can contain 106 to 113 separate notes. And Florence Bailey, in Chapman's *Handbook of Birds of Eastern North America*, wrote that its song is "full of trills, runs, and grace notes, it was a tinkling, rippling roundelay." The winter wren is one of the park's smallest birds, barely 4.25 inches (10.8 cm) in length, with dark reddish brown plumage and a very short tail.

Other birds seen or heard along the trail that morning included a merlin, hairy and pileated woodpeckers, northern flickers, eastern phoebes, eastern kingbirds, American crows, blue jays, black-capped chickadees, red-breasted nuthatches, cedar waxwings, yellow-rumped and black-and-white warblers, scarlet tanagers, and common grackles.

Cedar waxwings were nesting in a group of larch trees in the center of the marsh. They made numerous trips to and from this site. On each return trip they carried food to waiting nestlings; I could hear their anxious peeps with each delivery. Waxwings were fairly

Cedar waxwing

common along the edge of the marsh, and, because they are colonial nesters, other nests were probably nearby. Ornithologist Aretas Saunders once reported a total of 17 nests within a radius of 150 yards (137 m). These sociable birds spend all their lives in the company of other waxwings.

Cedar waxwings are one of our best-known songbirds, and images of this multicolored bird with a tall crest decorate many household items. Their name is derived from the bright red waxy substance exuded from the feather shafts of adult secondaries, although its function is unknown.

Most visitors to Pictured Rocks take County Road 58, which runs along the entire boundary of the park, with side roads to the lakeshore. The more popular stops along this route include Miners Castle, Chapel Basin, Little Beaver Lake, Kingston Lake, Log Slide, and Grand Sable Dunes. I spent several hours birding the Kingston Lake area one July morning. The loud "weep weep" notes of a **spotted sandpiper** greeted me almost immediately. One adult, with a heavily spotted breast, was discovered on a sandy island just offshore, where it probably was feeding young.

Spotted sandpipers are one of our most interesting shorebirds, for several reasons. They exhibit one of the most unusual breeding systems found in birds-polyandry; a female is likely to mate with more than one male. Polyandry occurs in less than 1 percent of all birds. A female will actually select her mates and fight off other females. The lopsided pairs jointly build the nests, incubate, and feed the young. The female can lay up to five clutches of four eggs each during the nesting season, but each clutch takes about 21 days to incubate. Completing all these incubations would be impossible for one pair. Having multiple mates allows the sandpiper to greatly increase her reproductive potential.

The spotted sandpiper is considered a pioneer species. Ehrlich and colleagues, in *The Birder's Handbook*, point out that it "quickly and frequently colonizes new sites, emigrates in response to reproductive failure, breeds at an early age, lives a relatively short time (breeding females live an average of only 3.7 years), lays many eggs per female per year, and has relatively low nest success." This method of reproduction is apparently successful; the spotted sandpiper is the most widespread sandpiper in North America.

Other birds found around Kingston Lake included several ring-billed gulls on the lake; numerous tree swallows were "flycatching" over the surface; song and white-throated sparrows sang from the surrounding shrubbery; and red-breasted nuthatches, yellow-rumped warblers, and ovenbirds were the most vocal birds in the adjacent forest.

Several open fields near the Grand Sable Visitor Center normally contain barn swallows, American crows, eastern bluebirds, indigo buntings, vesper and savannah sparrows, and eastern meadowlarks.

The 42-mile (68-km) Lakeshore Trail that runs between Munising Falls and Woodland Park passes through all the forest habitats, providing numerous birding opportunities.

One morning I walked the trail between Miners Castle Overlook and Mosquito Beach and found all of the common forest birds and a few surprises as well. At the Overlook area, cliff swallows were plying the air for insects to feed nestlings in their mud nests plastered on Miner's Castle and adjacent cliffs. Herring gulls floated like white corks on the lake surface. Song sparrows sang from the surrounding vegetation. A pileated woodpecker called from the forest. And an indigo bunting sang from the top of a nearby snag. Other birds detected from the parking area included American crows, black-capped chickadees, house wrens, wood thrushes, red-eyed vireos, chestnut-sided warblers, ovenbirds, American redstarts, and American goldfinches.

Between the Overlook and Miners Beach is a mature forest that was filled with birds. Black-throated green warblers were most evident from their husky "zee zee zee zee zoo see" songs. A veery sang a song that Wayne Peterson, in *The Audubon Society Master Guide to Birding*, describes as a "rolling series of descending, vibrant, breezy notes, 'da-veer-ur, vee-ur, veer.' "

I found a male red-headed woodpecker on a huge beech tree; its bright red head and black-and-white body seemed out of place in this dense forest. There, also, were blue jays; black-capped chickadees; red-breasted nuthatches; winter wrens; ruby-crowned kinglets; American robins; red-eyed vireos; parula, yellow-rumped, and black-and-white warblers; and ovenbirds. American crows, common ravens, and evening grosbeaks called overhead.

I stopped at a little overlook above Miner's Creek to investigate the bird activity across the creek. I spished slightly to bring the vocalists into view. White-throated sparrows were first to respond, but almost at the same time a male Nashville warbler popped out of an alder thicket with a sharp, metallic "tink" note. Through binoculars, I could see that it carried a fat, green larva in its sharp bill; feeding nestlings, no doubt. Its gray head with bold white eye rings, yellow throat and underparts, and yellow-green back were most distinct. And then, not more than 20 feet (6 m) above it on a little cedar was a beautifully marked Blackburnian warbler. I immediately switched my attention to this gorgeous creature which allowed me a long, superb look as it sat surveying its territory. Few birds are as striking as a breeding male Blackburnian. Its throat was almost an orange flame color, highlighted by the coal black rings around its eyes and cap. Additional orange striping ran from its eyebrows onto the back of the head and back to the throat. It suddenly sang a thin, wiry song, "sip sip sip titi tzeee."

Beyond Miner's Beach, the trail follows a roadway through a pine-dominated forest for about 1 mile (1.6 km). Pine warblers, chipping sparrows, and dark-eyed juncos called from the pines. The songs of these three birds are not always easy to distinguish, for they all contain extended trills. Pine warblers, all-yellowish birds with two prominent wing bars, sing a "slow, monotonous succession of soft sweet notes, given like the song of a Chipping Sparrow but slower, with longer intervals between the notes, and much softer," according to ornithologist Joseph Forbush in Griscom and Sprunt's The Warblers of America.

Chipping sparrows, little long-tailed sparrows with reddish crowns, sing a song that was described as "a series of chip notes, all on one pitch, sometimes given slowly, sometimes so rapidly they run together in trill," by John Terres in The Audubon Society Encyclopedia of North American Birds. And juncos, slate gray birds with white bellies and white edges on their black tails, sing musical trills, usually on a constant pitch, but sometimes including an abrupt change of pitch in the middle. One of the little "slate-colored" juncos that I was watching sang a rapid "cho cho cho cho cho," followed by a rapid trill.

Suddenly I was attacked by a sharp-shinned hawk that flew at me in a straight line from about 100 feet (30 m) away, calling sharp "kek kek kek" notes. At the last second it swerved away into the forest. In passing I had noticed its small size, rounded wings, and long, squared tail with a whitish terminal band. Although it did not return, it continued its incessant "kek kek kek" call as long as I remained in the vicinity. It undoubtedly had a nest or fledglings nearby.

Not far beyond, the trail climbed to the top of the cliff and entered a lush deciduous forest, typical of much of the Pictured Rocks landscape. Highlights of the next several miles included a hermit thrush that uncharacteristically remained still while I lingered long enough to see its reddish brown tail; a pair of mourning warblers carrying food; a great crested flycatcher that "wheeped" amid the high birch foliage; and several black-throated blue warblers.

The **black-throated blue warbler** has long been a favorite of mine, not only because of its impressive plumage and unique song, but also because of its personality. It is one of our tamest warblers, often allowing a surpringly close approach, but at other times shy and retiring. Also, unlike most warblers, it seems to have no established niche in the forest; one time it will be in the undergrowth and the next time in the canopy. But wherever it goes on its breeding grounds, its distinct song of two to seven syllables, like "sweee-sweee-sweee-sweee," "zur-zur-zur-zree," or "chur-chur-chur-chur," with an upward slur on the last syllable, is usually audible. Another interpretation of its short song is "I am la-zy."

A male black-throated blue is one of nature's most imaginable creations. In the shadowy forest it appears dark grayish blue above, with a black face and throat and white underparts. But perched on a maple and highlighted by a shaft of sunlight, it suddenly becomes a dazzling silver-blue bird with a coal black face and throat. Females are very plain, with an olive-green back and whitish underparts; they can be difficult to identify. However, both male and female possess a distinct white spot at the base of the primaries.

Other forest birds found along this stretch of trail included eastern wood-pewees; black-capped chickadees; brown creepers; wood thrushes; veeries; solitary and red-eyed vireos; chestnut-sided, yellow-rumped, and black-throated green warblers; American redstarts; ovenbirds; scarlet tanagers; rose-breasted grosbeaks; and white-throated sparrows.

Pictured Rocks' cliffs once held peregrine falcon aeries, but the entire Great Lakes population of peregrines disappeared by the

1960s. This loss was due to the effects of DDT, a deadly organochlorine pesticide that was finally banned in the United States and Canada in 1972. Since then, restoration programs at Isle Royale, Apostle Islands, and Pictured Rocks national park areas and Ottawa and Hiawatha National Forests have begun to pay dividends. Resource management specialist Brian Kenner told me that a pair of peregrines visited one of the old aeries in 1993, and he hopes for nesting in the near future.

Bald eagles have also made a comeback in the Great Lakes since the 1970s. At least one pair has nested within the park annually since 1987, producing fledged youngsters most years. Most sightings of this large raptor, with its all-white head and tail, are from the Beaver Lake area of the park.

Winter bird populations are only a fraction of spring, summer, and fall populations. Most of the park's breeding songbirds are Neotropical migrants that leave their nesting grounds in September or early October for warmer climes far to the south. Many migrate thousands of miles to Central America and South America. These migrants must find viable habitat, such as rain forest, in the tropics, if they are to survive and make the long journey back to their nesting grounds in the spring.

Winter birds are surveyed annually by Christmas Bird Counts, which provide an indication of what is present that time of year. The nearest count is done at Whitefish Point, just north of Grand Marais. In 1991, counters tallied 729 individuals of 29 species. The dozen most numerous birds, in descending order of abundance, included black-capped chickadee, oldsquaw, herring gull, pine grosbeak, common raven, common redpoll, red-breasted nuthatch, downy woodpecker and red crossbill (tied), hairy woodpecker, white-breasted nuthatch, and blue jay.

In summary, the park's "Central Upper Michigan" bird checklist (also includes Hiawatha National Forest and Seney National Wildlife Refuge) includes 264 species, of which 179 are listed as breeding. Of the 179 nesters, 39 are water birds (loon, grebe, cormorant, herons, waterfowl, rails, shorebirds, gulls, and terns), 18 are hawks and owls, and 23 are warblers.

Birds of Special Interest

Great blue heron. Watch for this tall, long-legged wader at water areas; it sports a bluish back, black-and-white head, and heavy, yellow bill.

Spotted sandpiper. This heavily spotted, little shorebird summers along the lakeshore; it teeters when walking and flies with stiff wing beats.

Winter wren. It can be common in the forest undergrowth, but is usually identified by its rapid, extended song, like tinkling bells.

Wood thrush. This is the forest thrush that sings an assortment of "ee-o-lay" songs; it has an all-reddish back and white breast with heavy black spots.

Cedar waxwing. One of our most common species, it is easily identified by its upright stance, tall crest, and yellow, buff, and black plumage.

Black-throated blue warbler. This little songster sings a short husky song and sports deep blue, black, and white plumage.

American redstart. One of the park's most common warblers, males possess black plumage with orange-red patches on their sides, wings, and tail.

Common yellowthroat. Males are distinguished by their all-yellow underparts, heavy black mask, gray forehead, and "witchity witchity witchity" songs.

Song sparrow. This heavily streaked, little bird can be expected in brushy areas throughout the park; its varied songs begin with three "sweet" notes and end with an extended trill.

White-throated sparrow. Its "old-Sam Pea-bod-y Pea-bod-y" song is well-known; adults possess a strongly marked black-and-white head with a yellow spot in front of each eye.

13

Sleeping Bear Dunes National Lakeshore, Michigan

We stopped at the Glen Lake Overlook on the Pierce Stocking Scenic Drive. Fluffy cumulus clouds provided a marvelous backdrop to the blue waters of Glen Lake and surrounding greenery. The color contrasts that mid-July day were intense. Through binoculars, I could see white ring-billed gulls soaring over the lake. Closer, a pair of barn swallows plied the air in their search for insects. Three cedar waxwings careened across the open sky on their way to some secret waxwing rendezvous. Red-eyed vireos sang loud whistle notes from the surrounding forest. And American crows called penetrating caw off to the right.

The vegetation directly below the overlook contained a family of American redstarts, flying here and there to search for insects and, in the case of the adults, to escape the incessant pleas of fledglings. It was difficult to get a good look at either adult because of constant movement. Finally, I was able to see the male's coal black plumage, with orange-red patches on its sides, wings, and tail. The female and youngsters were duller versions with yellow patches. I watched them "flycatching" by opening and closing their wings and tail like a butterfly, to startle insects into the air. Then they soared after the flying insects or grabed them off the foliage or branch with a snap of the bill.

Movement among the foliage at the upper left edge of the clearing attracted my attention. A chestnut-sided warbler, also "flycatching" by flying out after insects and returning to the same or adjacent foliage, provided me with a marvelous view of its bright chestnut sides, white cheeks surrounded with black, and golden yellow crown. While I was admiring this lovely warbler, it suddenly put its head back and sang a loud, clear song, which has been described as "so pleased, so pleased, so pleased to meet cha." Then it dived into the lower foliage and reappeared with an insect in its bill. It perched in full view, swallowed the insect whole, and sang once again: "so pleased, so pleased, so pleased to meet cha."

Another song seeped into my brain, and I realized that for the last several minutes an **indigo bunting** had been singing loudly and energetically. It took me another second or two to locate this little songster sitting on a dead branch in the clearing. Seen through binoculars, its indigo blue plumage gleamed in the bright sunlight. Its entire body was bright blue; only its wings and tail contained some black coloration. It continued singing its commanding song. I jotted down my interpretation, which took six or seven songs before I was satisfied: "swe-swee swe-swe ti-ti swee-swe ti-ti." At times it sang only part of a song, "swee swee ti-ti swee-swe." Peter Vickery, in *The Audubon Society Master Guide to Birding*, described its song as "a wiry, high-pitched, strident series of couplets, each pair at a different pitch, with the second pair of notes especially harsh 'swee-swee zreet-zreet swee-swee zay-zay seeit-seeit.' Considerable variation from individual to individual."

There are few better representatives of America's eastern deciduous forest clearings than the indigo bunting. At Sleeping Bear Dunes, it occurs at all the forest and field edges and appears on the park's checklist of birds as "common" in spring, summer, and fall. But it winters far to the south in southern Mexico, Central America, and the Greater Antilles, a true Neotropical migrant. However, unlike its warbler neighbors, which often depend on rain forest in winter, buntings spend their winters in fields and brushy areas. Also unlike the forest species, indigo bunting populations appear to be consistent year after year. Their annual summer residency at Sleeping Bear Dunes, therefore, seems assured.

The Park Environment
Located on the northeastern shore of Lake Michigan, the 71,000-acre (28,733-ha) Sleeping Bear Dunes National Lakeshore contains "out-

standing natural features, including forests, beaches, dune formations, and ancient glacial phenomena," according to the park's 1970 enabling legislation. Its name was derived from one of the park's extensive dunes, where Ojibwa Indian legend says a mother bear awaited her cubs after swimming across Lake Michigan to escape a forest fire; the cubs drowned.

The park is divided into five coastal segments and North and South Manitou islands. Unlike most national park areas, some of the park is still in private use and not accessible to the public. That continuing use, however, maintains a few habitats that are rarely present in other more complete park lands. The recently abandoned fields are still in an early stage of succession. Therefore, ten distinct plant associations have been identified: farmlands, old fields and meadows, orchards, stabilized dunes, heaths, aspen-birch forests, pine-oak-aspen forests, beech-maple forests, swamps-bogs-marshes, and lakes and ponds.

The beech-maple hardwood forest, commonly found on morainal hills, is considered the climax woodland. Dominant vegetation includes sugar maple and beech, with lesser amounts of basswood, ironwood, black cherry, red oak, and white ash. Hemlock and yellow birch are common in low, moist areas. The pine-oak-aspen forest communities, dominated by red, white, and jack pines, red oak, and aspens, form open woodlands.

Heaths occur inland on morainal bluffs and plateaus and are dominated by occasional cottonwoods and various shrubs, including sand cherry, common and creeping junipers, buffalo berry, bearberry, and chokecherry. On dunes stabilized by heaths, clumps of red, white, and jack pine occur, with an understory of mosses, creeping juniper, bearberry, and other shrubs.

Aspen, yellow and white birch, and white cedar normally occur at the edge of bogs and swamps; bogs are usually dominated by black spruce mixed with tamarack and surrounded with spaghnum and shrubs; cedar swamps contain white cedar mixed with yellow birch, balsam fir, and tamarack.

The park's only mainland visitor center is located in the village of Empire. It has an information desk, auditorium for orientation programs, exhibits, and a sales outlet; bird field guides and a checklist are available. Interpretive activities run throughout the summer and include ranger-guided walks and evening slide programs at D. H. Day and Platte River campgrounds.

The park also maintains the 7.4-mile (12-km) Pierce Stocking Scenic Drive as a self-guiding roadway. The 1.5-mile (2.4-km) Cottonwood Trail, at stop number four on the scenic drive, is also self-guiding. Brochures are available at the head of each.

Additional information can be obtained from the Superintendent, Sleeping Bear Dunes National Lakeshore, P.O. Box 277, Empire, MI 49630; (616) 326-5134.

Bird Life

Our next stop on the scenic drive was at the Picnic Mountain area, near the dune overlook. Another indigo bunting greeted us with its rollicking song; song sparrows sang from the shrubby edges; and American goldfinches called overhead in passing. An eastern wood-pewee sang its distinct "pee-wee;" more American redstarts appeared; chipping sparrows flew up from the lawn where they had been feeding; and a northern flicker called from the adjacent forest. A rose-breasted grosbeak sang its robinlike song from the adjacent shrubbery, and a family of **white-breasted nuthatches** searched for insects on the trunks of maple trees.

White-breasted nuthatch

The nuthatch family paid little attention to us while Betty video-taped their activities from about 12 feet (3.7 m) away. There were two adults and five or six youngsters that already looked much like their parents. Their all-white underparts and cheeks contrasted with their black cap and blue-gray back and wings. They stayed in constant communication by means of nasal "yank" calls and higher-pitched chattering. Their acrobatic behavior of walking up and down tree trunks and on the underside of horizontal branches was amazing. The law of gravity did not, apparently, apply to these nuthatches. Through binoculars, I could see their slightly upturned bill, used to pry pieces of bark loose in their search for insects. This bird is a full-time resident at Sleeping Bear and maintains the same feeding territory year-round.

I located a pair of **rose-breasted grosbeaks** feeding on a hackberry tree at the edge of the clearing. They, too, seemed unafraid and permitted an excellent look. The male was a brightly marked bird with a solid black hood, back, and tail, snow white underparts, and a rose red breast. The female lacked the male's bright colors and was mostly striped. But both sexes possessed the heavy bill that is used to strip thick husks from seeds. This bird, too, is a Neotropical migrant that overwinters in tropical forests; its heavy bill probably is more useful in the tropics, where there are plenty of large fruits, than in Michigan.

A bright red bird suddenly flew up from the undergrowth into a young maple. Immediately I recognized it as a male **scarlet tanager**, one of our most handsome songbirds. Its scarlet body, contrasting black wings and eyes, and silvery bill were unmistakable; females possess greenish upperparts and yellow underparts, a far cry from their lovely mates. But tanagers are forest birds, normally found in mature hardwood and mixed forests, seldom on the edge of clearings. I continued to watch this lone male, and within a few seconds it flew back into the shrubbery. I watched it pick a ripe raspberry, strip away the leafy bract, and swallow the fruit. No wonder it was foraging in the shrubbery. For the next several minutes it fed there, consuming a dozen or more raspberries.

Raspberries were growing at the edge of the picnic area clearing and along the adjacent roadside. Two dozen or more birds were taking advantage of the red delicacies. These included a great crested flycatcher, blue jays, white-breasted nuthatches, brown thrashers, red-eyed vireos, song sparrows, a female Baltimore oriole, and American goldfinches. A female and two immature eastern bluebirds hovered in the air while they delicately picked fruit. I, too, sampled the luscious raspberries.

Of all the birds recorded along the scenic drive, none was as numerous as the **red-eyed vireo.** However, they were more often heard than seen. Their whitish underparts and olive backs blend well with the greenery. The red-eye's most obvious feature is its head pattern: a grayish crown, white eyeline bordered with black, and blood-red eyes. But its constant songs are the most impressive, a "continuous series of short, robinlike phrases, given with rising inflection and separated by short pauses," according to Wayne Peterson in *The Audubon Society Master Guide to Birding.* To me, this bird sings a constant series of single and double notes with no recognizable melody.

Red-eyed vireo

Several other birds were found along the scenic drive: a red-tailed hawk flew across the roadway ahead of me; a female ruby-throated hummingbird was searching some flowering shrubs for nectar. Downy and hairy woodpeckers called from the forest, and northern flickers, with their yellow underwing linings, flew by. Black-capped chickadees were numerous throughout the area, and American robins flew up from the roadside. Black-throated green warblers sang husky "zee zee zee zoo zee" songs from the mixed forest areas, and ovenbirds sang a series of loud "teach" notes from the forest undergrowth.

Nearby Mill Pond, along Highway M-109 across from Glen Lake Picnic Area, provided an additional assortment of birds. Water birds on the pond included only a pied-billed grebe and an adult female and five young **wood ducks**. The gaudy wood duck drake was absent; it probably was molting in some out-of-the-way lake, less susceptible to prying eyes. I assumed that the young wood ducks had been fledged from a cavity nest in one of the many snags at the far edge of the pond. The hen wood duck was a rather drab, mottled brown bird with large, elliptical, white eye rings. For more about this bird's nesting capacity, see chapter 16 on Cuyahoga Valley.

A **common snipe** suddenly winnowed almost directly above me. It made two more wide circles and several more winnowing sounds before it dropped back into the grasses along the edge of the pond. This bird uses such a flight to stake out and defend its territory. A male or female snipe circles its breeding grounds, usually 300 to 360 feet (91-110 m) high, and every 10 to 20 seconds makes a slight dive to gain speed. It then spreads its outer tail feathers so that rushing air vibrates the distended feathers and produces a hollow, whistling sound. On the ground, the common snipe is a chunky bird with an extremely long, heavy bill. It feeds in soft earth by plunging its bill straight down into the ground and probing with the bill's pliable, highly sensitive ends for insects and larvae. They then move the food upward through their long bill by movement of spinelike projections. They also cast up indigestible parts of the food as pellets.

The cattails around the pond contained numerous common yellowthroats, evident by their loud "witchity witchity witchity" songs and the males' bright yellow throat and black mask. Several marsh wrens were also detected by their squeaky, cackling songs. They are short-tailed little wrens with bold white eyebrows, a streaked back, and an unstreaked crown. The willows and alders beyond the cattails and grasses supported an additional assortment of songbirds: black-capped chickadee, American robin, red-eyed and warbling vireos, yellow and black-and-white warblers, American redstart, rose-breasted grosbeak, song sparrow, common grackle, house finch, and American goldfinch.

The park's chief interpreter, Neal Bullington, suggested that I also bird the Otter Creek area between Esch Road and Otter Lake. I spent most of a morning along this route; it was superb! The birdiest part of the route was along the unimproved county road at the north end; it crosses the creek and follows the forested streambank for about 1 mile (1.6 km). Driving this road just after dawn produced a family of ruffed grouse and an American woodcock.

Ruffed grouse are upland gamebirds, best known for the male's drumming behavior in spring. By summer, the female is escorting her chicks through the forest, teaching them the edible foods and survival techniques. All eight or nine birds froze as I approached. I was fortunate to see them at the edge of the roadway, for their plumage provided wonderful camouflage. When I stopped, the hen began to herd her chicks away from the road and up the hillside. But one remained, and it was not until I continued that it suddenly arose with fast, whirring wing beats to catch up with the rest of the family.

The male ruffed grouse does not sing but performs a springtime display in a small clearing, often on a log. Naturalist Ernest Thompson Seton, in Frank Chapman's *Handbook of Birds of Eastern North America*, provides the best description:

> This loud tattoo begins with the measured thump of the big drum, then gradually changes and dies away in the rumble of the kettle-drum. It may be briefly represented thus: 'Thump—thump—thump—thump, thump; thump, thump-rup rup rup rup r-r-r-r-r-r-r-r.' The sound is produced by the male beating the air with his wings as he stands firmly braced on some favorite low perch, and it is now quite well known to be the call of the male to the female; an announcement that he is at the old rendezvous—a rendezvous that has perhaps served them for more than one season, and a place that in time become so fraught with delightful associations that even in autumn or winter the male, when he finds himself in the vicinity, cannot resist the temptation to mount his wonted perch and vent his feelings in the rolling drum-beat that was in springtime his song of love.

The American woodcock also displays for his lady in spring, but his courtship is very different. This chunky shorebird, which looks much like a common snipe, is among the earliest to commence courtship. It prefers dense woods and is crepuscular in nature, going about its territorial activities at dawn and dusk. For details about this bird's courtship display, see chapter 10 on Bruce Peninsula.

A few water birds were found along Otter Creek. Great blue herons, with their wide wingspan and long neck and legs, were flying over the creek or hunting the shoreline. A lone green heron flew up and crossed the creek, calling loud and emphatic "skouwp" notes. I also detected two pairs of mute swans, a brood of wood ducks, and at least two belted kingfishers which flew by with loud rattle calls.

Mute swans, our largest flying bird, are white and have an orange bill with a black knob at the base. They make a variety of low snorts and grunts, but are best known for their loud wing beats, swooshing "vaou vaou" sounds that are audible for up to a half mile (.8-km). Although they are one of the area's most spectacular full-time residents, this species is not native and undoubtedly affects the park's native waterfowl. Mute swans are fiercely territorial and will drive away any competitor, especially while nesting. The Traverse Bay population is the product of a single pair that was imported in 1919. In 1971, four individuals were transplanted to lakes in Illinois, but they returned on their own by the following winter.

At one point along the roadway, I found an adult mute swan and two small, brown-gray cygnets at a nest in a center island of the stream. The nest, made of various aquatic plants and rising 8 or 10 inches (20-25 cm) above the water, contained a single egg. According to waterfowl biologist Frank Bellrose, in *Ducks, Geese & Swans of North America*, mute swans do not nest until their third year, and most pairs mate for life. However, he stated, "separation occasionally occurs and some males have resorted to polygamy." Nesting territories normally are selected in March and early April, nests may be 5.5 feet across (1.7 m) and 3 to 4 inches (7.6-10 cm) deep. One to eight eggs are deposited and the average brood is 4.8 young. The male will "often care for the first hatched young while the female continues to incubate." Bellrose added that the brood often remains together until late fall, "when they are abandoned or forced away as the adults return to defend their nest territories."

Other birds found among the stream and riparian vegetation included downy woodpeckers; alder flycatchers calling slurred "rray-beea" notes, with emphasis on the "beea"; a willow flycatcher calling "fitz-bew"; a pair of eastern kingbirds; black-capped chickadees; American robins; numerous gray catbirds; a pair of chestnut-sided warblers; American redstarts; numerous song and a few swamp sparrows; a pair of Baltimore orioles; and American goldfinches.

One of the male **American goldfinches** was displaying, probably to impress a prospective mate. It circled high in the air for 20 seconds or so, then returned to the perch where it had begun. All the while it sang a clear, high whistle. Aretas Saunders, in *A Guide to Bird Songs*, described its territorial song very well: "saweet saweet saweet tototo ta tay tota tatay tata tseeo tilate tatate tototah." It sat for a moment before repeating the same display.

Between its singing bouts, I examined it carefully through binoculars. The male American goldfinch sports a bright yellow back and underparts and a coal black forehead, crown, and wings, with narrow white wing bars. Often called "wild canary," this finch decorates many household items. Finding a spectacular male like this is like meeting an old friend. After its third flight, it returned briefly to its perch, then flew off with its more typical undulating flight and flight song: "per-chik-o-ree."

Otter Creek road and trail passed through a number of other habitats. The mixed forest community supplied a pileated woodpecker; eastern wood-pewees; wood thrush; magnolia, black-throated green, and black-and-white warblers; and ovenbirds. From the pine-dominated community beyond I heard the singing of mourning doves, brown creepers, and pine warblers.

Wisps of fog hung over the surface of Otter Lake when I arrived. A belted kingfisher called from the far shore. A pair of eastern phoebes made short dashing flights over the lake edge to capture insects. A family of song sparrows sang their varied songs along the near shore or chased one another from thicket to thicket. And then, as if by magic, the lonesome wail of a common loon resounded across the water. Again.

It took me several minutes to locate it as it floated and dived near the center of Otter Lake. Its heavy bill and black-and-white plumage were most distinguished. Bullington had told me that this is the only lake in the park with a pair of loons, but resource management specialist Max Holden said that the loons are nesting. I can only hope that my common loon was signaling its young to stay hidden.

When I returned to where Otter Creek crosses under the roadway, I discovered local birders Bev and Clair Postmus checking the area. We talked about the park while we watched for birds, and I added a black-throated blue warbler to my growing list of park sightings. Then, based upon Bev's recommendation of the nearby Empire Bluff Trail, her favorite, I was soon walking through a cathedral of huge beech and maple trees.

This three-quarter-mile (1.2-km) trail terminates at a high bluff overlooking Lake Michigan and a good portion of Sleeping Bear Dunes. Although I added only a pair of red-bellied woodpeckers in the forest and a pair of northern rough-winged swallows at the bluff, it was a marvelous walk. In fact, I returned there at dusk to experience the evening sounds and mood.

The most impressive birdsongs were those of the **wood thrush**, which sang its flutelike "ee-o-lay" song over and over, each rendition slightly different. For instance, it would emphasize the first syllable, pause, then start again and emphasize the last syllable. Frank Chapman, in *Handbook of Birds of Eastern North America*, wrote: "The flutelike opening notes are an invitation to his haunts; a call from Nature to yield ourselves to the ennobling influences of the forest." He added that its "calm, restful song rings through the woods like a hymn of praise rising pure and clear from a thankful heart. It is a message of hope and good cheer in the morning, a benediction at the close of day."

On another morning I birded some field and forest edge habitats just north of Empire, from the park entrance to a huge red barn. Many of the species recorded were redundant: mourning dove, eastern kingbird, blue jay, American crow, American robin, gray catbird, brown thrasher, cedar waxwing, red-eyed vireo, American redstart, common yellowthroat, rose-breasted grosbeak, indigo bunting, chipping and song sparrows, red-winged blackbird, common grackle, Baltimore oriole, house finch, and American goldfinch.

But I also recorded a few additions. A Swainson's thrush sang its flutelike song from the far ridge. At least two prairie warblers were singing their ascending buzz song from the scattered young conifers;

this species has recently been listed as threatened in Michigan, according to Bullington. At the far edge of the field was a wild turkey hen. Several field sparrows were singing their distinct songs from the adjacent fields, clear, plaintive whistle followed by an accelerating trill. Two eastern meadowlarks flew across the field, their bright yellow bodies gleaming in the morning light. And among the cottonwoods, a yellow-billed cuckoo called guttural "ka-ka-ka-ka-ka" notes.

Most of the park's breeding birds depart in late summer and fall, leaving only the hardier full-time residents. A few species from farther north arrive in late October or November and stay for the winter. The winter bird populations are surveyed annually on Christmas Bird Counts at nearby Traverse City. In 1991, counters tallied 5,854 individuals of 63 species. The dozen most numerous birds, in descending order of abundance, included mallard, black-capped chickadee, rock dove, American crow, mourning dove, ring-billed gull, Canada goose, common goldeneye, American black duck, greater scaup, white-breasted nuthatch, and herring gull.

In summary, the park's bird checklist includes 261 species, of which 160 are listed as summer residents and assumed to nest. Of those 160 species, 26 are water birds (loon, grebe, waders, waterfowl, rails, shorebirds, gulls, and terns), 16 are hawks and owls, and 19 are warblers. The Bohemian waxwing is listed only in winter.

Birds of Special Interest

Mute swan. This huge, all-white bird has an orange bill with a black knob. Its wings make a loud "vaou vaou" sound as it flies.

Wood duck. Males are multicolored; females and young are drab with large, white, elliptical eye rings.

Ruffed grouse. Watch for this chickenlike bird along backcountry roads and trails; males display in springtime with a loud drumming noise.

Common snipe. This chunky shorebird may be seen flying over wetlands in spring. It produces winnowing sounds through its tail feathers in flight.

White-breasted nuthatch. One of the park's most common resident birds, it is distinguished by its white-and-black plumage and ability to walk up and down tree trunks.

Wood thrush. Its flutelike "ee-o-lay" songs are commonplace in the park's mature forests in spring and summer.

Red-eyed vireo. One of the park's most abundant songbirds, it sings loud whistle notes with no perceivable melody for long periods of time.

American redstart. Males of this common warbler species sport all-black plumage with orange-red patches on the sides, wings, and tail.

Scarlet tanager. The male of this forest bird is scarlet with contrasting black wings; females are yellowish.

Rose-breasted grosbeak. The male's rose red breast, all-black hood, and white belly are most distinguished.

Indigo bunting. This little all-blue songbird of the clearings sings loud, emphatic songs, often from high perches.

American goldfinch. The male's bright yellow-and-black plumage is unmistakable; this species is often called "wild canary."

14

Indiana Dunes National Lakeshore, Indiana

Rufous-sided towhees were the apparent overseers of the Inland Marsh Trail. A dozen or more crowded the thickets along the first stretch of the route, and they were only slightly less numerous along the remainder of the 2.5-mile (4-km) loop trail. Males were most obvious because of their bright plumage and loud calls. Their black hood, back, wings, and tail contrasted with their extensive rusty sides and white belly. And seen through binoculars, their blood-red eyes stood out like bright rubies against a velvety black background. The females were duller versions of the males. Whenever either would dive for cover, the last visible sign was the white tip of its otherwise black tail.

Many called grating "tow-heeee" notes from a favorite perch; their name was derived from this call. Others sang slightly different versions, including those sometimes interpreted as "drink-your-tea," with a trill on the last syllable. Arthur Bent, in *Life Histories of North American Blackbirds, Orioles, Tanagers, and Allies*, included other interpretations, such as "drink, drink, drink, tsit, tsit," "chipper-chee-e-e-e," and "lookout, ter-r-r." It was obvious from walking the trail that all of these interpretations and several others as well could apply.

I watched one searching for food amid the ground litter. Its "kick-foraging" behavior amounted to jumping backward, scratching and scattering the ground cover to reveal seeds and insects. It then searched the exposed ground, pecking at food. Another towhee was feeding on ripe blueberries among a dense thicket. From my perspective, the blueberry eater seemed the wiser of the two.

Rufous-sided towhee

Several of the towhees were in family groups of five to ten birds; the youngsters were generally distinguished by their dull brown plumage with streaked underparts. A few of the youngsters followed adults about, giving squeaky calls and soliciting handouts by quivering their wings. The adults, not yet ready to desert their fledglings, stuffed food into the open bills. But the brightly marked adult males quickly responded to my spishing by flying to the top of a shrub to scold me with loud, grating "tow-heee" notes.

The Park Environment

Indiana Dunes National Lakeshore contains a variety of habitats interspersed in a complex urban-industrial-residential-rural landscape. The sites are scattered along 13 miles (21 km) of the southern tip of Lake Michigan, between Michigan City and Gary, Indiana. Most of the sites are within 2 miles (3 km) of the lakeshore, but the Heron Rookery and Pinhook Bog units are 3 and 7 miles (4.8-11 km) inland, respectively. The park's approximately 14,000 acres (5,666 ha) extend from 100 feet (30 m) offshore inland to include dunes and other fascinating natural habitats within sight of steel mills and a power-generating plant. Indiana Dunes State Park, 2,200 acres (890 ha) of dunes, forest, and wetlands, is also within the designated boundary of the national lakeshore.

A profile of the park's geography includes lake, beach, and dunes, with scattered pockets of vegetation, interdunal depressions, forested ridges, and the lacustrine plain. Plant communities, as described by botanist Gerould S. Wilhelm of the Morton Arboretum, include aquatic, with the lake and water-filled depressions; bogs dominated by sedges, bog rosemary, leatherleaf, mountain-holly, and small cranberry; dunes and foredunes with grasses, trees, and shrubs that vary with the stability of the substrate; and marsh complex, a saturated habitat dominated by sedges and cattail.

Plant communities farther inland, according to Wilhelm, consist of mesophytic (medium moist conditions) forest, mesophytic prairie, pannes (wet interdunal depressions), savanna, and swamp. The mesophytic forest, considered the climax community for the area, is dominated by sugar and red maples, beech, American basswood, and red oak. In the savanna community, which dominates the western half of the park, black and white oaks, sedges, lupines, and prairies grasses are prominent.

The park has three visitor centers. The primary Dorothy Buell Memorial Visitor Center is on U.S. Highway 12 and Kemil Road; the West Beach Information Center is at West Beach; and the Paul H. Douglas Center for Environmental Education is at the entrance to Miller Woods. All three have an information desk, orientation programs, exhibits, and a sales outlet; bird field guides and a checklist, as well as the informative book *Birds of the Indiana Dunes* by Kenneth J. Brock, are available.

Interpretive activities through the spring and summer season include ranger-guided walks and occasional birding hikes, talks, and demonstrations. The park offers environmental education programs for school and youth groups throughout the year.

Additional information can be obtained from the Superintendent, Indiana Dunes National Lakeshore, 1100 North Mineral Springs Road, Porter, IN 46304; (219) 926-7561.

Bird Life

I detected several other songbirds along the Inland Marsh Trail during my morning walk. Blue jays flew from tree to tree, calling scratchy "jay jay jay" notes. Families of black-capped chickadees were calling "fee-bee" whistle notes. American robins were still feeding youngsters that trailed after the adults. One particularly bright male, with an orange-red breast, chipped loudly and flew at me when I got too close to a short-tailed youngster hidden in the grass along the trail. Dozens of cedar waxwings were flying from one clump of trees to another. Common yellowthroats sang "wichity wichity wichity" songs from many of the moist thickets; males had a lemon yellow throat and black mask. Bright red male northern cardinals sang "cue cue cue" songs from various perches. Field sparrow songs, clear whistles that accelerate into an extended trill, were commonplace, but the originators stayed out of sight. And **American goldfinches**, with the males' contrasting gold-and-black plumage, were everywhere.

Judging from the males' constant singing and displaying, the goldfinches undoubtedly were nesting; they are known to nest through August. Another clue was that most of my sightings were of males; females sit on the eggs 95 percent of the time, according to Paul Ehrlich and colleagues in *The Birder's Handbook*. The males feed the sitting females by regurgitation. Nests, woven from plant fibers and lined with thistledown and other soft plant parts, are placed in a fork or on a branch of a shrub or tree. Goldfinch songs vary from a flight song, usually described as "per-chick-o-ree," to a canarylike song consisting of a series of trills interspersed with "wee" notes.

Other less common birds found along the trail included a red-tailed hawk, which protested with a grating screech when disturbed from its perch; mourning doves; a black-billed cuckoo; ruby-throated hummingbirds; downy woodpeckers; northern flickers with their yellow underwings; eastern wood-pewees, still singing "pee-weee" songs; a silent *Empidonax* flycatcher, probably a willow flycatcher; a family of great crested flycatchers; brown thrashers; a sedge wren; red-eyed vireos singing their rambling whistle songs; yellow warblers; a black-and-white warbler; brown-headed cowbirds; common grackles; Baltimore orioles; and house finches.

Overhead I observed an American kestrel, flocks of rock doves, chimney swifts, a few pairs of purple martins, barn swallows, and American crows. Wood ducks and mallards were in ponded areas. Though I listened intently at each water area, I did not detect a sora or Virginia rail, two species that nest along this trail, according to Kenneth Brock. Nor did I find a **northern bobwhite,** the park's usually common quail. Often detected first by their "bob-white" call, males are distinctly marked with a white and reddish brown head pattern and striped flanks. They often call from posts, and during the nesting season, may allow a reasonably close approach. At other times, a flock (usually a family group), may suddenly fly up with loud, rapid wing beats and swiftly glide away to safety.

Cowles Bog is named for Professor Henry Cowles, of the University of Chicago, who did pioneering studies in plant ecology. Cowles Bog was designated as a National Natural Landmark in 1965. Today, a trail passes along the northern edge of the bog, loops over forested dunes, and circles interdunal ponds and marshes. It provides a pleasant walk and an outstanding birding route.

Song sparrows were common at the start of the trail, singing songs that began with "sweet sweet sweet," followed by a jumbled series of notes and a trill. These little sparrows normally respond immediately to spishing and come charging out to defend their territories. Song sparrows are brown and tan with a rather long tail, and their heavily striped breast shows a bold, dark stickpin in the center. For more details about this bird's incredible array of songs, see chapter 16 on Cuyahoga Valley.

The rapid "weet weet weet weet" song of swamp sparrows was evident, as well. This shy little bird, with a reddish cap and shoulders, seldom comes into the open. And a marsh wren sang a series of songs from the cattails. Park technician Dan McGuckin commented that it "sounds like he's warbling with water in his throat," an excellent description of the marsh wren's song. Like the swamp sparrow, this short-tailed, striped bird of the cattails rarely comes into the open.

But the aggressive **red-winged blackbird**, another wetland species, is seldom reluctant to voice its disapproval of any annoyance. This bird calls loud "chaeck" calls or sings "konk-a-reee" songs from open shrubs or cattails. If anyone approaches its nest, it immediately dives and hovers overhead with fluttering wings and shrill alarm notes, like "chee-e-e-e." Males are all-black with bright red wing patches (epaulets); females are duller, striped versions with only hints of red. In spring and summer, paired birds distribute themselves across the wetlands like a checkerboard, and defend their respective territories. But by late summer, after the young are fledged, they gather in huge flocks. They then seek weedy fields for food, returning to the cattails to roost overnight. John Terres, in *The Audubon Society Encyclopedia of North American Birds*, reported that the red-wing's year-round diet consists of 73 percent vegetable matter and 27 percent animal matter, including gypsy moths and forest tent caterpillars.

The Cowles Bog woodland is one of the best areas in the park to find veeries and wood thrushes in summer, according to geographic information specialist Eddie Childers. These two thrushes sing wonderful, but different, flutelike songs. The veery's song is "a rolling series of descending, vibrant, breezy notes, 'da-vee-ur, vee-ur, veer, veer,'" as described by Wayne Peterson in *The Audubon Society Master Guide to Birding*. The wood thrush sings a series of three notes, "eee-o-lay," that are repeated over and over, each time with a different tone and inflection. To hear both of these thrushes singing together is very special. And when the American robin, a third thrush, is also tuned up, the chorus can be out of this world.

The parking area for the Cowles Bog Trail is one of 50 stops included in the park's annual breeding bird survey, which is run by park volunteer Susan Bagby and research biologist Ralph Grundel. Ralph told me that the June 4, 1993, survey tallied 62 species, more than any other breeding bird survey in Indiana. Since this survey includes all of the habitats found at Indiana Dunes, it is an excellent indication of the park's overall breeding avifauna. This survey is designed for long-term monitoring.

The most numerous species recorded in 1993 was the **ring-billed gull**; herring gulls were present in smaller numbers by a ratio of about ten to one. Ring-bills are easily identified by their yellow bill with a black ring near the tip. Herring gulls are larger, with a heavy yellow bill having a reddish spot on the lower mandible.

Eleven of the 62 species recorded during the breeding bird survey were found on ten or more of the 50 survey stops: blue jay, tufted titmouse, American robin, gray catbird, red-eyed vireo, yellow warbler, common yellowthroat, northern cardinal, song sparrow, red-winged blackbird, and brown-headed cowbird. Birds recorded in the survey that were at the edge of their breeding range included chuck-will's-widow, Acadian flycatcher, and white-eyed vireo (which more typically nest south of Indiana Dunes) and veery and Canada warbler (which normally nest farther north).

Another morning I accompanied Ken Brock, Ralph, Eddie, and Dan into the Heron Rookery Unit, which contains the most mature deciduous forest in the national lakeshore. Although the main public access point is from the east side, off County Road 600 East, we entered from the west side and followed the Little Calumet River for about a half mile (.8 km). It was immediately apparent that the forest was full of birds. Songs and calls of downy woodpeckers, Acadian flycatchers, white-breasted nuthatches, blue-gray gnatcatchers, yellow-throated and red-eyed vireos, and American redstarts were among the first to greet us.

Acadian flycatchers were surprisingly abundant; I counted 13 or 14 in our two-hour walk. This little *Empidonax* flycatcher sings an "explosive and loud 'peet-sah' or 'peet-sup,' usually accented on the first syllable, sometimes with equal accent on both syllables," according to Kenn Kaufman in *Advanced Birding*. Acadian flycatchers are relatively plain birds with whitish underparts, greenish olive upperparts, and white eye rings. According to Kaufman, Acadians have the largest bill of the Empids, and the "lower mandible is almost always entirely pinkish yellow."

Distinguishing the songs of yellow-throated and red-eyed vireos can be tricky at first, but practice makes perfect. Red-eyes sing an extended series of rambling single notes or occasionally double notes, with a pause after each. **Yellow-throated vireos** sing a slower, deliberate song of slurred notes, usually two syllables, with a longer pause after each. Frank Chapman, in *Handbook of Birds of Eastern*

Yellow-throated vireo

North America, wrote: "If the Red-eyed Vireo is a soprano, the Yellow-throat is a contralto. He sings much the same tune, but his notes are deeper and richer, while they are uttered more deliberately and with greater expression than those of his somewhat too voluble cousin." The yellow-throat is a large, handsome vireo with a bright yellow throat, breast, and spectacles, white belly, and blackish wings with bold white wing bars. A novice birder might confuse this bird with a warbler, but the vireo's heavier bill and more deliberate manner help to distinguish it from the yellowish warblers.

A loud and emphatic "see-you see-you see-you chew chew to-wee" suddenly resounded from the streambank just ahead of us. A **Louisiana waterthrush**! It sang again. "Good, I wasn't sure whether it would still be singing," Ken said. Early August was late for this bird to be on territory. It called a loud "chink" and flew across the stream and back along the route we had just walked. This wetland warbler is a relatively large bird with long legs and a habit of teetering back and forth as it walks along a streambank. It is black-and-white with a dark back, striped whitish underparts, and heavy white eyebrows.

As we progressed along the riverbank we searched the high foliage for other warblers. I was especially interested in finding yellow-throated and cerulean warblers that nest in the sycamore trees along Little Calumet River. We did find several American redstarts, males with their black plumage with orange-red patches and females with their duller plumage with yellow patches; a lone yellow warbler, with its all-yellow plumage, including the underside of its tail; and a couple of ovenbirds singing their "teacher" song, with its two clear syllables, in a southern dialect. Yellow-throated and cerulean warblers eluded us; Ken pointed out that they "seem to disappear soon after nesting."

Indiana Dunes is the extreme northern edge of the breeding range of the **yellow-throated warbler**. Here it uses sycamores, but in the southeastern United States it nests in pines. Because of its affinity for sycamore trees, it once was known as "sycamore warbler." The yellow-throat is one of the loveliest warblers and one of the easiest to identify. Its bright yellow throat is bordered with black on the sides and with white below. Its black-and-white head pattern includes black cheeks and a bold white eye line. It has the longest bill of any warbler. And its song is very distinct and loud, like that of an indigo bunting or waterthrush. Paul Sykes, in *The Audubon Society Master Guide to Birding*, described the song as "a loud musical series of clear syllables given faster as they descend with abrupt higher note at end: 'tee-ew, tew-ew, tew-ew, tew-ew, tew-wi' or 'sweet-ie, sweetie, sweetie.' "

The **cerulean warbler** looks very different, although it too nests in the tall sycamores: a little blue-and-white bird with two broad white wing bars. Brock wrote, in *Birds of the Indiana Dunes*, that ceruleans "dwell in the treetops and are heard far more than seen; if its song is not recognized the summer Cerulean is almost impossible to locate among the dense foliage." Its song has been described as energetic and rapid, somewhat like that of a parula, "usually with 3-5 introductory short, chanted notes ending with a higher, drawn-out note. Variously transcribed as 'zray, zray, zray, zray, zreeee' and just a little sneeze. Like Black-throated Blue Warbler's song but faster and less slurred," according to Henry Armistead in *The Audubon Society Master Guide to Birding*.

In *The Warblers of America*, Frank Chapman quotes Ludlow Griscom's comments: "The Cerulean Warbler is sensitive to ecological change. . . . The bird disappeared the moment the big timbered swamps were logged" in Ohio and Missouri. Now, even "its wintering ground—temperate forest high in the Andes—is being cleared for Coca plantations," according to a 1993 article by Les Line in *National Geographic*.

Other birds found in the Heron Rookery Unit that morning included black-billed cuckoos, ruby-throated hummingbirds, red-bellied and downy woodpeckers, eastern wood-pewees, great crested flycatchers, blue jays, black-capped chickadees, tufted titmice, wood thrushes, American robins, scarlet tanagers, and northern cardinals. At one point, I thought I heard a distant pileated woodpecker call; Ken told us that this large woodpecker has increased in numbers in recent years and is likely to be found in the Heron Rookery Unit.

The area's dense floodplain forest also supports **barred owls**, which can usually be heard calling their wondrous hoots in spring and early summer. Although their deep, full-throated "who-cooks-for-you, who cooks-for-you-all" is most often heard in the evening and morning, during their nesting season in spring they may call throughout the daylight hours as well. This is a large, chunky, brownish owl with barring on its upper chest and streaks below, rounded facial disk, all-brown eyes, and no ear tufts. For additional details about this owl, see chapter 31 on Jean Lafitte.

One of the park's most accessible aquatic areas is Long Lake near West Beach. This is the best area to find water birds in summer. Pied-billed grebe, great blue and green herons, black-crowned night-heron, Canada goose, mallard, blue-winged teal, Virginia rail, sora, and American coot are most likely to be detected. Although great blue herons nest on the east side of the Heron Rookery Unit, which is closed that time of year, many of those birds feed along the shore of Long Lake and are often seen flying back and forth. In *Birds of the Indiana Dunes*, Brock mentions that this heronry is a well-established one, "at least fifty years old. The first birds return to the rookery about 12 March; young birds are present by early May; and fledging occurs in late July."

The much smaller, and more common, **green heron** can also be found along the shores of Long Lake and all the smaller interdunal ponds. This is the little heron with a greenish back, chestnut throat and chest, black cap, and dark bill. Great blues are much taller with long legs and neck and a very heavy yellow bill. Most often, the green heron is first seen when it flushes from a wet area near a trail, flying off with loud "kyowk" calls. A careful observer can sometimes find one perched along the shore. A fishing green heron strikes a pose over water, sometimes seeming so off balance that one would expect it to fall forward. Somehow they defy gravity and remain still for an incredibly long time. Sooner or later, a fish, frog, or other choice morsel passes by, and the heron strikes so fast its movement is little more than a blur. More often than not, it comes away with its prey held tightly in its bill. It then works its prey into position and swallows it whole. It either then resumes its fishing position or moves to another site.

Long Lake is most active during migration, when thousands of waterfowl are passing through the area. Canada geese, wood ducks, green-winged and blue-winged teal, mallards, northern pintails, northern shovelers, gadwalls, American wigeon, canvasbacks, red-heads, ring-necked and ruddy ducks, greater and lesser scaup, common goldeneyes, buffleheads, and hooded, common, and red-breasted mergansers can all be expected.

Spring migration at Indiana Dunes can bring waves of migrants. During clear and calm periods the migrants often pass overhead, but when there is a strong north wind, songbirds tend to follow the crest line of the dunes or congregate in pockets of vegetation where they can find food and shelter. There also is a hawk flight in spring, peaking during the first two weeks of April. Local birder Bobbie Squires has been monitoring hawk flights for 13 years and normally records 3,000 to 3,400 hawks each spring. She told me that most of the hawks recorded are red-tailed hawks, followed by a substantial number of sharp-shinned hawks, and a scattering of 11 other species: turkey vulture; bald and golden (rare) eagles; northern harrier; Cooper's, red-shouldered, broad-winged, and rough-legged hawks; American kestrel; merlin; and peregrine falcon. The fall hawk migration involves only a few immature red-tails and peregrines, generally following cold fronts.

The fall migration of other birds can be full of surprises. Local birders often gather along the shore in autumn when strong north winds create conditions that bring seabirds to the southern tip of Lake Michigan. These periods are locally called "jaeger days." Brock told me that on such a day in late September 1992, 13 jaegers were recorded, including one long-tailed that landed on the beach, six parasitics, and six unidentified jaegers.

Miller Beach is a popular birding location in fall. Chip Pretzman, in the *WildBird* article "Birder's Guide to the Indiana Dunes," stated: "North winds blowing on cold October and November days may bring in scores of birds off the lake, including Whimbrels, Red-throated and Arctic loons, Black-legged Kittiwakes, and both Parasitic and Pomerine jaegers." He adds, "Shorebirds seen here in early autumn include White-rumped, Baird's, and Purple sandpipers, Black-bellied Plovers, and Dunlins."

Brock points out that many southbound migrants following the shores are ultimately guided into the dunes area at the toe of the lake. He refers to this phenomenon as the "funnel effect," in explaining the unusual numbers of some species.

Most of the area's breeding birds join the southbound migration to the tropics for the winter. The winter bird population is only a fraction of what is present in spring, summer, and fall. Annual Christmas Bird Counts provide an indication of species present during the last weeks of December. In 1992, 11,367 individuals of 73 species were tallied in the 15-mile (24-km) diameter count area at the park. The dozen most common birds, in descending order of abundance, included ring-billed gull, herring gull, house sparrow, European starling, American crow, Canada goose, red-winged blackbird, dark-eyed junco, mallard, rock dove, black-capped chickadee, and house finch.

In summary, the park's checklist of birds includes 271 species, of which 108 are known to nest. Of those 108 species, 15 are water birds, 7 are hawks and owls, and 15 are warblers. Five species are listed for winter only: harlequin duck, oldsquaw, northern shrike, pine grosbeak, and common redpoll.

Birds of Special Interest

Green heron. This little greenish heron, with a deep chestnut throat and breast, occurs at all the ponds; it often calls a harsh "kwock" note when disturbed.

Northern bobwhite. The male possesses a white and reddish brown head pattern; it is most often detected by its loud "bob-white" call in spring and summer.

Barred owl. This large owl prefers dense floodplain communities; its call is a deep, haunting "who cooks for you, who cooks for you all?"

Acadian flycatcher. Watch for this little flycatcher along the floodplain; its call is an explosive "peet-suh."

Yellow-throated vireo. This forest vireo sings a slow, rather deliberate song from the high foliage; it is distinguished by a yellow throat and spectacles.

Yellow-throated warbler. Best detected in the high sycamores by its distinct song, it sports a bright yellow throat bordered with black.

Cerulean warbler. This is a little blue-and-white bird of the high sycamore foliage; its song is a rapid "zray, zray, zray, zray, zreeee."

Louisiana waterthrush. Watch for this long-legged warbler along streams; it sings a loud and emphatic "see-you see-you see-you chew chew to-wee."

Rufous-sided towhee. Most abundant at thickets, males have an all-black hood, bloodred eyes, and extensive rusty sides.

Red-winged blackbird. Males are all-black except for bright red wing patches (epaulets); females are duller versions with hints of red.

American goldfinch. This common bird of fields and woods is often called "wild canary"; males are bright yellow-and-black and sing "per-chick-o-ree" in flight.

15

Point Pelee National Park, Ontario

The Marsh Boardwalk provides a wonderful opportunity to see a freshwater marsh close-up. From the 3-story tower at the head of the trail, we could trace the boardwalk through the deep green forest of cattails, floating pads of yellow and white waterlilies, and open water for most of the 1-mile (1.6-km) loop. Back at ground level, we ambled along the boardwalk, taking our time, watching for whatever mammal, bird, fish, or other creature might appear.

We had already become acquainted with the two dozen or more barn swallows that were nesting and roosting on the tower. These

Barn swallow

forked-tailed swallows, with a chestnut throat and velvety black back, twittered constantly as they searched the air for insects. Their nests, constructed of tiny mud pellets pasted together to form a shallow cup, were fastened underneath the upper floors of the tower. And an occasional purple martin or tree swallow passed overhead or perched on a tree snag on the adjacent shore.

That summer day, the most obvious bird of the marsh was the **red-winged blackbird**. Males, with their black plumage with bright red wing patches (epaulets), were still defending territories along the boardwalk. Numerous youngsters followed their parents from place to place. The female and young red-wings were heavily striped, without the contrasting colors of the adult male. The adult females had a hint of red on their head and shoulders. With the abundance of youngsters, there was considerable chasing and begging. I found one still-energetic parent shoving insects into the gullet of a fully grown fledgling. Most of the communication involved a series of "chack" or "peeah" notes, but an occasional male still resorted to its territorial song, a loud "konk-ka-reee" or simply "konk-reeee," with a musical ending.

The shallow water of the marsh was mud-color, probably from the tremendous amount of roiling by at least two huge fish; I identified both carp and bullhead catfish. Carp were so abundant that in a few places several were visible at once. Their round mouths used to suck in plant parts, reminded me of a vacuum cleaner.

Suddenly, the "witchity witchity witchity" song of a **common yellowthroat** rang from the cattails. And a second or two later, two males charged out of the greenery. The first had apparently invaded the territory of the second and was being properly chastised. They zoomed right past me and continued the chase out of sight. Three other common yellowthroats, apparently family members, flew to the top of the cattails for a look around. These were the young of the year, with their all-yellowish dress and blackish wings. Then, almost immediately, the male returned. He was a gorgeous warbler with lemon yellow underparts, a coal black mask, and a grayish forehead. Apparently energized by the recent chase, he perched in full view, put his head back, and sang, "witchity witchity witchity."

A little marsh wren came to check out the disturbance. It climbed about in the cattail jungle, staying just out of our view, but teasing with occasional half views of its buff plumage, bold white eyebrows, and short tail. I was not completely sure about its identity until it sang a series of rasping, guttural notes, ending with a squeaky note and a rapid trill.

Just ahead we heard the rapid "weet weet weet weet weet" song, all on the same pitch but loudest in the middle, of a swamp sparrow. I moved closer, but it was now silent. After a couple of minutes of silence, I spished slightly to attract it into the open. Nothing. I spished again, a little louder, and it suddenly appeared on the rail of the board-walk, 30 feet (9 m) ahead of me. Through binoculars, I could see its reddish crown, shoulders, and wings, whitish throat, and grayish chest and belly. Another summer resident of Pelee's freshwater marsh.

We continued on the boardwalk loop, stopping now and then to watch a bird or examine some eye-catching animal or plant. A green heron flew ahead of us and disappeared into the cattails with a loud "kyowk." We had a short look at a muskrat before it vanished. Numerous green frogs sang single notes that sounded like plucked banjo strings. A painted turtle, with dark, shiny shell and orange cheeks, was observed on a clump of dead waterlilies before it slipped away into the dark water.

We climbed the stairs to the low viewing tower at the end of the short sidetrail and scoped the marsh. Three small flocks of ducks flew across the far horizon: groups of four and seven mallards and six American wigeon. Several ring-billed gulls flew toward the north as if they were heading for some secret gull rendezvous. Off to the right in the open water was a pair of Canada geese, and a lone pied-billed grebe surfaced nearby. Just beyond was a black tern that flew back and forth in its search for insects.

Then, a sora gave a high whinnying call just behind us. As I turned in that direction, an **American bittern**, rare at Point Pelee, suddenly flew up with a loud, hoarse "kok-kok-kok" call and flapped away. It probably had been there all along, but because of its wonder-ful camouflage we had missed it. As it continued across the open water, I could clearly see its broad wings with dark edges and heavily striped underparts. It landed at the edge of the cattails and immedi-ately pointed its bill skyward. If I had not been watching, it would have appeared to vanish; its pointed bill and striped body looked exactly like one more cattail in a sea of cattails. A wonderful ability to hide from predators and curious onlookers.

The Park Environment

Point Pelee has been described as the land where Canada begins, and as an area with an unrivaled collection of plants and animals. These superlatives are well deserved. The Pelee Peninsula, extending more than 12 miles (20 km) into Lake Erie, is the southernmost point of mainland Canada. It lies on the 42nd parallel, the same latitude as northern California and Cape Cod. Its southern geographic position, combined with the "lake effect" that maintains moderate winter temperatures, gives it the floristic character of eastern deciduous forest, an environment restricted to southern Ontario in Canada. The region is, in fact, locally known as "Carolinian Canada."

One of Canada's smallest national parks, Point Pelee National Park encompasses only 6 square miles (16 sq km) or 3,840 acres (1,564 ha) of the southern half of the Peninsula. The region north of the park is dominated by agricultural fields. In spite of its tiny size, Pelee contains one of the largest remaining natural areas in "Carolinian Canada." Two areas adjacent to the park have also received protected status: Hillman Marsh on the northeast side of the peninsula, and Holiday Beach, a migratory hawk observation center to the west.

The national park itself contains an amazing diversity of habitat considering its size: beach, field, savanna grassland, swamp forest, dry forest, and marsh. More than 12 miles (20 km) of beach lie along the dagger-shaped peninsula. Beyond the open beach are transition areas usually dominated by red cedar, staghorn sumac, hop tree, and wormwood. And along the eastern half of the peninsula, south of the marsh, swamp forest occurs in low areas between old beach ridges. Dominant swamp forest plants include silver maple and sycamore, while jewelweed and nettles grow profusely in the moist soil. In wet years, flooded areas are carpeted with duckweed.

Pelee's dry forest habitat most resembles the eastern deciduous forests to the south, in its types of trees and their height and density. Among the dominant hardwoods are hackberry, white ash, basswood, black walnut, shagbark hickory, sugar maple, sassafras, and red, chestnut, and chinquapin oaks. A few pine stands can be found on the drier open ridges along the western land base.

Pelee's marsh habitat covers 4 square miles (10 sq km) but is only a remnant of a much larger marsh that once stretched northeast as far as Hillman Creek. Its depth averages only 3 to 8 feet (1-2.5 m) and is regulated by the annual water level fluctuations of Lake Erie. Dominant marsh plants include cattail, waterlilies, and buttonbush.

Access through the park is by a narrow roadway that runs along the western edge of the marsh for about 4 miles (6.2 km) to the visitor center. From the visitor center to the Tip (1.2 mi. or 2 km), access is limited to trails or a public transit system that runs every 20 minutes. During the quieter winter months (November-March), the road is open. The visitor center contains an information desk, auditorium for orientation programs, exhibits, including a variety of children's exhibits, and a Nature Nook gift and book store operated by Friends of Point Pelee. Bird field guides and checklists are available.

Parks Canada interpreters offer a variety of programs during the summer season. Spring bird walks are provided in May, talks and demonstrations are scheduled on summer afternoons, and there is a Junior Naturalist Program in July and August. Other programs are available on request. Five park trails are self-guided: Marsh Boardwalk, the .8-mile (1.25-km) DeLaurier Trail, the .6-mile (1-km) Tilden's Woods Trail, the 1.7-mile (2.75-km) Woodland Nature Trail, and the .2-mile (.4-km) Tip Trail.

Additional information can be obtained from the Superintendent, Point Pelee National Park, R.R. 1, Leamington, Ont. N8H 3V4; (519) 322-2365.

Bird Life

Point Pelee is one of only about a dozen outstanding sites in North America that attract birders from across the continent; nearly 100,000 birders come to Pelee each spring to enjoy the spectacle of migration. The reasons for the extremely high numbers of migrants are varied, but most important, perhaps, is the peninsula's location at the northern convergence of two of North America's four flyways: Mississippi and Central. These two corridors dump millions of northbound birds into the midwestern states of Kentucky, Indiana, and Ohio. Many of these migrants are heading north to ancestral nesting sites in the Canadian forests. They either rest a few days in the United States or immediately strike out across the Great Lakes. In normal clear weather, especially with a tail wind, they pass over and come to land far beyond Point Pelee. However, less fortunate migrants may encounter cyclonic weather patterns over the Great Lakes, including temperature extremes and strong head winds, which force them to seek shelter and food before continuing their journeys. The Pelee Peninsula, protruding into Lake Erie, may be the first mainland site available. Some birds are so exhausted from their ordeal that they literally flop onto the ground or vegetation, unable to continue; they must rest even before they can begin to refuel. Those birds can actually be picked up and examined by hand, a rare treat but, for the bird's sake, not recommended. However, they soon begin to forage for food, and because of their exhausted condition, they may remain for several days before continuing. The park provides the only smorgasbord available; the area north of the park is dominated by agricultural fields. But the park's wide variety of habitats provide ample food for all species.

Park interpreter Tom Hince told me that he has experienced some spectacular fallouts. "My biggest day with really impressive numbers was on May 15, 1978. Between the road end and the Tip, there were 500 male scarlet tanagers and 200 cuckoos; I picked up 15 to 20 species of songbirds that were too exhausted to escape." He added, "on May 10, 1976, there were 34 species of warblers in that same area."

Tom explained that Pelee's spring migration generally occurs in three stages, with some overlap: "Migrant waterfowl reach us in March; in April we get birds that have overwintered in the eastern United States; and by late April and through May, our birds are dominated by Neotropical migrants."

My first visit to Point Pelee was in early May. Like all the other birders that day, I began along the Tip Trail, where the woods were filled with birds. For me, the most memorable thing about that morning was the chorus of birdsongs; it was almost overwhelming. It was impossible to identify more than a handful of songs because they seemed to blend together into one giant din of bird music. Even the loudest songs were evident only occasionally: those of northern cardinals, American robins, brown thrashers, mourning doves, red-eyed vireos, gray catbirds, yellow warblers, song sparrows, and house wrens, more or less in that order.

During the first morning I found 23 species of warblers, not the kind of morning that Hince undoubtedly had when he found 34, but a wonderful warbler morning, nonetheless. Most numerous were Tennessee, orange-crowned, Nashville, yellow, chestnut-sided, magnolia, yellow-rumped, black-throated green, Blackburnian, and black-and-white warblers; ovenbirds; and American redstarts. But some of the less numerous warblers, such as golden-winged, blue-winged, cerulean, and bay-breasted, were even more exciting. Several other songbirds provided special memories that morning, as well. I remember finding six swallow species together on an open snag: purple martin and tree, northern rough-winged, bank, cliff, and barn swallows. Five vireo species—solitary, yellow-throated, warbling, Philadelphia, and red-eyed—were gleaning insects together in a tall hackberry tree. And on one occasion I marveled at the contrasting colors of eastern kingbirds, American robins, yellow and black-throated green warblers, American redstarts, scarlet tanagers, rose-breasted grosbeaks, and indigo buntings, all together in one tree.

Spring migration normally peaks at Pelee from May 5-15, but the largest series of "good birds" depend upon the greatest concentration of birders. Park interpreter Laurel McIvor told me that the weekend of May 7-8, 1993, produced the highest number of reports. Sixty-three species were listed on the "Bird Observation" notebook at the visitor center. In reviewing that list, I was struck by the diversity of species reported. For example, the first 21 species noted (in the order recorded) included yellow-breasted chat, ruddy turnstone, semipalmated sandpiper, northern mockingbird, grasshopper sparrow, scarlet tanager, merlin, Louisiana waterthrush, black-billed cuckoo, eastern bluebird, white-eyed vireo, yellow-throated vireo, black-throated blue warbler, least bittern, wood thrush, solitary sandpiper, pine warbler, willet, brown thrasher, Cooper's hawk, and yellow-headed blackbird, truly a mixed assortment of birds.

By mid-May, the summer residents are defending their breeding territories, and Pelee's bird life takes on a very different appearance. A total of 121 species have nested in the park, according to Paul Pratt's *Point Pelee National Park and Vicinity Seasonal Status of Birds*, although typically only about 70 are found in a given year. To find the breeding birds, it is necessary to visit all the different habitats. My favorite route is the DeLaurier Trail; it passes through old field and orchard, second-growth, and swamp forest.

The fields and thickets of red cedar and staghorn sumac adjacent to the parking area are usually alive with birdsong. Most evident are American crows; house wrens, with their rapid bubbling songs; American robins, with their loud caroling; yellow warblers, which sing cheerful "tseet-tseet-tseet sitta-sitta-see" notes; and indigo buntings, with their strident series of double notes.

House wrens are unquestionably one of the park's most common and vocal songbirds, residing in all the wooded areas. It is a rather nondescript little bird with a reddish brown back and grayish brown underparts, indistinct eyebrows, and a lightly barred tail. But what it lacks in color, it more than makes up for in personality and song. It is an active and curious bird of the shadows that can often be enticed into the open with low spishing and squeaks. It then literally creeps to an open perch to check out the annoyance. When nesting, it usually chastises intruders with rapid grating and "sizzling" notes.

House wren

Its choice of nest sites varies so much that it is impossible to define a typical site. Most house wrens utilize natural cavities or woodpecker holes in stumps and trees, but John Terres, in *The Audubon Society Encyclopedia of North American Birds*, provides us with a fascinating list of additional sites: "empty cow skulls hung up in pasture; abandoned paper nests of hornets, deserted nests of swallows and other birds, in fishing creel hung in shed, in watering pots,

The Amisk Wuche Trail at Elk Island National Park loops through rich habitats and crosses wetlands on floating boardwalks. (Photo by R. Wauer)

Visitors to Ominnik Marsh in Riding Mountain National Park can easily identify two dozen or more birds. (Photo by R. Wauer)

Prince Albert National Park is a land of subtle but remarkable beauty, complete with hundreds of lakes and waterways. (Photo by R. Wauer)

Three common loons swim along the near shore of Waskesiu Lake in Prince Albert National Park. (Photo by R. Wauer)

Looking across the cattail marsh, with Black Bay in the background, from the Oberholtzer Nature Trail in Voyageurs National Park. (Photo by R. Wauer)

This beaver pond, complete with a lodge and dams, is a popular destination for interpretive nature trips at Voyageurs National Park. (Photo by R. Wauer)

A view of Rock Harbor from the Suzy's Cave Trail at Isle Royale National Park. (Photo by R. Wauer)

Ojibway Tower and Greenstone Ridge at Isle Royale National Park; notice the bull moose on the near lakeshore. (Photo by R. Wauer)

Halfway Lake, viewed from the mile-long circle-trail, is located next to
Hattie Cove Campground at Pukaskwa National Park. (Photo by R. Wauer)

Halfway Rock Point rises above Lake Huron's boulder-covered shore at
Bruce Peninsula National Park. (Photo by R. Wauer)

Looking northeast across Lake Superior from Squaw Bay at Apostle Islands National Lakeshore. (Photo by R. Wauer)

Lush green and light tan contrast vividly with the deep blue waters of Lake Superior at Pictured Rocks National Lakeshore. (Photo by R. Wauer)

Looking north over Lake Michigan and a portion of Sleeping Bear National Lakeshore from the Empire Bluff Trail. (Photo by R. Wauer)

Long Lake, a choice area for migrating waterfowl, nestles among sand dunes at Indiana Dunes National Lakeshore. (Photo by R. Wauer)

The Marsh Boardwalk at Point Pelee National Park affords a wonderful opportunity to see a freshwater marsh close up. (Photo by R. Wauer)

The Cuyahoga River floodplain is dominated by sycamore, cottonwood, buckeye, maple, ash, walnut, boxelder, and elm. (Photo by R. Wauer)

A view of the extensive grasslands in Frenchman River Valley from along Grasslands National Park's 17-mile-long Ecotour. (Photo by R. Wauer)

Devils Tower (867 ft.) dominates the surrounding landscape of ponderosa pine forest, deciduous woodland, and streamside riparian habitats. (Photo by R. Wauer)

Cottonwood Campground, a superb birding area, hugs the banks of the Little Missouri River in Theodore Roosevelt National Park. (Photo by R. Wauer)

Badlands formations and juniper slopes as seen from the Scenic Loop Drive, Theodore Roosevelt National Park. (Photo by R. Wauer)

Looking east over the Black Hills from Rankin Ridge Trail at Wind Cave
National Park. (Photo by R. Wauer)

Pronghorn are common on the extensive grasslands at Wind Cave
National Park. (Photo by R. Wauer)

Mount Rushmore, with the stone faces of Washington, Jefferson, T. Roosevelt, and Lincoln, from the visitor center's viewing terrace. (Photo by R. Wauer)

Badlands National Park encompasses large areas of lush grasslands and colorful, eroded badlands. (Photo by R. Wauer)

Looking across the Niobrara River wetlands toward the Fossil Hills Trail and Carnegie Hill at Agate Fossil Beds National Monument. (Photo by R. Wauer)

South Bluff provides a backdrop to the visitor center, Saddle Rock Trail, and access road at Scotts Bluff National Monument. (Photo by R. Wauer)

A view of the Current River from the highway bridge at Round Springs, Ozark National Scenic Riverways. (Photo by R. Wauer)

The Buffalo River, seen here at Pruitt, is one of the few major streams left undammed in the Arkansas Ozarks. (Photo by R. Wauer)

Tamaulipan scrub habitat, with sacahuista, cenizo, blackbrush acacia, and prickly pear cactus, on the shore of Amistad Reservoir. (Photo by R. Wauer)

Looking east across the seagrass-covered sand dunes toward the Gulf of Mexico at Padre Island National Seashore. (Photo by R. Wauer)

Longleaf pines, in the Hickory Creek-Savannah Unit of Big Thicket National Preserve, provide habitat for brown-headed nuthatches. (Photo by R. Wauer)

This boardwalk trail leads into the heart of the Mississippi River Delta wetlands of Jean Lafitte National Historical Park. (Photo by R. Wauer)

old hat, tin cans, teapots, in flower pots, old boots, shoes, nozzle of pump, in iron pipe railing, weather vane, holes in wall, in axle of automobile in use daily, etc." Yet it is the house wren's lovely song that is most enduring. Arthur Bent, in *Life Histories of North American Nuthatches, Wrens, Thrashers, and Their Allies*, described its song as "a burst of melody, a rather loud, hurried, strenuous, bubbling outpouring—shrill, ecstatic, and difficult to describe or to translate into written words." Bent mentions that the Chippewa Indians recognized this species for its marvelous song, by naming it *O-du-na-mis-sug-ud-da-we-shi*, meaning "a big noise for its size".

Farther along the DeLaurier Trail, **yellow warblers** flit in and out of the thickets and trees. Males are bright yellow with chestnut breast streaks; even the underside of their tail is yellow. Females are duller versions of the males without the chestnut streaks. This vocal little warbler's cheery song, a ringing "tseet-tseet-tseet, sitta-sitta-see," is commonplace around the visitor center parking area.

Another obvious bird of the clearings is the **indigo bunting**, a little finch whose song is usually interpreted as "swee-swee zreet-zreet swee-swee zay-zay seeit-seeit." The all-blue male often sits in the open, sometimes on the highest perch. A breeding male usually progresses from post to post along the outer edge of its territory. This is one of the many bird species that are heavily parasitized by brown-headed cowbirds, but some indigo buntings have learned to bury the cowbird eggs by building another bottom on their nest.

Other common breeding birds of the clearings and thickets include gray catbirds; brown thrashers; common yellowthroats; northern cardinals; chipping, field, and song sparrows; red-winged blackbirds; common grackles; house finches; and American goldfinches. This also is a good place to find ruby-throated hummingbirds feeding at the abundant flowering plants and purple martins and tree, northern rough-winged, and barn swallows plying the air for insects.

The **northern cardinal** is one of the park's "surprise birds" to Canadians, because its range extends north only to southern Ontario, southwestern Quebec, and southern New Brunswick and Nova Scotia. It has become a favorite in the park and is used to illustrate the park brochure as well as the "seasonal status" checklist.

The taller trees beyond the clearings often support another group of songsters, including American robins, cedar waxwings, European starlings, red-eyed vireos, yellow warblers, American redstarts, and Baltimore orioles. **Red-eyed vireos** are among the park's most vocal summer residents, but are rarely seen. Despite their fairly large size, about 6 inches (15 cm) long, finding one of these loud songsters in the canopy can be a real challenge. This vireo's rather dull plumage (whitish underparts and olive-green back, whitish eyebrows bordered with black lines, and red eyes) cannot compare with its distinct song. Aretas Saunders, in *A Guide to Bird Songs*, wrote: "The song of this bird really sounds more like talking than singing. The bird has been compared to a preacher. To me it sounds more like one of those persons who talks in short, choppy, interrogative and imperative sentences. 'Hulloa there—You, John Smith—where ya goin?—wait a minute—what's your hurry—come here—I want to talk to ya,' etc."

American redstarts are one of the flashiest of the summer birds. Males are all-black, except for orange-red patches on their wings, sides, and tail. They display these colors in their pursuit of insects, to startle them into moving. The redstart's slurred song can usually be heard all summer long, even after most other songbirds are quiet.

Other less common birds to watch for at the edge of clearings include great crested flycatchers, Carolina wrens, blue-gray gnatcatchers, warbling vireos, and orchard orioles.

The swamp forest provides habitat for a number of birds. The changing water level of the troughs often drowns mature trees, which then attract a variety of wood-boring insects. Red-headed and downy woodpeckers and northern flickers come to these sites to extract the larvae. They also may construct nests in the dying trees. They rarely use the nests beyond the first year, and the deserted nests are then claimed by other cavity-nesting birds. Great crested flycatchers, tree swallows, white-breasted nuthatches, house wrens, and European starlings take advantage of the smaller deserted cavities. And wood ducks utilize the larger and older cavities.

Other breeding birds of the swamp forest include eastern kingbirds, prothonotary warblers (rare), northern cardinals, common grackles, brown-headed cowbirds, and Baltimore orioles.

The dry forest looks in many ways like hardwood forests far to the south. It also supports a few of the same nesting birds: red-headed and downy woodpeckers; northern flicker; eastern wood-pewee; great crested flycatcher; blue jay; white-breasted nuthatch; Carolina and house wrens; blue-gray gnatcatcher; wood thrush; white-eyed, yellow-throated, and red-eyed vireos; American redstart; ovenbird; and scarlet tanager.

One of the most interesting groups of birds are the "Carolinian" species that are at the northern edge of their breeding range at Pelee: king rail, red-bellied woodpecker, Carolina wren, blue-gray gnat-cacher, white-eyed vireo, prothonotary warbler, yellow-breasted chat, and orchard oriole. Also of interest are Pelee's nesting ovenbirds; they sing the full "teacher" song that is typical of southern ovenbirds, rather than the shorter "teach" song of northern ovenbirds found only 250 miles (400 km) to the north at Bruce Peninsula National Park.

The **Carolina wren** is, perhaps, the best representative of the group. It is a full-time resident, although populations fluctuate from year to year. Christmas bird counters tallied 86 individuals on December 16, 1992. In July, I found it most common along the Woodland Trail. It was often detected first by its loud and ringing "teakettle, teakettle, teakettle, tea," "wheedle, wheedle, wheedle," or similar songs. Although this large wren is usually very secretive, with persistence one will eventually discover a reddish backed bird with bold white eyebrows. With binoculars, one can also see its rich buff underparts, barring on its narrow tail, and rather large bill.

The fall migration at Pelee can be just as exciting as that of spring, although it does not draw as many birders. Tom Hince told me that Pelee's fall migration lasts longer, from early July through mid-December, and "there tends to be more massive movements of birds in fall than in spring; they pass through in waves." A great variety of warblers and many shorebirds, including lesser yellowlegs; spotted, semipalmated, and least sandpipers; sanderlings; and short-billed dowitchers come through in August. Hawks are most numerous in September, as are northern flickers, blue jays, Swainson's thrushes, and a variety of warblers. And finches, such as white-throated sparrows, dark-eyed juncos, and rusty blackbirds, are more numerous during October.

A few species have a difficult time leaving the mainland and crossing Lake Erie. **Blue jays**, for example, mill around the Tip for days, starting across the lake then coming back. Hince described numerous incidents when flocks of several hundred blue jays leave the Tip, heading south, but almost immediately turn around when faced with the threatening expanse of Lake Erie and the lack of cover from predators. After numerous attempts, the jays eventually wander northwest along the shoreline to a point where they can turn south without crossing a major body of water. Hince also pointed out that these jays, so easily identified at ground level by their blue-and-white plumage and crest, appear uniformly pale gray high overhead.

The winter bird population at Point Pelee National Park is only a fraction of what it is in spring, summer, and fall. Christmas Bird Counts are undertaken annually in the park and adjacent area to the north to assess wintertime populations. In 1992, 29,525 individuals of 106 species were tallied. The dozen most numerous birds, in descending order of abundance, included European starling, American crow, horned lark, snow bunting, common merganser, house sparrow, herring gull, house finch, mourning dove, ring-billed gull, red-breasted merganser, and great black-backed gull.

In summary, the seasonal status checklist for the park includes 349 species, of which 122 are listed as breeding. Of those 122 species, 19 are water birds (loon, grebe, bitterns, waders, waterfowl, rails, and shorebirds), 10 are hawks and owls, and 6 are warblers.

Birds of Special Interest

American bittern. Watch for this large, secretive marsh bird along the Marsh Boardwalk; it hides among the cattails with its bill pointed skyward.

Ring-billed gull. This is the park's most common gull, best identified by its yellow bill with a dark ring near the tip.

Barn swallow. It has a long, forked tail, chestnut throat, and black back, and it nests on various structures.

Blue jay. This is the familiar blue-and-white, crested jay of the eastern forests, often detected first by its "jay jay jay" calls.

Carolina wren. Usually detected by its loud "teakettle" songs, this large wren is reddish above and buff below, with bold whitish eyebrows.

House wren. This common, nondescript, little bird of the underbrush sings a rapid and extremely variable, bubbling song.

Red-eyed vireo. Common in the forest canopy, it sings continual whistle notes with little melody.

Yellow warbler. This is the common, all-yellow little bird of the fields and edges; it sings a cheery song, "tseet-tseet-tseet, sitta-sitta-see."

American redstart. Males sport black plumage with contrasting orange-red patches on their wings, sides, and tail; females are duller versions with yellow patches.

Common yellowthroat. This little marsh bird sings "witchity witchity witchity" songs; males possess bright yellow underparts and a black mask.

Northern cardinal. The male is the all-red, crested bird that sings loud "cue cue cue" songs; females are dull versions with the typical cardinal red bill.

Indigo bunting. This little indigo blue bird of the clearings often sings from high, open perches.

Red-winged blackbird. A common wetland bird, males are all-black with red wing patches; females are heavily striped with only hints of red.

16

Cuyahoga Valley National Recreation Area, Ohio

There are few areas where bikers, joggers, and birds mix so well as along Cuyahoga Valley National Recreation Area's Ohio & Erie Canal Towpath Trail. One summer morning, I found more than three dozen bird species from the trail in the Beaver Pond area. Water and terrestrial species were divided fairly evenly. Great blue and green herons were probably the most obvious birds, although the larger number of wood ducks greatly helped their cause.

I found great blue herons feeding in the shallows or perched on snags. One was poised in the center of the pond, like a tall statue with a heavy yellow bill, black-and-white head pattern, long neck and legs, and bluish back. It remained frozen in place for several minutes before it struck down into the water with a lightning thrust of its lethal bill; it suddenly held a squirming frog. It seemed to examine its catch ever so slightly, then swallowed it whole. It then took three or four slow, deliberate steps forward on its stiltlike legs and again struck a pose, to wait for another passing morsel.

Green herons, less than half the size of the great blues, were hunting from perches along the water's edge. Their legs are much shorter, so they usually are unable to wade like their larger cousins. But their stout bills are just as lethal. I watched one poised on a dead log with most of its body over the water; how it was able to maintain balance without falling forward is a marvel of the bird world. Even in that seemingly off-balance position, it struck out and captured a passing fish with perfect aim and dexterity.

This little heron is probably heard more often than seen; it has a loud and rather sharp "skeow" call. Up close it sports a greenish back, rich chestnut head and sides, white belly, and orange-yellow legs. Its bill is dark, not yellow like that of the great blue heron. When nervous, it twitches its very short tail.

All the **wood ducks** along the towpath that day were females and immatures; the adult males were off by themselves. The male wood duck is well known for its multicolored plumage. The head, in particular, can properly be described as gaudy. Its iridescent green to purple crest is highlighted by a white line that runs from the back of its red bill to the top of the crest, which extends halfway down the burgundy-colored neck. A second white line forms the base of the crest, running from behind the eye to the tip of the crest. Additional white lines extend from its white throat onto the cheeks and halfway around the neck. The large red eyes seem to punctuate its velvety black cheeks. The body is an assemblage of white, burgundy, buff, and blues.

Wood duck

Conversely, the hen wood duck is a rather drab, mottled brown bird with large, elliptical, white eye rings. The wood duck is known to science as *Aix sponsa*, a mixed Greek-Latin phrase that means "waterfowl in wedding raiment," according to ornithologist S. Dillion Ripley, in *Water, Prey, and Game Birds of North America.*

Wood ducks are cavity-nesters that utilize natural sites in trees and other structures. Hens lead the search for a proper nest, with the male tagging along. The hunt may take several days. Normal clutch size is about 12, although as many as 50 eggs have been found in a single nest, with many of the eggs contributed by other hens. Frank Bellrose, in *Ducks, Geese & Swans of North America*, claims that a "nest with over 25 eggs is generally conceded to be a dump nest." As many as five wood duck hens may deposit eggs in a single nest, although only one hen does the incubation. The drake remains involved only until all the eggs are hatched. He then leaves to join bachelor flocks in more secluded places. The hen must entice the chicks, which are equipped with claws for climbing, out of the nest and down to the ground and then lead the family to the greater security of ponds.

The Park Environment

The 33,000-acre (13,355-ha) national recreation area, which lies between Cleveland and Akron, Ohio, contains 22 miles (35 km) of the Cuyahoga river and valley. According to the park brochure, Cuyahoga "allows us time and space to rediscover the beauty and meaning of nature, the peace of the countryside, or the substance of our past." It further describes the Cuyahoga River Valley landscape as "an enchanting diversity of river floodplain, steep and gentle valley walls forested by deciduous and evergreen woods, numerous tributaries and their ravines, and upland plateaus."

Vegetation varies from river floodplain, marsh, swamp forest, and old field to beech-maple, oak-hickory, and mixed forests. The Cuyahoga River floodplain is dominated by sycamore, cottonwood, Ohio buckeye, sugar maple, red ash, black walnut, boxelder, and American elm with an understory of common elderberry, poison ivy, clematis, and staghorn sumac. Marshes and swamp forest communities are scattered along the floodplain, especially in old oxbows. Marshes contain a wide assortment of water plants, including cattails and sedges. Swamp forests are dominated by black willow, American elm, white ash, red and sugar maples, and occasionally oaks and shagbark and shellbark hickories. The Ohio & Erie Canal runs in the floodplain for about 20 miles (32 km), the entire length of the park.

Mixed forest communities are dominated by sugar and red maples, beech, black cherry, white ash, shagbark and bitternut hickories, white oak, American hornbeam, tulip-tree, and red oak, with an understory of downy juneberry, common witch-hazel, alternate-leaf dogwood, pasture gooseberry, and mapleleaf viburnum. Beech-maple communities occur on old stream terraces, hemlocks dominate some ravines, and oak-hickory communities are scattered on thin rocky soils.

Visitor centers are located near both ends of the park: Canal Visitor Center lies at the north end, just off Interstate 77, about 15 miles (24 km) from Cleveland, and Happy Days Visitor Center lies in the southeastern corner of the park, just off Highway 8. Both have an information desk, orientation programs, exhibits, and a sales outlet; bird field guides and a checklist are available. Interpretive activities vary greatly during the summer months and include evening talks, nature walks, birding hikes, demonstrations, and concerts. Schedules are posted and listed in the *Schedule of Events*, available at visitor contact stations.

Additional information can be obtained from the Superintendent, Cuyahoga Valley National Recreation Area, 15610 Vaughn Road, Brecksville, OH 44141; (216) 650-4636 or (800) 257-9477.

Bird Life

The numerous wood ducks and a few mallards at Beaver Pond left trails through the green carpet of duckweed before disappearing into the wall of cattails. The cattails contained a very different assortment of birds. It was next to impossible to walk the Towpath Trail without hearing the "wichity wichity wichity" songs of the **common yellowthroats**; adults and youngsters were both abundant. The male yellowthroat is distinguished by its bright yellow throat and underparts, bold black mask, and gray forehead; the female is a drab yellowish bird without the black mask. In spite of its tiny size, the common yellowthroat can be extremely aggressive when nesting; it may fly at and circle anyone getting too close to a nest, calling repeated "chuck" notes. Yellowthroat pairs build large, bulky nests of plant materials attached to cattails and other plant stalks, lined with grasses, bark fibers, and hair.

The rather loud "weet weet weet weet weet" song from the marsh was that of the swamp sparrow, a shy bird with a reddish crown, shoulders, and wings, that usually remains concealed among the cattails. And the rapidly singing wren of the marsh is the marsh wren. A patient observer can usually attract it into the open with a few low spishing sounds. It can then be identified by its nervous behavior and conspicuous white stripes on its back and above the eye, buff to reddish back, and whitish underparts.

Red-winged blackbirds were also common around the marsh. Males possess black plumage with bright red wing patches (epaulets); females are duller versions with heavy stripes. These blackbirds were already in flocks, circling the marsh and diving into the cattails; I also found small flocks feeding in the adjacent cornfields. Earlier in summer, paired birds can be extremely territorial, even diving at and scolding passing bikers and joggers. Males often perch on the taller shrubs and cattails and sing loud "konk-a-reee" songs or call harsh "chuck" notes at passersby.

Other less common water birds during the summer can include pied-billed grebes, American and least bitterns, Virginia rails, soras, common moorhens, American coots, common snipes, and belted kingfishers.

Belted kingfishers were present in small numbers up and down the riverway; they nest in dirt banks and fish all the wetlands. I found a pair of kingfishers perched on dead snags between the Towpath and Riverview Road. Their sex was apparent from the male's single blue chest band and the female's blue band, plus a rusty belly band. The female suddenly dived from its perch at an exceedingly steep angle and hit the water, bill first, with barely a splash. For a second it was totally submerged. Then it emerged, with great flapping of wings and a fish gripped in its bill, and streaked off to the other side of the pond. The male quickly followed, with a loud rattle call. For details about this bird's fascinating nesting ability, see chapter 27 on Chickasaw.

I found several additional birds along the Towpath during the morning. The downy woodpecker, eastern kingbird, Carolina and house wrens, gray catbird, cedar waxwing, European starling, yellow warbler, northern cardinal, song sparrow, common grackle, orchard and Baltimore orioles, and American goldfinch probably owed their presence to the wetlands. Park interpreter Paul Motts told me that he found willow flycatchers in this area all summer.

The most vociferous bird of the group was the little yellow warbler, all-yellow except for the male's chestnut breast streaks. It seemed particularly partial to the patches of willows from which it sang a distinct "tseet-tseet-tseet sitta-sitta-see" song over and over. This is one of the easiest birds to attract up close. Faint spishing or squeaking sounds will usually immediately draw one of these inquisitive warblers.

Other birds seen or heard along the Towpath, probably due to the adjacent hardwoods or clearings, included mourning doves, a black-billed cuckoo (rare), hairy and pileated woodpeckers, northern flickers, eastern wood-pewees, great crested flycatchers, blue jays, black-capped chickadees, tufted titmice, white-breasted nuthatches, indigo buntings, and house finches. And a few Canada geese, a turkey vulture, a red-tailed hawk, and numerous American crows flew by during my walk.

Another morning I walked the Ledges Trail, which begins at the Happy Days Visitor Center. This 2.5-mile (4-km) loop route passes through a variety of forest habitats. The best representative of Cuyahoga's forest communities must be the **wood thrush**. Its most enchanting and memorable characteristic is its wonderful, flutelike music. Although its song contains only three syllables, "eee-o-lay," they are repeated over and over, each time with a slightly different emphasis. One time its song is rich and full, next it contains thin, liquid notes, only to be followed by undulating bell tones. Frank Chapman, also impressed with wood thrush songs, wrote in *Handbook of Birds of Eastern North America*, that its song is "an invitation to his haunts; a call from Nature to yield ourselves to the ennobling influences of the forest."

The wood thrush is not an easy bird to see, for it prefers the shadowy undergrowth and rarely comes into the open. During the early morning, however, it can sometimes be found searching for insects on the park's roads and trails. With patience, an observer will sooner or later see it well: it is a robin-sized bird with reddish brown upperparts, brightest on its crown and nape, white underparts with heavy black spots, and bold white eye rings. But its continual and varied songs on a summer morning or evening are what places this bird in a class by itself.

Several other forest birds of interest were encountered along the Ledges Trail. An American redstart greeted me near the head of the trail with a slurred "zee-zee-zee-zawaah" song. Several white-breasted nuthatches called nasal "yank" notes from the taller hard-woods. Four woodpecker species were recorded: numerous downy woodpeckers calling sharp "pik" notes; one hairy woodpecker, a downy look-alike, but larger; several red-bellied woodpeckers, with their barred, black-and-white backs, whitish underparts, and red nape; and a pair of pileated woodpeckers below the scenic overlook. Pileateds look like real Woody Woodpeckers, complete with a tall red crest that contrasts with their blackish back and a white line that runs from their cheek down the side of the neck.

Winter wrens sang from the dense undergrowth along the cooler north slopes; their rapid tinkling songs reminded me of distant bells. A waterthrush called a sharp "chink" note in the little drainage. I paused and chipped back, kissing the back of my hand; it took several chips before a Louisiana waterthrush approached, bobbing and walking along the stream. My chipping also attracted a male **hooded warbler** from the drier slope above. It approached close enough to give me a marvelous view. Its bright yellow face contrasted with its velvety black throat, cap, and nape; its back was olive-green. It soon lost interest in me and began searching for insects amid the open undergrowth, flicking its white-spotted tail, and dashing after flying insects like a flycatcher. Then, while I watched through my binoculars, it put its head back and sang "weeta weeta wee-tee-o," a short, emphatic, and swinging rendition.

I detected brown creepers, black-capped chickadees, tufted titmice, and a solitary vireo among the hemlocks near Ice-Box Cave. Then just ahead, among the tall hardwoods, a pair of great crested flycatchers called loud "wheep" notes. Blue jays screamed "jay jay jay" from the canopy. And a **scarlet tanager** sang a short song from the same area. Its song reminded me at first of a robin's song, but not so varied. Aretas Saunders, in *A Guide to Bird Songs*, wrote that its song "is delivered in a rather hoarse, high-pitched whistle. It consists of eight to twelve notes or slurs with slight pauses between them, each on a different pitch from the preceding one."

It took me several minutes to find this songster in the high canopy, but my search was worth the time and effort. The scarlet tanager is one of our most beautiful songbirds. The contrast of its scarlet body with its black wings, tail, and eyes and silvery bill makes it a wonder of the bird world. And seeing a scarlet tanager male among the forest green foliage is one of my most cherished memories.

Other birds detected during my morning walk on the Ledges Trail included an eastern screech-owl singing its whinny song on the hill behind the visitor center; several Acadian flycatchers, with their explosive "peet-sah" songs; Carolina wrens singing in the undergrowth; a lone yellow-throated vireo singing a deliberate and slurred series of whistle notes beyond Ice-Box Cave; and a pair of eastern phoebes chasing one another near the scenic overlook. Motts told me this trail is also a good place to find cerulean warblers in spring and summer.

Numerous old fields and shrubby edges are scattered throughout the park, but I found some of the best examples of this habitat along the Indigo Lake Trail, at Stanford Farm, and near Oak Hill Day Use Area. Summer resident birds in these habitats include mourning doves, ruby-throated hummingbirds, eastern kingbirds, blue jays, American crows, Carolina wrens, eastern bluebirds, American robins, gray catbirds, brown thrashers, cedar waxwings, white-eyed vireos, common yellowthroats, northern cardinals, indigo buntings, rufous-sided towhees, field and song sparrows, common grackles, house finches, and American goldfinches.

Song sparrows were especially numerous in the old field beside Stanford Farm Hostel. Youngsters followed their parents, begging for handouts with squeaky appeals. The adults scolded back with loud "chimp" notes. Occasionally, an adult sang a full song, which is heard more frequently earlier in the season. But whatever the time of year, there is something special about the song of the this bird.

Song sparrow

Ornithologist Margaret Nice, who spent several years studying song sparrow behavior, discovered that Ohio song sparrows knew at least six songs that were frequently used, and up to 18 others used occasionally. She found that there were at least seven notes per song, but believed there were others too high to be heard by the human ear. The most common rendition includes three to four short, clear notes, like "sweet sweet sweet," followed by a buzzy "tow-weee," then a trill. A bird typically sings all of its songs one after the other before starting over again. One of her study birds sang a total of 2,305 songs during a single day in May.

Nice named all her song sparrows with a letter and number. In *A World of Watchers*, Joseph Kastner provides us with a perspective on Nice's song sparrow studies: "Nice could hear 4M sing sporadically through the fall, and on Thanksgiving Day she heard him sing a last song. Then, she neither saw nor heard him again. During his eight years at Interpont, she had seen him go from spirited youth to sedate old age. He had had seventeen nests and eleven mates, was seven times a widower, and raised thirteen young."

The male **indigo bunting** has little competition for being the brightest and most visible bird of the old fields. This chunky, indigo blue bird often sits in the open singing a loud and spirited song. The best description of its song is provided by Peter Vickery in *The Audubon Society Master Guide to Birding*: "Song is a wiry, high-pitched, strident series of couplets, each pair at a different pitch, with the second pair of notes especially harsh; 'swee-swee zreet-zreet swee-swee zay-zay seeit-seeit.' " The female is an all-buff bird with only hints of blue on its neck, wings, and rump.

One of the park's best known birds is undoubtedly the yellow-and-black **American goldfinch**, a little finch that is particularly partial to weedy fields. It prefers seeds, especially those of the sunflower family, but will also eat buds and berries. Sometimes mistakenly called "wild canary," this bird has an undulating flight pattern and often sings a flight song, "per-chick-o-ree," with each undulation. It sings a very different territorial song when nesting: an extended melody described by Saunders as a "clear, high whistle weeto weeto weeto ta ta fa ta taweet taweet taweet toway toway toway."

Swallows were frequently sighted throughout the park. Barn swallows, with their long, forked tail and chestnut throat, were most numerous. I found several pairs of cliff swallows at the Bolanz Road Bridge, and two northern rough-winged and several bank swallows were sitting on the utility lines. Purple martins were present at various localities, as well. This large swallow, rare at Cuyahoga Valley, was undoubtedly en route to its wintering grounds in Brazil.

Other aerial specialists were few and far between: an occasional turkey vulture, with its two-tone underwings, bare red head, and wings held in a slight V-shape; red-tailed hawks, with their red tail; smaller broad-winged hawks, with their heavily barred, black-and-white tail; and tiny chimney swifts, with their sooty color and stiff, swept-back wings.

Most of the park's breeding songbirds leave for the winter, migrating to the southern United States, Mexico, Central America, northern South America, or the Greater Antilles. Those that cross the U.S.-Mexico border are true Neotropical migrants. Many, including most of our thrushes, vireos, warblers, and tanagers, spend the winter in tropical forests, where they must find suitable habitats if they are to survive and return in spring to brighten the Cuyahoga Valley with their wonderful songs and colorful plumage.

Only a fraction of the summer birds stay year-round; their population is supplemented by a small number of northern species that come for the winter. All the winter birds are censused each year as part of a continent-wide Christmas Bird Count. In 1991, Cuyahoga Falls counters tallied 26,730 individuals of 84 species. The dozen most numerous birds, in descending order of abundance, included European starling, house sparrow, Canada goose, house finch, ring-billed gull, rock dove, mourning dove, American goldfinch, northern cardinal, dark-eyed junco, black-capped chickadee, and blue jay.

In summary, the park's checklist of birds includes 231 species, of which 137 are listed as a year round or summer resident, and assumedly nest. Of those 137 species, 11 are water birds (waders, waterfowl, rails, and shorebirds), 8 are hawks and owls, and 12 are warblers.

Birds of Special Interest
Great blue heron. This is the tall, long-legged bird of the wetlands; two rookeries are in the valley, on Bath Road, and in Pinery Narrows.

Wood duck. Drakes are gaudy, multicolored creatures, while hens are drab with large, elliptical, white eye rings.

Belted kingfisher. Watch for this bluish bird with a banded chest along all the waterways; it nests in the dirt banks.

Wood thrush. Listen for the variable flutelike "eee-o-lay" song of this forest thrush; it has a reddish back and whitish underparts with heavy black spots.

Yellow warbler. This is the little, all-yellow bird (males also possess chestnut breast streaks) that sings a distinct "tseet-tseet-tseet sitta-sitta-see" song.

Common yellowthroat. Males have all-yellow underparts and a bold black mask; they sing an obvious "wichity wichity wichity" song.

Scarlet tanager. Look for this forest bird in the high canopy; males are scarlet with black wings.

Indigo bunting. This is the chunky, all-blue, little bird that sings from open perches at the edge of openings.

Song sparrow. It is most common at thicket and is best identified by its streaked breast with a central stickpin.

Red-winged blackbird. Males are all-black with a large bright red patch (epaulet) on each wing; females are heavily streaked with only a hint of red.

American goldfinch. This is the bright little yellow-and-black bird sometimes called "wild canary"; it flies in an undulated pattern.

GREAT PLAINS

Within one human lifetime, the prairies have passed from wilderness to become the most altered habitat in this country and one of the most disturbed, ecologically simplified and over-exploited regions of the world.

—Adrian Forsyth

17

Grasslands National Park, Saskatchewan

The Two Trees Interpretive Trail begins, most appropriately, at two isolated, wind-blown cottonwoods on the open prairie and follows an old roadway across the rolling hills. Grasses and blue, cloudless sky merge on the horizon. The foreground is dominated by waving grasses, a few wildflowers, and a mixture of birdsongs.

The loudest of the birdsongs that spring day was the lovely, flute-like gurgling of western meadowlarks. A few of these chunky individuals, perched on low sagebrush shrubs, provided wonderful views of their bright yellow breast crossed by a bold black, V-shaped band, and striped back and head. They called out deep "tweert" notes as I passed them by.

Horned larks were almost as numerous. These buff-colored songsters, with a black chest and black-and-yellow head markings, sang a jumbled song of tinkling notes. I stopped to watch one brightly marked male sitting on a nearby boulder, and could clearly see the black feathers rising above its head like two tiny horns. It then took flight, so that its whitish underparts and black tail with white edges were evident. It sang a short, but clear, "tsee-titi" song in flight.

I was suddenly attracted to two **vesper sparrows** just ahead that seemed to be in a real scrap. They appeared to be beating each other with their wings, then flew straight up for 4 or 5 feet (1-1.5 m). Suddenly, they landed and ran off through the grasses. One emerged 6 feet (1.8 m) beyond, clinging to a low sagebrush, where it sang a lovely song consisting of two sweet notes, followed by two higher ones and a descending trill. Peter Vickery, in *The Audubon Society*

GREAT PLAINS

Master Guide to Birding, describes this song as "here-here where-where all together down the hill." I had witnessed part of the vesper sparrow courtship, not a duel to the death, as I first assumed.

This grassland sparrow was abundant throughout the park and one of the most vociferous prairie species. Although it is not the most glamorous of birds, it possesses a subtle beauty of its own. The vesper sparrow is most readily identified as a streaked brown and gray bird with a white eye ring, chestnut shoulder patches, and distinct white outer tail feathers that are best seen in flight.

The all-black bird, except for its large snow white wing patches, was a male **lark bunting**. I had seen many along the highways en route to the park, but to find it in its natural setting was much more appealing. It, too, was courting, but its display was more impressive than that of the vesper sparrow. The lark bunting flew almost straight up into the air to about 35 feet (11 m), where it paused and then, with wings out, descended in awkward jerky motions, looking more like a butterfly than a bird, back to earth. But during its descent it sang a lovely, extended song of sweet notes rising in pitch, followed by slurred and falling notes. Arthur Bent, in *Life Histories of North American Cardinals, Grosbeaks, Buntings, Towhees, Finches, Sparrows, and Allies*, quotes a description of the song by John Zimmer: "'cheerp'-cheerp'-cheerp'-cheerp'-chee-ee-ee-ee-ee-hir'-ta-hir' ta-who-oo-oo-oo-oo-yor' da-yor' da-hurt'-hurt'-hurt'-ee-ee-ee-ee-ee-ee.'"

Eastern kingbirds, with their black cap, back, and tail, with a bold white terminal band, and snow white underparts, were also present. American crows flew across the trail, heading, no doubt, for some secret crow rendevzous. Mourning doves were common, either calling their sad songs from secluded posts or charging across the horizon. A pair of long-billed curlews called in the distance. Three brown-headed cowbirds flew by with loud, squeaky whistle notes, and a northern harrier and a Swainson's hawk cruised overhead.

At several points along the trail, **McCown's longspurs** arose from the ground and flitted away. Eventually, I discovered one on an open area of ground, frozen in place at my approach, so that I was able to see it well through binoculars. It was a brightly marked male with a black cap and chest, white throat, chestnut shoulder patches, and a distinctly marked black-and-white tail. In flight, it showed an upside-down black "T" on its otherwise all-white tail.

While I was admiring this lovely little grassland finch I detected high-pitched, musical tinkling notes ahead, near the end of the trail. The song was one I had never heard before: an incredibly sweet, descending sound, like the song of a distant veery or canyon wren. I moved up the trail near the spot where I believed the sound had come from. Nothing, only the continually singing meadowlarks, horned larks, and vesper sparrows. A distant crow caw and a common nighthawk called a loud "peent" to my left. I waited, searching all the exposed perches for my bird. Still nothing. I was just about to give up and move on, when the singing began again, so close I could almost feel it. But I still could not locate the perpetrator.

Suddenly I realized that the song was coming from above me. But it had a remarkable ventriloquistic quality that made it extremely difficult to pinpoint. I searched the sky, trying to determine the exact location. Suddenly, I discovered a tiny bird so high that I could barely see it. Viewed through binoculars, it looked very pale; white edges on its tail and single pale wing bars were visible against the lighter sky. It was flying, more or less, in a huge circle, and every 5 to 10 seconds it would glide, with its wings extended, and sing its wonderful song.

Only then it dawned on me that I was watching the courtship flight of a **Sprague's pipit**. Although I was familiar with this bird in winter, far to the south in Texas, where it does not sing, this was my first experience with it on its breeding grounds. That moment will forevermore be etched into my memory.

Sprague's pipit

The Park Environment

Grasslands National Park, located in two separate blocks in south-western Saskatchewan near the Montana border, is situated in an area that is "characterized by gently rolling hills, coulees, badlands, and wide-open spaces punctuated by ranch houses, small villages, and winding roads," according to the park's Interim Management Guidelines. About half of the eventual 576,000 acres (233,104 ha) of parkland (by the summer 1993) has been acquired since 1981. Access into the eastern Killdeer Badlands unit is minimal, but the western Frenchman River Valley unit, administered from a Parks Canada office in Val Marie, contains a full assortment of habitats and wildlife.

Parks Canada reports that the park contains one of the most extensive grassland associations in western Canada. Archibald Budd and Keith Best, in *Wild Plants of the Canadian Prairies*, refer to the area as "short-grass prairie, with blue grama grass, spear grass, June grass, Sandberg's blue grass, sedges, prairie selaginella, sagebrush, and cactus as the dominants."

The Frenchman River is undoubtedly the centerpiece of the western unit; its meandering channel attests to its once dominant force in shaping the landscape. The floodplain still contains a few isolated eastern cottonwoods and pockets of yellow willow, silver-berry, and Wood's rose, with an understory of grasses (most are non-native) and western snowberry. Shorter sandbar willows and saska-toon grow on the edges. And silver and big sagebrush, rubber rabbit-brush, greasewood, and bearberry dominate the drier areas.

The park's information center is in the village of Val Marie, on Saskatchewan Provincial Highway 4. It contains an information desk, an orientation room where video programs are available, and a few exhibits. There is no sales outlet at present. Interpretive activities are limited to nature walks on Sundays in July and August and other programs on request. The 1-mile (1.5-km) Two Trees Trail and the Frenchman River Valley Ecotour, a 17-mile (28-km) round-trip drive into the western unit, are self-guiding.

Additional information is available from the Superintendent, Grasslands National Park, P.O. Box 150, Val Marie, Sask. SON 2T0, Canada; (306) 298-2257.

Bird Life

In the last century, Sprague's pipits, whose entire nesting range is limited to the prairies from central Alberta to southern Manitoba, south only to northern Montana, and east to northwestern Minnesota, have lost most of their essential habitats to agriculture and grazing. However, their marvelous songs still echo across the landscape in places such as Grasslands National Park, which is dedicated to preserving remnants of the Great Plains.

Throughout my visit, once I had learned what to expect, I found this bird to be fairly common. It definitely prefers undisturbed prairie habitat; I did not find it in the arid bottomlands or on the Frenchman River floodplain. And in reviewing the literature on this bird, I discovered very little that was more recent than Arthur Bent's 1965 classic *Life Histories of North American Wagtails, Shrikes, Vireos, and Their Allies.* Two quotes from his book are worthy of inclusion:

Ornithologist Arthur Allen wrote that Sprague's pipit songs "resemble the syllables 'jingle, jingle, jingle, jingle,' rapidly repeated, beginning loud and high, and decreasing rapidly in strength and loudness, and are remarkable for their clear metallic ring, their song reminding one of the jingling sound of a light chain when slowly let fall into a coil." And ornithologist Elliot Coues wrote: "No other bird music heard in our land compares with the wonderful strains of this songster; there is nothing on earth in the melody, coming from above, yet from no visible source. The notes are simply indescribable; but once heard they can never be forgotten."

To truly experience Grasslands, take the Frenchman River Valley Road into the heart of the park. And to see this area at its best, early mornings and evenings are recommended; middays are warm, quiet, and less productive.

One early morning in mid-June, I drove the road slowly, watching for whatever might appear. Meadowlarks, horned larks, vesper sparrows, and mourning doves were most numerous. A northern harrier was hunting, flying back and forth, low over the grasslands; its white rump and wings held in a shallow V were obvious. I passed several common nighthawks, not yet ready to retire from their nocturnal wanderings.

I stopped along the roadway amid the open grasslands, got out of the vehicle, and scoped the surrounding terrain. A pair of pronghorns were watching me from almost a mile away. I was sure that I had been under their scrutiny since I first entered the park; wildlife depend upon keen eyesight and hearing for their survival. Something moved in the grass; a porcupine waddled away as fast as its short legs could manage. Then beyond the porcupine, perhaps 200 feet (61 m) from the road, the dark head and bill of a grouse appeared. It, too, was watching me intently. And when I scoped that general area I discovered a total of 11 grouse heads. Only one of these birds was positioned so that I could see the distinguishing features of a **sharp-tailed grouse**. When one of the birds flew off, its whitish tail substantiated my initial identification. During the several days that I explored Grasslands, I was to find several sharp-tails daily; I know of nowhere else where they are so obvious.

Here, too, were **sage grouse**. Betty and I discovered an adult with five chicks near the old corral during an evening drive. And the next day I located a flock of 18 in the sagebrush flat a quarter mile to the east. Sage grouse are the largest North American grouse and considerably larger than sharp-tails. They are best identified by their black belly. Although the two species can occur in proximity, sage grouse are closely associated with sagebrush, a primary food also used for nesting cover, while sharp-tails are often thought of as "prairie grouse" because of their use of grasslands. In late winter to early

Sage grouse

spring, the males of both species utilize traditional display grounds, called "leks," to attract a mate.

"The display of the male Sage Grouse is called 'strutting', and is different from the 'dancing' of Sharp-tailed Grouse or the 'booming' of prairie-chickens," states Terry Rich in *Birder's World*. Rich points out that sage grouse practice "the most extreme form of polygyny among birds." The male's courtship display permits the female to select her mate. "Perhaps 90 percent of the copulations will be obtained by only 10 percent of the males."

I stopped to identify a black-and-white bird perched on a thorny buffaloberry, a **loggerhead shrike**. It is a striking bird with a black mask, wings, and tail. I examined the nearby bushes for prey that it might have impaled there, but found nothing. I was sure its display post must be nearby. Shrikes are predators, and males display their prey by hanging it, usually head up from thorny shrubs or barbed wire. This behavior was once considered a way of killing and storing food, but researchers more recently have found that male shrikes do this primarily to impress prospective mates.

Shrikes lack the talons of most other avian predators, so they must use their heavy bill and available thorns to hold their catch. Although most of their prey species are small, such as insects and small mammals, birds, reptiles, and amphibians, they also take larger prey, such as bluebirds and mockingbirds. Their physical stature—a stout body and short, heavy bill—clearly suggests that this is a tough, aggressive predator. It is also known as "butcher bird."

The Frenchman River meanders along the southwestern edge of the valley, providing a very different habitat from other parts of the park. The willow stands reminded me of those I had visited in Grand Teton National Park. During the three hours or so I spent birding this habitat, I found about two dozen species, several of them numerous. Bright golden **yellow warblers** sang sweet songs from the willows; males, with their chestnut-streaked breasts, investigated my every movement. There was never a time when I was not in range of a singing yellow warbler; its song has been written as "tseet-tseet-tseet sitta-sita-see." At one point, while I was trying to attract a gray catbird into the open by spishing, I suddenly had three male yellow warblers within 20 feet (6 m) of me. They chipped and scolded me until one suddenly realized that the others had invaded its territory.

Then it totally ignored me and proceeded to fiercely drive off the others.

Brown thrashers were surprisingly common, too, flying across the openings or singing their rambling songs from the thickets. They were easily identified by their reddish upperparts, long tail, and heavily streaked underparts. Clay-colored sparrows sang buzzing songs from all directions; their songs included one, two, or three buzzes in varying lengths. Their striped head and back, clear grayish throat, and brownish cheeks were most distinguished. Eastern kingbirds, always paired and territorial, were among the willows and adjacent vegetation. And the "fitz-bew" songs of willow flycatchers were heard often. Several of these nondescript little *Empidonax* flycatchers were observed "flycatching" among the willows.

Other less numerous birds found within the riparian area included killdeers, willets, black-billed magpies, black-capped chickadees, house wrens, American robins, common yellowthroats, yellow-breasted chats, rufous-sided towhees, song sparrows, red-winged blackbirds, Brewer's blackbirds, common grackles, brown-headed cowbirds, and American goldfinches. And the waterway itself produced four duck species: mallard, northern shoveler, gadwall, and American wigeon. All these were lone females; I assumed that they had nests nearby.

The Frenchman River Valley Ecotour terminates at a huge prairie dog town along the west-facing slopes of a broad valley. Park biologist Vicki Sahanatien told me that researchers have estimated that population at about 2,000 dogs. I scoped the town for burrowing owls, which normally live alongside prairie dogs, often using vacant burrows, but to no avail. I actually walked the entire outer edge of the town without finding any of these little raptors. Leon Perrault, local outdoorsman, later explained that these owls are difficult to find in mid-June when they are with their young; then they leave their burrows only after dark. Sahanatien said that mid-July to early August is the optimum time to observe burrowing owls, when "adults and chicks sit near the burrows."

I did find a number of other birds, many of which are recognized for their use of prairie dog towns. The more numerous species (once more) were horned larks, western meadowlarks, vesper sparrows, American crows, and mourning doves, more or less in that order. In addition, long-billed curlews, Say's phoebes, eastern kingbirds, barn swallows, black-billed magpies, American robins, lark buntings, McCown's longspurs, Brewer's blackbirds, and brown-headed cowbirds were recorded.

Black-billed magpies were widely scattered through the town, picking at the ground or flying here and there to check on their companions or search for food. This 20-inch-long (51-cm) bird is difficult to miss because of its size and contrasting black-and-white plumage. In flight, it shows a rather spectacular white V-pattern on its back and rump. Individuals tend to follow one another, often by several hundred feet apart. Even when a number are flushed and fly off together, it is not long before they are trailing each other. Although a magpie's flight appears slow and measured, it is faster than it seems.

Magpies build bulky stick nests on woody trees and shrubs along the river, but hunt the entire park. Their favorite places seem to the prairie dog towns. Why do they spend so much time there? It could be that they just like the company of the cute little prairie dogs, but more likely, they find security in a dog town. Why be on constant vigil when there are so many other loud-mouthed lookouts?

There is much need for sentinels at prairie dog towns, which are choice hunting areas for all of the park's large predators: coyote, bobcat, badger, swift fox, long-tailed weasel, golden eagle, prairie falcon, and Swainson's and ferruginous hawks. Golden eagles are particularly adept at taking prairie dogs; they attempt to surprise their prey by utilizing the terrain to shield their approach whenever possible. And they can stoop at speeds of up to 200 miles (322 km) per hour. The park's largest avian predators, they have a wingspread of up to 7.5 feet (2.3 m).

The much smaller Swainson's hawk is more numerous in the park during the summer, but usually feeds on smaller prey, such as insects and mice. However, family groups are known to wait at the entrance of ground squirrel burrows and "seize them in their talons when they appear," according to John Terres in *The Audubon Society Encyclopedia of North American Birds*. This hawk also is one of the park's most attractive raptors, displaying bicolored wings and a rich brown bib in flight. Pete Dunne and colleagues, in *Hawks in Flight*, point out that soaring Swainson's hawks "greatly resembles a

Peregrine with its long, tapered wings, but when gliding, the wings are crooked like those of an Osprey. Swainson's hunts like a Harrier, migrates in large swirling flocks like a Broad-winged, and spends a good deal of time perched on the ground like the Ferruginous Hawk."

Swainson's hawks and most of the park's other breeding birds depart for warmer climes by early fall, leaving behind hardier species that are adapted to the severe winters. A few more northern species, such as bald eagles, rough-legged hawks, Bohemian waxwings, snow buntings, gray-crowned rosy finches, and common redpolls, arrive in the fall and stay for the winter. Some years, bald eagles can be found along the river. According to park warden Jacques Saquet, when eagles are present "you can depend upon seeing one, two, or three eagles perched on the lone cottonwood tree along the riverway."

Sage grouse begin their dramatic displays by late March, and the first meadowlark songs are heard by the first of April, ringing in the new season. Florence Miller, the park's visitor activities coordinator, told me, "The park seemingly goes from dormancy to new life all at once." The prairie music begins anew.

In summary, the park's preliminary bird list includes 183 species, of which 68 are known or assumed to nest. Of those 68 species, 6 are water birds, 11 are hawks and owls, and 3 are warblers: yellow warbler, common yellowthroat, and yellow-breasted chat.

Birds of Special Interest
Swainson's hawk. The park's most common grassland hawk is recognized by its bicolored, pointed wings, and dark bib.

Golden eagle. This is the park's largest raptor; adults are distinguished by their all-dark plumage and the golden sheen of their head feathers.

Sage grouse. Watch for this large grouse with a black belly in the sagebrush community.

Sharp-tailed grouse. This reasonably common grassland grouse sports a mottled plumage with a whitish belly and tail.

Horned lark. One of the park's most numerous birds, it is identified by its black, yellow, and white head pattern and black tail with white outer edges.

Black-billed magpie. This large, long-tailed, black-and-white bird gives loud "check" calls and can be found throughout the park.

Sprague's pipit. This is the grassland bird that sings a wonderful, high-pitched, descending song from great heights.

Loggerhead shrike. This black-and-white bird with a black mask is a predator that hangs its prey on thorny plants and barbed wire.

Yellow warbler. It is common along the river and is easily identified by its all-yellow plumage; males possess chestnut breast streaks.

Vesper sparrow. This common grassland bird has chestnut shoulder patches, white eye rings, and distinct white edges on its dark tail.

Lark bunting. Males are coal black with large snow white wing patches; they are most often found perched on posts along the roadsides.

McCown's longspur. Males are distinguished by a black cap, moustachial stripe, and bib; white throat and cheeks; chestnut shoulder patches; and black T-pattern on the tail.

Western meadowlark. One of the park's most abundant birds, it is best identified by its yellow breast, which is crossed by a bold, V-shaped, black band.

18

Theodore Roosevelt National Park, North Dakota

The dawn chorus was in full swing when I arrived at Cottonwood Campground. Sunlight was just beginning to crawl down the high slope toward the Little Missouri River and campground; few campers were stirring. The dominant birdsongs that June morning included the cheery caroling of American robins, the rapid rambling of house wrens, the whistle notes of red-eyed vireos, the "pkit-pkit-pkettle-ot" songs of western kingbirds, and the rich "hew-li" notes of Bullock's orioles, more or less in that order.

A few additional birdsongs blended with the chorus: mourning doves cooed "hoo hoo hoo-ooo"; northern flickers called loud "wik wik wik" notes from high snags; western wood-pewees whistled descending "peeer" songs; least flycatchers called "che-pek" over and over; eastern kingbirds cried harsh "dzzet"; and the clear, sweet songs of yellow warblers emanated from the high foliage. Common yellowthroats called "sweeta sweeta sweeta" from the surrounding underbrush, and yellow-breasted chats sang varied songs of whistles, squawks, rattles, and clucks. Lazuli buntings sang strident tunes of double notes; black-headed grosbeaks sang melodious, robinlike melodies; and orchard orioles sang a varied series of rich and squeaky notes.

Of all these, **western kingbirds** were the most evident, singing from open snags or "flycatching" about the huge cottonwoods. Their bright yellow belly, gray chest, and black wings and tail with rather distinct white outer edges stood out in the morning light. I discovered one carrying plant materials to a well-formed nest on a high cottonwood branch. But it was obvious that nest building was a lower priority than defending territories; ardent singing and chasing competitors took most of their time.

Eastern kingbirds were almost as numerous, though not so vociferous. These birds have a snow white throat and belly and coal black head and tail with a bold white terminal tail band, very different from their western cousins, but equally attractive. Based on the amount of cottonwood down being gathered off the ground, I surmised that they, too, were nesting. Their songs were a sputtering "tzitzee-tzi-tzee-tzi-tzee."

The nesting of the eastern and western kingbirds in such proximity clearly illustrates the considerable overlap of eastern and western birds on the Great Plains. And Cottonwood Campground, it seemed to me, was a microcosm of that interface.

Another good example was the two forms of "northern" orioles present. All but one of the orioles I found that morning were Bullock's orioles, of western affinity. The lone dissenter was a hybrid male with an all-black head and large, yellowish wing patches, undoubtedly part Bullock's and part Baltimore oriole, the eastern form of northern oriole. These orioles were lumped under the generic term "northern" oriole for several years because they hybridize within the Great Plains contact zone, but they split again in 1994.

There also were two forms of **northern flickers** in the campground: red-shafted and yellow-shafted. These flickers are essentially a repeat of the Bullock's and Baltimore oriole story, but have not been split. The red-shafted flicker is a western bird and the yellow-shafted flicker is of eastern affinity. One red-shafted northern flicker called from a high cottonwood snag that contained a nesting hole it was zealously guarding.

Of 34 species found that morning in Cottonwood Campground, half are known to nest across the country. However, seven forms were essentially of western affinity: northern (red-shafted) flicker, western wood-pewee, western kingbird, black-billed magpie, black-headed grosbeak, lazuli bunting, and Bullock's oriole. And ten forms were essentially of eastern affinity: red-headed woodpecker, northern (yellow-shafted) flicker, least flycatcher, eastern kingbird, red-eyed vireo, field sparrow, common grackle, orchard oriole, Baltimore oriole, and American goldfinch.

The Park Environment
This park contains a comfortable mix of grass-covered hills, arid badlands, wooded and brushy ravines, and the Little Missouri River and floodplain. Topographic relief is greatest in the smaller (24,070 acres or 9,741 ha) North Unit, 70 driving miles (113 km) north of the more popular South Unit (46,158 acres or 18,680 ha). Both units, however, are equally dedicated to America's 26th president, who once stated: "I never would have been president if it had not been for my experiences in North Dakota." The National Park Service further claims: "the park's natural resources played a significant role in shaping the life of Theodore Roosevelt during the era of the open range cattle industry, which consequently influenced his role as a conservationist during his term as president of the United States."

The park's mixed-grass prairie is part of North America's Great Plains and is dominated by little bluestem, western wheatgrass, green needlegrass, and blue grama. Scattered grassland shrubs include common juniper, big sagebrush, silver sage, spiny saltbush, and greasewood. Vegetation in the ravines varies with exposure. Ravines on the cooler northern slopes are often dominated by Rocky Mountain juniper, while those that flow into the floodplain contain a mixed woodland of Rocky Mountain juniper, green ash, and boxelder, with an understory of dwarf juniper, chokecherry, skunkbush sumac, and Wood's rose. The broad floodplain of the Little Missouri River, which includes the two park campgrounds, is clearly dominated by plains cottonwoods with a scattering of green ash, Rocky Mountain juniper, American elm, and boxelder.

Two visitor centers exist in the South Unit: Painted Canyon Visitor Center along Interstate 94, and Medora Visitor Center and park headquarters at the park entrance in Medora, North Dakota. The North Unit Visitor Center is at the Highway 85 entrance. All three centers contain an information desk, auditorium for orientation programs, exhibits, and a sales outlet; bird field guides and a park checklist are available.

Interpretive activities are varied. Daily ranger-led nature walks and nightly camp fire programs are conducted at both units. Ranger talks are presented each day in the South Unit and on weekends in the North Unit. Schedules are available on request. The Medora and

North Unit visitor centers are open daily except winter holidays.

Additional information can be obtained from the Superintendent, Theodore Roosevelt National Park, P.O. Box 7, Medora, ND 58645; (701) 623-4466.

Bird Life

That morning, the most outstanding bird at Cottonwood Campground was the **red-headed woodpecker**. Red-heads are one of the most distinct of all the woodpeckers; males possess snow white underparts, rump, and inner wing patches, coal black wings and tail, and a brick red hood. In flight, they show a large square patch of white on their rump and inner wings. Females are duller versions of the males. I counted at least six males during my walk around the campground loops; the females were undoubtedly sitting on nests out of sight. But the males were flying from tree to tree, calling hoarse "kweeer" or "kwee-arr" notes. Arthur Bent, in *Life Histories of North American Woodpeckers*, included a quote about this bird by John James Audubon: "With the exception of the mocking-bird, I know of no species so gay and frolicsome. Indeed, their whole life is one of pleasure."

Red-headed woodpecker

This colorful woodpecker was also present, but less numerous, at Squaw Creek Campground in the North Unit. The two areas differ in several ways. For instance, eastern kingbirds were far more common than western kingbirds in the North Unit. And the presence of American redstarts and ovenbirds in the Squaw Creek Campground was also a surprise. These two warblers were found only in the mixed woodland ravines in the South Unit; they were reasonably common behind the Peaceful Valley Picnic Area.

The **American redstart** is the more colorful and active of the two warblers; the male sports coal black plumage with orange-red patches on its sides, wings, and tail. Females possess a similar pattern, but are duller with yellow patches. Redstarts often hunt by flashing their wings and tail in an effort to startle insects. They also sing a lively song that Peter Vickery, in *The Audubon Society Master Guide to Birding*, has described as "zee-zee-zee-sawaah (down-slurred), zee-zee-zee-zee-zweee (up-slurred)."

Conversely, the ovenbird has a brown-olive back, white underparts with black streaks, bold white eye rings, and a broad orange crown stripe. But it is usually detected first by its loud and unique song: "teach teach teach TEACH TEACH," each note louder than the previous one. This chunky little warbler spends considerable time on the ground, walking with a teetering gait in its search for insects.

Other common species at Squaw Creek Campground and nearby Squaw Creek Nature Trail included mourning doves, northern flickers, American crows, house wrens, American robins, cedar waxwings, red-eyed vireos, rufous-sided towhees, chipping and field sparrows, and American goldfinches. Less numerous species included American kestrels, hairy woodpeckers, tree swallows, black-capped chickadees, blue jays, white-breasted nuthatches, gray catbirds, brown thrashers, warbling vireos, yellow and black-and-white warblers, yellow-breasted chats, black-headed grosbeaks, lazuli buntings, and brown-headed cowbirds.

One of the park's most numerous birds in all habitats but the open grasslands is the little **lazuli bunting**. This bird is named for the azure blue mineral lazurite, the color of the male's hood. A gorgeous bird, it also sports a mottled blue-brown back and wings, two white wing bars, white belly, and cinnamon breast and sides. The female is a dull two-tone brown. But what makes this bird special at Theodore Roosevelt is its spirited song, a series of loud, sweet notes that rise and fall, "swee swee che zee swee ti" or "swee swee swee che te tic." And one that eluded me at first along the Jones Creek Trail sang a different melody, which I interpreted as "I am right over this way, stu-pid."

Another common songster in brushy areas was the even smaller field sparrow, usually detected first by its distinct call, a series of clear whistles that accelerate into a trill. Although it is a secretive sparrow and usually feeds on the ground under sagebrush and other shrubs, it can readily be attracted with spishing. It then pops up into a shrub for a brief look around, providing the birder an opportunity to admire its subtle beauty. Field sparrows have a rust-orange crown, pink bill, distinct white eye rings, and gray to buff underparts.

But of all the park's brush-loving birds, none is as numerous and easily identified as the **rufous-sided towhee**. No matter where you are in the park, if you spish or make a squeaking noise, the first bird to respond will usually be this large-sparrow-sized towhee. More often than not, one will appear at the top of a nearby shrub or thicket and call "cheeee," or it will serenade you with a complete song that begins with "tink tink tink" and continues with an extended trill. What's more, it will often sit still for a while allowing a good look. The male possesses an all-black hood with blood-red eyes, black-and-white back and wings, chestnut sides, and a black tail with large white corners. When it finally dives for cover, its black-and-white tail will flash a quick farewell.

The park's numerous prairie dog towns often contain a very different assortment of birds. They are one of the best places to find a **black-billed magpie**, a 20-inch-long (51-cm) bird with an extremely long tail and black-and-white plumage. Biologist Morris Johnson, in *Black and White Spy: The Magpie*, claims its name is derived from "*margot* or *marquerite*, which is French and signifies 'chattering woman.' Apparently early observers in the Old World thought noisy women and magpies were alike." Although these birds do chatter quietly among themselves, their most common call is a hollow "chaeck" or a series, "chaech, chaeck, chaeck-chaeck, chaeck." For more on this bird's fascinating feeding behavior, see chapter 21 on Badlands.

Western meadowlarks are often found at prairie dog towns, singing loud "sweee-tee, swee ti me" or calling "jerk" or "trick" notes. This plump songster is easily identified by its very short tail, bright yellow throat and breast crossed with a bold black V, and striped head and back. The western meadowlark is the park's most common species, based on 12 breeding bird surveys, and it also was a Teddy Roosevelt favorite. According to the park's brochure, Roosevelt once wrote: "One of our sweetest, loudest songsters is the meadowlark. The plains air seems to give it a voice, and it will perch on top of a bush or tree and sing for hours in rich, bubbling tones."

Killdeers also frequent prairie dog towns. When disturbed, a killdeer calls its own name, "kill-dee kill-dee," over and over, then either runs off on long legs or flies away with much verbosity. It is an attractive bird with two black bands across its otherwise all-white breast, a head pattern of black, brown, and white, and a dull reddish-orange rump. This shorebird also frequents the river bottom, nesting on the bare ground amid bits of debris. When discovered at its nest, it may perform an outlandish display of injury, dragging a wing to draw a predator away. And just when it is about to be captured, it will stage a remarkable recovery and fly away unscathed.

Among other prairie dog town visitors are all-black, 17-inch (43-cm) American crows; smaller Brewer's blackbirds, black except for the male's yellow eyes; and horned larks, with yellow-and-black face, whitish underparts, and black tail with white edges. Barn swallows, with long, forked tails, are almost always present; mourning doves often feed about the colony; and western kingbirds chase insects overhead and from the ground. Well-marked lark sparrows can usually be found searching the ground for seeds and insects, and American goldfinches find seeds on the ground or on weedy plants.

The lucky observer may also encounter a burrowing owl, the little, brown, bare-legged owl that nests in vacated prairie dog holes. It has developed a fascinating technique for discouraging predators at the nest; it can utter a call that sounds like a rattlesnake. Its normal call is a high mournful sound, not unlike that of a mourning dove. A diurnal owl, it spends much time searching for prey, insects and other invertebrates, mice, small birds and snakes, and the like during daylight hours.

The **mountain bluebird** can be abundant about the dog towns or elsewhere on the open grasslands, especially after nesting, when family groups gather; these flocks sometimes number in the hundreds. Observant visitors to Theodore Roosevelt cannot help but see this beautiful songbird. The male can be almost turquoise blue, with paler underparts, although the female is a duller blue-gray color. They spend much time "flycatching" from snags, hovering over open ground, or even picking up insects on the ground. When berries ripen in late summer and fall, they also take advantage of that food supply. Nests are built in natural cavities or in deserted woodpecker nests. Although their most frequent calls are flutelike "terr" notes, they also sing a lovely song when nesting: a sweet and clear, warbling melody with "trually" and "tru-al-ly" ingredients, somewhat like the caroling of a robin.

The Little Missouri River is usually scarcely more than a shadow of its once mighty self, meandering north toward the larger Missouri River. Much of the river's waters are diverted for agriculture. Only a few water birds are normally present in summer: killdeers, great blue herons, an occasional Canada goose or wood duck, American white pelicans, and spotted sandpipers.

Another river bird is the **belted kingfisher**, usually located near a high dirt bank in which it may be nesting. Kingfishers are reasonably large, bluish birds with a heavy bill and white underparts crossed by a broad blue band. The female can be distinguished from the male by its reddish belly. They fish along the river, diving after prey from a considerable height and often becoming entirely submerged before they reappear with a fish, frog, or other prey in their bill. They then fly to a nearby perch, beat their catch against a branch to kill it, and swallow it whole. Occasionally, they capture a fish so long that they are unable to swallow it; it actually protrudes from the bill. However, nature has given them a digestive system that quickly dissolves the fish, so it soon dissappears down the gullet. For details about this bird's nesting behavior, aee chapter 27 on Chickasaw.

The park's arid badlands provide perfect habitat for the nondescript little **rock wren**, one of the area's most numerous birds. It usually is detected first by its distinct "tick-ear" call or by its varied song, usually an emphatic series of "cheer cheer cheer cheer cheer" notes. But it also sings a more extended song that Arthur Bent, in *Life Histories of North American Nuthatches, Wrens, Thrashers, and Their Allies,* described as "keree keree keree, chair chair chair, deedle deedle deedle, tur tur tur, keree keree trrrrr." Its gray-brown plumage, with tiny white specks on its back, blends in well with the badlands terrain.

The higher cliffs along the river provide nesting sites for at least two additional birds of interest: golden eagles and prairie falcons. Golden eagles nest early in the year, using high, inaccessible ledges. By summertime, their young are completely fledged and more or less on their own. One June morning I watched an adult and an immature eagle hunting along the high cliff behind Cottonwood Campground. Both hovered over the steep slope, and every now and then would dive on some prey below. The adult bird was gorgeous; its golden head feathers were clearly evident even at a distance. The immature bird was distinguished by its mottled appearance and white tail with a broad, dark terminal band. I could not tell what they were hunting, but it undoubtedly was small; I assumed I was watching a training exercise. This species is known for its diverse diet, which includes cottontails and hares, as well as smaller mammals, snakes, insects, and even carrion.

Prairie falcons also nest on the cliffs and hunt the adjacent prairie. During the several days I spent in the park, I found this raptor numerous times each day, usually flying away from me at a distance. But its large size, long, pointed wings, pale overall coloration, and black axillaries, or triangular patches that extend from the wing pits onto the underside of the wings, are distinct. One June morning in the North Unit, I found three prairie falcons flying over the scenic drive toward the Little Missouri River. At River Bend Overlook, I detected prairie falcon calls, screeched "keee keee keee" notes, below me to the right, where I assumed the male had just returned to its nest with prey for its incubating mate or nestlings.

A few additional soaring birds frequent these cliffs, taking advantage of the thermals rising from the warmer lowlands. Turkey vultures can be readily identified by their bicolored wings, bare red head, and unique flight pattern: they hold their wings in a shallow V and tilt their body slightly from side to side. The golden eagle flies in a straight-forward manner with wings held straight out. Red-tailed and Swainson's hawks are fairly common, as well. Red-tails possess a dull to brick-red tail, and Swainson's hawks are best identified by their bicolored wings (white wing linings and dark flight feathers), banded tail, and brown to buff breast. Northern harriers, Cooper's hawks, and American kestrels sometimes soar over the slopes, as well.

The riverway is busiest during migration, when thousands of birds follow this ancient route north or south. Park naturalist Bruce Kaye told me that Canada geese and sandhill cranes can be especially numerous in spring. The winter scene is very different. Most of the summer residents have gone south, and only a few more northern species come to stay. Most notable of these winter residents are rough-legged hawks, which hunt the open grasslands, and the hardier songbirds: Bohemian waxwing, northern shrike, American tree sparrow, and common redpoll.

The best indication of winter bird populations is provided by the Christmas Bird Counts, which have been undertaken annually at Medora since 1974, and at the North Unit since 1980. In 18 years, Medora counters tallied a total of 54 species, with 441 to 2,055 individuals of 16 to 35 species recorded per year. The dozen most numerous species recorded during the last five years, in descending order of abundance, are Bohemian waxwing (but totally missing some years), American robin, house sparrow, Lapland longspur, wild turkey, black-billed magpie, ring-necked pheasant, red-breasted nuthatch, gray-crowned rosy finch, sharp-tailed grouse, red crossbill, and European starling.

In summary, the park's bird checklist includes 185 species, of which 107 are known to nest or are probable nesters. Of these 107 species, 9 are water birds, 15 are hawks and owls, and 6 are warblers. Two species are listed for winter only: gray-crowned rosy finch and pine grosbeak.

Birds of Special Interest
Golden eagle. This huge, all-dark raptor hunts over the slopes and prairie; juveniles possess a white tail with a broad, dark terminal band.

Prairie falcon. It is distinguished by its pale plumage, long, pointed wings, and black "wing pits" that form an extended triangular pattern under the wings.

Killdeer. This noisy shorebird, with two black bands on its otherwise white underparts, is most common along the river and at prairie dog towns.

Belted kingfisher. Watch for this large-billed, bluish-backed bird along the river; females possess reddish bellies.

Red-headed woodpecker. This lovely red-headed bird, with black-and-white body and wings, is fairly common in the park campgrounds.

Western kingbird. Its yellow belly, gray hood, and black tail with white edges clearly distinguish this kingbird from the black-and-white eastern kingbird.

Black-billed magpie. Watch for this long-tailed, black-and-white bird along the roadways and at prairie dog towns; it has a harsh "chaeck" call.

Mountain bluebird. This turquoise blue bird may be found throughout the park; hundreds may gather after nesting on the open flats.

Rock wren. One of the park's most common, but inconspicuous, songbirds, it is often detected first by its loud "tick-ear" call or "cheer cheer cheer" song.

Lazuli bunting. Males possess an azure blue hood, cinnamon sides, and white belly; it is one of the park's most common species.

Rufous-sided towhee. This bird is abundant at brushy areas; males sport an all-black hood, blood-red eyes, and chestnut sides.

Western meadowlark. This plump, yellow-breasted bird sings a loud melodic song that domiantes the park's open grasslands.

19

Devil's Tower National Monument, Wyoming

Hundreds of white-throated swifts frequent the high cliffs of Devil's Tower in spring and summer. Their high-pitched, twittering call, a drawn-out, descending "skee-e-e-e-e," often is the first clue to their presence. They sometimes fly so high above the visitor center and trails that they appear as little more than dots in the blue sky. Especially in the early mornings, they usually stay at high elevations, preferring the eastern cliff face, which receives the earliest rays of sunshine; that is where they find the most insects. But as the day warms up, these speedy birds descend in elevation to hunt just above the forest canopy and over the visitor center parking area. Then, they may zip by the visitor at speeds in excess of 100 miles (161 km) per hour, sometimes so close that you can actually feel a rush of air.

White-throated swifts are easy to identify by their black-and-white plumage and swept-back wings, along with their almost constant twittering. They have been described as flying cigars due to their blunt shape. And their flight is very different from that of other birds; their wings are stiff and they fly with almost a twinkling effect. A careful observer might even see a pair copulating in midair; they may free-fall several hundred feet in a spin, wings out to slow their descent, and pull out of the fall barely before crashing to the ground.

Nests are built in narrow crevices high on the cliffs. The swifts construct tiny platforms with their own feathers, glued together with saliva. Their entire life is spent in the air or hanging onto the high cliffs. If they were to land on the ground, they would be unable to take off; their feet are too tiny and weak to push them off. Actually, their feet look very much like those of hummingbirds; they are members of the same order of birds, Apodiformes, Latin for "no feet." And like hummingbirds, they can withstand sudden cold temperatures by lowering their metabolism rate until warmer conditions occur. During extreme cold, they may huddle together like bees in a hive.

White-throated swift

Devil's Tower's white-throated swifts remain only until late summer and then go south. On their wintering grounds, such as Big Bend National Park in Texas, in Mexico, or Central America, hundreds may congregate in crevices like those in which they nest. However, shortly after the first insects are flying at Devil's Tower in the spring, they are right back on their nesting grounds.

The Park Environment
Devil's Tower has the distinction of being the very first national monument in the National Park System; it was created by President Theodore Roosevelt in 1906. Although the 867-foot (264-m) pillar looks like a gigantic petrified tree stump, the columnar structure is actually a lava intrusion, the core of an ancient volcano with the

softer outer materials worn away. Columns were formed as molten rock cooled, crystallized, and cracked inside the cone. The tower's base diameter is 1,000 feet (305 m), and its summit is 5,117 feet (1,560 m) above sea level. Peter Farb, in *Face of North America*, points out that the vertical columns possess "anywhere from three to eight sides, although the number is usually six. At the top of the tower the ends of the columns form a pattern that looks like the cracks that form in mud as it dries. Such cracks are the result of shrinking caused by the loss of water; when lava cools under certain conditions, it shrinks and cracks in the same way."

Devil's Tower clearly dominates the surrounding landscape of ponderosa pine forest, deciduous woodland, and streamside riparian habitats. The ponderosa pine community, which makes up approximately 62 percent of the park, contains a scattering of Rocky Mountain juniper and bur oak, and a sparse ground cover of grasses, common juniper, chokecherry, and skunkbush sumac. Patches of arrowleaf balsamroot are also common. A few aspens grow among the moisture-retaining boulder fields along the northern slopes. Below these habitats, on the southern slope and in a few lower ravines, is a deciduous woodland community dominated by bur oak, green ash, chokecherry, wild plum, and hawthorn. Open grasslands also checkerboard the lower slopes. And along the floodplain of the Belle Fourche River (pronounced bel'foosh), which crosses the southeastern corner of the park, is a riparian habitat with a scattering of huge eastern cottonwoods. The best example of this environment is found in the park campground, where the meandering river has formed a beautiful little valley, open on the north and with steep red banks to the south.

The 1,347-acre (545-ha) park is situated on the northwestern edge of the Black Hills, so it contains many of the same plants and animals found at Wind Cave and Jewel Cave parks. The differences relate primarily to the high, bare rock face of Devil's Tower. This tower also has become a center for rock climbers from across the country; visitors often spend considerable time watching climbers ascend the treacherous cliffs.

The visitor center is at the end of the park highway, 3 miles (4.8 km) beyond the entrance, near the western base of the tower. Trails provide easy access to the base of the tower and the surrounding forest. The 1.5-mile (2.4-km) Tower Trail circles the base; Red Beds Trail provides a longer (2.8-mi or 4.5-km) loop route around the tower, with a link trail to the campground; and the lower 1.5-mile (2.4-km) Joyner Ridge Trail, the northern edge of the park, crosses open grassland and passes through an upland riparian area locally known as the "green corridor."

The visitor center contains an information desk, auditorium for orientation programs, exhibits, and sales outlet; bird field guides and a checklist are available. Richard Peterson's *A Birdwatcher's Guide to the Black Hills and Adjacent Plains* is also available. Interpretive activities include evening talks at the campground amphitheater, daily nature walks, and visitor center talks three times daily. The Tower Trail and Joyner Ridge Trail are self-guiding.

Additional information can be obtained from the Superintendent, Devil's Tower National Monument, P.O. Box 8, Devil's Tower, WY 82714; (307) 467-5283.

Bird Life

Although the white-throated swift is far and away the most abundant bird around Devil's Tower, it is not the only species that resides on this granitic pillar. Violet-green swallows, which nest in crevices on the cliff face as well as in surrounding ponderosa pines, are fairly common and can be confused with swifts. About the same size as swifts, violet-greens have a normal swallow flight pattern and possess all-white underparts and rump spots and a violet-green back. In the right light their back can appear almost velvety green.

The park's most notable cliff bird is the much larger **prairie falcon**; a pair annually nests on Devil's Tower. It is easily identified by its size (17-20 in or 43-51 cm long with a wingspan of 40-42 in. or 102-107 cm), pale overall color, pointed wings, and distinct black underwing markings (axillaries) that form extended triangular patches. This is the same falcon used by the U.S. Air Force Academy as its official mascot. Like the larger and more powerful peregrine falcon, it declined drastically throughout its range while DDT was being used in the United States. But also like the peregrine, the prairie falcon has made a remarkable recovery since DDT was banned in the United States and Canada. The Devil's Tower birds spend much of their time soaring around the tower, although they hunt the adjacent grasslands.

Rock doves, the domestic pigeons so common in barnyards across the country, also occur on the high cliffs. This bird has adapted to the wild very well, nesting in high, inaccessible places and feeding on seeds, fresh leaves, and insects on the surrounding cliffs and in the lowlands. These large pigeons are also capable of performing impressive flights along the high cliff face. Rock climbers sometimes come face-to-face with this feral pigeon.

Watch also for the large, all-dark turkey vultures that soar over the tower and surrounding terrain utilizing the thermals that rise from the warmer lowlands. These broad-winged birds are easily identified by their bare red head, bicolored wings, and distinct flight pattern: they hold their wings in a shallow V and tilt their body slightly from side to side. Red-tailed hawks may also be present; their broad wings and dull to brick red tail are usually evident.

One morning in June, I walked the Devil's Tower Trail. **American robins** were the most obvious bird about the parking area. Some were building nests carrying billfulls of plant materials into the forest. One early bird was stuffing worms and insects into the mouths of two begging, heavily striped youngsters. Other robins sang from the forest; their loud caroling echoed across the parking area. They sang a distinct, flutelike song, "cheer-up, cheer, cheer, cheer-up," over and over. I looked closely at one particularly bright male, and in spite of my considerable familiarity with robins, I realized all over again how truly beautiful it was in the morning light. Its brick red breast contrasted with its black head, with slivers of white around the eyes, whitish throat, yellow bill, and brownish back. It suddenly flew off into the forest with sharp "tut tut tut" notes.

I was attracted to a smaller black-and-white bird that was walking straight down a ponderosa pine trunk, as if the law of gravity did not apply. This was a **white-breasted nuthatch**, one of two nuthatches common in the park's ponderosa pine community. Every now and then it called out a hollow knack. When it got to the bottom of the tree, it turned around and circled its way back up the trunk, probing into cracks in its search for insects. It seemed to ignore my admiration, providing me a wonderful look from about 30 feet (9 m). It had snow white underparts, except for a touch of buff on its belly, a solid black cap and nape, and a grayish blue back and wings. Also, it showed white corners on its blackish tail in flight.

The **red-breasted nuthatch**, also common in the forest, is slightly smaller and has buff to reddish underparts, black cap, and grayish blue back and wings. A red-breast also has a bold white eye line at the base of its black cap. Its call, more nasal than that of the white-breasted nuthatch, sounds like a toy horn. It, too, has the ability to walk up and down tree trunks and upside-down under branches. Amazing creatures.

Elsewhere, these two nuthatches seldom occur together on their nesting grounds. White-breasts prefer open ponderosa pine forests and riparian habitats, while red-breasts normally seek conifer forests at higher elevations. In the Rocky Mountains, red-breasts nest in the mixed forest and spruce-fir zones. Their togetherness in the Black Hills is but one more fascinating feature of this region. For more about the extraordinary ecology of the Black Hills, see chapter 20 on Wind Cave, Jewel Cave, and Mount Rushmore.

I located more than two dozen species during my walk that morning. Other common birds encountered along the loop route included western wood-pewees, with their plain appearance and descending "peeee" songs; black-capped chickadees, which sang "chick-a-dee-dee-dee"; solitary vireos, which stayed among the high foliage and sang two- to six-note phrases, "chu-wee cher-io"; yellow-rumped warblers singing a series of "sweee" notes high over the trail; and tiny pine siskins calling rising "tee-ee" notes.

Western wood-pewees were especially numerous. Their spirited songs rang out dozens of times along the trail. I discovered two nests, both on horizontal limbs of ponderosa pines 20 to 30 feet (6-9 m) above the ground. They stuck up about 2 inches (5 cm) above the limbs and appeared to be constructed of various soft plant parts woven together with lichen and spider webbing.

I also had several good looks at **yellow-rumped warblers**; these birds were "flycatching" from various snags along the trail. Their yellow, black, and white plumage was most obvious when they sailed out after a passing insect. The five yellow patches—on their cap, throat, sides, and rump—contrasted with their coal black chest and flanks. This little warbler was once called "Audubon's" warbler until ornithologists found the western Audubon's (with a yellow throat) interbreeding with the eastern "myrtle" warbler (with a white throat); then the two forms were lumped as one species and called "yellow-rumped" warbler, after their most obvious feature. Some birders refer to them as "butter-butts." Their song can be described as a rollicking "swee swee, swe swe swe de-eee," highest in the middle.

Several other less numerous birds were found along the Tower Trail that morning: mourning dove, hairy woodpecker, northern (red-shafted) flicker, violet-green swallow, brown creeper, rock and house wrens, mountain bluebird, Townsend's solitaire, ovenbird, western tanager, rufous-sided towhee, chipping and lark sparrows, dark-eyed (white-winged) junco, brown-headed cowbird, and red crossbill.

I discovered a pair of **mountain bluebirds** perched near a crevice in an old ponderosa pine along the south slope. They were bringing food to a anxious nestlings; I located the nest by the youngsters' high-pitched begging. Males are darker blue than the females, which are beautiful in their own right. But the brighter all-blue male glowed like a precious jewel in the morning light. I had earlier found this bird common along the entrance road, "flycatching" from fence posts or hovering over the ground. During the nesting season they pair off, but once their young are fledged these birds join other mountain bluebird families, often congregating over fields by the hundreds. They serve the farmers well; a large flock of bluebirds can consume tons of insects. For additional information about this lovely bird, see chapter 18 on Theodore Roosevelt.

Mountain bluebirds were also common in the open fields along the river. There they competed with the cliff and barn swallows that plied the air in their search for insects. Other birds that I found in both these habitats included hairy woodpeckers, northern flickers, western wood-pewees, black-capped chickadees, white-breasted nuthatches, house wrens, American robins, solitary vireos, chipping sparrows, and brown-headed cowbirds.

A few more species were found only in the campground or adjoining deciduous woodlands: American kestrel, red-headed woodpecker, eastern kingbird, cedar waxwing, European starling, red-eyed and warbling vireos, yellow warbler, black-headed grosbeak, common grackle, Bullock's oriole, and American goldfinch. A pair of American kestrels had a nest in a tall cottonwood near the campground entrance. I could hear the young pleading each time an adult approached the nest.

Black-and-white **eastern kingbirds** were common about the edge of the campground, sailing after insects and calling high-pitched, "stuttering 'kip-kip-kipper-kipper; dze-dzee-dzee' and 'dzeet' " notes, as described by Wayne Peterson in *The Audubon Society Master Guide to Birding*. This flycatcher has a coal black cap, snow white underparts, and dark back, wings, and tail, except for the broad, white terminal band.

I was most surprised by the large number of **red-headed woodpeckers**, at least four pairs in the campground proper. In a 1992 bird survey along the river, the park's resource specialist Jane Gyhra and colleagues located 11 individuals. I found the campground red-heads searching the furrowed trunks of cottonwoods for insects, flying here and there about the taller trees, or calling distinct notes, like "kweeer" or "kwee-arr." Male red-heads possess snow white underparts, rump, and large patch on their wings; coal black back, wings, and tail; and a spectacular all-red head.

The general loss of open riparian woodlands throughout the red-headed woodpecker's range, along with increased populations of nonnative European starlings and extensive use of biocides, has led to serious declines of this wonderful and easily recognized species. Although the woodpecker's habitat is protected in the national monument, several starlings were nesting in holes that might otherwise be used by woodpeckers.

Bullock's orioles were also common among the high cottonwoods. I watched a pair chasing each other from tree to tree. Every now and then the male would stop and sing a loud, flutelike song. Biologists Joseph Grinnell and Robert Storer, in Arthur Bent's *The Life Histories of North American Woodpeckers*, described its song as a "slightly varying series of syllables, rhythmically accented, like 'hip-kip-y-ty-hoy-hoy,' but with a peculiar quality impossible to describe; also a mildly harsh 'cha-cha-cha-cha,' etc., in rapid sequence, and a single clear note, 'kleeek.' Female and young give simple harsh blackbird-like notes." The male is a gorgeous creature, sporting a brilliant pattern of fiery orange cheeks, eyebrows, and chest, with a black crown, back, tail, and wings and large white wing patches. Females are overall yellowish with a whitish belly.

The fairly large blackbird seen about the campground and along the river was the **common grackle**, best identified by its keel-shaped tail. Males possess yellowish eyes, while the duller females have black eyes. Devil's Tower is close to the western edge of this bird's range; it is common throughout the East, but does not breed west of eastern Wyoming, central Colorado, and central and southeastern New Mexico, according to the American Ornithologists' Union 1983 Checklist.

A few other species were common about the campground: plain western wood-pewees; house wrens singing rapid, bubbling songs from the undergrowth; yellow warblers singing spirited songs, "tseet-tseet-tseet sitta-sitta-see," from the surrounding vegetation; and chipping sparrows contributing fast trills, all on one note. I also observed numbers of hairy woodpeckers; northern flickers; violet-green, cliff, and barn swallows; black-capped chickadees; cedar waxwings; red-eyed and warbling vireos; black-headed grosbeaks; red-winged blackbirds; brown-headed cowbirds; and American goldfinches.

Most of the park's breeding birds leave for the winter. Only the full-time residents and a few more northern species remain. The more common winter resident birds include rock doves; hairy and downy woodpeckers; blue, gray, and pinyon jays; black-billed magpies; black-capped chickadees; white-breasted and red-breasted nuthatches; brown creepers; Townsend's solitaires; American tree sparrows; red crossbills; and pine siskins.

In summary, the park's bird checklist includes 119 species, of which 88 are listed as summer residents and assumedly nest. Of these 88 species, 5 are water birds, 8 are hawks and owls, and 5 are warblers. Eight species are listed as winter residents only: Cooper's and rough-legged hawks, golden eagle, sharp-tailed grouse, Steller's jay, rosy finch, Harris' sparrow, and common redpoll; a few of these must also occur as migrants.

Birds of Special Interest
Prairie falcon. Watch for this large, pale, pointed-wing raptor soaring along the high cliff face.

White-throated swift. This fast-flying, black-and-white bird with stiff, swept-back wings emits high-pitched twittering calls.

Red-headed woodpecker. It is common in the campground; the male is easily identified by its black-and-white body and all-red head.

Western wood-pewee. This bird is common throughout the park and best identified by its plain gray-brown plumage and descending "peeee" song.

Eastern kingbird. Watch for this black-and-white flycatcher in the lowlands; it is most common along the river.

White-breasted nuthatch. This bird is a year-round resident in the forest and campground; it has all-white underparts and a black back and can walk up and down tree trunks.

Red-breasted nuthatch. This is the smaller nuthatch with buff to reddish underparts and a white line through its otherwise all-black cap.

American robin. It can be common throughout the park and is easily identified by its red breast and dark head.

Yellow-rumped warbler. This little yellow, white, and black bird has five yellow patches: on its cap, throat, sides, and rump.

Common grackle. It is common in summer about the campground; notice its long, wedge-shaped tail and the male's whitish eyes.

Bullock's oriole. This orange, black, and white bird is seen in the campground and deciduous habitats; males spend much time chasing one another about the high foliage.

20

Wind Cave National Park, Jewel Cave National Monument, and Mount Rushmore National Memorial, South Dakota

Wind Cave's visitor center grounds contained an amazing diversity of birds. I found more than two dozen species there in about two hours one early June morning. From the parking lot, American robins, house wrens, rufous-sided towhees, and common grackles were most obvious. The caroling of American robins, "cheerily, cheery, cheerily, cheer," resounded from all sides. Several of these red-breasted birds, with black head, partial white eye rings, and

American robin

bright yellow bill, were searching the front lawn for worms. They ran here and there, stopping to cock their head for a better look, then reaching down to pull out long, fat breakfast worms. One duller female was feeding a pair of spot-breasted youngsters.

Common grackles were also plentiful about the lawn and parking lot; their glossy purple plumage, pale yellow eyes, and wedge-shaped tail helped to identify these waddling blackbirds. The much smaller, elusive house wrens sang their rapid, bubbling songs from the adjacent undergrowth. Rufous-sided towhees remained near cover, but a few were perched on the low stone wall or adjacent chokecherry shrubs. One brightly colored male sat in the open, singing its distinct song, "clip clip cheee" over and over. Its all-black hood and blood-red eyes, black-and-white back and wings, and rufous sides gleamed in the morning light. A truly lovely bird.

I followed the edge of the parking lot toward the picnic area, identifying various birds along the way. A yellow warbler sang a distinct "tseet-tseet-tseet sitta-sitta-see" song from the thicket, but came within easy viewing distance when I spished faintly. It was a male with chestnut streaks on its otherwise all-yellow chest. A pair of eastern kingbirds flew across the parking area; their black-and-white plumage and sharp, stuttering flight songs were obvious. Another flycatcher, a western wood-pewee, sang its descending "peeee" notes from a pine across the road. Then a Lewis' woodpecker flapped across the road, its black wings and reddish belly gleaming in the morning light. Several pine siskins flew over, calling rising "tee-ee" notes, and four barn swallows, with long, forked tails, worked the parking area for insects.

The fluty whistles of a male black-headed grosbeak attracted my attention to a juniper across the little drainage. Through binoculars, I admired this brightly marked songster; its black head, black-and-white wings and tail, and orange-brown underparts and collar gave it a striking appearance. There, too, was a yellow-and-black American goldfinch male. And at the base of the juniper were two chipping sparrows; their small size and reddish caps were obvious. Farther up the ravine I detected the sharp "chuck" of a brown thrasher.

Suddenly, only a few feet away among the dense foliage of a juniper, a bird let out a series of squawks and grunts. It moved higher and emerged into the open, where I had a wonderful look at a yellow-breasted chat. Chats are large warblers with an olive-brown back, lemon yellow breast, white spectacles, and heavy bill. All the while it sang its wild song, an elaborate repertoire of whistles, grunts, cackles, mews, and rattles. All of a sudden it seemed to realize that it was being watched and disappeared into the undergrowth. Once hidden, it called a series of loud "caw" notes.

Several other birds were detected during my morning walk: The low, mournful calls of mourning doves were common; a red-shafted northern flicker flew across the skyline; and a black-billed magpie called loud "chaech" notes from behind the visitor center. Calls of red-breasted and white-breasted nuthatches emanated from the pines across the road; a pair of mountain bluebirds were "flycatching" on the hillside above the cave entrance trail; and a pair of European starlings streaked across the sky. Several yellow-rumped warblers sang from the pines; a pair of brown-headed cowbirds called squeaky whistle notes in passing; and numerous red crossbills, calling loud "jib jib" notes, passed overhead. A pair of Bullock's orioles chased one another in the high cottonwood foliage across the road, and all the while, western meadowlark songs echoed from the grasslands beyond.

In a sense, the birds found near the Wind Cave visitor center that morning represented a microcosm of the most common species in South Dakota's Black Hills.

The Park Environment
Wind Cave, Jewel Cave, and Mount Rushmore lie within a 30-mile (48-km) radius of one another. All are situated in the southern portion of the Black Hills, an area that occupies the southwestern corner of the Missouri Plateau and runs about 125 miles (201 km) north-south and 60 miles (97 km) east-west. Named for the deep green vegetation that covers much of the higher slopes, the Black Hills rise almost 4,000 feet (1,219 m) above the Missouri Plateau and contain a varied terrain.

The 28,292-acre (11,450-ha) Wind Cave National Park is largely rolling hills, except for Rankin Ridge, which rises 5,013 feet (1,528 m) above sea level. The limestone cavern contains more than 70 miles (113 km) of explored passageways with extensive boxwork and calcite crystal formations. The 1,275-acre (516-ha) Jewel Cave

National Monument lies between 5,100 and 5,740 feet (1,554-1,750 m) elevation. This limestone cavern, the world's fourth longest, contains more than 90 miles (145 km) of passageways, including a series of interconnecting chambers with many side galleries and fine calcite crystal encrustations. And the 1,300-acre (526-ha) Mount Rushmore National Memorial lies between 5,180 and 5,725 feet (1,579-1,745 m) elevation. It is famous worldwide for the sculptured busts of U.S. Presidents George Washington, Thomas Jefferson, Theodore Roosevelt, and Abraham Lincoln.

The predominant tree in all three units is the ponderosa pine, often growing in relatively pure stands as well as scattered patches on canyon walls. Rocky Mountain juniper is often associated with the taller pines. A few deciduous trees such as cottonwood, aspen, and white birch, with an understory dominated by chokecherry and snowberry, occur in ravines. Riparian habitats occur at Wind Cave, where additional broadleaf trees and shrubs such as American elm, boxelder, American plum, and skunkbush sumac are common. Wind Cave's grassland communities represent the mixed prairie environment where western wheatgrass and green needlegrass are most abundant; buffalo, little and big bluestem, and grama grasses are also common.

National Park Service visitor centers are in all three units. Each has an information desk, orientation programs, exhibits, and a sales outlet; bird guides, a checklist, and Richard Peterson's useful little book, *A Birdwatcher's Guide to the Black Hills and Adjacent Plains*, are available.

Cave tours are the principal interpretive activity at Wind Cave and Jewel Cave, although nightly camp fire programs, visitor center demonstration programs, occasional "night prowls," and prairie hikes are scheduled at Wind Cave during the summer. At Mount Rushmore, evening sculpture lighting programs are presented throughout the summer. In addition, the Black Hills Parks & Forest Association offers a variety of adult field seminars in summer and fall, including a three-day session on bird finding and identification. Details are available by calling (605) 745-4600.

Additional park information can be obtained from the Superintendents: at Wind Cave National Park, RR 1, Box 190-WCNP, Hot Springs, SD 57747-9430; (605) 745-4600; at Jewel Cave National

Monument, Route 1, Box 60AA, Custer, SD 57730; (605) 673-2288; at Mount Rushmore National Memorial, Keystone, SD 57751-0268; (605) 574-2523.

Bird Life

The ponderosa pine forest communities at Wind Cave, Jewel Cave, and Mount Rushmore look much like those throughout the Rocky Mountains. Their bird life is similar, including such species as common nighthawk, hairy woodpecker, northern flicker, western wood-pewee, dusky and cordilleran flycatchers, western kingbird, violet-green swallow, white-breasted nuthatch, Townsend's solitaire, brown creeper, house wren, American robin, solitary and warbling vireos, yellow and MacGillivray's warblers, western tanager, black-headed grosbeak, chipping sparrow, brown-headed cowbird, red crossbill, and pine siskin. But there are some fascinating differences. Missing from the Black Hills are breeding broad-tailed hummingbirds, Hammond's flycatchers, Steller's jays, mountain chickadees, and Grace's warblers. And the pygmy nuthatch, abundant in the Rockies, is rare in the Black Hills.

However, the red-headed woodpecker, least flycatcher, eastern kingbird, blue jay, red-eyed vireo, American redstart, ovenbird, and common grackle, all birds of eastern affinity, and the gray jay, red-breasted nuthatch, and yellow-rumped warbler, species that nest primarily in higher elevation spruce-fir forests in the Rocky Mountains, can be found in the Black Hills' ponderosa pine communities.

Also, for many years ornithologists believed that the Black Hills' white-winged junco was a unique species, due to its uncharacteristic whitish wing bars. However, because it breeds with other juncos along the edge of its range, it was lumped with the other North American juncos in 1973; it is now only a subspecies of the dark-eyed junco. Richard Peterson, in his bird guide, points out that its range overlaps with the "pink-sided" form in Wyoming's Big Horn Mountains and with the "gray-headed" form in Wyoming's Medicine Bow Mountains. In the Black Hills, it is common throughout the ponderosa pine forests, where it remains a most glamorous bird.

Red crossbills are also common in the Black Hills. Dozens were flying over Jewel Cave's parking area and along Wind Cave's Rankin Ridge during my visits. Their loud "jip jip" flight notes are often the first clue to their presence. They also have a distinct undulating flight pattern with rapid wing beats. Male crossbills possess all-red plumage with blackish wings; females are yellowish. But their most interesting feature is their crossed bill, shaped like fat, overlapping forceps. They utilize their forceps bill to pry seeds out of pinecones.

Another colorful bird of these areas is the yellow, black, and red **western tanager**. Males possess a striking pattern of lemon yellow underparts, rump, collar, and wing bars, coal black back, wings, and tail, and bright red head. Their song at first resembles a robin's song, but is more gutteral, "querit, queer, queery, querit, queer." Arthur Bent, in *Life Histories of North American Blackbirds, Orioles, Tanagers, and Allies*, remarked that its song carries a "suggestion of wildness and freedom." Its call often heard throughout the summer, is a sharp "pit-ic" or "prit-titic."

The **yellow-rumped warbler** was especially numerous among the ponderosa pines at the viewing terrace of Mount Rushmore's visitor center. A brightly marked male was "flycatching" directly in front of the crowds of people viewing the granite sculptures. The bird's five yellow patches, on its throat, cap, sides, and rump, contrasted with its black-and-white plumage. Several more were singing along the edge of the huge parking lot and along the trails: "chwee-chwee-chwee," followed by an energetic trill at a lower pitch. Other species detected from the viewing terrace included western wood-pewees,

Yellow-rumped warbler

black-capped chickadees, red-breasted nuthatches, American robins, dark-eyed juncos, and pine siskins.

High over the sculpted cliff was a mixed flock of white-throated swifts and violet-green swallows. The swallows showed all-white underparts and dark, triangular wings in flight, while the faster swifts showed black-and-white bodies and stiff, swept-back wings. The latter bird, closely related to the hummingbird, can fly more than 100 miles (161 km) per hour. Both species nest in crevices on the high cliffs and capture insects in flight.

One morning I walked a couple of miles on Wind Cave's Centennial Trail, which follows a little valley filled with riparian vegetation below the drier slopes of ponderosa pine. Songs of house wrens, American robins, western wood-pewees, black-capped chickadees, solitary vireos, and red-breasted nuthatches greeted me at the trailhead. As I crossed the first grassy flat, I detected the "witcha witcha witcha" songs of common yellowthroats in the chokecherry bottom ahead. It was easy to spish an adult male into view; its bright yellow underparts, coal black mask, and whitish forehead were obvious. Rufous-sided towhees sang "chip chip cheee" songs nearby. And from the tall cottonwood trees came the songs of warbling and red-eyed vireos.

Two bison stood in the trail around the first bend, so I gave them plenty of space, circling through the tall grasses and wildflowers. Suddenly, a **mountain bluebird** hovered ahead of me, apparently searching for insects in the meadow. I froze in place so as not to frighten it away; it continued to "flycatch" while I watched. That morning, the sunlight gave it a special glow, like a bright jewel. It was all-blue except for its black eyes and bill. Twice it called a mellow "flew" note.

Farther on I watched a dozen or so violet-green swallows flying about some tall ponderosa snags; they were using vacant woodpecker nests and other crevices. High overhead I detected the twittering calls of white-throated swifts. It took me several seconds to find these fast-flying birds. And while searching for the swifts I discovered an American kestrel hovering over the open slope.

The boxelders and cottonwoods along the little creekbed contained several more songbirds: bright yellow warblers were singing spirited melodies; an American redstart sang a wheezy, slurred song;

a pair of black-headed grosbeaks were eating cottonwood buds; an American goldfinch sang a series of trills and "swee" notes; and there were numerous American robins about.

Suddenly, from the drier hillside to my right, I detected an ovenbird's "te-cher te-cher te-cher" song, very different from the typical "teacher" song of eastern forest ovenbirds. I decided to find this little warbler and slowly climbed the slope toward the ovenbird. I had not gone more than 200 feet (61 m) before a Townsend's solitaire flew up ahead of me; it probably was nesting on the grassy slope. It seemed strange to find this western thrush so far east. But it had the same grayish plumage, black eyes, white-edged tail, and buff wing bars as its cousins that nest about the high cirques at Rocky Mountain National Park.

The "swee-seet" song of a cordilleran flycatcher attracted my attention, and I found this yellowish *Empidonax* flycatcher singing from a branch alongside a tall rock outcropping, where I assumed it was nesting. It gave a jerk of its tail and dashed after a passing insect.

I continued upward toward the ovenbird's song, "te-cher te-cher te-cher TE-CHER TE-CHER," each double note louder than the last. I reached a point on the ridge where I could see across a little ravine; the song emanated from that area. I sat down and watched. Another cordilleran flycatcher flew by. A house wren sang a short way up the ravine. Farther up the slope I detected a "churr" call of a red-naped sapsucker. Then, a bird flew from a perch midway up a ponderosa to a snag almost at ground level. There it was, my ovenbird; it sat still, allowing me to study its olive-brown back, heavily striped under-parts, bold white eye rings, and rust crown stripe. Then it sang again: "te-cher te-cher te-cher TE-CHER TE-CHER."

I also visited one of Wind Cave's many prairie dog colonies, unique communities in their own right. Betty and I had pulled off the road to watch these fat little mammals. She was videotaping a mother with five pups, while I scoped the surrounding terrain. So long as we stayed in the vehicle, we were ignored.

A flock of American crows attracted my attention far across the colony; they seemed to be hassling another creature. Through my binoculars, I could see that a golden eagle had made a kill, probably a young prairie dog, and was consuming its prey. The eagle's head was golden in the sunlight, even at that distance. The crows were doing all they could to divert the eagle's attention, probably so one of them could steal the eagle's dinner. But the eagle would have none of it and remained in full control. At one time I counted 21 crows surrounding the eagle. In about a half hour, enough time for the eagle to finish its meal, the crows began to drift away.

The bird that dominated the grasslands, including prairie dog colonies, was undoubtedly the **western meadowlark**; several of these wonderful songsters could be heard at any given time across the prairie. Their liquid gurgling songs were pure delight. One interpretation is "Oh, yes, I am a pretty-little-bird," almost a musical yodel. This heavyset bird has bright yellow underparts crossed by a heavy black V on its chest. In flight, it shows its stubby tail with white outer edges. For more about this grassland bird, see chapter 23 on Scotts Bluff.

The **horned lark** was almost as numerous on the prairie, but less obvious because of its smaller size and high-pitched song. In flight, it shows light underparts and a black tail. A close-up view of a male reveals a contrasting yellow-and-black face with elongated black feathers over the eyes that look like tiny horns. During courtship the horns are erected, the wings are drooped, and the male struts before his lady and performs an elaborate flight display. See chapter 22 on Agate Fossil Beds for details.

Several other birds are found on Wind Cave's prairie. The long-legged upland sandpiper is usually detected first by its distinct call, a rolling "pulip pulip." The larger long-billed curlew also occurs on the prairie, but in smaller numbers. These two grassland shorebirds are most numerous along Highway 5, which crosses the eastern half of the park.

Three sparrows also inhabit the prairie: Lark sparrows, with chestnut, white, and black heads, white corners on the tail, and a black breast spot, occur along the edges where they sing from invading trees and shrubs. Also found are vesper sparrows, with streaked head, back, and sides, rufous shoulders, and white edges on the tail, and little grasshopper sparrows, with stubby tail, pale central head stripe, and buff chest. For details about vesper and grasshopper sparrows, see chapter 17 on Grasslands and chapter 22 on Agate Fossil Beds.

Prairie dog colonies attract numerous predators, from coyotes and badgers to raptors. The largest of these raptors is the golden eagle, but Swainson's, red-tailed, and ferruginous hawks and prairie falcons also take advantage of this rich food supply. **Prairie falcons** are the fastest of these raptors and, according to Pete Dunne and colleagues, in *Hawks in Flight*, use "low, swift, coursing flight" to locate prey. "A Prairie Falcon on patrol will cruise over suitable terrain to avoid detection, hoping to surprise a ground squirrel or to flush a Horned Lark. Less frequently (though with no less skill), the Prairie Falcon will hunt from a soar, in the manner of a Peregrine, executing a long, calculated, shallow stoop on sighted prey."

Wind Cave's prairie falcons are full-time residents that frequent the same territories year-round. Their favorite prey is, undoubtedly, horned larks, also present all year, but they also take young prairie dogs when possible. Most sightings of this large falcon are of a bird flying away across the prairie. They can be identified by their overall pale body, with dark, almost triangular axillaries (wing pits) and long, pointed wings. Dunne and colleagues also mention the obvious contrast between their light tail and darker upperparts. "A Peregrine shows no such contrast," they state.

No visitor should leave the prairie without getting acquainted with the **burrowing owl**, a summer resident of the prairie dog colonies. One of only a few owls that are active during daylight

Burrowing owl

hours, it often sits at the edge of its burrow or on a rock or shrub. It nests in a deserted prairie dog burrow, which it enlarges by kicking dirt backward with its strong feet. Its burrow can often be identified by the bison dung scattered at the entrance. It uses the dung, along with grasses, to line the nest cavity. Paul Johnsgard, in *Birds of the Great Plains*, points out that the manure is "placed near the burrow entrance, apparently to provide scent camouflage." Also, this owl has learned to imitate a rattlesnake's rattle to frighten away intruders.

Burrowing owls are relatively small owls, about 9.5 inches (24 cm) high, with a wingspan of 20 to 24 inches (50-60 cm). The bird has long, unfeathered legs, a stubby tail, and light tan plumage that can make it resemble a prairie dog from a distance. When nervous, it bobs up and down and often emits a sharp alarm call, "a chattering 'cack-cack-cack' or 'quick-quick-quick,' given by both sexes on ground and in flight," according to Julio De La Torre, in *Owls: Their Life and Behavior*. Courting males sing an emphatic "coo-cooo" song, not unlike the cooing of a dove, "but higher pitched and delivered at smart pace," according to De La Torres.

Prey species include all the smaller creatures that reside in the prairie dog colony, from meadowlarks and horned larks to mice and snakes, crickets and dragonflies, as well as young prairie dogs. By September, the family unit moves south to warmer climes about the same time that many of its prey species are also migrating south.

South Dakota winters can be harsh, and the resident bird life is only a fraction of what it is in spring and summer. Prairie dogs practice a partial hibernation, remaining active on mild winter days. The park's winter bird population comprises the permanent residents and a few more northern species that come for the winter, such as the winter wren, Bohemian waxwing, northern shrike, American tree sparrow, Lapland longspur, snow bunting, gray-crowned rosy finch, purple finch, and common redpoll.

In summary, the combined checklist of birds for the three parks includes 199 species, of which 122 are listed as permanent or summer residents and assumedly nest. Four of these are water birds, 15 are hawks and owls, and 7 are warblers. Seven species are listed as winter residents only: winter wren, northern shrike, American tree sparrow, snow bunting, gray-crowned rosy finch, purple finch, and common redpoll; a few of these must also be present as migrants.

Birds of Special Interest
Prairie falcon. This year-round resident hunts the prairie; it is a large raptor with pointed wings, long tail, pale plumage, and black wing pits.

Burrowing owl. Watch for this little owl in prairie dog colonies; it has pale plumage and bare legs.

Horned lark. A prairie bird that spends most of its time on the ground, it has pale plumage and a yellow-and-black head with tiny black feather horns.

Mountain bluebird. This bird has all-blue plumage and is often found hovering in midair watching for insects.

American robin. This abundant, red-breasted bird feeds on the ground; it sings a caroling song in spring and summer.

Yellow-rumped warbler. One of the most common forest birds, it is best identified by five yellow spots, on its crown, throat, sides, and rump.

Ovenbird. This elusive little warbler sings a spirited "te-cher" song, each double note louder than the last.

Western tanager. Males are one of the area's most colorful songbirds; they have all-yellow underparts, black wings, and a red head.

Rufous-sided towhee. This bird sings "chip chip seee" from the thickets; males have a coal black hood and blood-red eyes.

Western meadowlark. A common grassland bird with yellow underparts, crossed by a black V on its chest, it sings continually in spring and summer.

21

Badlands National Park, South Dakota

The black-billed magpie and the rock wren are two of Badlands' most common birds. Yet they are as different as any two birds can possibly be. The magpie is outgoing and mischievous, often associating with people. It hangs around the visitor center and campgrounds and can become a real beggar. What's more, it seems to have designated itself as Badlands' official avian ambassador; it is one of the first birds that visitors see when entering the park. Conversely, the rock wren is normally shy and elusive, although undoubtedly more numerous in the park than the magpie. The rock wren prefers bare rock and dirt slopes, the epitome of the park's badlands.

Black-billed magpie

Physically, the two birds are as different as night and day. Magpies are almost 20 inches (51 cm) long, although about half of that length is tail; the rock wren is a chunky bird barely 6 inches (15 cm) in length. Magpies possess striking black-and-white plumage, a snow white belly and shoulders, and an all-black hood, bill, back, wings, and tail. Their wings and tail often have an iridescent greenish sheen. In flight, magpies show a bold, white V-pattern on their wings and rump. Rock wrens are plain, almost nondescript birds with a gray-brown back with white specks, whitish underparts, buff flanks, and a long bill.

The two birds' voices are also very different. Magpie vocalizations are mostly limited to "chaeck," "cack cack," or whining notes, although they communicate among themselves with a steady chatter. Rock wrens possess a variety of calls and songs that range from their "tick-ear" call notes and basic "chee chee chee chee chee" song to a more extensive song consisting of buzzes and trills. Arthur Bent, in *Life Histories of North American Nuthatches, Wrens, Thrashers, and Their Allies*, describes its full song thus: "chair chair chair chair, deedle deedle deedle deedle, tur tur tur tur, keree keree keree trrrrrrrrrr."

When it comes to nests, the two birds also part ways. Magpies build huge, domed stick nests in trees and may reuse for several years. Although the outside of the nests appears messy, they are well-protected and waterproof. Paul Ehrlich and colleagues, in *The Birder's Handbook*, point out that the core nest is a "bowl of mud or cow dung, lined with rootlets, fine plant stems, and hair." Magpies are often colonial in nature; several pairs may nest in a particular grove or line of trees. At Badlands, they utilize cottonwoods, junipers, and green ash most often. I located one nest wedged in the lower crotch of a cottonwood tree just behind the Cedar Pass Campground.

As might be expected, rock wrens nest in holes and crevices in the rocky terrain. Their ground nests are lined with whatever fine materials are available; grasses and other plant parts are most popular. But nest preparation does not stop there. Rock wrens actually decorate their nest entrance with tiny pieces of rock, bone, and other materials, creating an elaborate front porch. For additional details about this bird's fascinating nesting behavior, see chapter 23 on Scotts Bluff.

The black-billed magpie is a year-round resident at Badlands, so it will be there to greet you in summer or winter. Conversely, the rock wren is a summer resident only, migrating south to warmer climes for the winter. But in summer, no visitor to Badlands should leave without getting acquainted with both of these wonderful birds.

The Park Environment
As suggested above, Badlands National Park contains two distinct habitats: badlands and grasslands. The "badlands" term probably was first used by the Lakota Indians as *mako sica*, or "a hard place to travel." Other Lakotas claim the area's name is *Paha ska*, or "white hills." Geologists use the badlands term today to describe classic erosion. But it was this colorfully grotesque and dissected landscape, along with its considerable number of animal fossils that date from 26 million to 37 million years ago, that enticed Congress to designate the area a national monument in 1939. Since then, increased awareness of the area's grasslands and wildlife prompted Congress, in 1976, to set aside 64,250 acres (26,002 ha) of the area as the Badlands (locally known as Sage Creek) Wilderness Area. And in 1978, an enlarged area of 243,302 acres (98,463 ha) was redesignated a national park. Also important for the greater protection of the park's grasslands is the surrounding 591,000-acre (239,174-ha) Buffalo Gap National Grassland, administered by the U. S. Forest Service.

To the nature lover, the essence of Badlands is its broad expanse of grasslands. Prairie comprises about 177,000 acres (71,631 ha) or 73 percent of the park. In combination with Buffalo Gap National Grassland, the area represents the largest intact mixed-grass prairie under federal protection in the United States. Continentwide, the mixed-grass prairie forms a broad north-south belt that dominates the province of Saskatchewan and North Dakota, South Dakota, Nebraska, Kansas, Oklahoma, and central Texas. This grassland was described by Lauren Brown in *The Audubon Society Nature Guides Grasslands:*

> On its western edge, the tallgrass prairie grades into a broad north-south belt dominated by grasses of medium height—those that are approximately two to four feet tall. This area is primarily called the midgrass prairie, the mixed-grass prairie, the bluestem bunchgrass prairie, or the Great Plains. Some feel that the mixed prairie should not exist as a separate province, arguing that it merely represents a transition zone between the

tallgrass and shortgrass prairies. If the mixed prairie is a transition zone, however, it is an extremely broad one: It is wider than either of the two zones it is supposed to bridge. Furthermore, the mixed prairie has a distinct look of its own, and possesses certain discrete characteristics that set it apart.

More than 50 kinds of grasses have been found in the park, but four species are dominant: buffalo and needle-and-thread grasses, blue grama, and western wheatgrass. A few shrubs, such as meadowrose, common chokecherry, skunkbush sumac, rubber rabbitbrush, and various sagebrush species, are scattered across the landscape. Trees occur only in a few wet depressions, such as pre-park stock ponds, along creeks, and in ravines. The resultant riparian vegetation includes cottonwood, willow, and green ash, and Rocky Mountain juniper dominates the higher ravines, especially in the Sage Creek area.

Two visitor centers are in the park: the principal visitor center and park headquarters at Cedar Pass, at the eastern edge of the park, and a temporary structure at White River, at the south entrance. Both centers have an information desk and orientation programs, but exhibits and a sales outlet, which offers bird field guides and a checklist, are limited to Cedar Pass. A campground, outdoor amphitheater, lodge, and gift store are also at Cedar Pass.

Interpretive activities include evening talks at Cedar Pass Campground, three ranger-guided walks daily, and afternoon talks at the Cedar Pass Visitor Center throughout the summer. Three self-guiding trails are available: Cliffs Shelf Nature Trail, near the visitor center; Door Trail, near the Cedar Pass entrance; and Fossil Exhibit Trail on Highway 240. Detailed information is available in the park's newspaper, *The Prairie Preamble*, available at entrance stations and visitor centers.

Additional information can be obtained from the Superintendent, Badlands National Park, P.O. Box 6, Interior, SD 57750; (605) 433-5361.

Bird Life

Early mornings on Badlands' grasslands are like nowhere else. The liquid gurgling songs of western meadowlarks resound from all directions. The tinkling flight songs of horned larks, the soft calls of mourning doves, and the melancholy "pee-ee" songs of Say's phoebes are commonplace. Overhead, cliff and barn swallows ply the air in their search for insects, and the loud "peent" calls of common nighthawks echo across the landscape.

I left my vehicle at a parking area along the highway and walked north, intending to make a wide, sweeping loop across the undulating prairie. I could see a tall cottonwood in the distance, perhaps a half mile away; I would head in that direction. It was immediately apparent that, to avoid stepping on the abundant flowers and ground-hugging cacti, it would be best to follow one of the animal trails. Pronghorn were plentiful; I located four individuals or family groups by making a 180-degree sweep of the terrain with my binoculars.

Only 100 (30 m) feet ahead of me was a **western meadowlark**; its bright yellow breast, crossed by a bold, black V, gleamed in the morning light. It was clucking at me like a rooster, and I wondered if I was too close to its nest. It jerked its stubby tail with each sharp "jert" note. I took a few more steps and it took flight. A plump, striped bird with short, almost triangular wings, landed on top of a little hill, jerked its tail, and repeated more "jert" notes. Neighboring meadowlarks were singing loud, melodic songs that are often interpreted as "Oh, yes, I am a pretty-little-bird."

The buzzing trill of a grasshopper sparrow attracted my attention. It took me several seconds to locate this tiny, short-tailed bird. It was sitting on top of a dead plant stalk at a considerable distance; its breezy trill song carried much farther than I would have expected. As I got closer, I could see its buff face and chest, whitish eye ring, and striped head. A most attractive grassland sparrow, but often overlooked because of its small size and inconspicuous voice. Unless you are aware of its song, you might pass it off as an insect.

I crossed a little hill where I had a good view of the grassy flat below. A pair of red-winged blackbirds were perched on the meadowrose shrubs; the female called "clip-zee" notes; the male spread its wings to highlight its bright red epaulets and sang "konk-ka-ree." Just then, an eastern kingbird settled on a nearby sumac. It pumped its tail several times and called a harsh "dzeet" note. Its black-and-white plumage, black back and white underparts, with a broad, white terminal band on its otherwise all-black tail, provided an interesting comparison with the slightly larger red-wing.

My cottonwood tree was much closer now, and I detected more birds among the foliage or perched on the bare snags on top. There were two more eastern kingbirds, a western kingbird, a pair of mourning doves, a brightly marked lark sparrow, several common grackles, and a **loggerhead shrike**. I checked the branches for carcasses of small rodents or insects that the shrike might have placed there, but to no avail. Loggerhead shrike males, although barely larger than a sparrow, are efficient predators that decorate a favorite perch with their prey. This behavior apparently attracts females.

I studied this 9-inch (23-cm) songbird for several minutes, and I could readily comprehend its powerful character. It was a stocky bird with little or no neck and a very short and heavy, slightly hooked bill. Sitting still, it showed all-whitish underparts, grayish back and cap, and black mask, wings, and tail. It flies in a distinct, straight-ahead manner with rapid but sporadic wing beats. According to chief park naturalist Joe Zarki, this bird is reasonably common all summer but leaves for the winter.

Just beyond the cottonwood tree was a little check dam, a remnant of the ranching years. It still held a half-acre pond that was partly overgrown with weedy plants. But something about this little pond attracted water birds; I identified five species of ducks and a lone sora. Once I realized the pond was there, I moved extremely slowly, barely looking over the edge so as not to frighten any residents. There were four pairs of northern pintails with eight youngsters; eight or nine gadwalls with four youngsters; a pair of northern shovelers; three blue-winged teal; and a green-winged teal male. It surprised me to find so many ducks in one little pond, but the summer nesting season is short on the prairie, and there is lots of competition that requires taking advantage of every available pond.

Later that morning I visited nearby Thistle Reservoir along Quinn Road at the edge of the park, where I found more ducks. Thistle Reservoir contained the same species as in the pond in much greater numbers, plus a pair of Canada geese, many mallards, and a few ruddy ducks. Pied-billed grebes, American coots, killdeers, and Wilson's phalaropes were also present in substantial numbers. And several common yellowthroats sang "witcha witcha witcha" songs from the brushy edges.

All during my walk through the grasslands I watched unsuccessfully for sharp-tailed grouse, the local "prairie chicken" without the neck sacs. When I asked at the visitor center about the best place to find this bird in June, I was told to try the isolated grasslands of the Sage Creek Wilderness Area. The following morning found me at Sage Creek (no water) Campground. It was a gorgeous day with a slight breeze and big fluffy clouds on the horizon.

I decided to take the same kind of loop route as I had the previous day, to cover as much area as possible in a 3 to 4-mile (5-6.4-km) walk. However, I immediately discovered that the riparian vegetation along South Fork Creek was filled with birds. During the first hour or so I found more than 30 species: American kestrel; mourning dove; common nighthawk; northern flickers (red-shafted and yellow-shafted); eastern phoebe; western and eastern kingbirds; northern rough-winged, cliff, and barn swallows; black-billed magpie; house wren; mountain bluebird; American robin; brown thrasher; cedar waxwing; loggerhead shrike; warbling vireo; yellow warbler; yellow-breasted chat; black-headed and blue grosbeaks; rufous-sided towhee; chipping and lark sparrows; red-winged blackbird; western meadowlark; brown-headed cowbird; orchard oriole; and American goldfinch.

The **American kestrels** were standing guard on a high snag of a cottonwood tree. From the racket they made when I approached the tree, I assume that they were tending nestlings. The male had a very reddish back and tail that contrasted with its slaty gray wings; the female was a duller version of the male. Both possessed distinct double black lines on their white cheeks.

I found American kestrels several times during my visit, most often over the grasslands or along the edge of the badlands. They sometimes take advantage of thermals and breezes to help them hover as they search the ground for prey. Their normal hunting procedure is to hover 20 to 30 feet (6-9 m) above the ground until they locate a prey species; the they will stoop or glide down with outstretched talons. Since kestrels are reasonably small falcons, their prey is limited to mice and other small rodents, insects, and so forth.

I followed an open drainage that gradually narrowed to a ravine filled with junipers on the north slope. Numerous rufous-sided towhees were active along the drainage; a pair of brown thrashers flew out ahead of me; a black-capped chickadee called "chick-a-dee-dee-dee;" chipping sparrows sang their trill songs from the junipers; a lone olive-sided flycatcher, probably a late migrant, perched on a tall juniper snag; and field sparrows sang their distinct songs all around. Suddenly, almost at my feet, a field sparrow flew out of a sagebrush bush. Within seconds I had located its nest, about 10 inches (25 cm) above the ground. It contained four bluish-green eggs spattered with brown and one larger, grayish egg spattered with brown. The larger egg belonged to a brown-headed cowbird that had laid its egg there so the field sparrow would raise the larger cowbird baby along with its own. Most often the more aggressive cowbird becomes the dominant nestling and the rightful babies are underfed or shoved out of the nest and perish.

The most numerous bird of this habitat was the **rufous-sided towhee**. Its song, a distinct "chink chink treeeee," was commonplace. Many of these large sparrows flew into the chokecherry thickets or junipers as I approached. But they were easy to coax into the open; with only the slightest spishing they would reappear at the top of the shrub. The males' coal-black hood, blood-red eyes, black-and-white back and wings, and rufous sides were obvious. This is another of Badlands' common summer residents.

I continued to keep watch among the junipers for sharp-tailed grouse, as well as long-eared owls; ornithologist Carolyn Hull-Sieg had found this normally rare owl to be reasonably common in this habitat year-round. She also reported, "Sharp-tailed grouse prefer grasslands interspersed with woody cover; juniper woodlands play a role in providing cover and, perhaps, food at certain times of the year." But despite my vigilance, neither grouse nor owl was found.

I also spent a couple of hours at Roberts Prairie Dog Town, along the Sage Creek Rim Road. I set up my spotting scope on my vehicle window and watched the colony and surrounding skies. Prairie dog burrows were scattered over an area of about 2 square miles (3.2 sq km), and the dogs were outdoors enjoying the lovely spring day. Western meadowlarks were the most abundant bird in the town, and horned larks were second. These sparrow-sized larks were easily identified by their yellow and black face and black tail with white edges. A few red-winged blackbirds lurked around the edges, and barn and cliff swallows captured insects overhead.

The largest bird of this community was the long-legged **long-billed curlew**. I counted at least three pairs within my viewing area. They stood out like sore thumbs because of their size and loud, ascending "cur-lee" calls that echoed across the compound. I watched one poke its extremely long bill into various holes; I never did see any food that it might have retrieved. And on another occasion, one suddenly flew at its assumed mate, and they both flew together in a high and wide circle, cinnamon wing linings visible, and landed in about the same spot where they had begun. It seemed strange to find this large shorebird, which I had so often seen on pastures in east Texas in winter, on a prairie dog town in South Dakota.

In spite of Badlands' extensive grasslands, many visitors are interested only in seeing the more sterile badland formations. That habitat is readily accessible along Highway 240, the Badlands Loop Road. But even this environment, as hostile as it seems, attracts birds. Foremost is the little rock wren, with its varied songs and strange nesting behavior.

The largest and probably the most visible of the badlands birds is the **turkey vulture**. This dark bird with a bare red head and bicolored wings, darker on the front half, has a 69-inch (175-cm) wingspan. In flight, even at a distance it can easily be identified by the way it holds its wings in a shallow V and tilts its body slightly from side to side. It nests on isolated ledges of the badlands so it is more obvious at midday, when thermals rise above the cliffs from the warmer slopes, creating drafts on which this bird can soar for hours, barely flapping its wings. Vultures are often misidentified as golden eagles because of their size, but eagles have feathered heads and seldom soar on local thermals. In flight, eagles hold their all-dark wings practically straight out and do not tilt.

These same thermals attract other soaring birds at various times of the year. One is the broad-winged red-tailed hawk, easily identified by its reddish tail and mottled underparts. Two other broad-winged hawks to look for in summer are the Swainson's and ferruginous hawks. And in winter, rough-legged hawks replace Swainson's and ferruginous hawks.

Watch also in summer for the much smaller **white-throated swifts** about the cliffs. This black-and-white, cigar-shaped bird with swept-back wings zips by at more than 100 miles (161 km) per hour, sometimes so close that you can feel the wind. This swift is especially common over the Cliff Shelf Nature Trail. It nests in high crevices on the cliffs, building a tiny nest platform of its feathers glued together with saliva. It is often detected first by its high-pitched, descending twittering in flight. For more about this unique species, see chapter 19 on Devils Tower.

Another interesting bird of the badlands is the exotic rock dove, or domestic pigeon, which has gone wild and learned to nest in secure crevices. The cliffs provide nesting sites for other species as well: Prairie falcons nest here but hunt the grasslands for prey; barn and great horned owls utilize crevices and ledges; Say's phoebes construct mud nests on narrow ledges; cliff and barn swallows construct their mud-pellet nests under protected ledges; and mountain blue-birds use crevices and deserted cliff swallow nests.

Say's phoebes blend in so perfectly with the clay-colored terrain that they often go undetected. But this little flycatcher is not shy; it often "flycatches" along the edge of parking areas or at picnic and camping areas, with little concern for onlookers. It is often detected first by its mournful "pee-eee" call; during the breeding season it will repeat that call over and over.

The little square-tailed **cliff swallows** are among the park's most abundant birds. Although their nesting sites are rather limited, they fly considerable distances to feed, so they can be expected anywhere

Cliff swallows

in the park. They are particularly active after spring and early summer rains, when mud puddles form near their nesting sites. Then, they may congregate by the hundreds, grabbing bits of mud in their bills and molding them into tight little balls for use as building blocks for their nests. A completed nest, fastened to a cliff or some other structure, looks much like a retort with a small opening at the lower end. The long-tailed barn swallows also build mud nests, but theirs are open at the top.

Cliff swallows are true Neotropical migrants, which spend their summers in the temperate region of North America and their winters in the tropics; they overwinter as far south as South America, from Paraguay south to Brazil and central Argentina. And yet, as soon as the spring days at Badlands are warm enough to produce flying insects, they are right back on their nesting grounds.

Wintertime is an ecological low point for birds in the Badlands. Although full-time residents, such as the prairie falcon, black-billed magpie, horned lark, and American robin, remain, most of the breeding birds are gone. A few more northern species, such as the rough-legged hawk, northern shrike, dark-eyed junco, and American tree sparrow, appear and stay for the winter. The best indication of the wintertime bird populations is the annual Christmas Bird Count. In 1992, ten observers tallied 1,673 individuals of 27 species. The dozen most numerous birds, in descending order of abundance, included horned lark, house sparrow, American tree sparrow, Lapland longspur, rock dove, Townsend's solitaire, American robin, black-billed magpie, dark-eyed junco, northern flicker, wild turkey, and black-capped chickadee.

In summary, the park's bird checklist includes 217 species, of which 73 are listed as nesters. Eleven of the 73 are water birds, 11 are hawks and owls, and 3 (yellow warbler, common yellowthroat, and yellow-breasted chat) are warblers. Only 2 species, snowy owl and snow bunting, are listed as winter residents only.

Birds of Special Interest

Turkey vulture. This large, all-dark bird soars over the badlands; in flight, it holds its wings in a shallow V and tilts its body slightly from side to side.

American kestrel. It is often found hovering in midair, searching the ground for prey; males possess a reddish back and slaty wings.

Long-billed curlew. Watch for this large bird with long legs and an extremely long, curved bill at prairie dog towns; it shows cinnamon wing linings in flight.

White-throated swift. This little black-and-white speedster frequents cliff areas; it is often detected by its high-pitched, descending trill.

Cliff swallow. One of the park's most abundant birds, it builds mud nests on the cliffs and is distinguished by its black and reddish throat, buff rump, and square tail.

Black-billed magpie. This long-tailed, black-and-white bird frequents the campgrounds and other visitor areas.

Rock wren. Watch for this tiny, all-gray-brown bird at bare rocky areas; it sings a variety of songs and has a short "tick-ear" call.

Loggerhead shrike. This little black-and-white bird with a stout profile and fast flight is most common in the lower grasslands, such as along Conata Road.

Rufous-sided towhee. It is common at all the thicket areas of the park; males possess an all-black hood, blood-red eyes, black-and-white back and wings, and rufous sides.

Western meadowlark. This is the park's most obvious bird; it is easily identified by its plump body, yellow breast crossed with a bold, black V, and wonderful songs.

22

Agate Fossil Beds National Monument, Nebraska

Hundreds of swallows cruised over the wetland at the head of Fossil Beds Trail. Most were cliff swallows, distinctly marked with a chestnut and black throat, pale forehead, black cap, and square tail. There also were a few bank, northern rough-winged, and barn swallows. The bank and rough-wings were undoubtedly nesting in the dirt banks scattered along the Niobrara River. Barn and cliff swallows require cliffs or other tall structures; at Agate Fossil Beds, they were utilizing the same rocky bluffs that still hold secrets of ancient mammals.

The loudest birdsongs that morning emanated from a dozen or so red-winged blackbirds, evenly spaced out along the broad flood-plain. Male red-wings called sharp "chip-zee" or "chack" notes from both sides of the boardwalk and occasionally sang a distinct "konk-a-reee" song. I focused my binoculars on one bright male just as it raised its head and sang a grating "konk-a-reee." Its all-black plumage, except for the bright red and yellow shoulder patches, seemed almost velvety in the morning light.

It then took flight, fluttering from its cattail perch with tail spread and feathers puffed out, descending to another perch a short distance away. Then, I noticed the basketlike nest fastened onto the cattails just below its new perch. It was a remarkable structure, woven of grasses and sedges, and large enough to easily hold an adult and several nestlings. A female red-wing, a duller, striped version of the male, suddenly flew to the nest with a long strip of grass. Nest construction was still under way. No wonder the male red-wings were so vocal. Although territories apparently had been selected, it was still necessary to proclaim their rights and defend their turf.

The male red-wing suddenly took off again, but this time it quickly gained altitude and aggressively pursued another male that apparently had come too close. Within a few seconds it was back. It flipped its tail, spread its wings and tail, and sang its territorial song once again: "konk-a-reee."

The Park Environment

Agate Fossil Beds National Monument is best known for its paleontological treasury: it is the site of a great mammalian boneyard containing hundreds of skeletons of creatures that perished during a drought about 19 million years ago. The 2,700-acre (1,093-ha) park was established in 1965 to protect the most significant sites.

The park, which lies along the banks of the Niobrara River in northwestern Nebraska, contains a relatively open floodplain and low hillsides with scattered sandstone outcroppings. The gradually sloping landscape above the floodplain contains a short-grass prairie environment that is carpeted primarily with grasses, like prairie sandreed, blue grama, little bluestem, and needle-and-thread. Common woody plants include soapweed yucca, skunkbush sumac, sand and fringed sagebrush, and wild prairie rose. Sandbar willow dominates the floodplain, although cattail, American rush, and cottonwoods are common.

The National Park Service visitor center, located 3 miles (4.8 km) east of Highway 29, has an information desk, orientation programs, exhibits, and sales outlet; bird guides and a checklist are available. Interpretive activities are limited to the self-guided Fossil Hills Trail just behind the visitor center, the Daemonelix Trail near State Highway 29, and ranger-led programs by prior request.

Additional information can be obtained from the Superintendent, Scotts Bluff National Monument, P.O. Box 27, Gering, NE 69341-0027; (308) 436-4340.

Bird Life

Another prominent bird of the Niobrara River wetland was the little **common yellowthroat**. Its "witchity witchity witchity" songs rang out loud and clear. I located one of these vociferous songbirds perched at the top of a willow near the boardwalk. The male's bright yellow underparts contrasted with its coal black mask. At one time I could hear five different yellowthroats, but they stayed hidden among the cattails.

Two other little songsters were evident in the immediate area: marsh wren and yellow warbler. The **marsh wren's** song was very different from the yellowthroat's. Peter Vickery, in *The Audubon Society Master Guide to Birding*, described it as "reedy, not musical: 1 or 2 low grinding, scraping, guttural notes, followed by a squeak and then a rapid, rasping trill." To me, marsh wren songs include all the squeaks, grunts, gurgles, and bubbling sounds imaginable. Few birds are so excitable and animated as this short-tailed marsh dweller. Also, few marsh birds possess such perfect camouflage for their cattail residency; their plumage has all the right tones to blend perfectly with their environment. A good look will reveal a brown back with whitish stripes, whitish eyebrows, light underparts, and cinnamon flanks. This mite prefers the shadowy haunts of the marsh and rarely ventures far into the open.

Conversely, the little **yellow warbler** is easily observed; it will perch and sing in the open. And its all-yellow plumage, except for the male's chestnut breast streaks, makes identification especially easy. If it is not already in the open, a few chips with your lips on the back of your hand will usually attract this warbler. It also sings a loud and lively song, "tseet-tseet-tseet sitta-sitta-see." Frank Chapman, in *The Warblers of North America*, described a varied song: "Now it is 'sweet sweet sweet sweet sweeter sweeter,' now 'sweet sweet sweet sweetie,' again 'wee-chee, we-chee, wee-i-u'; once more 'wee-che, chee, chee, chur-wee.' " Chapman also referred to this bird as "a bit of feathered sunshine. In his plumes dwells the gold of the sun, in his voice its brightness and good cheer."

American goldfiches, with their striking yellow-and-black plumage, were also present among the willows. Eastern and western kingbirds were "flycatching" nearby. A willow flycatcher sang its distinct "fitz-bew" song. A pair of mourning doves careened across the sky. Three brown-headed cowbirds flew over, calling squeaky whistle notes. And a number of common grackles flew by.

Several larger water birds were also recorded that morning. A pied-billed grebe sang its strange grunting song. An American bittern called out "oonk-a-lunk" from the cattails; its deep calls reminded me of the sound of an old pump. The distinct "kid kidick" calls of a Virginia's rail resounded from the same area. A spotted sandpiper flew up and across the wetland, then settled back into some secluded site. Suddenly, I heard the winnowing sound of a **common snipe**. It took me several seconds before I located this long-billed shorebird as it circled high overhead. Then I was able to follow it with my binoculars. Every 10 to 20 seconds it would dive slightly and spread its tail feathers, producing a strange winnowing sound, almost like a distant screech-owl call or the bleating of a goat. The sound is produced by the air rushing through the bird's outer tail feathers. The snipe utilizes the flight and sound as a territorial display for attracting a mate, and also to warn competing males.

I crossed the boardwalk and began the gradual climb across the grassland. Just before the first interpretive sign, I found a place where I could scope an open wet area and pond on the floodplain far to the left. I could see a few more water birds: a great blue heron frozen in place, waiting for prey to get close to its large, lethal bill; several mallards, the males' with all-green heads; a male green-winged teal; a pair of blue-winged teal; several killdeers, with their loud "kill-dee" calls; and a Wilson's phalarope female.

The rattle call of a **belted kingfisher** attracted my attention, and I turned just in time to see this bluish, heavy-billed bird flying past at about eye level. It was a female, evident by its rust-colored belly. I wondered if it was nesting nearby. Kingfishers actually dig tunnels which may be 15 feet (4.6 m) long and tilted slightly upward, in dirt banks. A nest chamber 6 to 10 inches (15-25 cm) deep is constructed at the end of the tunnel. For more about this fascinating bird, see chapter 27 on Chickasaw.

The prairie habitat along the trail supports a different group of birds from those of the wetland, and several of these were reasonably easy to locate and identify. Most obvious was the **western meadowlark**, a robust, short-tailed bird with a bright yellow breast crossed by a broad, black band. Several were perched on top of yucca stalks or in flight. Their loud, liquid gurgling songs echoed across the terrain. They were by far the dominant bird of the grassland. Most of the songs that morning were typical of those of western meadowlarks farther west, but I also detected eastern meadowlark songs. I was reminded that this portion of the Great Plains produces considerable avian hybridization, and I wondered if these meadowlarks were hybrids, or only western meadowlarks that had learned to sing eastern songs; either is possible.

Horned larks were also common along the trail. I had a good look at one that walked ahead of me. It was a brightly marked bird with a yellow-and-black face, black chest, and little black "horns." The horns are only tufts of black feathers that protrude over the head. The remainder of its plumage was clay-colored, except for its black tail with white edges, evident only in flight. I could not help but think how perfectly its coloration helped it blend into the terrain. My little lark finally flew up the trail and landed out of sight. Several others were singing along the trail, a high-pitched twittering or a jumble of tinkling notes.

Horned lark

This bird performs an elaborate flight display that John Terres, in *The Audubon Society Encyclopedia of North American Birds*, describes thus: "flight song is begun silently on climb into sky from 270 to more than 800 feet [82-244 m], where he circles singing 'pir-wir, wee-pit, pit-wee, wee-pit'; closes song with headlong drop to earth with wings closed."

Another common bird that morning was the little **grasshopper sparrow**, most evident by its insect-like buzzy song. This high-pitched song was heard every couple of hundred feet; grasshopper sparrow territories were evenly spaced like squares on a checkerboard. A few of the singing birds sat on top of yucca stalks or shrubs. It took me several minutes to locate one close enough to get a good view. Through binoculars, I finally could see its buff chest and striped head. It was a chunky, tiny bird with a relatively flat head and extremely short tail. I was watching one individual, head thrown back, singing its buzzy song, when suddenly, without interruption, it began singing a very different song. Its new song, which lasted about two seconds, consisted of a series of beautiful, melodic notes that reminded me of a weak house wren song. That morning I detected that same song several times; it was my first exposure to this song. An truly incredible experience.

A few other birds were detected along the trail. A red-tailed hawk passed over. I also observed a pale ferruginous hawk at a distance. Cliff and barn swallows were flying low over the grasslands, searching for insects. A Say's phoebe was "flycatching" nearby; its pale buff underparts and black tail were obvious. A loggerhead shrike was perched on a distant utility pole. And nearby, a pair of lark sparrows, with boldly marked faces, flew ahead of me. One of the lark sparrows sang a jumbled song of trills mixed with flutelike notes.

As I approached Carnegie Hill, I detected the songs of a **rock wren** emanating from that rocky bluff. It sang various songs while I circled the hill. Most of these were the typical "kra-wee kra-wee kra-wee" songs, but at one point it sang a full repertoire of songs like those that Arthur Bent described in *Life Histories of North American Nuthatches, Wrens, Thrushes, and Their Allies*: "krree keree keree, chair chair chair, deedle deedle deedle, tur tur tur, keree keree trrrrr." One of these nondescript little wrens came within 25 feet (7.6 m) of me as I was reading the interpretive sign at the far side of Carnegie Hill. Its gray-brown back with tiny white flecks, lighter underparts, and long bill were obvious. It seemed to totally ignore me at first, then suddenly discovered my presence and flew to a nearby perch with a sharp "tick-ear" call. For information about this wren's fascinating nesting behavior, see chapter 23 on Scotts Bluff.

Springtime at Agate Fossil Beds can produce a wide variety of birds, and the Fossil Hills Trail provides a superb transect through choice habitats. Wintertime is very different; the Niobrara River is frozen and all the songbirds, so obvious in spring and summer, are on their wintering grounds to the south. Park interpreter Anne Quintard told me that only a few species, such as dark-eyed juncos and a few other hardy northern birds, frequent the area.

In summary, the park checklist of birds contains 139 species, of which 96 are listed as either permanent or summer residents and assumedly nest. Eleven of those are water birds, 16 are hawks and owls, and 4 are warblers. Six species are listed as winter residents only: hairy and downy woodpeckers, gray-crowned rosy finch, dark-eyed junco, American tree sparrow, and snow bunting.

Birds of Special Interest
Common snipe. Listen for its winnowing flight over the wetland in spring and early summer; it has a plump body that is heavily streaked and a long bill.

Belted kingfisher. Watch for this bluish, heavy-billed bird along the riverway; it captures prey by diving for it in the water.

Horned lark. This little bird with a yellow-and-black face and black tail is common on the open prairie and performs an elaborate flight display.

Cliff swallow. It is common over the wetlands and easily identified by its chestnut and black throat, pale forehead, black cap, and square tail.

Rock wren. Watch for this little gray-brown bird with buff sides and a long bill on rocky bluffs; it often bobs and moves in a jerky fashion.

Marsh wren. It occurs only among the cattails, where it sings a rapid series of rambling notes; its plumage is light brown and heavily striped.

Yellow warbler. This is the little all-yellow bird of the willows; males possess chestnut breast streaks.

Grasshopper sparrow. Watch for this tiny, short-tailed bird on the short-grass prairie; it usually is detected first by its high-pitched buzzy song.

Red-winged blackbird. Males are all-black with red and yellow wing patches; females are dull versions of the males. It is most numerous in the wetlands.

23

Scotts Bluff National Monument, Nebraska

Few birds stand out like the black-billed magpie. Several of these large, showy birds were along the park entrance road when I arrived. Three were frolicking amid the row of junipers below the visitor center. I pulled into the parking area and walked back along the bicycle trail to view these long-tailed, black-and-white Corvids (crow family). Their coal black hood, bill, back, tail, and wings and snow white underparts, shoulders, and primaries gave them a striking appearance. Seen through binoculars, the back and tail showed an iridescent green sheen. In flight, a magpie's long, wedge-shaped tail streams behind it for more than half of the bird's length, and the white markings on its wings and rump form an obvious V-pattern.

Magpies feed on an extremely diverse assortment of foods. Although Paul Ehrlich and colleagues, in *The Birder's Handbook*, consider it the "most insectivous" of any Northern American Corvid, John Terres, in *The Audubon Society Encyclopedia of North American Birds*, reports that, although it "eats insects throughout the year, including flies and their larvae and pupae from carrion," it also "cleans up roadside carcasses of dead animals; picks and eats ticks from back of elk, mule deer, bighorns; eats remains of animals killed by coyotes and other carnivores; sometimes pecks flesh at sores or cuts on back of horses, cows, sheep; takes some eggs and young of small birds in spring; also eats mice, snakes, some grain and fruit." Scotts Bluff resource management specialist Robert Manasek told me that staff members once watched a magpie kill a cottontail. It "used its heavy bill to peck the back of the cottontails head, at the base of its skull."

I located a magpie nest on one of the junipers. It was a bulky, rounded structure of sticks and debris about 2 feet (61 cm) across with an opening on one side. It seemed poorly constructed, with sticks protruding in all directions, but I knew that inside was a secure bowl of mud and grass, well protected from the elements. Although magpies usually build new nests each year, they may "use old nests for nighttime brooding during cold weather," according to Paul Johnsgard in *Birds of the Great Plains*.

My presence near the nest apparently disturbed the owners, because two of the birds began to scold me vehemently, flying back and forth just behind the junipers. Their loud, emphatic "chaeck" calls created so much havoc that I decided to retreat and leave them in peace. But as I walked back to the visitor center, they continued the uproar; their "chaeck" and "chek-chek-chek" calls were audible almost to the parking area.

The Park Environment

Scotts Bluff is best known for its historical significance as an important landmark on the Oregon and California trails, a place that marked the end of the Great American Desert and the beginning of the Rocky Mountains. Its name is a reference to Hiram Scott, an employee of the Rocky Mountain Fur Company, who, according to legend, died near the bluff in 1828.

The bluff rises 800 feet (244 m) above the North Platte River, serving as a centerpiece to the park's nearly 3,000 acres (1,214 ha). Dominant prairie vegetation consists of numerous grasses, especially needle-and-thread, western wheatgrass, downy brome, and side-oats grama, and pricklypear cactus, kochia, yucca, fringed and sand sages, winterfat, rubber rabbitbrush, skunkbush sumac, and snowberry. Cottonwood, willow, chokecherry, snowberry, and gooseberry are common in the ravines and along the river. And ponderosa pine and Rocky Mountain juniper occur on the upper slopes of Scotts Bluff, as well as South Bluff on the park's southern boundary.

Vehicular access into the park is available only via Highway 92, 3 miles (5 km) southwest of Gering, and a 1.6-mile (2.6-km) road to the summit of Scotts Bluff. The National Park Service visitor center is at the junction of Highway 92 and the Summit Road. There can be found an information desk, auditorium where orientation programs are presented hourly, numerous exhibits, including a display of paintings by noted pioneer photographer and artist William Henry Jackson, and a sales outlet; bird field guides and a checklist are available. Interpretive activities include Thursday evening campfire programs during the summer and the self-guided Summit Trail at the end of Summit Road.

Additional information can be obtained from the Superintendent, Scotts Bluff National Monument, P.O. Box 27, Gering, NE 69341-0027; (308) 436-4340.

Bird Life

Highway 92 and the Saddle Rock Trail, the foot trail between the visitor center and summit, provide the best opportunities for finding grassland birds. Year-round, the single most common bird in this habitat is the **western meadowlark**. Its plump body, bright yellow throat, yellow breast crossed by a bold, black V, striped head and back, and extremely short tail with white edges are most obvious. But what makes this bird most appealing is its familiar song, a surprisingly loud, flutelike, gurgling melody. Arthur Bent, in *Life Histories of North American Cardinals, Grosbeaks, Buntings, Towhees, Finches, Sparrows, and Allies*, quoted Claude Barnes's description of its song as " 'tra la la traleek'; the traleek was a jumble of sounds, short, emphatic.' " Another common description is "Oh, yes, I am a pretty-little-bird." But for me, a western meadowlark's song always reminds me of my mother's description; she told me that the meadowlark sings: "Salt Lake City is a pret-ty little city." To my ears, the Salt Lake City song sounds right.

A few additional birds can be found on the grasslands with more effort, although the presence of most of these is due primarily to the woody plants scattered along the ravines. True grassland birds are mostly limited to the common nighthawk, usually seen flying at dusk and dawn; horned lark, a little bird with a black-and-yellow head and black tail with distinct white edges; vesper sparrow, with chestnut shoulders and white edges on its rather long tail; lark sparrow, with its black, white, and tan face and large white corners on its tail; and lark bunting, with the male's coal black body and a large, white patch on each wing.

I found several "ravine birds" along the Saddle Rock Trail one spring morning. Most common were **rufous-sided towhees**, singing slurred "chup-chup-zeee" notes from various perches. One brightly marked male, perched at the top of a rabbitbrush bush, literally glowed in the morning light. Its all-black hood, blood-red eyes, black-and-white back and wings, and rufous sides were most distinguished. When I approached too close, however, it gave a loud "wank" and dived for cover with a flash of the white corners of its long, dark tail.

Another song was at first reminiscent of that of a mockingbird, but more rambling. The singer, a **brown thrasher**, was sitting on top of a juniper snag farther up the ravine. Through binoculars, I saw this bird's yellowish eye, all-reddish back, heavily striped breast, and long tail. I stood still and listened to its varied songs, which seemed to go on and on. Ornithologists believe the brown thrasher has more than 1,100 song types, more than any other North American songbird. A member of the mockingbird family, Mimidae, it can mimic other birds and various other sounds and can modulate its voice from whispers to loud, wild, rollicking sounds. John Terres, in *The Audubon Society Encyclopedia of North American Birds*, mentions that they usually sing in pairs, and that one listener likened the brown thrasher's song to a telephone conversation: "Hello, hello, yes, yes, who is this? who is this? I should say, I should say, how's that? how's that?" My bird continued its monologue long after I passed by.

Other birds found that morning along the Saddle Rock Trail included a lone American kestrel hovering over the grassland in search of prey, and several mourning doves. I located one dove singing its mournful song from a distant juniper snag. A Say's phoebe sailed out after a passing insect; several barn swallows crisscrossed the grasslands in search of insects; and a red-breasted American robin sang its cheery song from a cottonwood snag. A brightly colored indigo bunting male flew up from the side of the trail and disappeared in the direction of the visitor center, and a pair of brown-headed cowbirds, social parasites of the bird world, called squeaky whistle notes as they flew by.

As the trail ascended the rocky slope of Scotts Bluff, I began to find other birds. **Rock wrens** were surprisingly common; their varied songs of melodic trills and buzzing notes resounded all around me.

Rock wren

One called, "tick-ear tick-ear tick-ear"; I found it along an open ledge reasonably close by. It walked in a jerky fashion and bobbed up and down every few seconds. Its dull, grayish plumage, with only a hint of buff sides, did not match its fascinating behavior. Suddenly it sang a very different and lovely song, one that Bent, in *Life Histories of North American Nuthatches, Wrens, Thrashers, and Their Allies*, has described as "keree keree keree, chair chair chair, deedle deedle dee-dle, tut tur tur, keree keree trrrrr."

I watched this little wren move along the steep rocky slope for several minutes, waiting for it to sing again, but it did not. I wondered if it had a nest nearby, and I searched the slope for debris that might give its nest site away, but to no avail. This bird actually lines the entrance to its nest with stones and other materials. Terres points out that "one passageway of a hole in earth to nest was lined with 1,665 items, of which 492 were small granite stones, 769 bones of rabbits, fishes, birds, and nesting materials."

As I progressed up the trail I began to hear the sweet songs of **house finches** echoing down the slopes above me. Their lovely songs were described by J.V. Remsen, Jr., in *The Audubon Society Master Guide to Birding*, as "a scrambling series of rhythmic notes usually lasting 3 or more seconds. Song slower, less monotonic, less fluid, and higher than that of Cassin's or Purple finch; often end on distinctive ascending note." It took considerable time to locate these vociferous birds, but I finally found a pair perched on a juniper, apparently trying to outsing each other. The males reddish head and throat, mottled brown body, and striped underparts were obvious. The female was a duller version.

As I moved higher, I detected a few other birds: a pair of rock doves circling overhead, probably nesting somewhere along the cliff; several mourning doves; a northern flicker calling off to my left; the sad song of a Say's phoebe; a pair of black-capped chickadees singing from the ponderosa pines ahead; an American robin caroling; chipping sparrows singing dull trills; and more brown-headed cowbirds.

Suddenly, a black-and-white bird shot by at an incredible speed; I could actually feel the wind as it passed close by. It continued its dive down the slope, and then, just as swiftly, ascended straight up into the sky so high that I needed binoculars to see it. It was a **white-throated swift**, one of the common summer residents of Scotts Bluff. As I continued up the trail, I heard several more swifts calling shrill, descending, twittering sounds high overhead. I also got several more good looks as one or more zoomed by, flying at speeds in excess of 100 miles (161 km) per hour. The white-throated swift is perfectly adapted to such flight: its cigar-shaped body and stiff, swept-back wings give it the aerial ability to careen along the bluff to capture insects. When it is flying high, its stiff wing beats create a twinkling effect. It nests in crevices on the cliff face, utilizing its own saliva to glue its feathers together into a small nesting platform. For additional information about this fascinating bird, see chapter 19 on Devil's Tower.

The much larger soaring birds over Scotts Bluff were **turkey vultures**. This all-dark, broad-winged bird with a bare, red head is able to soar for long periods of time without flapping its wings, simply by using the thermals rising from the warmer valley. It is sometimes mistaken for an eagle, but the golden eagle is rare in the park and soars with wings flat, not tilted slightly in a shallow V like those of the turkey vulture. Also, eagles soar straight on, while vultures tip slightly side to side. Turkey vultures can be expected almost anywhere in the park; they are scavengers that feed on carrion.

In some years, prairie falcons frequent the Scotts Bluff cliffs and hunt the grasslands along Highway 92. This raptor nested on the face of Eagle Rock, behind the visitor center, for several years. But in 1993, its nest site was usurped by a great horned owl, according to local birder Alice Kenitz.

A relatively small prairie dog colony exists on the nearly inaccessible western edge of the park. A few burrowing owls reside there, as well. Ornithologist Martha Jeanne Desmond of the University of Nebraska has surveyed these ground-dwelling owls for several years; she estimates the population at five nesting pairs.

The monument is bordered on the north by the North Platte River, but access into this area is difficult. The riverine habitat, however, is different from other habitats in the park. Ornithologists Mike Cox and William Franklin surveyed this habitat in the summers of 1986 and 1987, and published their findings in 1989. They recorded 60 bird species, 23 of those listed as common or abundant: great blue heron; mallard; mourning dove; northern flicker; downy woodpecker; northern rough-winged, cliff, and barn swallows; black-billed magpie; black-capped chickadee; house wren; American robin; European starling; yellow warbler; common yellowthroat; yellow-breasted chat; lazuli bunting; rufous-sided towhee; red-winged blackbird; common grackle; brown-headed cowbird; American goldfinch; and house sparrow.

A few of the less common birds found in this habitat include double-crested cormorant, Canada goose, wood duck, green-winged and blue-winged teal, common merganser, red-tailed hawk, killdeer, yellow-billed cuckoo, belted kingfisher, eastern and western kingbirds, blue jay, blue grosbeak, and orchard and Bullock's orioles.

Winter birds are very different from those found in spring and summer. The Neotropical migrants, such as the flycatchers, swallows, warblers, grosbeaks, and buntings, have departed for warmer climes south of the United States. But a few more northern species move into the area for the winter; bald eagles, geese, and ducks frequent the river and lakes. The best indication of species present at that time of year is the annual Christmas Bird Count that is undertaken in the Scotts Bluff area. In 1991, eight counters tallied 9,563 individuals of 43 species. The dozen most numerous species, in descending order of abundance, included mallard, Canada goose, red-winged blackbird, house sparrow, European starling, American crow, horned lark, rock dove, dark-eyed junco, American robin, house finch, and black-capped chickadee.

In summary, the Scott Bluff bird checklist includes 96 species, of which 40 are known to nest. Only 2 (Canada goose and mallard) of the 40 species are water birds, 4 are hawks and owls, and 1 (yellow-breasted chat) is a warbler.

Birds of Special Interest

Turkey vulture. This large, all-dark bird is usually seen soaring overhead; it has a bare, red head and tilts slightly from side to side in flight.

White-throated swift. Common in summer about the high cliffs, this bird has a black-and-white body and swept-back wings; its high-pitched descending trill also helps with identification.

Black-billed magpie. This long-tailed, black-and-white bird is common along the entrance road; its call is a "chaeck" note.

Rock wren. These little grayish birds frequent the rocky slopes; their typical call is a sharp "tick-ear."

Brown thrasher. Watch for this reddish, long-tailed bird along the ravines and at other shrubby areas; it sings marvelous and diverse songs.

Rufous-sided towhee. This is the bird of shrubby areas; males have an all-black hood, blood-red eyes, black-and-white back, and rufous sides.

Western meadowlark. This common grassland bird has a bright yellow breast, crossed with a bold, black V, and a wonderful song.

House finch. Males possess a reddish-brown head and throat and streaked underparts; they sing a lively, continual song in spring and summer.

SOUTHERN

The wild things on this earth are not to do with as we please. They have been given to us in trust, and we must account for them to the generations which will come after us and audit our accounts.

—William T. Hornaday

24

Ozark National Scenic Riverways, Missouri

The morning birdsong along the riverway was intense. It seemed to peak soon after we put in, and it continued through most of the morning. Although we saw only a fraction of the choir, its wonderful music added considerably to our leisurely canoe trip down the aqua-colored Current River.

The loud "jibbidy jibbidy jibbidy" song of a Carolina wren emanated from the thicket near the beach. It seemed as if this large wren was watching over the cadre of canoers that July morning. I caught sight of one that came out of hiding as if to bid us farewell. Its reddish back, buff underparts, and bold white eyebrows were most distinguished. Then, as if to bid us luck, it sang again: "jibbidy jibbidy jibbidy" and ducked into a tangle of grapevines.

A male northern cardinal, all-red except for a black face, with a tall crest, flew across the river ahead of us. A family of blue jays, calling scratchy "jay jay jay" notes, trailed one another through the streamside vegetation. Cedar waxwings were "flycatching" from snags. A downy woodpecker called thin rattle notes nearby. The "peter peter" notes of tufted titmice rang out from the streamside. And Carolina chickadees called "fee-bay" notes overhead.

Then, perched on an open sycamore branch hanging over the riverway was another all-red bird, a male **summer tanager**. Its darker wings, black eyes, and yellowish bill were also evident. It gave a dry "pit-a-tuck" call and disappeared into the higher foliage. We encountered several other summer tanagers that morning, perhaps because of their affinity for the riparian vegetation along the waterway. Once

Summer tanager

we watched a female, evident by her greenish-yellow plumage, chase and capture a cicada. She then flew back into the foliage to consume breakfast, the cicada buzzing loudly in defense.

Summer tanagers also feed on wasps and bees and their larvae. Arthur Bent, in *Life Histories of North American Blackbirds, Orioles, Tanagers, and Allies*, includes a report from Gray's Summit, Missouri, of a summer tanager that, for two full weeks, fed its young on paper wasp larvae taken from nests under the eaves of an old barn. Another time, a summer tanager captured wasps in midair by diving on them, grasping them with its bill, and beating them to death before swallowing them whole. "After repeating the attack several times, the wasps all suddenly disappeared, whereupon the Tanager alighted on the nest, rapidly tore the upper protecting layers away and attacked the comb." Bent also points out that the summer tanager "feeds largely on beetles, caught on the wing or in trees." He adds that it eats "beetles so large that it seems impossible for it to swallow them. After these insects are digested, the indigestible feet, legs, and shells are rolled into a ball by the bird's stomach and disgorged."

Nests are normally placed on a horizontal limb, 10 to 35 feet (3-

11 m) high, oftentimes over a roadway or waterway, constructed of bits of weeds, leaves, bark, and grasses, and lined with fine grasses. Youngsters look like the drab female, but males acquire their all-red plumage (at first blotched with yellow) by the following season. Tanager families remain together for a few weeks, but leave their breeding ground as early as late August. They are Neotropical migrants that travel to Central America and northern South America for the winter. There they must find suitable habitats if they are to survive long enough to return in the spring to their ancestral nesting sites along the Ozark Riverways.

The Park Environment
The authorized boundary of Ozark National Scenic Riverways, America's first (1964) national scenic riverway, contains 81,790 acres (32,900 ha) and 134 miles (216 km) of the Current and Jacks Fork rivers. About 12 percent of the area is still in private ownership and not accessible to the public, except for a 300 foot (91 m) wide strip on the riverbank accessible for sight-seeing.

Most visitors come to canoe or float the river; many camp in the seven developed and more than 50 primitive campgrounds along the river. Other activities include swimming, fishing, hiking the Ozark Trail, hunting and trapping in season, and visiting a number of historic and natural sites. Alley Roller Mill, Klepzig Mill, CCC Cabins, Suzie Nichols Farm, and Buttin Rock School are historic areas, and Big Spring, Devils Well, and Rocky Falls are the prominent natural areas.

The park landscape is largely riverbank and floodplain with many rocky bluffs, wetlands, and adjacent forested hillsides. Vegetation is all second-growth with scattered stands of mature hardwoods. Dominant floodplain plants include maples, sycamore, eastern cottonwood, American elm, shellbark hickory, hackberry, black cherry, and a variety of oaks. Mature hardwood forest communities include beech, maples, blackgum, bitternut hickory, and numerous oaks. Shortleaf pine is also present in drier or sandy soils, such as along the entrance road to Big Spring.

There are no operational visitor centers in the park, although park headquarters at Van Buren is open daily. This center contains an information desk and sales outlet; bird field guides and a park checklist are available. Interpretive activities include a variety of walks, talks, and evening programs from Memorial Day to Labor Day; check the schedules on campground bulletin boards.

Additional information can be obtained from the Superintendent, Ozark National Scenic Riverways, Box 490, Van Buren, MO 63965; (314) 323-4236.

Bird Life

The largest bird found on our canoe trip was the **great blue heron**. We discovered one sitting on a high sycamore limb over the river; it seemed to be monitoring our progress. It had spread its bluish wings, probably to take a sunbath, and it reminded me of a large dishrag hung out to dry. Its blue, black, and white neck and head and huge yellow bill were obvious. This large heron usually is found along the shore, poised over a shallow place ready to strike at a passing fish, frog, or other prey. When disturbed, it will fly off with loud, grating squawks. It nests in colonies in a few protected places along the river. The smaller green heron, with a chestnut neck and breast and black cap, was also seen during the morning. It has shorter legs than the great blue, so it usually fishes from sticks or rocks along the waterway.

During our morning trip I recorded a variety of birds. Eastern kingbirds sat on the tips of snags; eastern wood-pewees called thin "pee-wee" notes; and gray catbirds called scratchy "meow" notes from the thickets. American robins were reasonably common; red-eyed vireos called whistle notes continually from the high foliage; and a parula warbler sang a song of ascending notes ending with a sharp, descending "jip." We startled a Louisiana waterthrush along the riverbank; it flew ahead of us with loud "chink" notes; several American goldfinches passed overhead; and indigo buntings sang their songs from all the open areas.

The **eastern kingbirds** provided us several good views sailing overhead with their characteristic quivering flight, calling out stuttering "kip-kip-kipper-kipper" notes, or "flycatching" low over the waterway. We could see their two-tone pattern of all-white underparts, coal black cap and dark back, and a white terminal band on the otherwise all-black tail. The other flycatcher seen along the river was the smaller, nondescript eastern wood-pewee. Its paler underparts, olive-brown upperparts, a slight crest, and paler underparts are its principal features.

The bird of our trip was undoubtedly a **belted kingfisher** that startled us with its loud rattle call when it suddenly took flight from a limb hanging less than 50 feet (15 m) over our canoe. Neither of us had seen it until its rollicking departure. But we watched it fly down-river and alight on another limb in full view. And as we closed the distance, we got a much better look. It was a female with a broad rusty belly band; males possess only the blue chest band. Its plumage included an all-blue back and a white throat, collar, and underparts. We also could see its high crest and heavy bill.

This bird captures its prey-fish, frogs, and other water creatures by diving headfirst from 30 or 40 feet (9-12 m) above the surface, and often becoming completely submerged. It then brings its catch out of the water and carries it to a favorite perch, where it beats it to death before swallowing it headfirst. For details about this bird's nesting behavior, see chapter 27 on Chickasaw.

Another morning in August, I birded the Big Spring area, a microcosm of the entire park. Fog was rising from the river and the grass was wet with dew. **American robins** were most numerous, searching the lawns for earthworms and insects. Several speckled youngsters were following the adults, no doubt learning the art of worm hunting. The adults' bright red breast contrasted with their black head, whitish throat, and yellow bill. I could not help but admire their stately appearance as they ran here and there in their never-ending search. A few were apparently still feeding nestlings, as I watched one carrying long fat worms into the high sycamore foliage.

A **wood thrush** sang a dozen or so "eee-o-lay" songs from the adjacent forest, each rendition slightly different from the previous ones, but containing the same exquisite, flutelike quality. The wood thrush is closely related to the robin, but, unlike its red-breasted cousin, is a bird of the shadows rather than the sunlight. This robin-sized bird has a cinnamon back and white underparts with large black spots. It also has narrow white eye rings and dusky cheeks. But its song is what makes this bird special; in spring and summer it may sing all day. Walking through the forest can be like visiting a huge cathedral with a great choir.

Blue-gray gnatcatchers were rarely still, flying from tree to tree and sailing after passing insects. They looked at first like miniature mockingbirds, with their blue-gray back, distinct white eye rings, and long blackish tail with white outer edges. I watched one that had captured a large damselfly spend considerable time dewinging it with several sharp blows before it swallowed the remainder whole. It flipped its long tail here and there during the entire process, and upon completion, gave a typical high-pitched, buzzy "zpeeee zpeeee" call.

The edges of the clearings and the weedy areas near the river produced numerous indigo buntings, a few gray catbirds, brown thrashers, common yellowthroats, and a family of yellow-breasted chats. **Indigo buntings** were especially common, singing from high posts or searching for food along the roadside and adjacent vegetation. The adult males were gorgeous birds with all indigo blue plumage, except for some black in front of their eyes and on their wings. The females and young were a duller brown with only hints of blue on their neck and tail; the youngsters also showed faint breast streaks. The males sang loud, penetrating songs that could be heard for several hundred feet: "swee-swee zreet-zreet swee-swee ti-ti che-che," a distinct song of couplets on different pitches.

The shortleaf pines and associated vegetation near the entrance to the area produced several more birds. **White-breasted nuthatches** called nasal "yank" notes as they searched the pine bark for food, probing every crack as they walked up and down the trunks and upside-down under the larger branches. This is a 6-inch (15-cm) bird with white underparts, black cap, and grayish back and wings. Through binoculars, I could see its slightly upturned bill, used to pry up loose bark in its continuing search for insects. It is a cavity-nester that inhabits unused woodpecker nests and other natural cavities.

Pine warblers are rarely found anywhere except on pines, where they spend much of their time searching for insects among the outer boughs. They are yellowish warblers with an olive-green back and wings and two prominent white wing bars. And their song is a distinct sweet, clear musical trill with little change in tone.

Hackberry trees were full of fruit, and I discovered a bird party of more than a dozen songbirds feeding on the tiny ripe berries. Carolina chickadees, tufted titmice, blue-gray gnatcatchers, red-eyed and warbling vireos, indigo buntings, and several warblers: blue-winged, parula, yellow, prairie, cerulean, worm-eating, Swainson's, and Kentucky, and American redstart and ovenbird were all present. The male cerulean warbler was most exciting, for this bird is normally associated with high foliage and not easily seen. Accompanied by three poorly marked birds, undoubtedly a family group, the male showed a lovely, almost frosty blue on its crown and back, with a narrow blue breast band and bold white wing bars.

The Swainson's warbler was also special because this rather nondescript bird, with grayish underparts, olive-brown back and bold whitish eyebrows, is a state endangered species. The park's biological technician, Michael Gossett, told me that it is under study by Brian Thomas of the University of Missouri, who found 14 nests in the park in 1993, all in canebrake habitats along the river.

Once the sun warmed the ground enough to produce thermals, turkey vultures and red-tailed hawks began to soar. The turkey vultures, all-black except for their bare, red heads, were easily distinguished from the smaller red-tails, with their whitish underparts and red tails. The flight patterns of these two birds also differ: turkey vultures soar with their wings held in a slight V and rock slightly from side to side; red-tailed hawks soar with their wings straight out and do not rock. Other aerial specialists we saw included several chimney swifts, much smaller gray-black birds that fly with stiff, nervous wing beats; barn swallows, with their long, forked tail and chestnut throat; and a pair of purple martins, with the male's purplish plumage and the female's whitish underparts.

Other birds recorded during my morning's exploration of the Big Spring area included a pair of wood ducks near the Big Spring Lodge boat landing; a yellow-billed cuckoo at the johnboat river access site; several ruby-throated hummingbirds; red-bellied woodpeckers, evident by their loud "churr" calls; a crow-sized pileated woodpecker; numerous Acadian flycatchers and a great crested flycatcher in the forest; numerous American crows; three eastern bluebirds chasing insects near the craft center; and two common grackles feeding on the lawn. And in the old fields across from the campground entrance, I found several white-eyed vireos, a family of yellow-breasted chats, a male blue grosbeak, and a pair of rufous-sided towhees.

I birded several other locations during my August visit and discovered some exciting birds. At Akers, I watched a black-billed cuckoo feeding on tent caterpillars that it was extracting from a "tent" on a black walnut branch. At Round Spring, an immature broad-winged hawk sat on a tall oak tree close to the walkway over the river, screaming high-pitched whistles. Betty videotaped this bird for several minutes, and it was still screaming when we finally departed. At Alley Spring, a yellow-throated vireo sang its methodical whistle song from a tall sycamore next to the roller mill. At Two Rivers, a pair of eastern phoebes were still attending fledglings near the campground station. And from the Powder Mill Bridge, I found a willow flycatcher among the willows on the floodplain, and a scarlet tanager among the hardwoods in front of the unmanned visitor center.

During the winter, bird populations are only a fraction of what they are in spring, summer, and fall. Gossett told me that bald eagles are frequently found along the river in winter. The best perspective on winter bird life can be obtained by examining the results of the annual Christmas Bird Counts. The 1992 Big Spring Christmas Count produced 963 individuals of 44 species. The dozen most numerous birds, in descending order of abundance, included dark-eyed junco, northern cardinal, blue jay, American robin, American crow, Carolina chickadee, tufted titmouse, eastern bluebird, song sparrow, northern flicker, European starling, and downy woodpecker.

In summary, the park's checklist of birds includes 196 species, of which 97 are listed as nesting. Of those 97 species, 8 are water birds (herons, waterfowl, and shorebirds), 9 are hawks and owls, and 17 are warblers.

Birds of Special Interest
Great blue heron. This is the large, long-legged, long-necked heron of the riverways; notice its great yellowish bill.

Belted kingfisher. It is most often found flying away or across the river, giving loud rattle calls; it has an all-blue back and blue bar across its white chest.

Eastern kingbird. This white-and-black flycatcher has a white terminal band on its black tail and is common along the rivers.

White-breasted nuthatch. Watch for this black-capped bird that walks up and down tree trunks while probing crevices for insects; it has a nasal "yank" call.

Carolina wren. This reddish wren of the thickets sings a loud "jibbidy jibbidy jibbidy" song.

American robin. It is most often found on the lawns; it has an all-red breast and black head.

Wood thrush. This forest bird is more often heard than seen; it sings a flutelike "eee-o-lay" song with many variations.

Blue-gray gnatcatcher. It is a tiny bird with bluish gray plumage and white outer edges on its long, loose-appearing tail.

Summer tanager. This is the all-red, noncrested bird common along the riverways; its call is a distinct "pit-a-tuck."

Indigo bunting. One of the park's most abundant songbirds, males are bright blue and sing a lively song with distinct couplets.

25

Buffalo National River, Arkansas

Tyler Bend is probably the best bird-finding area in the entire park, due undoubtedly to the diversity of habitats at this location. River, floodplain forest, mixed lowland forest, oak-hickory upland forest, and old field communities are all present.

The Tyler Bend Visitor Center grounds, which overlook the Buffalo River floodplain, yielded more than two dozen species during one summer morning visit. From the parking area, the sorrowful songs of mourning doves, "caw caw caw" calls of American crows, "jay" calls of blue jays, "cue cue cue" of northern cardinals, descending trills of field sparrows, and emphatic songs of an **indigo bunting** were most audible. I located the male indigo blue bunting singing from the top of an oak tree. Through binoculars, I could see the blackish patch behind each eye, darker wings, and short, conical bill. As I watched, it put its head back and sang a song of couplets, "swee-swee zreet-zreet swee-swee zay-zay seeit seeit." It was undoubtedly on its territory, announcing to the world, "This area belongs to me."

During the several days that I spent along the Buffalo River, the indigo bunting was one of the most abundant birds encountered. In fact, Douglas James and Joseph Neal, in *Arkansas Birds: Their Distribution and Abundance*, note that it is the "commonest breeding bird" at Buffalo National River. It especially favors old fields and forest edges.

Male indigo buntings sing continually from high posts, while the females, drab brownish birds with a hint of blue on their neck and tail, seemed to spend most of their time in the lower shrubbery. They undoubtedly had nests hidden amid the dense tangles. But with any disturbance they were quick to respond, calling sharp "tsisk" notes.

I also found a pair of **blue grosbeaks** in the weedy field to the right of the visitor center. Although the male blue grosbeak can initially be mistaken for the smaller indigo bunting, a good sighting will reveal a different bird. The male blue grosbeak is truly blue, not indigo blue, and it has a distinct rusty patch on each shoulder. Additionally, its bill is considerably heavier than the bunting's, a "grosbeak" capable of cracking larger seeds. And its song is also different, with a number of single short notes and slightly longer trills, without the distinct couplets of the indigo bunting song. Arthur Bent, in *Life Histories of North American Cardinals, Grosbeaks, Buntings, Towhees, Finches, Sparrows, and Allies*, quotes two descriptions of its songs by birdsong specialist Aretas Saunders: " 'ray ree ray totah ray reeray to see see totay' and 'truray truray tritray tritray tro tro.' "

A third blue bird was also near the visitor center, an **eastern bluebird**. A pair of these lovely birds were "flycatching" over the open field, dashing after passing insects, and calling rich "chur-lee" notes. Both sexes possessed a blue back and rusty underparts, but the male had a bright blue back, head, and tail, with a reddish rust chest and sides, while the female's head and underparts were more buff than rust. Bluebirds are one of our better known and most loved songbirds.

Yet bluebirds declined to as few as one-tenth of their former numbers during the last several decades. This decline was generally due to habitat destruction and nest-site competition. Paul Zimmerman, in a 1993 article in *Birder's World*, points out that countless nest cavities were destroyed by development or eliminated by the use of metal fence posts. And the increased numbers of competitors like house sparrows and European starlings seriously curtailed bluebird reproduction. However, the public came to their rescue by putting up bluebird nest boxes along the edges of fields across the eastern and central United States. The eastern bluebird's recovery is living proof that songbirds are an important part of our daily lives.

The Park Environment
The Buffalo River is one of the few major streams left undammed in the Arkansas Ozarks. It flows easterly for 150 river miles (241 km),

dropping in elevation from 2,385 to 375 feet (727-114 m), from near Fallsville to Buffalo City. There it joins the White River, then the Black and Arkansas rivers, and eventually enters the Mississippi River near Cleveland, Mississippi, to continue southward to the Gulf of Mexico. Buffalo National River contains 95,730 acres (38,741 ha) of both swift-flowing and placid riverway, rocky beaches, numerous bluffs, and steep and gentle hillsides and ridges. It also includes three wilderness areas: Upper Buffalo, near Boxley; Ponca, below Ponca; and Lower Buffalo, between Buffalo Point and the confluence of the Buffalo and White rivers.

Major vegetation types in the park include floodplain, mixed hardwood, oak-hickory, oak-pine, cedar glade, and beech communities, according to botanist Edward Dale of the University of Arkansas. The floodplain is composed mostly of American elm, green ash, silver leaf maple, and boxelder, with lesser amounts of sycamore, river birch, black willow, and eastern cottonwood. Gravel bars are dominated by Ward's and sandbar willows. The mixed hardwood communities, usually located between the floodplain and oak-hickory, oak-pine, or cedar glade areas, are dominated by American elm, green ash, and silver leaf maple, with numerous sweetgum, white ash, bitternut hickory, hackberry, black gum, black walnut, and oaks.

The oak-hickory communities, principally on south-facing slopes and hilltops, contain post, blackjack, and black oaks and mockernut hickory; dogwoods frequently dominate the understory. Patches of oak-pine areas, predominantly shortleaf pine, occur in the uplands. Cedar glades, dominated by red cedar, invade the old fields. And small scattered patches of beech also exist.

The National Park Service operates ranger stations at Pruitt and Buffalo Point and a visitor center at Tyler Bend. The visitor center and ranger stations contain an information desk, orientation programs, exhibits, and a sales outlet; bird field guides and a checklist are available. Interpretive activities are provided from Memorial Day to mid-August and include ranger-guided walks (including an occasional bird walk) and talks and evening programs at Ozark Pavilion, Tyler Bend, and Buffalo Point. Schedules are posted at park bulletin boards and are available on request.

Several hiking trails wind through the park, ranging from the .3-mile (5-km) Morning Star Loop Trail at Rush to the Buffalo River

Trail that runs for 25 miles (40 km) along the upper river from Ponca to Pruitt. The Ozark Highlands Trail runs for 165 miles (266 km) from Lake Ft. Smith State Park to Tyler Bend. The 2.1-mile (3.4-km) Lost Valley Trail is self-guided. Fourteen park campgrounds lie along the river, and backcountry camping is also permitted. Additional information can be obtained from the Superintendent, Buffalo National River, P.O. Box 1173, Harrison, AR 72602-1173; (501) 741-5443.

Bird Life
Several other birds were found near the Tyler Bend Visitor Center that summer morning. **Carolina wrens** called loud "jibbidy jibbidy jibbidy" notes from the adjacent undergrowth. I located one singing from an open limb; its reddish back and buff underparts, bold whitish eyebrows, and long bill were readily apparent. It normally is a nervous and secretive bird, a skulker of the dense thickets that is more often heard than seen. It possesses a variety of songs that range from a "jibbidy" version to "tea-kettle, tea-kettle, tea-kettle" to a softer "whee-udel, whee-udel, whee-udel." Paul Ehrlich and colleagues, in *The Birder's Handbook*, point out that male Carolina wrens "sing 27 to 41 different song types, singing one song repeatedly before switching to a different song type; neighboring males frequently match song types. Males and females duet."

Red-bellied and downy woodpeckers, eastern kingbirds, Carolina chickadees, tufted titmice, blue-gray gnatcatchers, brown thrashers, summer tanagers, brown-headed cowbirds, orchard orioles, and American goldfinches were also evident near the visitor center. The **blue-gray gnatcatcher** is a fascinating little bird with a blue-gray back, bold white eye rings, whitish underparts, and a long black tail with distinct white edges. It is one of the few birds that, even at a distance, can be identified by its behavior of flipping its tail about when foraging on foliage. It looks much like a miniature mockingbird.

Below the visitor center are old fields that are slowly returning to forest, except where they are maintained for hay cropping, camping, and other visitor activities. This is where I found northern bobwhites; ruby-throated hummingbirds; eastern kingbirds; northern rough-winged and barn swallows; American robins; northern mockingbirds; yellow-breasted chats; more blue grosbeaks and indigo buntings; rufous-sided towhees; chipping, field, and lark sparrows; red-winged blackbirds; eastern meadowlarks; common grackles; brown-headed cowbirds; orchard orioles; and American goldfinches. The little gold-and-black **American goldfinches** were especially numerous, flying up from the adjacent weedy areas as I passed and flying off with deep undulating flights while singing "per-chic-o-ree." Few birds are as distinctly marked as the male goldfinch; the female is a duller version without the black cap. Goldfinches also have the distinction of waiting until late summer to nest, when all the plants they need for nests and food are readily available. Ehrlich and colleagues described this bird's nest thus: "In branch fork, oft woven so tightly that nest holds water; of forbs, other pliable veg, lined with plant down. Caterpillar webbing and spider silk oft used to bind outer rim. Male may collect some nest material and give to female."

The floodplain forest at Tyler Bend contained additional species: yellow-billed cuckoo; red-bellied, downy, and hairy woodpeckers; eastern wood-pewee; great crested flycatcher; white-breasted nuthatch; white-eyed and yellow-throated vireos; and several warblers. The warblers were of special interest for they were still on their nesting territories and singing. Black-and-white warblers sang a series of high, thin "wee-see" notes. Parula warblers sang a short ascending buzz that ended abruptly with a lower note. And high in a sycamore I detected loud, musical song of a yellow-throated warbler. Paul Sykes, in *The Audubon Society Master Guide to Birding*, provides the best description of this bird's song: "a loud musical series of clear syllables given faster as they descend with abrupt high note at end: 'tee-ew, tew-ew, tew-ew, tew-ew, tew-wi' or 'sweetie, sweetie, sweetie.'" I stared into the high canopy for along time before I found this lovely creature near the top of the tree. Through binoculars, I could see its bright yellow throat edged with black, black-and-white head pattern, bold white eyebrows, and white belly with black streaks on its flanks.

I also located a Kentucky warbler singing a loud and emphatic song in the dense undergrowth. I recognized the song immediately, but it took me several minutes of searching the undergrowth before it came into the open for a look around. Its bright yellow throat, eyebrows, and underparts contrasted with its black forehead, cheeks, and sideburns. It stayed only a second before it dropped back into the undergrowth with a loud "chuck." A few seconds later it sang again, a clear whistled "tory, tory, tory, tory, tory."

Two other "ground" warblers occur along the riverway in summer: prothonotary warbler and Louisiana waterthrush. The prothonotary warbler frequents riverbottom wetlands, while the Louisiana waterthrush prefers small, fast side streams. Both species are heard more than seen. The prothonotary warbler sings an emphatic "peet, zweet, zweet, zweet" song, all on the same key. The Lousiana waterthrush sings a loud "see-you see-you see-you chew chew to-wee" song.

I was suddenly aware that a pair of **eastern screech-owls** were singing descending whinny songs in the mixed forest directly across the river; the male was singing on a lower pitch than the female. They sang for only about 2 or 3 minutes and then were silent; I was unable to solicit any further response. But later I found a mounted specimen in the exhibits at the visitor center, a red-phased bird about 8 inches (20 cm) tall with ear tufts. Although this little owl is reasonably common throughout the park, it is rarely seen. It is wholly nocturnal, going about its business after dark and retiring before daylight. It is known to feed on almost any kind of small creature, from insects to fish, reptiles, birds, and mammals. James and Neal report that in fall and winter insects make up 84 percent of its diet.

A few other nocturnal birds also nest in the park. Great horned owls are reasonably common in open areas; their calls are normally a series of three to eight deep hoots, "hoo hoo hoo-hoo." The slightly smaller barred owls reside along riverways; they also possess a distinct call, "who-cooks-for-you, who-cooks-for-you-all?" Park interpreter Rhonda Terry told me that a pair of barred owls live near Pruitt Ranger Station; she hears their "who-cooks-for-you" songs often. In addition, three nightjars also nest in the park. Common nighthawks are often seen flying overhead at dawn and dusk; their grayish brown plumage with a broad white band near the tip of each wing and their territorial "peent" notes are easy to recognize. Chuck-will's-widows, summer residents of the lowland forest communities, sing a song that sounds like their name. And whip-poor-wills sing "whip-poor-will" songs from the drier ridges.

The middle-sized **red-bellied woodpecker** was seen numerous times on snags and flying back and forth across the river. It called loud "churr" notes on numerous occasions. This woodpecker is distinguished by its finely barred black-and-white back, whitish underparts, and red nape; males also possess a red crown. Its faint red belly patch is difficult to see.

One of the most accessible forest habitats encountered was along the Ozark entrance road, which transects upland and lowland forest communities. Although many of the birds found there replicate those found on the floodplain, a few more species were recorded: broad-winged hawk; Acadian flycatcher; Carolina chickadee; wood thrush; white-eyed, yellow-throated, and red-eyed vireos; worm-eating and hooded warblers; American redstart; ovenbird; and scarlet tanager. The voice of the "deep forest" was undoubtedly that of the wood thrush, its flutelike "eee-o-lay" songs were repeated over and over, each time with a slightly different inflection. Acadian flycatchers, plain little birds with loud, explosive "PEET-sah" calls, were common as well.

The most obvious songster in the forest, however, was the **red-eyed vireo**, which continually sang single and double whistle notes with no particular tune. This is a bird of the high foliage that rarely ventures into the lower layers of vegetation. It is a real challenge to locate this 6-inch (15-cm) songster, which is well camouflaged by its olive-green back and lighter underparts. But seen in the right light, it possesses a subtle beauty. Its head pattern is most distinct: gray crown bordered with thin black lines, bold whitish eyebrows, and red eyes. It also is interesting to realize how abundant this bird is; James and Neal report that it is the "most numerous bird inhabiting the oak-hickory forest in the upper part of Buffalo National River."

Stop anywhere along the Ozark entrance road in spring and summer, and you can usually hear three or four birds singing close by and others in the distance. Since only male vireos sing, sometimes right on the nest, one can appreciate not only their abundance, but also how this species has divided the forest. Territories are established like a giant checkerboard. "Summer population studies in southern Arkansas showed a population of seventy-eight singing males per one hundred acres of forest stream bottomland, and thirty-five per one hundred acres of upland forest," James and Neal wrote.

On another mid-September visit to Buffalo River, I canoed from Buffalo Point to Rush Landing, a beautiful stretch of the river with high bluffs and deep green forests. Migration was well under way, and many of the birds recorded were only passing through, following the riverway on their route south for the winter. The most memorable bird of the trip was a common summer resident, a **green heron**, that flew just ahead of us for a long stretch. Each time it was disturbed it flew off with loud "kyowk" calls, chastising us for interfering with its business. We sort of herded it downriver. Its green back, black cap, and deep chestnut throat and sides were obvious. This little heron normally is found along the bank, poised over shallow water and waiting for a passing fish, frog, or other prey. It builds a stick nest in the trees along the riverway.

We also found a number of **eastern phoebes** along the river; they were especially common at rocky bluffs, where they probably had nested earlier in the season. Their calls were rather monotonous "fee-bee" or "pewit" notes. These middle-sized flycatchers, with a black cap and white to yellowish underparts, have a tendency to wag their tails, in addition to the typical tail jerking exhibited by most flycatchers.

Other birds found along the river during that autumn canoe trip included great blue herons; Cooper's and broad-winged hawks; spotted sandpipers; red-bellied, downy, and pileated woodpeckers; eastern wood-pewees; olive-sided, Acadian, and scissor-tailed flycatchers; eastern kingbirds; blue jays; American crows; Carolina chickadees; tufted titmice; white-breasted nuthatches; Carolina and house wrens; blue-gray gnatcatchers; gray catbirds; solitary, red-eyed, and warbling vireos; Nashville, parula, yellow, yellow-rumped, black-throated green, black-and-white, and hooded warblers; ovenbirds; summer tanagers; rose-breasted grosbeaks; and chipping sparrows.

Of all these birds, none was as welcome as the **pileated woodpecker** that we encountered near our lunch stop at a secluded beach. It was working at extracting insects from a deep cavity it had dug in an oak snag directly across the river; perhaps it felt safe with the river between us. It continued with little apparent attention to the six intruders with three shiny canoes. It was a male with a bright red crest, red malar patch, white throat, and bold white line that ran from below its black mask into its cheeks and down onto its shoulder. The remainder of the bird was blackish brown, except that it showed a large white underwing patch in flight. It is our largest

Pileated woodpecker

North American woodpecker and the model for the Woody Woodpecker cartoon character.

Pileated woodpeckers normally utilize year-round territories and mate for life. Nest cavities are constructed in dead trees, usually 28 to 35 feet (8.5-10.7 m) above the ground, according to Terres in *The Audubon Society Encyclopedia of North American Birds*. Ehrlich and colleagues described an incident in which a female transferred eggs from a fallen nest tree to a second nest, and the pair succeeded in raising the brood.

They often dig huge gaping holes into dead and dying trees for insects, which make up about 75 percent of their diet; fruits and nuts make up the remainder. Their winter diet, especially during colder winters when most insects are unavailable, may be mostly ants. Their tongue is equipped with tiny barbs to aid in capturing insects, and they use it to probe into cavities dug with their sharp, heavy bill.

Our pileated woodpecker stayed for 20 minutes or more and then, apparently completing its lunch, flew off into the forest, flapping its broad wings like a huge bat. It called a loud "kuk kuk kuk kuk kuk," and immediately a second pileated, undoubtedly its mate, responded with a similar, but slightly higher-pitched, call from the forest beyond.

By midmorning, when the thermals began to rise along the forested slopes, a few soaring birds appeared in areas of open sky along the riverway. Turkey vultures, with their bicolored underwings and bare, red head, were most numerous. Stubby-tailed black vultures were present as well, flapping rapidly to gain elevation. But the only soaring hawk encountered that day were two red-tailed hawks, evident by their brick red tail and broad whitish wings with black edges. Later in the year, bald eagles can sometimes be found along the river and at adjacent lakes.

Many of the songbirds found along the river that September day were Neotropical migrants en route to the tropics for the winter. Only a fraction of the birds found in spring, summer, and fall remain through the winter. A few more northern nesters sometimes join them. The winter birds are surveyed annually as part of the Christmas Bird Counts that are taken during the holidays throughout North America. The 1992 Buffalo National River Christmas Count tallied 4,687 individuals of 64 species. The dozen most numerous birds, in descending order of abundance, included dark-eyed junco, American crow, eastern bluebird, Carolina chickadee, European starling, American robin, northern cardinal, tufted titmouse, white-throated sparrow, blue jay, northern flicker, and white-breasted nuthatch.

In summary, the park's bird checklist includes 189 species, of which 99 are listed as either permanent or summer residents and assumedly nest. Of those 99 species, 5 are water birds, 8 are hawks and owls, and 17 are warblers.

Birds of Special Interest
Green heron. Watch for this little heron along the riverway; it has a green back, black cap, and chestnut throat and breast.

Eastern screech-owl. This little forest owl with ear tufts is heard more often than seen. Its call is a whinney.

Red-bellied woodpecker. A medium-sized woodpecker with whitish underparts and a barred black-and-white back, it has a distinct "churr" call.

Pileated woodpecker. This is our largest woodpecker, a Woody Woodpecker look-alike.

Carolina wren. A large wren with reddish upperparts, buff underparts, and bold whitish eyebrows, it sings a loud and often continual "jibbidy" or "tea-kettle" song.

Blue-gray gnatcatcher. This long-tailed little bird looks like a miniature mockingbird and has a high-pitched buzzy call.

Eastern bluebird. Watch for this bird with a blue back and rusty underparts "flycatching" over fields.

Red-eyed vireo. Heard more than seen, it sings a series of single and double notes continually during spring and summer.

Blue grosbeak. Males are large-billed birds with all-blue plumage, except for rusty shoulder patches, they sing a series of sweet single notes.

Indigo bunting. Males are little indigo blue birds that sing loud songs of couplets from high posts in spring and summer.

American goldfinch. This is the common, bright yellow-and-black little bird of the fields; it flies in an undulating pattern.

26

Hot Springs National Park, Arkansas

Blue jays are everywhere at Hot Springs: along the Grand Promenade, at Gulpha Gorge Campground and Picnic Grounds, at the park's many overlooks, and on the trails. No other bird is so abundant as this blue-and-white, crested jay, with its harsh, scratchy "jay jay" calls and incongruous personality. It can be extremely secretive, sneaking up on a picnicker with great stealth one minute, and raising a loud, obnoxious fuss the next. Blue jays are members of the Corvidae, a widely distributed family of birds that includes 103 species worldwide. Other North American Corvids include ravens, crows, magpies, and Clark's nutcracker. All of these birds have evolved a high degree of intelligence. John Terres, in *The Audubon Society Encyclopedia of North American Birds,* points out that captive crows "can count up to three or four, are keen, wary birds, good at solving puzzles and at performing astonishing feats of memory, and quick to associate various noises and symbols with food."

Nesting blue jays are usually shy and place their nests in well-concealed locations. They utilize a wide variety of sites, from horizontal tree branches to dense tangles of vines. They also construct a false nest prior to building their true nest. And there are several records of blue jays appropriating the already constructed nests of another species, such as an American robin. However, most blue jay nests are built by the territorial pair, using plant materials like pieces of bark, sticks, moss, lichens, and grass. But they also take advantage of whatever might be available, such as pieces of paper, rags, and string. All this is cemented together with mud. Although the female

Blue jay

blue jay does most of the incubation, the male is usually nearby, and he often feeds his mate on the nest.

Their diet is primarily (about 75%) vegetable matter (acorns, fruit, nuts, and seeds), according to a study of 292 blue jay stomachs by ornithologist F.E.L. Beal, described in Arthur Bent's *Life Histories of North American Jays, Crows and Titmice.* The remainder of their diet is animal matter, including "insects, with a few spiders, myriapods, snails, and small vertebrates, such as fish, salamanders, tree frogs, mice and birds." Beal also reported that mineral matter (tiny pebbles) made up over 14 percent of the contents. These help to grind up hard seeds and beetle parts in the gullet. Blue jays also take advantage of the summer harvest by storing food in the soil, under litter, and in trees, for later use.

But despite blue jays' fascinating behavior, it is their voice that makes them most conspicuous. They are both mimics and ventriloquists. Although the typical "jay jay" call is best known, they possess an amazing repertoire of other calls and songs. Terres points out that the blue jay has a high pitched shriek when discovers enemy such as owl in daytime roost; utters great number of calls, including bell-like 'tull-ull,' ringing double note during which jay lowers and raises its head; mostly female utters rapid clicking call; also 'teekle' (like word "teacup"), and others; in concealment of evergreen will sing soft, barely audible, sweet, lisping notes; also utters exact imitation of screams of red-shouldered and other hawks; reported to mimic songs or calls of black-capped chickadee, eastern wood-pewee, northern (Baltimore) oriole, gray catbird, American goldfinch, and others. In some parts of the country, blue jays are migratory. At Hot Springs, they are present year-round. Although they once were wild birds of the forest, they have adapted to civilization and now are among our most popular avian neighbors.

The Park Environment
Hot Springs National Park has the distinction of being the oldest in the entire national park system. The U.S. Congress establishd "Hot Springs Reservation" in 1832, 40 years prior to Yellowstone National Park, "to protect the numerous hot springs at the base of Hot Springs Mountain." It was redesignated a national park in 1921, and has since been expanded to 5,543 acres (2,243 ha).

The park is in the Zig Zag Mountains on the eastern edge of the Ouachita (Watch-a-taw) Range. Fordyce, Sugarloaf, West, North, Hot Springs, and Indian mountains form a sort of horseshoe around the town of Hot Springs, with the open end to the northeast. Although the vegetative cover is mostly second-growth, much of the forest has reached mature conditions. Botanist Edward Dale, Jr., of the University of Arkansas, classified the Hot Springs forests into four categories: upland hardwoods, pine-oak-hickory, oak-hickory-pine, and mixed forest.

Upland hardwood communities lie along the ridge tops and gentle slopes. Dominant tree species include white, blackjack, black, and red oaks and mockernut hickory, with a few shortleaf pine and bitternut hickory. Pine-oak-hickory communities occur on the south-facing slopes near the ridge tops and are dominated by shortleaf pine, post and blackjack oaks, and black hickory. Similar oak-hickory-pine communities are dominated by post, blackjack, and red oaks and shortleaf pine. The mixed forest communities, such as those that occur along Gulpha Creek and in various upland ravines, include shortleaf pine and sweetgum with lesser numbers of blue beech, sycamore, beech, white oak, and black gum.

The visitor center is in downtown Hot Springs along Bath House Row in the historic Fordyce Bathhouse. It contains an information desk, orientation program, exhibits, 24 restored rooms, and a bookstore; bird field guides and a checklist are available. Interpretive activities include ranger-guided walks and evening programs at the Gulpha Gorge Campground Amphitheater. Schedules are posted at the campground and visitor center.

Additional information can be obtained from the Superintendent, Hot Springs National Park, P.O. Box 1860, Hot Springs, AR 71902-1860; (501) 623-1433.

Bird Life

Blue jays were not the only active birds at Gulpha Gorge Campground during my summer morning visit. American crows, Carolina wrens, American robins, brown thrashers, and northern cardinals were almost as numerous. The **American crows** were searching the lawns for scraps from the previous day. One family had usurped a garbage can that apparently had been raided by raccoons the night before, leaving a string of trash behind. They seemed to spend more time fending off other crows than eating breakfast.

Carolina wrens called "teadle teadle teadle" songs from the undergrowth. These wrens possessed reddish upperparts, bold whitish eyebrows, and buff underparts. Several young birds were chasing adults here and there for handouts. One especially aggressive fledgling had only a nub of a tail and pinfeathers protruding from its head. Apparently, it had not yet learned any of the numerous Carolina wren songs, as it offered little more than squeaky call notes. This wren is known to sing up to 41 different song types. For additional details about its vocal ability, see chapter 26 on Chickasaw.

Several young **American robins** with heavily spotted breasts were in company with the more brightly marked adults. I watched one adult, with its deep red breast and contrasting black head and yellow bill, searching for worms. It would run a few steps and then cock its head as if listening. Actually, ornithologists tell us that robins cock their heads to better see movement on the ground, not to hear. But whatever hunting method it was using, it seemed to work, because during the 3 or 4 minutes I watched the robin, it captured three large earthworms in about 30 square feet (2.8 sq m) of ground. At least one adult was apparently still on territory, for its loud caroling, "cheerily cheer-up cheerio," emanated from the high foliage of a sycamore.

Brown thrashers were also busy searching for breakfast. These long-tailed birds, with reddish backs and buff underparts with heavy dark streaks, stayed close to protective shrubbery instead of foraging on the open lawn like the robins. The brown thrasher is a nervous bird that darts into the thickets with the least provocation. From its hiding place it often calls sharp, scrappy "wheeu" notes. However, in spring and early summer, it fills the air with some of the finest bird-song imaginable, richer even than that of the closely related mock-ingbird. Thrasher songs consist of a series of phrases of two to four syllables, musical and varied, each one delivered as a separate state-ment of its own. Arthur Bent, in *Life Histories of North American Nuthatches, Wrens, Thrashers, and Their Allies,* quoted an interpreta-tion by Mrs. H. P. Cook: "'Hello, hello, yes, yes, yes, Who is this? Who is this? Well, well, well, I should say, I should say, How's that? How's that? I don't know, I don't know, What did you say? What did you say? Certainly, Certainly, Well, well, well, Not that I know of, Not that I know of, Tomorrow? Tomorrow? I guess so, I guess so, All right, All right, Goodbye, Goodbye.'"

One of the **northern cardinal** females in the campground was partially albino with a high white collar. It looked as if its head had been ducked into white paint, except that its bill had somehow retained its reddish color. Its mate possessed the typical bright red male plumage, except for its black face.

Several other less numerous species were found in the camp-ground. Tufted titmice called "peter peter peter" from the oaks. A mourning dove sang its sorrowful "whoo hooo-hoo" notes over and over. Blue-gray gnatcatchers were also present, evident from their wheezy songs. Downy and red-bellied woodpeckers called "peeet" and "chuur" notes, respectively. A pair of all-black common grackles were walking about the lawn searching for food. Carolina chickadees called thin "fee-bay" notes from the high foliage. The nasal "yank" notes of a white-breasted nuthatch echoed down from a high pine tree. And I also detected the "wheep" call of a great crested flycatcher.

As I crossed Gulpha Creek, a Louisiana waterthrush flew up from the stream bank with emphatic "chink" notes and landed on a rock downstream 75 feet (23 m) or so. Through binoculars, I could see its black-and-white body, bold whitish eyebrows, and long legs as it teetered up and down in its characteristic way. Farther up the creek, near the old stone bridge, an eastern phoebe called its distinct "fee-bee" song. And from the slope above the creek, a pileated wood-pecker called loud "wuk wuk wuk wuk" notes; a second pileated responded farther away. This is our largest woodpecker, a Woody Woodpecker look-alike with an all-dark body, black-and-white face pattern, and bright red crest. For more about this fascinating bird, see chapter 25 on Buffalo River.

The entire slope above the campground is dominated by short-leaf pines with a scattering of oaks and a few other hardwoods. I detected many of the same birds in this area as in the campground, plus a few others. The most outstanding was a wood thrush that sang a single "eee-o-lay" song and then was silent. It flew from its perch to the ground, where I watched it search for insects, very robinlike. Through binoculars, its reddish upperparts and whitish underparts with large black spots, were obvious. I could not help but think how uncharacteristic my sighting was, because this bird is usually in the deep forest, singing its flutelike song over and over. Each series of "eee-o-lay" notes is presented with a slightly different emphasis and tone. It is one of our most outstanding songsters.

Another bird encountered that morning was the **pine warbler**, a common species that is almost totally dependent upon pines. From the Goat Rock Overlook, I had a good view of a pair of these yellow-ish warblers searching the pine boughs almost at eye level. Their yellow underparts with faint streaks, their unstreaked, olive-green back, two distinct white wing bars, and dark tail with prominent white edges were obvious. While I was watching, the male put its head back and sang a musical trill. Paul Sykes, in *The Audubon Society Master Guide to Birding*, describes its song as "like Chipping Sparrow's song but softer, lower, and less rapid: 'zit, zit, ziz-ziz-ziz-ziz-ziz-ziz-ziz-ziz-ziz-ziz.' "

I encountered several other songbirds in the forest along the Goat Rock and Dogwood (upper loop) trails that morning: eastern wood-pewees, Acadian flycatchers, red-eyed and warbling vireos, black-and-white warblers, American redstarts, ovenbirds, and summer tanagers. And high overhead, numerous chimney swifts and a few purple mar-tins circled about in their search for high-flying insects.

The **American redstarts** were most impressive. Males are all-black except for orange-red patches on their sides, wings, and tail;

females are duller versions with yellow patches. Their song is a strident series of rapid notes that Paul Vickery, in *The Audubon Society Master Guide to Birding*, describes as "zee-zee-zee-zawaah (down-slurred), zee-zee-zee-zee-zweee (up-slurred)." The redstart exhibits distinct behavior when foraging for insects; it fans its tail and spreads its wings to flash its contrasting colors in an attempt to solicit movement of insects. And it often flutters down, almost parachutelike, in pursuit of flying insects.

Sunset Trail on West Mountain provides easy access into the upland hardwood community, as well as a pleasant hiking environment. Spring and early summer are the best times to find large numbers of birds. Common nesting forest birds here include mourning doves; ruby-throated hummingbirds; red-bellied, downy, hairy, and pileated woodpeckers; northern flickers; eastern wood-pewees; Acadian and great crested flycatchers; blue jays; Carolina chickadees; tufted titmice; Carolina wrens; blue-gray gnatcatchers; wood thrushes; American robins; red-eyed vireos; black-and-white warblers; American redstarts; ovenbirds; summer tanagers; northern cardinals; and chipping sparrows. Less numerous forest species include yellow-billed cuckoos, eastern screech-owls, great horned owls, and chuck-will's-widows. And at clearings, such as rights-of-way, eastern kingbirds, gray catbirds, brown thrashers, white-eyed vireos, yellow-breasted chats, indigo buntings, and rufous-sided towhees can also be found.

Blue-gray gnatcatchers were uncommonly abundant during an early June walk on the Sunset Trail to Music Mountain. Their wheezy songs seemed to emanate from all directions, and they immediately responded to any spishing or squeaking noise. At one time I had four within about 20 feet (6 m) of me, each scolding me with excited "tseeeeit" notes and flicking its long black-and-white tail up and down. It was easy to see why this bird is sometimes called "little blue-gray wren"; the movement of its tail is very wrenlike. Besides its small size and black tail with white outer edges, it has a bluish gray back, blackish cap, narrow white eye rings, and thin bill. It also is often characterized as a miniature mockingbird.

Blue-gray gnatcatchers are summer residents only at Hot Springs, migrating south for the winter months; they are one of our Neotropical migrants. Terres reported that a gnatcatcher banded in

Pennsylvania on "May 9, 1969, was killed by a boy with a slingshot at Llano Grande, Jalisco, Mexico, Nov. 1, 1970, when at least 2½-3 years or more old."

The **black-and-white warbler** is also a Neotropical migrant, and a fairly common nesting bird in Hot Springs' forest communities. It spends its winter months from south Texas to northern South America and the Greater Antilles. I have found this species wintering in mangrove forests in the Virgin Islands. Black-and-whites behave differently from most other warblers, foraging over tree trunks and branches like creepers, actually walking upside-down in their pursuit of insects. They are distinctly marked with black-and-white streaks and bold white eyebrows. Males possess a black throat, while the duller females have a white throat. And their songs are also unlike those of other warblers: "Unhurried, high, thin song of 6-8 'wee-see' couplets, with stress on first syllable," according to Vickery.

On another morning in mid-August, I walked this same trail to Music Mountain, finding only a fraction of the breeding birds. A great horned owl, not yet retired for the day, called a distant "hoo hoo hoo-hoo." Blue jays, Carolina wrens, American robins, and a mourning dove were at the parking area. Several chimney swifts and purple martins and a pair of common grackles flew overhead. Carolina chickadees and tufted titmice were detected along the start of the trail. A pair of pileated woodpeckers called from the north slope.

My only good series of bird sightings occurred near the summi,t where I encountered a party of early migrants. As might be expected, blue jays, tufted titmice, and northern cardinals were included. Blue-gray gnatcatchers, red-eyed vireos, and indigo buntings were most numerous. There were a few black-and-white warblers, summer and scarlet tanagers, and yellow-billed cuckoos. A single ruby-throated hummingbird, blue-winged and worm-eating warblers, and orchard oriole were in the party, as well. It was obvious that southbound movement had begun.

More **purple martins** were detected overhead, and I soon realized these birds were all moving in a southwesterly direction. Several were birds of the year, evident by their mousy plumage. I wondered where all these birds had nested, perhaps in martin houses at Hot Springs or in adjoining states to the north. But I was sure they all were en route south to Brazil's Amazon Valley, where they gather in great congregations, feeding on flying insects as well as ants and a few other ground insects. By the first of the year, however, they begin to move north, and a few reach the United States by late January. Many migrate up the coast into Mexico's Yucatan Peninsula, cross the Gulf of Mexico to Florida, Alabama, Mississippi, Louisiana, or Texas, and then disperse west, north, and east.

Purple martin males reach Hot Springs by mid to late February and immediately establish territories in anticipation of the females' arrival several days later. By late March, nesting is well under way, and a new crop of purple martins is out and about by mid-June.

With so many of the songbirds gone south, winter birding at Hot Springs is limited to permanent residents and a few species that come from father north for the winter. Examples include yellow-bellied sapsuckers; red-breasted nuthatches; brown creepers; winter wrens; cedar waxwings; yellow-rumped warblers; dark-eyed juncos; white-throated, fox, and song sparrows; and pine siskins.

Christmas Bird Counts, taken annually at Hot Springs, provide the best perspective on the winter bird populations. The 1992 Hot Springs Village Christmas Count tallied 2,149 individuals of 61 species. The dozen most numerous birds reported, in descending order of abundance, included dark-eyed junco, American crow, northern cardinal, eastern bluebird, eastern meadowlark, European starling, mourning dove, white-throated sparrow, American goldfinch, blue jay and Carolina chickadee (tied), and tufted titmouse.

In summary, the park's bird checklist includes 90 species, of which 64 are listed as either permanent or summer range and assumedly nest. Of those 64 species, 2 are water birds (green heron and yellow-crowned night-heron), 7 are hawks and owls, and 7 are warblers.

Birds of Special Interest
Purple martin. Few birds are so well-known and loved as these large swallows that utilize houses built especially for them.

Blue jay. This blue-and-white, crested bird, with a distinct "jay jay" call, can be found throughout the park year-round.

American crow. Watch for this all-black bird, usually in small flocks, about the campground and town; it has a loud "caw" call.

Carolina wren. This large wren with a reddish back, buff underparts, and bold whitish eyebrow frequents dense thickets.

Brown thrasher. A long, thin bird with a reddish back and buff underparts with many dark spots, it sings a wonderful song.

American robin. This well-known thrush spends much of its time searching for earthworms on lawns or singing cheery songs from high posts.

Blue-gray gnatcatcher. Like a miniature mockingbird, it has a long, loose tail, blue-gray back, and dark head with thin, white eye rings.

Black-and-white warbler. This black-and-white forest bird creeps about the woody vegetation, and sings a distinct song of high "wee-see" notes.

Pine warbler. It occurs only on pines, where it forages on the outer boughs; its song is a musical trill.

American redstart. Males are all-black with orange-red patches on their sides, wings, and tail; females are duller with yellow patches.

Northern cardinal. Males are all-red except for a black face, and females are duller versions with a red bill; these crested birds sing "cue cue cue."

27

Chickasaw National Recreation Area, Oklahoma

The Bromide Pavilion area was alive with birdsong that early spring morning. The melodic caroling of American robins was loudest. I listened to these red-breasted birds pour out their spirited whistles, "cheerily cheer-up cheerio," over and over again. Several were feeding on ripe fruits of a mulberry tree. At least two were young of the year; their heavily spotted breasts were obvious amid the fresh green foliage. Several of the adult robins were running here and there, cocking their heads to better see movements of their earthworm prey.

Carolina chickadees' thin, four-note whistles and "chick-a-dee-dee-dee" songs rang out from numerous locations in the canopy. Several members of a new family of these little tits flew from one tree to another, one after the other. The recently fledged youngsters were undoubtedly trying to keep up with their parents, all the while begging for handouts. Their coal black caps and throats, white cheeks, and long tails gleamed in the morning light.

The whistle songs of **tufted titmice**, loud and slurred "keter keter keter" notes, echoed from the adjacent vegetation. I located a pair of these crested birds, barely larger than the chickadees, but all-gray to whitish except for a tint of buff on their flanks and their black eyes. They were searching for insects, gleaning one leaf after the other. One held a green caterpillar in its bill and suddenly flew off, assumedly to feed youngsters in some nearby cavity nest.

Several other birds were singing from the row of trees bordering Rock Creek. I detected the hollow "wheep" and "whe whe whe" notes of a great crested flycatcher; the "que que que" of northern cardinals; the stuttering "jay" notes of blue jays; and the high-pitched "pik" of a downy woodpecker. A pair of brown-headed cowbirds, calling squeaky whistle notes, rushed overhead. I heard the rolling "churr" of a red-bellied woodpecker, and the "kuk kuk kuk" of a yellow-billed cuckoo. A red-eyed vireo sang a series of short whistle notes and the "teedle teedle teedle" of a Carolina wren resounded from the undergrowth.

The **Carolina wren** suddenly flew to an open branch of a nearby redbud tree, providing me with a wonderful view of this lovely song-ster. Its reddish back, buff underparts, and bold whitish eyebrows were highlighted by the morning light. It sang again in full view, as if it was putting on a show for my benefit only; its "jibbidy jibbidy jib-bidy" sounded somewhat different from its earlier song. It suddenly discovered a caterpillar on an adjacent leaf and captured it with a deft grab of its long bill. For a second or two it seemed to carefully examine its catch, then it dropped into the undergrowth out of sight. I wondered if it was feeding young in some secret cavity. Then it called again, even louder than before: "jibbidy jibbidy jibbidy."

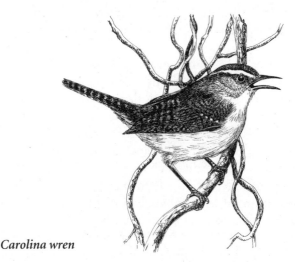

Carolina wren

The Park Environment

Chickasaw was one of the first-established federal preserves; it has a fascinating history. Early Indian inhabitants, the Caddos, Wichita or

Comanche, called it "the peaceful valley of rippling waters." The area became part of the Chickasaw Nation in 1855. But in 1902, 640 acres (259 ha) were transferred to the United States and named Sulphur Springs Reservation. In 1906, according to the park brochure, "the area was renamed Platt National Park in honor of Sen. Orville Hitchcock Platt. During the 1930s, the Civilian Conservation Corps built pavilions and roads, laid out trails, engineered waterfalls, and planted half a million trees and shrubs. In 1976, Platt National Park was combined with Arbuckle Recreation Area and additional lands to create a new national recreation area in honor of the land's long-time inhabitants: the Chickasaws."

The 9,931-acre (4,020-ha) Chickasaw National Recreation Area is dominated by Lake of the Arbuckles, a recreational area popular with boaters, fishermen, swimmers, and water-skiers. The original Travertine District, which lies along the southern edge of the town of Sulphur, contains Rock and Travertine creeks, numerous springs, 17 miles (27 km) of trails, and the Travertine Nature Center. This structure, built in 1969, contains an information desk, exhibits that include a few live animals, an auditorium where films are shown throughout the day, and a sales outlet; bird guides and a checklist are available.

The Travertine Nature Center serves as the centerpiece of the park's varied interpretive activities. Programs include nature walks and evening talks, as well as occasional owl talks and nighttime strolls.

Chickasaw is situated along the northern edge of the Arbuckle Mountains and is dominated by flat and rolling uplands, numerous creeks, and broad valleys. The higher and drier areas produce a variety of arid land plants, including cacti, yucca, Ashe juniper, hackberry, and blackjack and post oaks. The lower, more mesic areas contain a rich assortment of eastern forest trees and shrubs. The more common species include boxelder, dogwood, chinkapin and black oaks, black walnut, black hickory, sycamore, buttonbush, cottonwood, and willows.

Additional information can be obtained from the Superintendent, Chickasaw National Recreation Area, P.O. Box 201, Sulphur, OK 73086; (405) 622-3165.

Bird Life

Chickasaw's Carolina wrens sang a variety of songs during my May visit. I heard everything from the typical "tea-kettle" songs, commonly sung by East Coast birds, to "ka-dek ka-dek ka-dek" and "teddle teddle teddle," often ending with short "tek" notes. Paul Ehrlich and colleagues, in *The Birder's Handbook*, point out that male Carolina wrens "sing 27 to 41 different song types, singing one song repeatedly before switching to a different song; neighboring males frequently match song types. Males and females duet."

Carolina wrens were also common along the Antelope Springs Trail. One was singing near the parking area at the Travertine Nature Center. Its song seemed to blend with the louder songs of **northern cardinals**. At least three of these all-red birds were loudly proclaiming the new day. One male was perched on the nature center roof; its red plumage, black face, and tall crest made it stand out like a Christmas tree ornament. A second bird then joined the male, a female with dull reddish and buff plumage and a red bill. But when a blackish-billed youngster put in its appearance, begging for food, both adults flew off into the adjacent vegetation. The juvenile trailed along with thin "cue cue cue" notes.

The northern cardinal, sometimes called "red bird," for obvious reasons, is one of Chickasaw's most abundant birds. These full-time residents utilize feeders whenever possible. Park interpreter Chris Czazasty told me that cardinals frequent the bird feeder behind the nature center, especially in winter. She said that purple finches and American goldfinches are also abundant at that time of year. The northern cardinal is used as a symbol on directional signs along the Antelope Spring Trail.

A second all-red bird was also present at the nature center, the noncrested **summer tanager**. I found a pair of these birds chasing one another about the upper branches of the huge cottonwood tree that partly shades the building. The male's brilliant rose red plumage contrasted with that of the yellowish female; both birds had a yellowish bill. They called "ki-ti-tuck" time and again during a game of tag. Finally, after one particularly fast chase, the male sat alone at the tip of the tree and sang a lovely, robinlike song with clear, sweet phrases. But immediately after a second chorus, it dived from its perch to pursue its lady again. For information about this bird's strange diet, see chapter 24 on Ozark Riverways.

A white-breasted nuthatch also appeared on the tall cottonwood. I watched this bird walk straight down the tree trunk, pausing now and then to search the deep furrows for insects. What an incredible bird is the nuthatch, seemingly able to defy gravity by walking up and down or upside-down on trunks and high limbs.

I was then attracted to an **eastern phoebe** perched on the edge of the nature center roof. It held a large insect tightly in its bill and was pumping its tail with great enthusiasm. Through binoculars, I identified its prey as one of the beautiful black-and-green damselflies so common along the trail. I watched that eastern phoebe beat the wings off its prey with several strokes against the roof and then swallowed the rest. It flipped its long tail again, then sang a typical phoebe song, "fe-bee," with a slight buzz on the "ee." It remained just long enough to flip its tail again before flying off after another insect. Its blackish hood, gray-brown back and tail, and whitish underparts were most distinguished; in fall and winter, its underparts become yellowish.

Carolina chickadees, tufted titmice, American crows, blue jays, red-eyed vireos, red-bellied and downy woodpeckers, and a pileated woodpecker were all heard from the nature center. I detected more birds along the trail.

A **belted kingfisher** called in the distance; its dry rattle echoed through the forest. At one point along the trail, it flew up the creek, passing me with an added rattle call. I assumed it was nesting nearby in the dirt creek bank. This large bird actually tunnels up to 15 feet (4.5 m) into dirt banks at a slightly upward angle. At the end of the tunnel, it constructs a 6- to 10-inch-deep (15-25 cm) nest chamber. It digs with its bill and pushes the loose dirt out with its small, strong feet. The construction takes three days to three weeks, depending on the type of soil. The chamber is then lined with grass, feathers, and material from its pellets.

Kingfishers prey on fish, frogs, crayfish, and other aquatic species along Travertine Creek, usually by diving into the water to capture prey. Like many other birds that swallow their prey whole, kingfishers regurgitate pellets of undigested materials, bones, and scales.

The 1.5-mile (2.4-km) round-trip trail passes through a dense riparian habitat with trees up to 35 feet (11 m) in height. This same trail is used after dark for the park's "Down a Path Darkly" nature walk. According to Czazasty, the highlights of these strolls include barred owls, usually heard hooting up close; chuck-will's-widows, which call their names over and over after dark and hunt along the trail; and beavers, the park's construction engineers, which maintain the little side ponds along the creek.

Three short side trails that loop onto the adjacent hillside add drier habitat to a bird walk. I found four warblers along the central loop: black-and-white, prairie, and hooded warblers and an ovenbird. **Black-and-white warblers** were reasonably common, judging by the number of songs I detected along my route, although I observed only one. I attracted that songster out of the high foliage by imitating an eastern screech-owl. It was a brightly marked male with a coal black throat, white underparts, and black-and-white streaks elsewhere. It carefully looked me over before flying back into the canopy. Then, it sang again, a high, thin song of six to eight unhurried, but melodic "wee-see" notes.

The ovenbird sang a very different song, a loud and distinct "teach teach teach TEACH TEACH," each note louder than the previous one. I detected the hooded warbler by its metallic "chip," about halfway up the slope. It allowed me one quick look before it slipped away into the vegetation. And the prairie warbler, found among the drier juniper trees along the ridge, sang a song that was different again, a series of rising, thin, buzzing notes, "zee, zee, zee, zee, zee, zee, zee, zee."

Several other birds utilize the drier, more open country: I detected the deep "hooo hooo hooo" call of a greater roadrunner; a family of American crows cawed from a distant clump of junipers; and a northern mockingbird sang a variety of songs. A pair of brown thrashers were scratching among the leaf litter for food; at least two painted buntings were singing their spirited songs; a field sparrow sat singing at the top of an Ashe juniper; and several common grackles flew off as I approached.

Antelope Springs gushes out of the base of a rocky ridge to form a fast-flowing creek that joins Travertine Creek just above the Buffalo Spring confluence. I found the bird of the day en route back toward the nature center. I first detected the loud and emphatic "see-you see-you see-you" song some distance ahead. I walked slowly toward the song, trying to locate the perpetrator on the streambank through the vegetation. Then suddenly, it chipped and flew down the creek; I continued to follow. I finally reached an opening on the trail where I could clearly see along the creek bank, and I froze in place. For there, not more than 20 feet (6 m) away, was a **Louisiana waterthrush**. Its long, orangish legs, streaked underparts, dark brown back, and bold white eyebrows were obvious. It moved along the rocky creek bank in a jerky fashion, teetering in its search for insects. It suddenly stopped and sang a complete song, "see-you see-you see-you chew chew to-wee." Its song rang loud and clear above the rushing waters of Travertine Creek. Then it ran forward a few feet, grabbed an insect, and, with a sharp "tich" call, flew down the creek out of sight. I assumed it was delivering food to a waiting family.

Later in the morning I visited Bromide Hill, where I walked the short distance to an overlook above Rock Creek and the surrounding area. Several purple martins, probably nesting in martin houses in Sulphur, cruised over the little valley. Chimney swifts were present, too; their swept-back wings and cigar-shaped bodies allow them to fly much faster than the purple martins. Turkey and black vultures were soaring on the thermals above the steep ridge. Then a broad-winged hawk appeared, flying lower over the canopy; its dark back and banded tail were visible from my perch.

Purple martins are spring and summer residents only at Chickasaw, departing in mid to late summer for their wintering ground far to the south in Brazil. They are Neotropical migrants, which nest in the United States and spend the other half of their lives in the tropics. These wonderful birds, our longtime harbingers of spring, are threatened by a variety of human activities, such as overuse of pesticides. Their continued survival depends on the protection they receive in both their homes.

About the same time that the purple martins and a few other early migrants depart, species from farther north begin to trickle through the Chickasaw area. The fall and spring migrations can be exciting times for bird finding. A wide variety of water birds can be expected at area lakes and ponds. Common waterfowl at these times of year include Canada geese, green-winged and blue-winged teal, mallards, northern pintails, northern shovelers, gadwalls, American wigeon, redheads, lesser scaup, buffleheads, ruddy ducks, and common mergansers. Other migrant water birds include eared grebes, American white pelicans, double-crested cormorants, American coots, common moorhens, and Franklin's gulls. At times, Franklin's gulls are the most numerous bird about area lakes.

Many of these water birds remain all winter. In addition, up to ten bald eagles frequent Lake of the Arbuckles, fishing the waters or searching for carrion along the shore. They remain into April, and then depart for their northern breeding grounds. About that time, the earliest purple martins arrive from the south, checking their old haunts or scouting out new nesting sites. The breeding season begins once again.

In summary, the park (area) checklist of birds includes about 260 species; of those, 140 are listed as either permanent or summer residents and assumedly nest. Twenty-one of the 140 species are water birds (cormorant, waterfowl, waders, rails, and shorebirds), 15 are hawks and owls, and 14 are warblers. Sixty-seven species are listed as winter visitors only, but many of these must also be migrants.

Birds of Special Interest
Belted kingfisher. Watch for this heavy-billed bird along the creeks where it nests in the dirt banks and captures prey by diving headfirst into the water.

Eastern phoebe. This little flycatcher often nests on buildings; it flips its tail and sings spirited "fe-bee" songs.

Carolina chickadee. One of the park's most common birds, its coal black cap and throat, white underparts, and long tail are its most obvious features.

Tufted titmouse. This is the common little grayish bird with a tall crest; it often sings a loud "keter keter keter" song.

Carolina wren. This reddish songster with bold whitish eyebrows is one of the park's most common residents, but it is usually shy and secretive.

American robin. It prefers open, grassy areas and is easily identified by its all-red breast and upright stance.

Black-and-white warbler. This little warbler usually stays in the canopy and is best detected by its distinct, high-pitched song, a series of thin, but melodic, "wee-see" notes.

Louisiana waterthrush. Its loud and emphatic song can be heard along the creeks in summer; it is distinguished by its long, orangish legs, streaked underparts, and bold whitish eyebrows.

Summer tanager. Males are rose red with a yellowish bill; they frequent the canopy of cottonwoods and other broadleaf trees in summer.

Northern cardinal. A full-time resident, it has a tall crest and reddish bill; the male's plumage is bright red.

28

Amistad National Recreation Area, Texas

The dawn literally exploded with birdsong. Northern cardinals, yellow-breasted chats, northern mockingbirds, and painted buntings were the earliest birds to the songfest. Chats and mockingbirds had sung their territorial songs throughout much of the night. But with the dawn, other nesters joined the choir. As daylight began to spread, a dozen or more lesser nighthawks dominated the air, swooping and circling with fluttering wing beats. Their low, purring trills were all prevailing.

From where Spur 406 road runs into the reservoir, I walked slowly up the road through the campground and surrounding vegetation. The mournful calls of mourning doves were detected next. Then Bewick's wrens and Bell's vireos added their voices to the concert. Bewick's wrens sang rather complex songs of variable notes ending with musical trills. Bell's vireos' songs were distinct because of their habit of asking then quickly answering questions. A house finch joined in. Red-winged blackbirds called "konk-a-ree" from the adjacent shoreline. And from far across the little bay, I detected the distinct gobbling of a wild turkey. But still, only the nighthawks were visible.

Suddenly, a **yellow-breasted chat** arose from a nearby acacia. I watched as it flew 40 or 50 feet (15-18 m) into the air, and then, with wings flapping like a huge butterfly, it fluttered downward. Its descending display included an amazing series of whistles, mews, grunts, and groans. And when it alighted on a secluded perch it continued its barrage of calls. I moved to the far side of the road, where I could clearly see this highly vocal warbler. Its bright yellow breast and throat contrasted with its olive-green back and bold, white spectacles.

By now birds were moving over the water. Three great egrets flew by, their long white wings beating slowly. A great blue heron, with its even slower wing beats, passed over in the opposite direction. Five blue-winged teal zoomed across the water and landed among the snags on the far shore. Through binoculars, I could see the males' distinct white crescent patch in front of each eye. Nearby was a pair of pied-billed grebes, and farther to the right was a flock of **American coots**. These plump, all-black water birds with white bills were bathing and preening, preparing for the new day. Coots are members of the rail family (Rallidae), not ducks. They can be extremely aggressive with each other. One may actually grab a neighbor with a clawed foot, slap with the other foot, and jab with its heavy bill. Paul Ehrlich and colleagues, in *The Birder's Handbook*, point out that the aggressor's aim is "to push the opponent onto its back and, in some cases, hold it underwater." These coots seemed too docile to have earned such a reputation; they are among the reservoir's most visible and abundant residents.

American coots

On the near shore was a pair of mallardlike ducks. I studied these two carefully because mallards are winter residents at Amistad only; they should be far north by now, in late April. Neither has the typical green head of a mallard drake, and both showed dark blue speculums bordered with white on their wings. Then I realized that they were Mexican ducks, a subspecies of mallard that was once a separate species. These birds apparently had not interbred with the dominant mallard. They exhibited true Mexican duck traits: Both sexes were heavily streaked above and spotted below, the male had a yellow-orange bill with a dark ridge, and the female possessed an unmarked yellow-green bill. My identification was further confirmed when I discovered three more Mexican duck pairs that morning.

Altogether, I found 52 species from the roadway in about 3 hours. Most interesting was the diversity of species within that patch of riparian habitat. For instance, both the western Bullock's oriole and the eastern orchard oriole were present, chasing one another about the mesquite and huisache in typical oriole courting fashion. Northern bobwhites, apparently at the western edge of their range, were common there, too, delivering their loud "bob-white" calls with great vigor. I also discovered a few brown-crested flycatchers and long-billed thrashers and numerous olive sparrows. These three are Mexican birds that range north only to south Texas and up the Rio Grande only so far, apparently, as Amistad.

The Park Environment
Amistad National Recreation Area is best known as a boating and fishing reservoir that extends from Del Rio, Texas, up the Rio Grande for 74 miles (119 km) beyond the dam. Elevations range from 900 to 1,500 feet (274-457 m) above sea level. Amistad Reservoir, with its 850 miles (1,368 km) of shoreline, backs up into the Devil's River for 25 miles (40 km) and the Pecos River for 14 miles (22 km). The non-flooded riparian zones, as well as a few side canyons, contain remnants of the original environment.

The riparian zones comprise scattered stands of giant and common reeds and cattail, honey mesquite, willows, seepwillow, tree tobacco, and tamarisk, with an understory dominated by skeletonleaf goldeneye. Drainages that flow into the reservoir are often narrow and insignificant, but a few, such as lower California Creek (on Spur

406) and Lowry Spring, possess a luxuriant growth of trees and shrubs. Most common species in this habitat are honey mesquite, blackbrush acacia, huisache, catclaw guajillo, little walnut, Texas mountain-laurel, Texas persimmon, little-leaf leadtree, and seepwillow.

The open, drier flats above the reservoir are influenced by Chihuahuan Desert flora to the west and Tamaulipan Scrub flora to the southeast. Indicator species of the Chihuahuan Desert region include lechuguilla, candelilla, creosote bush, tarbush, ocotillo, and mariola. Indicator plants of the Tamaulipan Scrub region include blackbrush acacia, cenizo, desert yaupon, and Texas mountain-laurel. Common widespread species include guayacan, wolfberry, brush myrtlecroton, sacahuista, sotol, and yuccas.

Park headquarters, located on Highway 90 just north of Del Rio, has an information desk and a sales outlet; bird guides and a checklist are available. The Rough Canyon Ranger Station has an information desk and exhibits. The International Boundary and Water Commission Visitor Center on the U.S. side of Amistad Dam, which contains a few exhibits on the construction of the dam, is operated by the National Park Service in summer.

Interpretive activities during the winter months include one or two evening programs and one or two daytime activities weekly. Other programs are available on request. The park has three self-guiding trails: at Diablo East, Mouth of the Pecos, and Parida Cave.

Additional information can be obtained from the Superintendent, Amistad National Recreation Area, P.O. Box 420367, Del Rio, TX 78842-0367; (210) 775-7491.

Bird Life

Amistad's riparian vegetation, like that at Spur 406 Campground, supports the most birds in spring and summer. Besides those birds mentioned above, this is where you are most likely to find the outstanding **vermilion flycatcher**. Males sport bright red underparts and crown, which contrast with their deep brown back, tail, wings, and cheeks; females are duller versions of the males. Because of the male's fiery plumage, in Latin America it is known as *la brasita de fuego*, or "little coal of fire." During the breeding season, males perform amazing aerial displays much like those of the neighboring chats. They fly

high in the air and descend with wings pumping while singing a tinkling song, "pit-a-see pit-a-see."

Two *Myiarchus* flycatchers can be found in this habitat, the
brown-crested flycatcher and the slightly smaller and more common
ash-throated flycatcher. But neither can match the vermilion flycatcher in dress and personality. Brown-crested and ash-throats are
brownish above and possess a gray to ashy throat, yellowish belly,
and buff tail and wings that show a reddish tinge. They can be difficult to tell apart, but the brown-crested flycatcher is a bulkier bird
with a heavier bill and a distinctly yellow belly. In addition, brown-
crested flycatchers produce sharp "whit" or "queet" calls, while ash-
throat calls are two-syllabled, "ka-brick" or "ka-wheer." Both are cavity-nesters that utilize vacant woodpecker nests and natural holes in
trees and shrubs. Vermilion flycatchers construct small grass and
twig nests on the lower branches of woody plants; they are usually
easy to locate.

Two additional flycatchers frequent these areas as well. Scissor-
tailed flycatchers, with their long, deeply forked tails, often can be
found perched on wires, tall poles, or trees in the open. The smaller
black phoebe usually perches on snags over the water. Its all-black
body and snow white belly make identification easy.

I also spent several hours at Lowry Spring, located along a paved
roadway northeast of Rough Canyon. Betty and I had the place all to
ourselves; apparently it is remote enough to receive little use. But the
bird life was almost a duplicate of what I had found at the Spur 406
Campground area, with a few additions. Several tall Vasey shin oaks
in the rocky drainage apparently enhanced the habitat enough to
attract tufted titmice, blue-gray gnatcatchers, white-eyed vireos, and
summer tanagers.

Painted buntings were abundant along the drainage, singing
their spirited songs from various shrubs. Males perched in full view
so that their contrasting, almost gaudy, plumage was obvious. Their
bright blue head, red underparts, and greenish yellow back stood
out. Through binoculars, I could also see their red eye rings and
short, conical bill. A truly gorgeous creature. Females possess a lime
green back and duller underparts. And their songs rang out in clear,
musical couplets, "pew-eate, pew-eata, j-eata, you-too."

Also along the drainage I discovered a **great horned owl** perched on a tree branch. It watched me intently, but remained still as I approached. Partly concealed by foliage, it apparently did not feel threatened. A large (18-25 in or 46-64 cm) owl with ear tufts and yellow eyes, it is sometimes seen perched on utility poles along highways at dusk and dawn. Its loud song, a deep "hoo hoo hoo-hoo," can usually be heard throughout the night.

The great horned owl is one of several birds that nest on the high limestone cliffs along the many canyons, even the deep canyons of the Rio Grande, Pecos, and Devils rivers. Great blue herons; black and turkey vultures; red-tailed hawks; cliff, cave, and barn swallows; and rock and canyon wrens also nest there.

When nesting, **great blue herons** can usually be detected from a considerable distance. They emit terrible grunts and groans that echo off the cliff and seem to permeate the entire area. They select small, secure ledges, often with small shrubs, where they build bulky stick nests. Several nests were visible on the cliff ledges across the Pecos River from the Pecos River Picnic Site overlook one spring day.

Great blue herons, tall, skinny birds with long legs and neck, a huge yellow bill, and black-and-white plumage, fish the shoreline of the reservoir year-round. Although they are most active during the morning and evening hours, they can be busy all day and all night when feeding young. They usually fish by standing perfectly still over shallow water, beak poised for a instant thrust at passing prey. They capture small fish in their bill sidewise, but they actually spear larger fish. And like most predators, they are opportunists that will take a wide variety of prey, ranging from insects to other birds, reptiles, amphibians, and even mammals like mice and rats.

The open shoreline of the reservoir is seldom without the constant "kill-dee" calls of **killdeers**, another common year-round resident. If disturbed, this shorebird can cause a tremendous fuss, especially when nesting. Then it may actually pretend injury by dragging a wing, as if broken, as it runs in the opposite direction from its nest. Thus, a predator like a coyote or badger may be enticed away from the nest. But just when the predator is about to close in, the killdeer will "recover" and fly off to safety.

Although killdeers are most numerous along the moist shoreline of the reservoir, they occasionally are found in drier sites some distance from the water. Even there, they may fly up with great agitation, loudly calling their piercing "kill-dee" or "dee-dee-dee" cries.

To the inexperienced eye, the drier shoreline beyond is an uninviting desertscape devoid of wildlife, where the dominant vegetation consists of thorny or armored shrubs. But the naturalist, or anyone who takes time to walk out into the desert scrub, will find this habitat alive with birds. Especially in spring, when birds are most active in their territorial defense, a short walk can easily produce a dozen or more species.

Cactus wrens and northern mockingbirds are likely to be detected first, primarily due to their loud singing and habit of perching on top of the tallest shrubs. The **cactus wren** sings a rollicking, throaty "chug-chug-chug-chug" or "cora cora cora cora" song that is more a series of grunts than a melodic aria. Its song is usually delivered with so much enthusiasm that it can hardly be ignored. Its bulky, football-sized nest apparently stuck haphazardly among the thorny branches of an acacia or the protective spines of a cactus, is easily seen. The male usually constructs a second nest while the female is incubating. The second nest is used for a second clutch or for roosting; the nests normally are maintained year-round.

Cactus wren

The cactus wren is a robin-sized, chunky bird with a heavy bill, dark brown spots on its whitish underparts, streaked back, rusty crown, and bold, whitish eyebrows. Its behavior also helps with identification. Besides singing from the tops of shrubs, it exhibits fascinating feeding behavior. It actually pries up pieces of debris to search underneath for insects. But its diet is not limited to insects. This aggressive wren captures small lizards and frogs, and when cactus fruit is ripe it takes advantage of those delicacies, as well.

I suspect there is unending competition between the cactus wren and the mockingbird for which can be more obnoxious during the nesting season. The **northern mockingbirds**, true to its ame, often mimics cactus wren songs. Then suddenly, it switches to a totally different song, often one with various phrases and a melody. Besides being just as loud as the neighboring wrens, the mockingbird often sings off and on throughout the night, after the cactus wren has retired. Aretas Saunders, in his classic book, *A Guide to Bird Songs*, wrote that the "song is made up of imitations of other birds, and not only these, but of other kinds of animal life and of inanimate sounds. These are interpolated into the middle of the song, and sometimes songs are largely made up of imitations. The bird often sings in flight, and commonly does this on moonlight nights, at time apparently singing almost all night long." It has been called our "national songbird." And in Texas, it is the official state bird.

The mockingbird is one of our most recognized birds, slim, gray-and-white, with a long tail. Often found in gardens and fields, it also is a common bird of the southwestern deserts. There it feeds on a wide variety of foods, from insects to fruit. When searching for insects, it often uses its contrasting plumage to advantage. "Wing flashing," or quickly opening and closing its wings while perched on a shrub or on the ground, tends to flush insects. This behavior may also be used to distract predators.

There are several other common desert birds at Amistad. The smallest is the verdin, with gray body, yellow face, and chestnut wing patches. One of the largest is the curve-billed thrasher, brownish gray with lightly spotted underparts and yellow-orange eyes. The black-throated sparrow possesses a black throat and white stripes above and below the eyes; it seems to prefer the most arid habitats. Conversely, the nondescript Cassin's sparrow appears only after high to moderate rainfall; it is best detected by its constant singing from a perch or while "sky larking." The rufous-crowned sparrow may be one of the shyest of sparrows. This bird sings a song of jumbled whistle notes and prefers rocky terrain. And the lark sparrow can be abundant in spring and summer; this large sparrow is easy to identify by its chestnut, white, and black head, white underparts with a central breast spot, and black tail with conspicuous white corners.

Another common arid land bird is the **pyrrhuloxia**, a species that closely resembles the cardinal, but lacks the all-red body and bill. Pyrrhuloxia males have a red face, throat, tip of the crest, belly, and tail but otherwise are a subtle tan. Females are duller versions of the males, but both have a yellow bill.

Amistad's desert quail is the **scaled quail**, sometimes called "cottontop" because of its whitish crest, which looks like a tuft of cotton. It also is known as "blue quail" because of its overall bluish color. However, seen up-close, its breast feathers appear scaled, providing its proper name. In spite of its relative abundance, it is more often heard than seen. This bird has a loud, nasal, almost obnoxious "pe-cos" call, not like the clear "bob-white" call of that quail.

Most of Amistad's dry land birds are full-time residents, remaining on preferred territories year-round. Fall migrants and wintering species often substantially add to the bird life in areas with abundant seeds and fruit. And by late fall, northern water birds begin to arrive. Many remain all winter, while others continue south to favored sites in Mexico. Various species of ducks stay until spring, feeding around the lake and flocking in deeper water overnight. The most common species include mallard, northern pintail, American wigeon, and ring-necked duck. Smaller numbers of blue-winged teal, northern shovelers, gadwalls, redheads, common goldeneyes, buffleheads, and ruddy ducks can also be expected. American white pelicans also fish the reservoir in winter; according to Superintendent Robert Reyes, they are most common at Pecos River, Rio Grande, Cow Creek, and San Pedro Canyon.

Winter bird populations are censused each year in Christmas Bird Counts. The Del Rio Count includes only a portion of the park, but provides the best indication of the area's species abundance. For example, the 1991 count produced 9,386 individuals of 125 species. The dozen most numerous species, in descending order of abundance, included American coot, double-crested cormorant, great-tailed grackle, house sparrow, red-winged blackbird, meadowlarks (western and eastern), white-crowned sparrow, house finch, killdeer, brown-headed cowbird, ring-billed gull, and European starling.

In summary, the park checklist of birds includes 204 species. Ninety-six of those are listed for summer and presumedly nest. Of those 96 species, 14 are waterbirds, 7 are hawks and owls, and 3 are warblers.

Birds of Special Interest

Great blue heron. This tall, long-legged wader with a 6-foot wingspan can be expected anywhere in the park; it nests on high cliffs.

American coot. Small to huge flocks of these chubby all-black birds with white bills occur along the shore and in secluded bays of the reservoir year-round.

Killdeer. This shorebird is best recognized by its loud "kill-dee" calls; it is a year-round resident that frequents moist areas surrounding the reservoir.

Scaled quail. Locally called "blue quail" because of its overall bluish appearance, it has a loud, obnoxious call, "pe-cos."

Great horned owl. This large "horned" owl is often seen perched on high posts or heard singing deep "hoo hoo hoo-hoo" songs after dark.

Vermilion flycatcher. With its fiery red underparts and dark brown back, this little songbird cannot be mistaken for any other species; it prefers open acacias near wetlands.

Cactus wren. This is the plump, all-brown bird of the arid landscapes; its song is a distinct, rollicking "chug chug chug chug" or "chur chur chur chur."

Northern mockingbird. One of our best-known birds, it can imitate almost any bird or sound and is common throughout Amistad's arid landscapes.

Yellow-breasted chat. A common summer resident at riparian areas, it sings a wild assortment of notes and possesses all-yellow underparts, olive-green back, and white spectacles.

Pyrrhuloxia. This is the cardinal look-alike without the all-red plumage; it is overall tan with a red chest, crest, and tail and a yellowish (not red) bill.

Painted bunting. Males are gorgeous little birds with a bright blue hood, rose red underparts and rump, and yellow-green back.

29

Padre Island National Seashore, Texas

Orioles decorated the willows like bright ornaments on a Christmas tree. Their black-and-orange plumage contrasted with the fresh green leaves. I counted over 50 orioles before I gave up and estimated the flock at about 115 birds. They were flying back and forth among the willows and the weedy surroundings. Most of the orioles were males, although I also saw a few much duller females. At least two males were western Bullock's orioles; the remainder were the more brightly colored, eastern Baltimore orioles.

I had a wonderful view of the willows and surrounding area from my vehicle, which I had pulled off the Bird Basin Road. The vehicle made a superb blind; the birds appeared to be oblivious to my presence after the first few seconds. With binoculars, I had a ringside seat.

Several other bird species were there among the willows. At least 35 orchard orioles were flying with the larger northern orioles, perhaps members of the same flock of migrants. Two western kingbirds were perched on the nearest treetop; their yellow and gray underparts and black tail with white outer edges were obvious. Four eastern kingbirds, two scissor-tailed flycatchers, and a rose-breasted grosbeak male were perched nearby. All the birds amid the outer branches were hanging on tight as the willow swayed with the strong north wind.

The smaller birds stayed among the lower branches and at the base of the willow: male painted and indigo buntings, male blue grosbeaks, gray catbirds, and a lone veery, warbling vireo, chipping sparrow, male summer tanager, and northern cardinal. Also during that hour, I identified six warbler species: two black-throated greens and lone Tennessee, yellow, black-and-white, and hooded warblers; common yellowthroat; and northern waterthrush. In the middle of all this, a huge flock of dickcissels, as many as 200 of these active finches, suddenly descended onto the willows. Their yellow, black, and brown plumage added to the myriad of colors before me. It became a kaleidoscope of birds, shifting about to accommodate the buzzing newcomers.

As I watched with wonder, I realized that I was witnessing a fall-out of migrants. Many of my willow tree ornaments were undoubt-edly following the island northward, from one shrub or tree to the next. But several of the other birds had probably flown across the gulf from Mexico's Yucatan Peninsula, turning inland when they encountered the strong north winds of a storm front. That late April afternoon had produced all the right conditions for a spectacular fallout. But the following morning when I returned, the willows were bare of birds. Overnight, all had apparently continued their north-ward journey.

The Park Environment

Padre Island National Seashore "is one of the longest stretches of primitive, undeveloped ocean beach in the United States," according to the park brochure. Here along the Texas gulf coast is 70 miles (113 km) of "white sand-and-shell beaches, picturesque windswept dunes, wild landscapes of grasslands and tidal flats teeming with shore life, and warm offshore waters." Here, also, is a bounty of wildlife, includ-ing the Kemp's Ridley sea turtle, one of the world's most endangered vertebrates, and more than 335 species of birds.

Padre Island contains a variety of habitats, from the murky waters of the Gulf of Mexico to a broad, white-sand beach, 30-foot (9-m) dunes, expanses of waving grasses, scattered freshwater wet-lands, open tidal flats, and the blue waters of Laguna Madre with its line of spoil islands. The spoil islands are products of dredged mate-rials deposited along the Intracoastal Waterway, a man-made channel that follows the coastline for 1,116 miles (1,796 km) between St. Marks, Florida, and Brownsville, Texas.

Vegetation on the beach is sparse, due to continuous salt spray and tidal effects, but the foredunes and backdunes support several hardy plant species. These include a few grasses and pigweeds, beach tea, beach evening-primrose, morning glory, and sea ox-eye. Sea oats often provide picturesque groupings on the higher dunes. Aquatic and marsh vegetation fills swales and depressions, especially in wet years, when rushes, sedges, waterlilies, and cattails can be common.

Much of the island is dominated by vast expanses of grass, although scattered shrubs and small trees grow on a few drier sites. Fred Jones, in *Flora of the Texas Coastal Bend*, lists two dominant groups of grasses: buffalo, three-awn, and the taller silver bluestem on the clay soils, and seacoast and big bluestems, tanglehead, and trichloris on sandy soils. Honey mesquite, pricklypear cactus, hackberry, live oak, and black willow are a few of the infrequent woody plants.

Access to the national seashore by land is limited to Highway 358 (Padre Island Drive) from Corpus Christi, or Highway 361 from Port Aransas to Park Road 22, which crosses the Kennedy Causeway to the island and extends south into the park for only 12 miles (19 km). An additional 55 miles (88-km) of the Gulf beach is open to four-wheel-drive vehicles, and a 5-mile (8-km) closed section of beach lies to the north. Paved Park Road 22 ends at Malaquite Beach, the site of the park's visitor center, an observation deck, changing rooms, snack bar, gift shop, and campground. The visitor center has an information desk, orientation program, a few exhibits, and a sales outlet; bird field guides and a checklist are available.

Interpretive activities include evening programs and beach walks in the summer and the Grasslands Nature Trail, located amid the dunes near the park entrance.

On April 8, 1968, Lady Bird Johnson, then First Lady of the United States, dedicated this new national seashore with these words: "Her treasure is the gold of her sun, the silver of her moonlight, and the sapphire of her pearl-crested waves. This treasure requires no iron strong box. It is safe from the greedy hands of man . . . I dedicate it with the hope that we—as its stewards—will be worthy of the trust."

Additional information can be obtained from the Superintendent, Padre Island National Seashore, 9405 South Padre Island Drive, Corpus Christi, TX 78418; (512) 949-8068.

Bird Life

Of the millions of migrant birds that pass through Padre Island in spring and fall, none is as carefully monitored as the **peregrine falcon**. Peregrines and Padre Island have become synonymous; more of these magnificent creatures can be found here during migration than anywhere else in North America. Raptor biologist Thomas Maechtle reported in 1988, that Padre Island is "the only known locality in the Western Hemisphere where Peregrine Falcons can be found in concentrations during the spring migration." In spring of that year, Maechtle and colleagues observed 1,497 peregrines in 770 hours; that fall, they observed 953 peregrines in 656 hours. They captured birds that had been banded in Greenland, on the Seward Peninsula and along the Colville and Kuskokwim rivers, Alaska, on Florida's Dry Tortugas, on Assateague Island, Maryland, and in New Jersey. A female peregrine banded at Padre Island on October 17, 1987, raised two young in 1988 on the Lower Yukon River, near Holy Cross, Alaska.

Peregrine falcon

In 1980, raptor biologist Grainger Hunt studied peregrine food habits on Padre Island, identifying 77 prey species. These included mourning doves (11), cattle egrets (6), blue-winged teal (6), white-winged doves (5), purple gallinules (4), indigo buntings (4), gray cat-birds (3), yellow-breasted chats (3), soras (2), common moorhens (2), northern shovelers (2), and an American avocet, blue grosbeak, thrushes, sparrows, and orioles.

Most sightings of this large falcon here are from the broad tidal flats, with a moderate number of sightings from the beach and dunes. The windswept flats are studded with small vegetated sand dunes, creating ideal perches. But the most exciting observations are of hunting birds. One of the world's fastest creatures, the peregrine, can stoop at more than 200 miles (322 km) per hour. Watching a peregrine in a power dive or chasing down its prey is an unforget-table experience.

One April morning, I walked Malaquite Beach for about 2 hours, recording all the birds encountered. As expected, the scene was dom-inated by gulls, terns, and shorebirds. Most numerous were the **laughing gulls**, medium-sized gulls with a black hood with slivers of white above and below the eyes, deep red bill, gray back, slate gray wings with black tips, and a snow white neck and belly, its full breed-

Laughing gull

ing plumage. In winter, these gulls lose their all-black hood and red bill color. But that day, the brightly marked gulls were practically everywhere I looked, sitting along the beach or flying overhead and as far out over the gulf as I could see.

Laughing gulls are undoubtedly among the best representatives of the wide assortment of gulf coast birds. They occur in abundance along the entire southeast coast, and scattered populations also exist along the Atlantic coast as far north as Nova Scotia. Their name is derived from their laughlike call, a drawn-out "hah-ha-ha-ha" or "ka-ha ka-ha."

I also identified several terns on my walk. **Royal terns** were most numerous and easily identified by their moderate size, a couple of inches larger than laughing gulls, and their orange-red bill, solid black cap, white forehead and underparts, and high-pitched "keer" call. A few Caspian terns, a similar but somewhat larger, more robust bird with a bloodred bill, were also present.

Sandwich terns were common, as well. These smaller terns were distinguished by their black bill with a yellow tip. I watched several of these gregarious terns fishing amid the waves just offshore. Flying 30 to 40 feet (9-12 m) above the water they suddenly wheeled and plunged headfirst into the surf, going under for 2 to 4 seconds before emerging with a fish held tightly in their bill. I also saw numerous Forster's terns, with their orangish bill with a black tip; tiny least terns, with their nervous flight; and gull-billed terns, which resemble gulls.

Shorebirds were abundant along the surfline, running here and there to retrieve tiny creatures left by the retreating waters. That day, The most abundant shorebird was the **sanderling**, a whitish bird with black shoulders; breeding birds become rust-colored. But the Padre Island sanderlings were still in their pale winter plumage. Except for a few that seemed asleep, with their head resting along their body, all the three hundred or so that I saw on my walk were actively feeding. I could not help but think of Ralph Palmer's description of a feeding sanderling in Matthiessen and Palmer's *The Shorebirds of North America*: "It gives an impression almost of desperation—as though striving mightly to snatch tiny animals from the wet sand the moment they are exposed and before they can settle beneath the surface." Palmer added that "in addition to snatching, the Sanderling has a trick of probing rapidly and repeatedly, without halting, with bill-tip open a couple of millimeters."

Willets were almost as numerous, but solitary instead of in flocks. Willets are much larger than sanderlings and stand upright on long bluish legs. They possess dull, somewhat mottled gray plumage and a fairly long, black bill. However, once they fly or spread their wings, they show a striking black-and-white pattern on their wings and tail. And if disturbed, they can be extremely noisy; they may carry on excessively with loud and obnoxious calls, like "will-it will-it," "kuk kuk kuk, wek wek wek," or "kip kip kip." These resident shorebirds nest among the wetland grasses in isolated areas.

Other shorebirds found that morning included a number of ruddy turnstones, with a black throat, reddish back, bright orange legs, and slightly upturned bill; black-bellied plovers, a few of which sported a solid black belly, representing breeding plumage; one closely packed flock of about 40 red knots; smaller numbers of spotted and least sandpipers; and one piping plover.

I detected other birds moving north, flying along the beach or dunes or some distance at sea: a flock of about 35 northern pintails, scattered flocks of cattle egrets, a few great blue herons, a couple of ring-billed gulls, and a herring gull.

Many of these birds also frequent the tidal flats along the Laguna Madre. Several other species can also be expected there. The shallow, warm lagoon and spoil islands attract some fascinating birds, such as the **reddish egret**. At Bird Island Basin, one can almost always spot a reddish egret running about with wings spread to entice prey to make a dash for it. Once the prey is flushed, this tall, reddish blue egret grabs or spears the fish, frog, or crustacean with its long, flesh-colored (with a black tip) bill. This wader also tends to drag a foot when hunting, a habit that also helps stir up prey.

Reddish egrets exhibit two different color phases, the typical reddish phase and an all-white phase. Both phases exhibit the bicolored bill and bluish legs. The all-white birds can be confused with Padre Island's two other all-white egrets: great and snowy egrets. But these three waders can easily distinguished. Great egrets are larger (38 in or 97 cm) birds with a 55-inch (140-cm) wingspan, a bright yellow bill, and black legs and feet; snowy egrets are smaller (20-27 in or 51-69 cm) with a wingspan of about 38 inches (97 cm), a black bill and legs, and bright yellow feet. Reddish egrets stand about 29 inches (74 cm) tall and have a wingspan of about 46 inches (117 cm). In addition, feeding snowy and great egrets are stalkers that use patience to capture their prey; they usually are found poised along a ditch or over a wetland waiting for prey to pass by. Neither utilizes the unique flushing behavior of the reddish egret.

From the end of Bird Island Basin Road, near the boat ramp, I used a spotting scope to view hundreds of egrets, herons, ibis, gulls, terns, and a handful of other birds milling about the long spoil island across the bay. A few were nesting on the stubby vegetation or on the open shore. The most obvious nesting birds, perhaps because of their large size, were **great blue herons**. They seemed to dominate the higher nest sites. I could clearly see their long necks, black-and-white head pattern with long black plumes, and heavy, yellow bill. Great blues are even larger than great egrets, with a body length of 42 to 52 inches (107-132 cm) and an 84-inch (213-cm) wingspan.

The large pink birds with a long, flattened bill, were **roseate spoonbills**, a tropical species that normally reaches the United States only along the gulf coast. They nest on spoil islands, but feed in the freshwater wetlands on the island. Although this bird's bill is shaped like a spoon, the bill is not used as a scoop "but as a supersensitive forceps," according to Harry Oberholser in *The Bird Life of Texas*. "The network of nerves in the bill allows the bird to feed in clouded water or probe in mud where invisible prey must be felt to be caught. As the Roseate wades in shallows, it swings its partially open spoonbill in lateral arcs through the water and mud; with this scything motion, it seizes its prey. The bird then raises and slightly shakes its head to guide the food down the bill to the gular pouch, which is about midway down on the lower mandible."

Both white-faced and white ibis, tricolored herons, an American white pelican, four or five black skimmers, and several great-tailed grackles were also present on the spoil island. The **great-tailed grackles**, almost crow-sized, seemed to fill up all the empty spaces. They not only were perched on the shrubs amid the nesting waders, but also crowded the shoreline. A dozen or so were walking along the near-shore only a few feet from where I was scoping the island. Their shiny black, almost purple plumage, long keel-shaped tail, and the males' creamy eyes were obvious. Territorial males put on a great show by pointing their bill skyward, only inches away from an opponent, and giving great "clacks" and whistles. Their incredible calls were described by John Terres, in *The Audubon Society Encyclopedia of North American Birds*: "loud, piercing 'cha-we' note or 'may-ree, may-ree!' and high falsetto squeal, 'quee-ee, quee-ee,' much like flicker's 'week-it, week-it' call."

The gated road directly across Park Road 22 from the Bird Island Basin Road provides access to open grasslands and freshwater pond and marsh habitats. Expected species in this area include all of the previously mentioned waders as well as pied-billed grebes, green herons, mottled ducks, black-bellied whistling-ducks, black-necked stilts, king rails, common moorhens, American coots, killdeers, black-necked stilts, greater and lesser yellowlegs, marsh wrens, common yellowthroats, savannah sparrows, eastern meadowlarks, and red-winged blackbirds. Smaller numbers of American and least bitterns can sometimes be found. Gulls and terns are always overhead, as are cliff and barn swallows, and at dawn and dusk, common nighthawks.

Eastern meadowlarks are almost always evident on the grasslands, where their slurred whistle notes can dominate the scene. Their bright yellow breasts, crossed with a bold black line, stand out like beacons during the morning. They often sit on top of higher vegetation, singing their distinct songs that Roger Tory Peterson, in *A Field Guide to the Birds of Texas*, describes as "tee-yah, tee-yair (last note skewy and descending)."

In winter, the grasslands support an additional assortment of birds, including northern harriers, that cruise back and forth in their search for prey; the little, reddish-backed American kestrels; and tall, stately **sandhill cranes**. Some winters, sandhills number in the thousands, according to park interpreter John Lujan. Then, family groups to larger congregations can be observed easily from the roadside. Adults possess gray plumage with a whitish face and reddish crown; immatures are brownish with a dark crown. Some adults show a brownish stain on their underparts and neck in early winter, from the iron-rich mud of their breeding grounds far to the north. But this stain normally disappears by mid to late winter.

Some years this national seashore is censused during the annual Christmas Bird Counts and those surveys provide the best indication of the park's winter birds. In 1990, counters tallied 14,472 individuals of 75 species. The dozen most numerous birds, in descending order of abundance, included double-crested cormorant, northern pintail, lesser scaup, laughing gull, American white pelican, ring-billed gull, redhead, bufflehead, red-winged blackbird, Canada goose, herring gull, and eastern meadowlark.

In summary, the Padre Island bird checklist includes 336 species, of which 35 are considered to nest. Twenty-six of the 35 species are water birds (waders, ducks, rails, shorebirds, gulls, and terns), none are hawks and owls, and none are warblers.

Birds of Special Interest

Great blue heron. This tall, stately bird, with blue, white, gray, and black plumage and a heavy yellow bill, can be expected anywhere.

Reddish egret. Watch for this bird in the shallow bay waters, where its unique behavior of flushing prey by running with wings spread helps with identification.

Roseate spoonbill. This large, pink wader with a long, flattened bill nests on the Bird Basin spoil islands, but feeds in shallow wetlands.

Peregrine falcon. It is most numerous during the spring and fall migrations, especially on the tidal flats. It is best distinguished by its large size, slaty back, black sideburns, and pointed wings.

Sandhill crane. This long-legged, long-necked bird with gray plumage frequents the grasslands in winter.

Willet. One of the most common of the large shorebirds, it shows a contrasting black-and-white wing pattern in flight.

Sanderling. This little shorebird has pale plumage with blackish shoulders; it is abundant along the surf most of the year.

Laughing gull. The park's most common gull species, breeding birds sport an all-black hood with white slivers below and above the eyes, deep red bill, and black-tipped wings; winter birds have blackish bills and gray heads.

Royal tern. This large tern has a solid black cap, white forehead and underparts, and orange-red bill.

Sandwich tern. A medium-sized tern with a black crest and black bill with a yellow tip, it is fairly common along the beach in spring and summer.

Eastern meadowlark. This bird has a bright yellow breast crossed with a bold, black V; it is usually common in the grasslands.

30

Big Thicket National Preserve, Texas

There is something magical about ponds, especially woodland ponds. The surrounding trees and shrubs not only insulate ponds from outside influences, but also help maintain the sites as viable wildlife habitats. The value of such ponds, therefore, is largely devoted to nature, where human use is generally limited to wildlife appreciation.

Such a magical pond exists at the head of the Woodlands Trail in Big Thicket's Big Sandy Creek Unit. Collin's Pond began as a stock tank, dammed early in the century by a rancher. Once the National Park Service acquired the land in 1974, cattle were removed and the pond was allowed to return to nature. Today, Collin's Pond looks as natural as if Mother Nature had done it all.

I approached the pond with all the stealth I could muster, so as not to frighten any of its inhabitants. Birdsongs sounded from all sides, the most obvious were those of Carolina chickadees, tufted titmice, Carolina wrens, white-eyed vireos, and northern cardinals. The deep hooting of a barred owl echoed from the distance. A pair of American crows suddenly flew up from the pond's far shore, cawing a reprimand at my appearance. Their departure seemed to trigger further response. A pair of wood ducks lifted off the pond with squealing "wee-e-e-ek" calls, and a little blue heron flapped across the surface and disappeared over the far pines.

I froze in place, trying to blend into the dense vegetation. It took 3 to 4 minutes before birdsongs continued as before. Parula warblers were singing their slightly ascending songs. One brightly marked male, with its lemon yellow throat and chest, crossed with a rust to black band, was gleaning the bright green leaves of a red maple. A pine warbler sang its trilling song from the high pine foliage; I watched it search the long needles for insects. Nearby were a pair of "wheezing" blue-gray gnatcatchers, a nervous ruby-crowned kinglet, and a yellow-rumped warbler that chipped as it settled on a branch after sailing after a passing insect.

Suddenly, the lovely song of a **wood thrush** resounded from the forest beyond the pond. Its distinct "eee-o-lay" notes, seemingly delivered by a velvet flute, seemed to put all the other birdsongs to shame. I pictured this robin-sized thrush with a cinnamon crown and back and white underparts with large dark spots. I also wondered if it was already on its breeding territory or if it had only stopped along its migration route to rest and refuel. I stood there in admiration as it sang again and again. Then, just as suddenly as it had begun, it was silent.

The "tic-tic-tic" call of a black-and-white warbler came from the foliage of a black willow near where I stood. I focused my binoculars on this neatly groomed little bird, a male, evident by its black throat and bold markings. This was another Neotropical migrant that might stay and nest.

I followed the narrow trail around the pond, watching carefully for any movement and listening for birdsong. A red-eyed vireo was singing high in a sweetgum tree across the pond. I also detected a singing eastern wood-pewee and a great crested flycatcher to my left. There, too, and somewhat closer, was the "weeta, weeta, wee-tee-o" of a hooded warbler. I "chipped" with the back of my hand to my lips, trying to attract this yellow-and-black warbler into view. Again, and louder, but to no avail. But my chipping did attract another bird. A Louisiana waterthrush appeared less than a dozen feet (3.6 m) away from me, teetering on a thin branch only a foot (30 cm) above the ground. I could see its bold white eyebrows, heavily streaked chest, white throat, and long, pinkish legs. Another migrant on its way to a nesting site, perhaps in the Appalachians? Or was this one going to remain and nest?

All of these migrants had stopped at Collin's Pond for a few hours, or a few days, to rest and feed. I wondered if woodland ponds have special appeal to birds, as they do to humans. But one thing was

sure, Collin's Pond and the few others in the protected national preserve, can offer shelter and food to prepare them for the next leg of
their long journey.

The Park Environment

The Texas Big Thicket is often described as a "biological crossroads
of North America" for a good reason. Numerous eastern and western, northern and southern plant species reach the edge of their
ranges here, where eastern forests, southeastern swamps, central
plains, and southwestern deserts overlap.

The original Big Thicket covered about 3.5 million acres
(1,416,431 ha), from Louisiana west to what is now Houston, and
from the coastal plains of the Gulf of Mexico north to the upper
watersheds of the Trinity, Neches, and Sabine rivers. Only about
300,000 acres (121,408 ha) of "The Thicket" remain today, with just
86,000 acres (34,804 ha) protected in the national preserve. Edwin
Way Teale stated, in an article in *Audubon:* "This shrunken fragment
of the great wilderness still contains green solitude and untamed
beauty and regions that are remote and mysterious, filled with contrast and surprise."

According to the park brochure, the national preserve contains
"85 tree species, more than 60 shrubs, and nearly 1,000 flowering
plants, including 26 ferns and allies, 28 orchids, and four of North
America's five types of insect-eating plants." In addition, the region
has produced 56 state and 15 national champion trees, the tallest
known specimens of each species.

Eight distinct plant associations were described for the Big
Thicket by Geyata Ajilvsgi in *Wild Flowers of the Big Thicket.* These
include mixed-grass prairies, most common along the western edge
of the park, "mainly on the uplands between Pine Island Bayou and
the Trinity River." Along the river bottoms are palmetto-oak flats on
"the lowest, flattest terrain;" sweetgum-oak floodplains, which are
dominated by sweetgum and chestnut, willow, water, and red oaks.
Sweet bay-gallberry holly bogs are widely scattered in wet depressions of varying size. Pine-black gum savannas "are broad, grassy
flatlands with a widely spaced overstory of longleaf pine and small,
stunted black gum, while loblolly pine and sweetgum are recent
invaders," Longleaf-bluestem uplands are best represented in the

northern, hillier portion of the preserve. Beech-magnolia-loblolly slopes contain a "magnificent mingling of deciduous, broad-leaved evergreen, and coniferous trees" and are scattered throughout the preserve. Finally, oak-farkleberry sandy lands occur in deep sands or gravels, and possess an overstory of various oaks and an understory dominated by farkleberry.

Big Thicket National Preserve contains 13 units scattered over a 2,500 square-mile (965 sq-km) region. Several units are connected by river or stream corridors. Trails provide access into several of these. The Kirby Nature Trail, at the southern tip of the Turkey Creek Unit, is the best introduction to the park. It winds through a diverse mixture of hardwoods and pines, and past cypress sloughs and floodplains along Village Creek.

A small information station, located in a historic house at the trailhead, contains a few exhibits and a sales outlet; bird field guides and a park checklist are available.

Additional information can be obtained from the Superintendent, Big Thicket National Preserve, 3785 Milam, Beaumont, TX 77701; (409) 839-2689.

Bird Life

I recorded 32 species of birds along the 5.4-mile (6.7-km) Woodlands Trail that early April morning. Park naturalist David Baker had suggested this trail because of its diversity of habitats. Besides Collin's Pond, the loop trail passes through floodplain, hardwood and pine forests, and old pastures being reclaimed by nature. In addition to species at the pond that morning, I found red-shouldered and broad-winged hawks; mourning doves; ruby-throated hummingbirds; red-headed, red-bellied, downy, hairy, and pileated woodpeckers; Acadian flycatchers; blue jays; gray catbirds; yellow-throated warblers; white-throated and swamp sparrows; and brown-headed cowbirds.

The **red-shouldered hawk** was one of the most vocal birds, crying loud "kee-you" calls on several occasions. Although red-shouldered hawks are more often heard than seen, I was able to study one well-marked bird as it fed on a small rodent while perched on an open tree limb. Its rufous shoulders, barring on its chest and breast, and black-and-white banded tail were obvious. According to Arthur

Red-shouldered hawk

Bent's classic *Life Histories of North American Birds of Prey*, this hawk possesses a "strong attachment to its nesting territory"; succeeding generations of one pair occupied the same tract for 45 years. Bent also points out, "Along the Neches River one can often count anywhere from 10 to 15 in the air at one time" during the "courtship season, which begins in February and...lasts for about a month. At this season the birds may be seen circling in pairs over the treetops, calling almost constantly."

The surprise of the day was finding two pairs of red-headed woodpeckers, along the far end of the trail among the oldest hardwoods. This portion of Big Sandy Creek was once owned by Carter Mainline Lumber Company, which used it as an employee recreation area; timber cutting was therefore excluded, and some of the oldest beech, hickory, and oak trees were saved. Those ancient trees were now being utilized by a dwindling population of red-heads.

While watching the red-headed woodpeckers, I wondered if these woods had once supported ivory-billed woodpeckers. Like the proverbial "canary in the mine," this large woodpecker was one of our first birds to disappear after European settlement. The original

Big Thicket was once home to this wonderful woodpecker, now extinct. According to ornithologist James Tanner's 1942 summary report, *The Ivory-billed Woodpecker*, the last positive ivory-bill sighting in east Texas was in 1904. Tanner reported that the bird's demise closely corresponded with logging of the swamp hardwoods.

My visit to the Woodlands Trail was too early in the season to find several of the typical breeding birds. The yellow-billed cuckoo; chuck-will's-widow; Swainson's, prairie, and Kentucky warblers; yellow-breasted chat; American redstart; summer tanager; blue grosbeak; and indigo bunting apparently had not yet arrived from their wintering grounds.

A few days later, local birder and long-time friend, Bill Graber, accompanied me on the Confluence Trail, on the westernmost edge of the preserve. We drove down Forest Park Road, which begins behind the 6 Lakes Store, on Highway 2610 above Romayor, stopped at a small parking area, and walked a quarter mile (.4 km) or so to a lovely overlook above the confluence of the Trinity River and Menard Creek. The river level was high, and the sandbar normally visible near the far shore was underwater. This was the same place that Lance Rosier, Big Thicket patriarch and self-educated naturalist, took the late Supreme Court Justice William O. Douglas during his tour of the Big Thicket in the early 1960s. Douglas wrote about this site in his book *Farewell to Texas*, exclaiming about the numerous shrubs that were blooming at the time: "cross vine, yellow jasmine, hawthorn, azalea, rhododendron, and dogwood." Azalea and dogwood were blooming for Bill and me, as well.

Several great and snowy egrets and a couple of great blue and little blue herons were feeding along the muddy shoreline. A purple martin and several tree, northern rough-winged, and barn swallows quartered back and forth, catching insects over the river, swollen and muddy from recent rains. A pair of double-crested cormorants and a American wigeon flew by. Then a red-shouldered hawk called from the forest.

A pair of **wood ducks** suddenly flew up from the flooded edge of Menard Creek with loud, squealing "wee-e-e-ek" calls. The male's contrasting colors and crest were obvious. The female was drab in comparison, although its bold, elliptical eye rings were also evident. I wondered if this pair of "tree ducks" had already begun to nest in some hidden cavity along the creek. Wood ducks utilize tree cavities 30 feet (9 m) or more above the ground and 10 to 19 inches (25-48 cm) deep, with an entrance at least 10 square inches (6.5 sq cm). Males remain to help with the initial nesting chores, but desert their mates before the young leave the nest; they retire to bachelor flocks in secluded ponds. The hen must coax the chicks, which are equipped with claws for climbing, out of the high nest and down to the ground. All of their early training is left to the hen. Broods of up to fifty eggs have been recorded in a single nest, with many of the eggs contributed by other hens. The "dumping" of eggs into one nest is a fairly common occurrence with wood ducks. Up to five hens are known to participate, but only one hen and drake incubate the clutch.

Several other birds were found along the Confluence Trail: High in the canopy were a number of Carolina chickadees, tufted titmice, ruby-crowned kinglets, blue-gray gnatcatchers, cedar waxwings, red-eyed vireos, and parula and yellow-rumped warblers. Noisy Carolina wrens sang from the thickets, and a prothonotary warbler sang a loud and ringing "zweet, zweet, zweet, zweet" song from the flooded shore.

First-time visitors to the Big Thicket should begin at the visitor information station on Highway 420, at the southern end of the Turkey Creek Unit. The 2.5-mile (4-km) Kirby Nature Trail (interpretive booklet available at the station) provides a wonderful introduction to the park. Betty and I walked this trail one spring morning, savoring the lush atmosphere and abundant birdsong. A few dogwoods and hoary azaleas were still blooming. Gray squirrels cavorted amid the canopy.

The most abundant birds that morning included red-bellied woodpeckers; American crows; Carolina chickadees; tufted titmice; Carolina wrens; blue-gray gnatcatchers; white-eyed and red-eyed vireos; parula, pine, and hooded warblers; and northern cardinals. We recorded smaller numbers of ruby-throated hummingbirds; downy, hairy, and pileated woodpeckers; eastern wood-pewees; great crested and Acadian flycatchers; blue jays; Swainson's, hermit, and wood thrushes; solitary and yellow-throated vireos; black-throated green, yellow-throated, black-and-white, and prothonotary warblers; American redstarts; Louisiana waterthrushes; summer tanagers; and indigo buntings.

The most outstanding find was the **pileated woodpecker** that we observed from about 75 feet (23 m), as it searched on a rotting tree trunk for insects. It made great whacks into the soft wood, breaking off large pieces in its effort to locate larvae that it apparently knew were there. We stopped and admired this huge, dramatic bird. Its black back and bright red crest were unmistakable. Its black forehead and the absence of a red patch behind the bill identified it as a female. Then a loud "wuck-a-wuck-a-wuck" call resounded from the forest beyond, and our lady woodpecker flew off with batlike wing beats toward its apparent mate.

The greatest diversity was found at the baldcypress slough, about midway on the trail. The most common songster there was the little parula warbler, singing slightly ascending songs, each ending in a sharp lower note. But the most impressive warblers that morning were a pair of **prothonotary warblers**. These birds seemed to be on their breeding territory, because they sang constantly while we were there. Their loud, emphatic "zweet, zweet, zweet, zweet" songs reverberated through the woods. Their golden heads, coal black eyes, bluish wings, and yellowish underparts gave them a special countenance. For more details about this lovely bird, see chapter 31 on Jean Lafitte.

Swainson's warblers also nest in the Big Thicket, but this species is local in occurrence. Birder Mary Reed, who leads bird walks in the Thicket, told me that she has the greatest success in finding this warbler along the Turkey Creek Trail, just south of the Gore Store Road. And Bill Graber told me that he has found it along this trail just north of the Gore Store Road, the same location described by Mike Austin in a 1991 *Birding* article, "Finding Nesting Red-cockaded Woodpeckers, Swainson's Warblers, and Bachman's Sparrows in East Texas." Austin wrote: "The bird's loud, ringing song can be heard from mid-April through May. The songster uses a variety of perches, from ground level to about eight feet [2.4 m] up. It prefers the densest cover and, because it usually cohabits with the cottonmouth and a variety of thorned bushes, commando-type excursions to view it are not recommended." Its song, described by Paul Sykes, in *The Audubon Society Master Guide to Birding*, is a loud and clear melody, "tee-o, tee-o, whit-sut-say, bee-o, tee, toot-sut-say, bee-o." And Frank Chapman, in *The Warblers of North America*, added that its song "has an indescribable tender quality that thrills the senses after the sound has ceased."

Paul Ehrlich and colleagues, in *The Birder's Handbook*, pointed out that the Swainson's warbler "forages for insects on or near ground by flipping leaves and probing [its] long heavy bill into soil." It is one of the Neotropical migrants that winter in the Bahamas, Cuba, Jamaica, Belize, and southeastern Mexico, and nest only in the southeastern United States.

Bachman's sparrow, another of the Big Thicket specialties, is rarely seen in the park, but it does occur in open pine stands along the boundary. Graber and I found it along Highway 420, just west of the Turkey Creek Information Station.

Betty and I also spent several hours on the nearby 1 mile-long (1.6-km) Sundew Trail in the Hickory Creek-Savannah Unit, just

Brown-headed nuthatch

west of Highway 69. The trail passed through a little bog that was filled with pitcher-plants; a few of the greenish yellow flowers, shaped like ragged, upside-down umbrellas, were still in bloom. Many old and a few new leaves, standing erect like hollow trumpets, were scattered about the depression. A variety of wildflowers grew along the trail. Birds were less numerous here than on the Kirby Nature Trail, but we had excellent looks at brown-headed nuthatches and pine warblers among the longleaf pines.

Brown-headed nuthatches were flying from pine to pine, walking up and down the scaly trunks, and gleaning the long pine needles. All the time they were uttering thin "pee-you" calls in constant communication with their neighbors. This nuthatch was one of the first birds recognized for its use of tools; it uses a flake of bark like a crowbar to pry up other pieces of bark to retrieve insects underneath. Unmated males are known to assist paired birds with feeding nestlings and fledglings.

The **pine warblers** stayed in the upper pine foliage, so good looks at these little birds required considerable neck strain. Their distinct song usually gives them away first. Paul Sykes, in *The Audubon Society Master Guide to Birding*, described the song as "a musical trill varying slightly in pitch, like chipping sparrow's song, but softer, lower, and less rapid: 'zit, zit, ziz-ziz-ziz-ziz-ziz-ziz-ziz-ziz-ziz-ziz.' " Singing pine warblers were our constant companions along the trail. Occasional views of these songsters revealed small birds with yellowish underparts, olive-green upperparts, and darker wings with two prominent white wing bars.

We also kept a sharp eye out for red-cockaded woodpeckers or their "candle trees" along this trail. This endangered woodpecker is between a downy and a hairy woodpecker in size, with bold white cheeks and, on the male, tiny red ear tufts. It prefers open stands of mature longleaf pines (80-120 years old) whose heartwood has been destroyed by a fungus. The woodpeckers excavate cavities into the living trees; a colony may use the hole for several decades. Resin "wells" are excavated and maintained around the cavity entrance so that the sticky resin repels predators like rat snakes. Because the dripping resin resembles melting wax, the trees are called "candle trees." Although a colony can include up to 30 cavity trees, only one cavity is utilized by a single pair of breeding birds. Other mature birds serve as helpers.

Red-cockaded woodpeckers have declined drastically throughout their range, even after being listed as endangered in 1970. The reasons for the decline range from habitat removal to overprotection of habitat, such a fire suppression. When the surrounding understory gets tall enough to allow predators to reach the nest, these woodpeckers desert the site. Ehrlich and colleagues, in *Birds in Jeopardy*, point out that the current range is only 10 percent of the original, and the world's population is "about 7,400 individuals."

The National Park Service has developed a fire management program designed to restore and maintain certain areas, such as the Hickory Creek-Savannah Unit, for this woodpecker. It is now extremely rare in the area, and protection of the few remaining colonies is of utmost important.

Winter birding can also be exciting in the Big Thicket because of the park's southern latitude and its diverse habitats, which support a wide variety of wintering northern species. And, three Big Thicket specialties—red-cockaded woodpecker, brown-headed nuthatch, and Bachman's sparrow—are year-round residents. All the park's wintering birds are surveyed annually in the Turkey Creek Christmas Bird Count. The 1991 count tallied 4,558 individuals of 72 species. The dozen most numerous birds, in descending order of abundance, included American robin, yellow-rumped warbler, northern cardinal, American goldfinch, eastern bluebird, American crow, cedar waxwing, ruby-crowned kinglet, blue jay, Carolina chickadee, turkey vulture, and tufted titmouse.

In summary, the Big Thicket checklist of birds contains 177 species, of which 97 are considered to nest. Of these, 16 are water birds, 7 are hawks and owls, and 14 are warblers.

Birds of Special Interest
Wood duck. Watch for this duck at quiet ponds and waterways; it often is detected first by its squealing "wee-e-e-ek" calls.

Red-shouldered hawk. This year-round resident sports reddish shoulders, barred underparts, and a black tail with narrow white bands.

Red-cockaded woodpecker. An endangered species, it prefers open stands of mature longleaf pines; males have bold white cheeks with tiny red ear tufts.

Pileated woodpecker. The loud "wuck-a-wuck-a-wuck" calls and the all-black back and red crest of this huge woodpecker are unmistakable.

Brown-headed nuthatch. This little bird is usually found walking up and down the trunks and branches of pines; it often emits thin "pee-you" calls.

Wood thrush. Its loud, flutelike "eee-o-lay" song, reddish back, and white breast with bold black spots help identify this large thrush.

Prothonotary warbler. Watch for this golden yellow bird at bald-cypress sloughs; its loud, emphatic "zweet, zweet, zweet, zweet" song is also diagnostic.

Swainson's warbler. This rare bird, with an all-brown back, pale eyebrows, and whitish underparts, prefers wet thickets; it is often found along the Turkey Creek Trail.

Pine warbler. One of the park's most common birds, it resides in pines and sings a distinct, musical, buzzing trill.

31

Jean Lafitte National Historical Park, Louisiana

The new spring foliage was bright green that early morning as I prepared to walk the Bayou Coquille Trail. The spirited trill of a parula warbler, gleaning insects from a swamp red maple, provided a most welcome greeting. A pair of Carolina wrens and a northern cardinal sang from an adjacent thicket. I detected the distant "wik wik wik" notes of a pileated woodpecker. The whistle screech of a red-shouldered hawk hung in the still air. Then, the loud, emphatic "sweez, sweez, sweez, sweez" of a prothonotary warbler resounded from a flooded depression near the trailhead. And when the deep, almost haunting calls of a pair of barred owls echoed from the forest, any doubt about the kind of environment I was about to experience evaporated.

Barataria's Bayou Coquille Trail provides a wonderful excursion into the Mississippi River Delta wetlands, representative of the southern swamp and riverine forests. Barataria is one of the few reasonably intact forested wetlands left in the delta; much of this habitat has been lost to development. The Bayou Coquille Trail is considered the most accessible walking trail into the heart of Louisiana's 2.5 million acre (1,011,736 ha) wetland ecosystem.

I focused my binoculars on the parula warbler and watched it capture a tiny caterpillar from the underside of a maple leaf. The bird moved constantly in its search for food. Every 10 to 20 seconds it would lift its head and sing. A parula's song is one of the most easily identified in the bird world, a slightly ascending trill, "zzzzzzzzzzeurip," almost always ending with a sharp lower note.

Northern parula warbler

However, I was soon to learn that Louisiana's parulas often sing slightly different patterns. Although they all sing a buzzing trill, usually ending with a sharp lower note, I discovered birds that broke up their songs into two, three, or even four parts.

Barataria's parula warblers do possess the same bright plumage as parulas throughout eastern North America, lovely shades of yellow, rufous, black, gray, green, and white. When viewed from below, their yellow throat and chest is crossed by a black to rufous band. And when seen from the top, they show a greenish yellow patch on their otherwise all-gray back. But parulas are undoubtedly detected and identified more often by their spirited and distinct songs. They are one of our most persistent and lovely songbirds.

I identified more than three dozen species along the Bayou Coquille Trail that morning. Several had apparently just arrived from their wintering grounds in the tropics. They would likely remain a few hours or a few days to rest and refuel before continuing their journeys. Both the parula and prothonotary warblers are Neotropical migrants, as well several others found along the trail: eastern wood-pewee; Acadian and great crested flycatchers; wood thrush; red-eyed vireo; yellow-throated, black-and-white, worm-eating, and Kentucky warblers. They spend their winters in Mexico, Central America, South America, or the West Indies and migrate north to the temperate forests to nest and raise their families. They remain in North America about four to five months and then return south. All of the

Neotropical migrants, therefore, depend upon healthy and protected wintering and nesting homes, as well as stopover sites along their migration routes, for their long-term survival.

The Park Environment

The Barataria Preserve Unit is the only one of Jean Lafitte's four separate units that contains significant natural resources. The New Orleans Unit interprets the rich history and culture of the city, including the 66-block original city founded in 1718. The Chalmette Unit, 6 miles (10 km) east of New Orleans, commemorates the Battle of New Orleans; a 1.5-mile (2.4-km) tour road provides access to the battlefield site and national cemetery. The Acadian Unit contains three separate cultural centers in the towns of Lafayette, Eunice, and Thibodaux, Louisiana.

The 11,500-acre (4,654-ha) Barataria Preserve Unit, about 15 miles (24 km) south of downtown New Orleans, preserves examples of all the freshwater natural habitats found in the Mississippi Delta. Eight miles (13 km) of boardwalk and hard-surfaced trails and over 20 miles (32 km) of canoe trails exist. The Bayou Coquille Trail (named by early French settlers for the mounds of clam shells, *coquilles*) passes through good examples of four distinct habitats. According to the park's *Barataria Trails* brochure, "hardwoods, including the majestic live oak, grow on the natural levee. The wetter soils of the backslope are thick with dwarf palmettos under a canopy of swamp red maple. The swamp, a flooded forest of baldcypress, water tupelo, and pumpkin ash, is encountered next. Near the end of the trail the trees thin out, revealing the open marsh, a floating prairie of freshwater grasses, sedges, and aquatic plants." Other common plants found in the park include abundant Spanish moss, giant blue iris, dewberry, red rattlebox, poison ivy, muscadine, trumpet creeper, American elm, hackberry, sweetgum, and buckbrush.

The Barataria Visitor Center is on Highway 45, in the heart of the unit. It has an information desk, exhibits, an auditorium where the 25-minute film "Jambalaya A Delta Almanac" is shown continually, and a sales outlet. Books, including bird field guides and a checklist, and other informational materials are available. *A Bird Finder's Guide to Southeastern Louisiana*, published by the Orleans Audubon Society, includes a short chapter on birding the Barataria

Preserve Unit. Ranger-guided interpretive trips include walking tours on the Bayou Coquille Trail and weekend canoe trips; contact the visitor center for details.

Additional information can be obtained from the Barataria Unit Manager, Jean Lafitte National Historical Park, Barataria Preserve Unit, 7400 Highway 45, Marrero, LA 70072; (504) 589-2330.

Bird Life

The Mississippi Delta can literally be crawling with migrants in spring. Anytime from mid-March to early May, waves of songbirds can arrive from the south. When a severe storm or strong north winds tire the trans-Gulf migrants, thousands of birds might suddenly "fall out" of the sky. At such times, the trees and shrubs are filled with migrants, all in need of rest and food. Although Neotropical migrants to the west of the delta include birds that may have traveled overland up the Texas coast, most migrants that appear in the delta and eastward along the gulf coast are trans-Gulf migrants. These birds fly nonstop across the Gulf of Mexico from Mexico's Yucatan Peninsula, departing in the evening and arriving on the Louisiana coast the following day; peak arrival time is midafternoon. For additional details about the trans-Gulf migration, see chapter 30 on Gulf Islands National Seashore in *The Visitor's Guide to the Birds of the Eastern National Parks: United States and Canada* (John Muir Publications, 1992).

The **prothonotary warbler** is a Neotropical migrant that epitomizes America's southern swamp forests. Wherever stands of baldcypress are found, the golden prothonotary warbler may be found. Especially where boardwalks have been constructed into the baldcypress cathedrals, so that visitors can penetrate those hallowed sites, prothonotary warblers seem to lose their normal fear and flit about, almost underfoot. Their bright golden-mantled bodies, bluish wings, and black piercing eyes are not easily missed. And their loud, penetrating songs, "sweez, sweez, sweez, sweez," in a slightly different dialect from that of their East Coast cousins, are most distinguished.

Prothonotary comes from a Latin word *protonotarius*, for the yellow hood or cape worn by some church officials. The bird also is sometimes known as "golden-swamp warbler," a most appropriate name for this lovely creature.

As I continued down the Bayou Coquille Trail, I began to realize that one of the most vocal songbirds that morning was the **Carolina wren**, and that I was hearing an unbelievable variety of songs. After tracking down several of these large, reddish wrens to be sure of my identification, I wrote down my interpretation of each song. The most common rendition was "sweety sweety sweety," but that was sometimes reduced to "sweet sweet sweet" or "swee swee swee." I watched one sing "sweet sweet sweet" and follow that with a sharp "pee-de." A high-pitched "teacher teacher teacher" was heard on one occasion. Other common songs included "clewy clewy clewy" and "tweedly, tweedly, tweedly," with a number of variations. And "too too too" was also expressed on several occasions. I never did hear the typical "tea-kettle" song so commonly sung by Carolina wrens on the East Coast. For more details about this bird's singing ability, see chapter 27 on Chickasaw.

Barataria's Carolina wrens possess a rufous back and buff underparts with bold white eyebrows; they are a particularly striking bird. I could not help but think how advantageous their color pattern is as I watched them play peekaboo among the reddish-barked shrubs. Carolina wrens are full-time residents in southern Louisiana and one of the area's most obvious birds in winter.

Another loud-mouthed songster along the trail was the **white-eyed vireo**. This little bird was extremely secretive; it was seldom seen in the open. But from the abundance of its scolding calls and songs, it seemed to be one of the most common species present that day. Most of its songs were three or five notes, "chip-whee-oo" or "chick-a-per-weeoo-chik." At one place along the trail I spished loudly and a brightly marked white-eyed male suddenly appeared about 5 feet (1.5 m) away among the foliage of a waxmyrtle. It scolded me vehemently with harsh, scratchy notes. Then, just as suddenly, as if to show me who was truly in charge, it seemed to say, "Who are you, eh?"

I was attracted to a lovely melody coming from near the top of a baldcypress. "See-we, see-we, see-we, swee, swee swee." I immediately identified the songster as a yellow-throated warbler, but it took several minutes to find this bird, in spite of its almost continual singing. It was rather frustrating, but this little warbler, with a lemon yellow throat and contrasting black side patches, was truly ventriloquistic.

At one point along the trail, a **red-shouldered hawk** flew up from a low tree where it had been perched. It circled back overhead with a loud antagonistic screech, "kee-ah," giving me a wonderful view. Its reddish underparts and shoulders gleamed in the morning sunlight. Through binoculars, I also could see its black-and-white wings and banded tail. Later in the day, I watched one soaring in circles over the forest; its relatively long wings provided sufficient lift to keep it airborne with only occasional flapping.

At the point where the Bayou Coquille Trail joins the Marsh Overlook Trail, which follows Kenta Canal to a wooden platform, are a number of black willows. Apparently, it was the height of their flowering season; hundreds of insects were savoring the sweet catkin pollen. The insects had, in turn, attracted predators, birds and reptiles alike. Parula warblers were most obvious, due to their high-pitched songs. Pairs of Carolina chickadees and tufted titmice were busy searching the catkins for insects. Several yellow-rumped warblers were "flycatching" from the higher branches. A lone black-and-white warbler was literally creeping along the branches in its search for insects. An orange-crowned warbler and two ruby-crowned kinglets were inspecting clusters leaves. And a male ruby-throated hummingbird danced up and down as it captured insects in midair.

A 6-inch (15-cm) green anole was also taking advantage of the abundant insects. I watched this bright green lizard as it slowly crawled along a high limb into the center of several catkins, where it could grab passing insects. It then moved to a bare branch and began to do push-ups, its orangish dewlap expanding to attract the notice of a female. I could not find a second anole, but anole secrets are not readily available to humankind.

The Kenta Canal was alive with tiny creatures, a living broth in support of higher life forms. The highest order predators seen that day were the American alligators; most were in the 3- to 4-foot (.9 to 1.2-m) range. But all those I found could have been asleep, if alligators sleep with their eyes open, because they simply floated like logs. At one point, a double-crested cormorant lifted off from the canal, after a lengthy takeoff, and made a huge circle to land back in the canal out of sight. At another point, I watched a great egret for several minutes as it poised perfectly still on the shoreline, waiting for some unfortunate prey to come within striking distance. Its all-white plumage and heavy yellow bill made it seem statuelike.

The marsh overlook platform, at the end of the .9-mile (1.4-km) route, provides an outstanding view of the extensive floating prairie beyond. A swamp sparrow dived for cover below the overlook. Blue jays squawked from the line of trees on the canal bank beyond. Then, a brown thrasher sang a rambling melody at the edge of the marsh. And the avian flybys included a half dozen little blue herons, a great blue heron, a pair of double-crested cormorants, a soaring red-tailed hawk, and a number of boat-tailed grackles.

The most obvious and numerous birds visible from the overlook were **red-winged blackbirds**. Many of the taller grass stalks in the marsh supported singing red-wings. Several made dramatic charges at others that got too close. Nesting, or at least territorial defense, was apparently well under way. Each time a male red-wing sang, it would show off its bright red epaulets. This lovely bird seldom receives the recognition it deserves, perhaps because it is so common.

Later, during the nesting season, the vegetation along the canal will support several other birds, including great crested flycatchers, eastern kingbirds, painting buntings, and orchard orioles. The most attractive of these is the gaudy **painted bunting**. Male painted buntings sport an unbelievable combination of rose red underparts and rump, purple-blue head, green wings, and yellow-green back. Females are greenish overall, darker on their backs, and much lighter underneath. These sparrow-sized birds sing extended songs that Paul Skyes, in *The Audubon Society Master Guide to Birding*, described as "pew-eata, per-eata, j-eata-you-too."

A few days later, I visited the same open marsh and canals by boat with David Muth, the supervisory park ranger and knowledgeable birder. At one stop we left the boat and walked into the marsh. Our footing was fairly solid, but it was like walking on a huge wet sponge. Bulltongue was the most obvious plant, with its green, spatulate leaves. David said that by August the marsh vegetation gets 4 to 5 feet (1.2-1.5 m) tall. But in spring, when the growth is just beginning, the various marsh birds are more visible. During our 3-hour visit we either saw or heard great blue, little blue, and green herons; great and snowy egrets; white and either glossy or white-faced ibis (both occur here); a mottled duck; several king rails; common moorhens; a pair of black-necked stilts; greater yellowlegs; and common yellowthroats. Least bittern and purple gallinule also occur here during the nesting season.

Another afternoon, I walked the Ring Levee Trail with David, who seemed to know its every nook and cranny. He pointed out that the drier areas were the best places to find hooded warblers, and that Swainson's warblers occasionally are found along the wetter portion of the adjacent Plantation Trail. We had several outstanding views of **hooded warblers**, one of my all-time favorite songbirds. Actually, we first heard one singing its loud and clear song, "weeta, weeta, weetee-o." Early naturalist Frank Chapman, in *Handbook of Birds of Eastern North America*, wrote that the hooded warbler sings, "You must come to the woods, or you won't see me." To my ear, its song is lovely and sweet, but all too short; it seems to end just at its height. The male's bright yellow face, coal black cap, collar, and throat, and its habit of flicking its white-spotted tail, give it a special character.

The Ring Levee Trail follows an abandoned oil exploration road and circles the partially flooded drill site. David pointed out Mississippi mud, painted, and red-eared turtles, as well as several banded water snakes. Bird-voice treefrogs sounded like distant pileated woodpeckers, except a bit more melodic.

At the far end of the trail loop is a huge baldcypress with a great hole, probably from a lost limb, that apparently was being utilized by nesting **barred owls**. "They always perch nearby," I was told, and we readily located one. The owl's rounded head, all-brown eyes, and barred chest were obvious. David mentioned that Barataria's barred owls were already feeding young, and crayfish was a significant part of their diet.

During the several days that I roamed the Barataria Unit, I was amazed that barred owls were calling so constantly throughout the day, although they were most vocal at dawn and dusk. And they delivered a great variety of calls. John Terres summarized barred owl calls in *The Audubon Society Encyclopedia of North American Birds*: "antiphonal hootings of pair more emphatic and slightly higher-pitched than moan of great horned owl; usually call in series of eight accented hoots ending in oo-aw, with downward pitch at end; sometimes rendered phonetically as 'Who cooks for you? who cooks for you-all!' "

Barred owl

We also located several pairs of **wood ducks** in the duckweed ponds around the Ring Levee. Male wood ducks are among the world's most gorgeous creatures. Their glossy green crests, white throats, blood-red eyes, and maroon, blue, tan, and white bodies give them a tropical appearance unlike that of any other duck. Year-round residents in Barataria's swamps, they nest in vacant pileated woodpecker cavities and other hollows up to 50 feet (15 m) high in baldcypress, live oak, and other swamp trees. All of the birds observed were already paired, and in spite of the male's bright plumage, most of the birds were not detected until they flew away with loud "whoo-eek" calls. For more details about this lovely creature, see chapter 30 on Big Thicket.

Only wood and mottled ducks nest in the park, but winter populations of waterfowl can be extensive, especially on the larger bodies of water like Lake Salvador. A Christmas Bird Count, undertaken on the Barataria Unit in 1981 by Muth and three colleagues, tallied 10,258 individuals of 80 species. Of the 80 species recorded, the dozen most numerous birds, in descending order of abundance, included scaup (both lesser and greater), red-winged blackbird, yellow-rumped (myrtle) warbler, tree swallow, laughing gull, common grackle, American goldfinch, European starling, ring-billed gull, killdeer, boat-tailed grackle, American pipit, and four species tied for 12th: Carolina chickadee, American robin, ruby-crowned kinglet, and swamp sparrow.

In summary, Barataria's bird checklist contains 228 species; 60 of those are known to nest. Twelve of the 60 nesting birds are water birds, 6 are hawks and owls, and 6 are warblers. Only 2 species—merlin and Bonaparte's gull—are listed as winter residents only.

Birds of Special Interest

Red-shouldered hawk. Usually detected first by its whistle screech, it sports reddish underparts and shoulders and a black-and-white banded tail.

Wood duck. This year-round resident prefers wooded ponds and flooded swamps; the male's multicolored plumage and crest are unmistakable.

Barred owl. A dominant predator of Barataria's swamps, its loud hooting may be heard anytime during the night and day.

Pileated woodpecker. This is the Woody Woodpecker look-alike, a huge, red-crested woodpecker with a black back and white neck stripes.

Carolina wren. The loud songs and reddish plumage of this year-round resident of the thickets can hardly be missed.

White-eyed vireo. This secretive little bird, with yellow sides and eye lines, sings a harsh "chick-whee-oo" song.

Parula warbler. The smallest of warblers, it is best identified by its song, a slightly ascending trill that ends with a distinct lower note.

Hooded warbler. The males has a bright yellow face and a coal black cap, collar, and throat; its song is a loud, clear "weeta, weeta, wee-tee-o."

Prothonotary warbler. This golden bird with bluish wings frequents the swampy forests from late April to September. It sings a loud, emphatic "sweez, sweez, sweez, sweez" song.

Painted bunting. Males sport multicolored plumage: rose red underparts and rump, purple-blue head, and greenish yellow back.

Red-winged blackbird. Most common in the open marsh, males are easily identified by their black bodies with bright red wing patches.

Checklist of Birds Occurring Regularly in the Central National Parks

LOONS
__ Red-throated loon
__ Pacific loon
__ Common loon

GREBES
__ Least grebe
__ Pied-billed grebe
__ Horned grebe
__ Red-necked grebe
__ Eared grebe
__ Western grebe
__ Clark's grebe

PELICANS
__ American white pelican
__ Brown pelican

CORMORANTS
__ Double-crested cormorant
__ Neotropical cormorant

DARTERS
__ Anhinga

FRIGATEBIRDS
__ Magnificent frigatebird

BITTERNS AND HERONS
__ American bittern
__ Least bittern
__ Great blue heron
__ Great egret
__ Snowy egret
__ Little blue heron
__ Tricolored heron

__ Reddish egret
__ Cattle egret
__ Green heron
__ Black-crowned night-heron
__ Yellow-crowned night-heron

IBIS
__ White ibis
__ Glossy ibis
__ White-faced ibis
__ White-faced ibis

SPOONBILLS
__ Roseate spoonbill

STORKS
__ Wood stork

SWANS, GEESE, AND DUCKS
__ Fulvous whistling-duck
__ Black-bellied whistling-duck
__ Tundra swan
__ Trumpeter swan
__ Mute swan
__ Greater white-fronted goose
__ Snow goose
__ Ross' goose
__ Canada goose
__ Wood duck
__ Green-winged teal
__ American black duck
__ Mottled duck
__ Mallard
__ Northern pintail
__ Blue-winged teal
__ Cinnamon teal

__ Northern shoveler
__ Gadwall
__ American wigeon
__ Canvasback
__ Redhead
__ Ring-necked duck
__ Greater scaup
__ Lesser scaup
__ Harlequin duck
__ Oldsquaw
__ Black scoter
__ Surf scoter
__ White-winged scoter
__ Common goldeneye
__ Barrow's goldeneye
__ Bufflehead
__ Hooded merganser
__ Common merganser
__ Red-breasted merganser
__ Ruddy duck

VULTURES
__ Black vulture
__ Turkey vulture

HAWKS AND EAGLES
__ Osprey
__ American swallow-tailed kite
__ White-tailed kite
__ Mississippi kite
__ Bald eagle
__ Northern harrier
__ Sharp-shinned hawk
__ Cooper's hawk
__ Northern goshawk
__ Harris' hawk
__ Red-shouldered hawk
__ Broad-winged hawk
__ Swainson's hawk
__ White-tailed hawk
__ Red-tailed hawk
__ Ferruginous hawk
__ Rough-legged hawk
__ Golden eagle

FALCONS
__ Crested caracara
__ American kestrel
__ Merlin
__ Peregrine falcon
__ Gyrfalcon
__ Prairie falcon

GROUSE, TURKEY, AND
QUAIL
__ Gray partridge
__ Ring-necked pheasant
__ Spruce grouse
__ Blue grouse
__ Ruffed grouse
__ Sage grouse
__ Greater prairie-chicken
__ Lesser prairie-chicken
__ Sharp-tailed grouse
__ Wild turkey
__ Northern bobwhite
__ Scaled quail

RAILS, GALLINULES, AND
COOTS
__ Yellow rail
__ Black rail
__ Clapper rail
__ King rail
__ Virginia rail
__ Sora
__ Purple gallinule
__ Common moorhen
__ American coot

CRANES
__ Sandhill crane
__ Whooping crane

PLOVERS, STILTS, AND
AVOCETS
__ Black-bellied plover
__ American golden-plover
__ Snowy plover

__ Wilson's plover
__ Semipalmated plover
__ Piping plover
__ Killdeer
__ Mountain plover
__ American oystercatcher
__ Black-necked stilt
__ American avocet

SANDPIPERS, PHALAROPES,
AND ALLIES
__ Greater yellowlegs
__ Lesser yellowlegs
__ Solitary sandpiper
__ Willet
__ Spotted sandpiper
__ Upland sandpiper
__ Whimbrel
__ Long-billed curlew
__ Hudsonian godwit
__ Marbled godwit
__ Ruddy turnstone
__ Red knot
__ Sanderling
__ Semipalmated sandpiper
__ Western sandpiper
__ Least sandpiper
__ White-rumped sandpiper
__ Baird's sandpiper
__ Pectoral sandpiper
__ Sharp-tailed sandpiper
__ Dunlin
__ Stilt sandpiper
__ Buff-breasted sandpiper
__ Short-billed dowitcher
__ Long-billed dowitcher
__ Common snipe
__ American woodcock
__ Wilson's phalarope
__ Red-necked phalarope

SKUAS, GULLS, AND TERNS
__ Pomarine jaeger
__ Parasitic jaeger

__ Laughing gull
__ Franklin's gull
__ Little gull
__ Bonaparte's gull
__ Ring-billed gull
__ California gull
__ Herring gull
__ Thayer's gull
__ Glaucous gull
__ Great black-backed gull
__ Black-legged kittiwake
__ Gull-billed tern
__ Caspian tern
__ Royal tern
__ Sandwich tern
__ Common tern
__ Forster's tern
__ Least tern
__ Black tern
__ Black skimmer

PIGEONS AND DOVES
__ Rock dove
__ Band-tailed pigeon
__ White-winged dove
__ Mourning dove
__ Inca dove
__ Common ground-dove

CUCKOOS
__ Black-billed cuckoo
__ Yellow-billed cuckoo
__ Greater roadrunner
__ Groove-billed ani

OWLS
__ Barn owl
__ Eastern screech-owl
__ Western screech-owl
__ Great horned owl
__ Snowy owl
__ Northern hawk-owl
__ Northern pygmy-owl
__ Elf owl

__ Burrowing owl
__ Barred owl
__ Great gray owl
__ Long-eared owl
__ Short-eared owl
__ Boreal owl
__ Northern saw-whet owl

NIGHTJARS
__ Lesser nighthawk
__ Common nighthawk
__ Common poorwill
__ Chuck-will's-widow
__ Whip-poor-will

SWIFTS
__ Chimney swift
__ White-throated swift

HUMMINGBIRDS
__ Buff-bellied hummingbird
__ Ruby-throated hummingbird
__ Black-chinned hummingbird
__ Broad-tailed hummingbird
__ Rufous hummingbird

KINGFISHERS
__ Belted kingfisher
__ Green kingfisher

WOODPECKERS
__ Lewis' woodpecker
__ Red-headed woodpecker
__ Acorn woodpecker
__ Golden-fronted woodpecker
__ Red-bellied woodpecker
__ Yellow-bellied sapsucker
__ Red-naped sapsucker
__ Ladder-backed woodpecker
__ Downy woodpecker
__ Hairy woodpecker
__ Red-cockaded woodpecker
__ Three-toed woodpecker
__ Black-backed woodpecker
__ Northern flicker
__ Pileated woodpecker

FLYCATCHERS
__ Olive-sided flycatcher
__ Western wood-pewee
__ Eastern wood-pewee
__ Yellow-bellied flycatcher
__ Acadian flycatcher
__ Alder flycatcher
__ Willow flycatcher
__ Least flycatcher
__ Dusky flycatcher
__ Cordilleran flycatcher
__ Black phoebe
__ Eastern phoebe
__ Say's phoebe
__ Vermilion flycatcher
__ Ash-throated flycatcher
__ Great crested flycatcher
__ Brown-crested flycatcher
__ Western kingbird
__ Eastern kingbird
__ Scissor-tailed flycatcher

LARKS
__ Horned lark

SWALLOWS
__ Purple martin
__ Tree swallow
__ Violet-green swallow
__ Northern rough-winged swallow
__ Bank swallow
__ Cliff swallow
__ Cave swallow
__ Barn swallow

JAYS, MAGPIES, AND CROWS
__ Gray jay
__ Steller's jay
__ Blue jay
__ Scrub jay
__ Clark's nutcracker
__ Black-billed magpie
__ American crow
__ Fish crow
__ Chihuahuan raven
__ Common raven

TITMICE
___ Black-capped chickadee
___ Carolina chickadee
___ Boreal chickadee
___ Tufted titmouse

VERDINS
___ Verdin

BUSHTITS
___ Bushtit

NUTHATCHES
___ Red-breasted nuthatch
___ White-breasted nuthatch
___ Pygmy nuthatch
___ Brown-headed nuthatch

CREEPERS
___ Brown creeper

WRENS
___ Cactus wren
___ Rock wren
___ Canyon wren
___ Carolina wren
___ Bewick's wren
___ House wren
___ Winter wren
___ Sedge wren
___ Marsh wren

KINGLETS AND GNATCATCHERS
___ Golden-crowned kinglet
___ Ruby-crowned kinglet
___ Blue-gray gnatcatcher
___ Black-tailed gnatcatcher

SOLITAIRES, THRUSHES, AND ALLIES
___ Eastern bluebird
___ Western bluebird
___ Mountain bluebird
___ Townsend's solitaire
___ Veery
___ Gray-cheeked thrush
___ Swainson's thrush
___ Hermit thrush
___ Wood thrush
___ American robin
___ Varied thrush

MOCKINGBIRDS, THRASHERS, AND ALLIES
___ Gray catbird
___ Northern mockingbird
___ Sage thrasher
___ Brown thrasher
___ Long-billed thrasher
___ Curve-billed thrasher

PIPITS
___ American pipit
___ Sprague's pipit

WAXWINGS
___ Bohemian waxwing
___ Cedar waxwing

SHRIKES
___ Northern shrike
___ Loggerhead shrike

STARLINGS
___ European starling

VIREOS
___ White-eyed vireo
___ Bell's vireo
___ Black-capped vireo
___ Gray vireo
___ Solitary vireo
___ Yellow-throated vireo
___ Warbling vireo
___ Philadelphia vireo
___ Red-eyed vireo

WOOD WARBLERS
___ Blue-winged warbler
___ Golden-winged warbler

__ Tennessee warbler
__ Orange-crowned warbler
__ Nashville's warbler
__ Virginia's warbler
__ Parula warbler
__ Yellow warbler
__ Chestnut-sided warbler
__ Magnolia warbler
__ Cape May warbler
__ Black-throated blue warbler
__ Yellow-rumped warbler
__ Black-throated gray warbler
__ Black-throated green warbler
__ Blackburnian warbler
__ Yellow-throated warbler
__ Pine warbler
__ Prairie warbler
__ Palm warbler
__ Bay-breasted warbler
__ Blackpoll warbler
__ Cerulean warbler
__ Black-and-white warbler
__ American redstart
__ Prothonotary warbler
__ Worm-eating warbler
__ Swainson's warbler
__ Ovenbird
__ Northern waterthrush
__ Louisiana waterthrush
__ Kentucky warbler
__ Connecticut warbler
__ Mourning warbler
__ MacGillvray's warbler
__ Common yellowthroat
__ Hooded warbler
__ Wilson's warbler
__ Canada warbler
__ Yellow-breasted chat

TANAGERS
__ Summer tanager
__ Scarlet tanager
__ Western tanager

GROSBEAKS, CARDINALS, AND ALLIES
__ Northern cardinal
__ Pyrrhuloxia
__ Rose-breasted grosbeak
__ Black-headed grosbeak
__ Blue grosbeak
__ Lazuli bunting
__ Indigo bunting
__ Painted bunting
__ Dickcissel

TOWHEES, SPARROWS, AND ALLIES
__ Olive sparrow
__ Green-tailed towhee
__ Rufous-sided towhee
__ Canyon towhee
__ Bachman's sparrow
__ Cassin's sparrow
__ Rufous-crowned sparrow
__ American tree sparrow
__ Chipping sparrow
__ Clay-colored sparrow
__ Brewer's sparrow
__ Field sparrow
__ Vesper sparrow
__ Lark sparrow
__ Black-throated sparrow
__ Lark bunting
__ Savannah sparrow
__ Baird's sparrow
__ Grasshopper sparrow
__ LeConte's sparrow
__ Sharp-tailed sparrow
__ Seaside sparrow
__ Fox sparrow
__ Song sparrow
__ Lincoln's sparrow
__ Swamp sparrow
__ White-throated sparrow
__ White-crowned sparrow
__ Harris' sparrow
__ Dark-eyed junco

__ McCown's longspur
__ Lapland longspur
__ Smith's longspur
__ Chestnut-collared longspur
__ Snow bunting

BLACKBIRDS AND ORIOLES
__ Bobolink
__ Red-winged blackbird
__ Eastern meadowlark
__ Western meadowlark
__ Yellow-headed blackbird
__ Rusty blackbird
__ Brewer's blackbird
__ Great-tailed grackle
__ Boat-tailed grackle
__ Common grackle
__ Bronzed cowbird
__ Brown-headed cowbird
__ Orchard oriole
__ Hooded oriole
__ Baltimore oriole
__ Bullock's oriole

FINCHES
__ Gray-crowned rosey finch
__ Pine grosbeak
__ Purple finch
__ Cassin's finch
__ House finch
__ Red crossbill
__ White-winged crossbill
__ Common redpoll
__ Hoary redpoll
__ Pine siskin
__ Lesser goldfinch
__ American goldfinch
__ Evening grosbeak

OLD WORLD SPARROWS
__ House sparrow

Common and Scientific Plant Names

Acacia, blackbrush. *Acacia rigidula.*
Alder. *Alnus rugosa*
Alder, green. *Alnus crispa*
Alder, mountain. *Alnus crispa*
Alder, river. *Alnus tenuifolia*
Alder, speckled. *Alnus rugosa*
Ash, green. *Fraxinus pennsylvanica*
Ash, mountain. *Fraxinus decorum*
Ash, pumpkin. *Fraxinus tomentosa*
Ash, red. *Fraxinus pennsylvanica*
Ash, white. *Fraxinus americana*
Aspen. *Populus tremuloides*
Azalea, hoary. *Rhododendron canescens*
Baldcypress. *Taxodium distichum*
Balsamroot, arrowleaf. *Balsamorhiza sagittata*
Basswood. *Tilia sp.*
Basswood, American. *Tilia americana*
Bay, sweet. *Magnolia virginiana*
Beach tea. *Croton punctatus*
Beech. *Fagus americanus*
Beech, blue. *Carpinus caroliniana*
Bearberry. *Arctostaphylos uva-ursi*
Birch, paper. *Betula papyrifera*
Birch, white. *Betula papyrifera*
Birch, river. *Betula nigra*
Birch, swamp. *Betula pumila*
Birch, yellow. *Betula allegheniensis*
Blackberry. *Rubus allegheniensis*
Blackgum. *Nyssa sylvatica*
Blueberry. *Vaccinium angustifolium*
Blueberry, velvetleaf. *Vaccinium myrtilloides*
Blue grass, Canada. *Poa compressa*
Blue grass, Sandberg's. *Poa secunda*
Bluestem, big. *Andropogon gerardi*
Bluestem, little. *Andropogon scoparius*

Bluestem, seacoast. *Andropogon sp.*
Bluestem, silver. *Andropogon sacchardoides*
Boxelder. *Acer negundo*
Brome, downy. *Brome tectorum*
Buckbrush. *Symphoricarpos occidentalis*
Buckeye. *Aesculus glabra.*
Buckeye, Ohio. *Aesculus glabra*
Buffalo berry. *Shepherdia argenta*
Buffalo grass. *Buchloe dactyloides*
Bulltongue. *Scirpus sp.*
Buttonbush. *Cephalanthus occidentalis*
Cactus, pricklypear (Great Plains). *Opuntia polyacantha.*
Cactus, pricklypear (Gulf States). *Opuntia lindheimeri*
Candelilla. *Euphorbia antisyphilitica*
Cattail. *Typha sp.*
Cedar, red. *Juniperus virginiana*
Cedar, white. *Thuja occidentalis*
Cenizo. *Leucophyllum frutescens*
Cherry, black. *Prunus serotina*
Cherry, sand. *Prunus depressa*
Chokecherry. *Prunus virginiana*
Chokecherry, red-fruited. *Prunus arbutifolia*
Cinquefoil, shrubby. *Potentilla fruitilla*
Clematis. *Clematis sp.*
Cordgrass, prairie. *Spartina pectina*
Cottonwood. *Populus deltoides*
Cottonwood, eastern. *Populus deltoides*
Cottonwood, plains. *Populus deltoides*
Cranberry. *Viburnum sp.*
Cranberry, high-bush. *Viburnum opulus.*

Cranberry, long-bush. *Viburnum edule*
Cranberry, small. *Viburnum oxycoccus*
Creeper, trumpet. *Campsis radicans*
Creosote bush. *Larrea tridentata*
Dewberry. *Rubus trivialis*
Dogwood, alternate-leaf. *Cornus alternifolia*
Dogwood, flowering. *Cornus florida*
Dogwood, red-osier. *Cornus stolonifera*
Duckweed. *Lemna* sp.
Elderberry. *Sambucus* sp.
Elderberry, common. *Sambucus canadensis*
Elderberry, red. *Sambucus pubens*
Elm, American. *Ulmus americana*
Elm, white. *Ulmus americana*
Evening-primrose, beach. *Oenothera drummondii*
Farkleberry. *Vaccinium arboreum*
Fir, balsam. *Abies balsamae.*
Goldeneye, skeletonleaf. *Viguiera longifolia*
Gooseberry, pasture. *Ribes cynosbati*
Gooseberry, wild. *Ribes oxyacanthoides*
Grama, blue. *Bouteloua gracilis*
Grama, side-oats. *Bouteloua curtipendula*
Grass, June. *Koeleria cristata*
Grass, needle-and-thread. *Stipa comata*
Grass, spear. *Stipa comata*
Grass, three-awn. *Aristada longiseta*
Greasewood. *Sarcobatus vermiculatus*
Guayacan. *Porlieria angustifolia*
Guajillo. *Acacia berlandieri*
Gum, black. *Nyssa sylvatica*
Hackberry. *Celtis occidentalis*
Hackberry, spiny. *Celtis pallida*
Hawthorn, round-leaved. *Crataegus rotundifolia*
Hazelnut. *Corylus americana*

Hazelnut, beaked. *Corylus cornuta*
Hemlock. *Tsuga canadensis*
Hickory, bitternut. *Carya cordiformes*
Hickory, black. *Carya texana*
Hickory, mockernut. *Carya tomentosa*
Hickory, shagbark. *Carya ovata*
Hickory, shellbark. *Carya laciniosa*
Holly, gallberry. *Ilex glabra*
Honeysuckle. *Lonicera* sp.
Honeysuckle, bush. *Diervilla lonicera*
Honeysuckle, twinning. *Lonicera* sp.
Hop tree. *Ptelea trifoliata*
Hornbeam. *Ostrya virginiana*
Huckleberry, black. *Gaylussacia baccata*
Huisache. *Acacia farnesiana*
Iris, giant blue. *Iris virginica*
Ironwood. *Carpinus caroliniana*
Jewelweed. *Impatiens capensis*
Juneberry. *Amelanchier alnifolia*
Juneberry, downy. *Amelanchier arborea*
Juniper, Ashe. *Juniperus ashei*
Juniper, common. *Juniperus communis*
Juniper, dwarf. *Juniperus communis*
Juniper, Rocky Mountain. *Juniperus scoplorum*
Kochia. *Kochia americana*
Labrador tea. *Ledum groenlandicum*
Larch. *Larix laricina*
Laurel, bog. *Kalmis polifolia*
Leadtree, little-leaf. *Leucaena retusa*
Leatherleaf. *Chamaedaphne calyculata*
Lechuguilla. *Agave lecheguilla*
Magnolia. *Magnolia* sp.
Magnolia, cucumber. *Magnolia acuminata*
Maple, Manitoba. *Acer negundo*
Maple, mountain. *Acer spicatum*
Maple, red. *Acer rubrum*
Maple, silver. *Acer saccharinum*

Maple, sugar. *Acer saccharum*
Mariola. *Parthenium incanum*
Meadowrose. *Rosa blanda*
Mesquite, honey. *Prosopis glandulosa*
Mountain-holly. *Nemopanthus mucronata*
Mountain mahogany. *Cercocarpus montanus*
Morning glory. *Ipomoea pes-caprae*
Moss, spaghnum. *Spaghnum* sp.
Moss, Spanish. *Tillandsia* sp.
Mountain-holly. *Nemopanthus mucronata*
Mountain-laurel, Texas. *Sophora secondiflora*
Mulberry. *Morus microphylla*
Muscadine. *Vitis rotundifolia*
Nanny berry. *Viburnum lentago*
Needlegrass, green. *Stipa spartae*
Ninebark. *Physocarpus opulifollus*
Nolina. *Nolina erumpens*
Oak, black. *Quercus velutina*
Oak, blackjack. *Quercus marilandica*
Oak, bur. *Quercus macrocarpa*
Oak, chestnut. *Quercus prinus*
Oak, chinkapin. *Quercus muehlenbergii*
Oak, chinquapin. *Quercus prinoides*
Oak, live. *Quercus virginiana*
Oak, post. *Quercus stellata*
Oak, red. *Quercus rubra*
Oak, Vasey shin. *Quercus havadrii*
Oak, water. *Quercus nigra*
Oak, white. *Quercus alba*
Oak, willow. *Quercus phellos*
Ocotillo. *Fourquieria splendors*
Ox-eye, sea. *Borrichia frutescens*
Palmetto, dwarf. *Sabal minor*
Partridgeberry. *Mitchella repens*
Persimmon, Texas. *Diospyros texana*
Pine, jack. *Pinus banksiana*
Pine, loblolly. *Pinus taeda*
Pine, ponderosa. *Pinus ponderosa*
Pine, red. *Pinus rubra*
Pine, shortleaf. *Pinus echinata*

Pine, white. *Pinus strobus*
Pincherry. *Prunus pensylvanicus*
Pitcher-plant. *Sarracenia alata*
Plum, American. *Prunus americana*
Plum, wild. *Prunus americana*
Poison ivy. *Rhus radicans*
Poplar, balsam. *Populus balsamifera*
Possumhaw. *Ilex decidua*
Rabbitbrush, rubber. *Chrysothamnus nauseosus*
Rattlebox, red. *Ludwigia alternifolia*
Redbud. *Cercis canadensis*
Reed, common. *Phragmites communis*
Reed, giant. *Arundo donax*
Rose, prickly. *Rosa acicularis*
Rose, wild prairie. *Rosa blanda*
Rose, Wood's. *Rosa woodsi*
Rosemary, bog. *Andromeda glaucophylla*
Rush, American. *Scirpus americana*
Sacahuista. *Nolina texana*
Sagebrush, big. *Artemesia tridentata*
Sagebrush, fringed. *Artemesia frigida*
Sagebrush, sand. *Artemesia filifolia*
Sagebrush, silver. *Artemesia cana*
Saltbush, spiny. *Atriplex confertifolia*
Sandreed, prairie. *Calamovilfa longifolia*
Sassafras. *Sassafras albidum*
Saskatoon. *Amelanchier alnifolia*
Sarsparilla. *Aralia hispida*
Sea oat. *Uniola paniculata*
Sedge. *Carex* sp.
Seepwillow. *Baccharis glutinosa*
Selaginella, prairie. *Selaginella densa*
Silverberry. *Elaeagnus commutata*
Snowberry. *Symphocarpos occidentalis*
Snowberry, few-flowered. *Symphocarpos* sp.
Snowberry, thin-leaved. *Symphocarpos albus*
Snowberry, western. *Symphocarpos occidentalis*
Sotol. *Dasylirion texanum*

Spruce, black. *Picea mariana*
Spruce, white. *Picae glauca*
Spurge, leafy. *Euphorbia esula*
Squashberry. *Viburnum edule*
Squawberry. *Viburnum edule*
Squawbush. *Rhus trilobata*
Sumac, skunkbush. *Rhus aromatica*
Sumac, staghorn. *Rhus typhina*
Sweetgum. *Liquidambar styraciflua*
Sycamore. *Platanus occidentalis*
Tamarack. *Larix laricina*
Tamarisk. *Tamarisk* sp.
Tanglehead. *Heteropogon contortus*
Tarbush. *Flourensia cernua*
Thimbleberry. *Rubus parviflorus*
Three-awn. *Aristida roemericana*
Tobacco, tree. *Nicotiana glauca*
Trichloris. *Trichloris pluriflora*
Tulip-tree. *Liriodendron tulipifera*
Tupelo, water. *Nyssa aquatica*
Viburnum, mapleleaf. *Viburnum acerifolium*
Walnut, black. *Juglans nigra*
Walnut, little. *Juglans microcarpa*
Waterlily. *Nymphaea* sp.
Wheatgrass, western. *Agropyron smithii*
Willow, beaked. *Salix bebbiana*
Willow, black. *Salix nigra*
Willow, sandbar. *Salix exigua*
Willow, smooth. *Salix leiolepis*
Willow, ward's. *Salix caroliniana*
Willow, yellow. *Salix lutea*
Winterfat. *Eurotia lanata*
Wintergreen, redberry. *Arctostaphylos uva-ursi*
Witch-hazel, common. *Hamamelis virginiana*
Wolf-berry. *Symphoricarpos occidentalis*
Wolfberry. *Lycium berlandieri*
Wolf-willow. *Elaeagnus commutata*
Wormwood. *Artemisia caudata*
Yaupon, desert. *Schaefferia cuneifolia*

Yew. *Taxus canadensis*
Yew, American. *Taxus canadensis*
Yew, Canadian. *Taxus canadensis*
Yucca. *Yucca glauca*
Yucca, soapweed. *Yucca glauca*

Bibliography

Able, Kenneth P. 1991. Migration Biology for Birders. *Birding* (April): 64-72.

Ajilvsgi, Geyata. 1979. *Wild Flowers of the Big Thicket.* College Station: Texas A&M University Press.

American Ornithologists' Union. 1983. *Check-list of North American Birds.* A.O.U. Lawrence, Kans.: Allen Press.

Armistead, Henry T. 1983. Cerulean Warbler. In *The Audubon Society Master Guide to Birding* Vol. 3, ed. John Farrand, Jr., 158. New York: Alfred A. Knopf.

Austin, Mike. 1991. Finding Nesting Red-cockaded Woodpeckers, Swainson's Warblers, and Bachman's Sparrows in East Texas. *Birding* (April): 74-78.

Bellrose, Frank C. 1976. *Ducks, Geese and Swans of North America.* Harrisburg, Pa.: Stackpole Books.

Bent, Arthur Cleveland. 1958. *Life Histories of North American Blackbirds, Orioles, Tanagers, and Allies.* Washington, D.C.: Smithsonian Institution.

_____. 1961. *Life Histories of North American Birds of Prey.* New York: Dover Publications.

_____. 1963. *Life Histories of North American Flycatchers, Larks, Swallows, and Their Allies.* New York: Dover Publications.

_____. 1963. *Life Histories of North American Wood Warblers.* New York: Dover Publications.

_____. 1964. *Life Histories of North American Woodpeckers.* New York: Dover Publications.

_____. 1964. *Life Histories of North American Jays, Crows, and Titmice.* New York: Dover Publications.

_____. 1964. *Life Histories of North American Thrushes, Kinglets, and their Allies.* New York: Dover Publications.

_____. 1964. *Life Histories of North American Nuthatches, Wrens, Thrashers, and Their Allies.* New York: Dover Publications.

_____. 1965. *Life Histories of North American Wagtails, Shrikes, Vireos, and Their Allies.* New York: Dover Publications.

_____. 1968. *Life Histories of North American Cardinals, Grosbeaks, Buntings, Towhees, Finches, Sparrows, and Allies.* Washington, D.C.: Smithsonian Institution.

Bjork, Jennifer. 1988. Peregrine Falcon Monitoring at Padre Island. *Park Science* (Summer): 7-8.

Brock, Kenneth J. 1986. *Birds of the Indiana Dunes.* Bloomington: Indiana University Press.

Brockman, C. Frank. *Trees of North America.* New York: Golden Press.

Brooks, Paul. 1980. *Speaking for Nature*. San Francisco: Sierra Club Books.

Brown, Lauren. 1947. *The Audubon Society Nature Guides: Grasslands*. New York: Alfred A. Knopf.

Budd, Archibald C., and Keith F. Best. 1969. *Wild Plants of the Canadian Prairies*. Ottawa: Canada Department of Agriculture.

Canadian Parks Service. 1990. *State of the Parks 1990 Report*. Gloucester, Ont.: T&H Printers.

Canadian Parks Service. 1990. *State of the Parks 1990 Profile*. Gloucester, Ont.: T&H Printers.

Carson, Rachel. 1962. *Silent Spring*. Boston: Houghton Mifflin.

Chadwick, Douglas H. 1990. The Biodiversity Challenge. *Defenders* (May/June): 19-31.

Chapman, Frank M. 1966. *Handbook of Birds of Eastern North American Birds*. New York: Dover Publications.

_____. 1968. *The Warblers of North America*. New York: Dover Publications.

Clark, Jim. 1991. Silent Chorus. *Birder's World* (Oct.): 25-29.

Clark, William S., and Brian K. Wheeler. 1987. *A Field Guide to Hawks of North America*. Boston: Houghton Mifflin.

Clements, James F. 1991. *Birds of the World: A Check List*, 4th ed. Vista, Calif.: Ibis Publishing.

Cuthbert, Calvin W., Jean I. Horton, Mamie W. McCowan, Barbara G. Robinson, and Borman G. Short. 1990. *Birder's Guide to Southwestern Manitoba*. Brandon, Manitoba.: Brandon Natural History Society.

Cook, Francis R., and Dalton Muir. 1984. The Committee on the Status of Endangered Wildlife in Canada (COSEWIC): History and Progress. *The Canadian Field-Naturalist* 98:63-70.

Correll, Donovan Stewart, and Marshall Conring Johnston. 1970. *Manual of the Vascular Plants of Texas*. Renner: Texas Research Foundation.

Council on Environmental Quality and Department of State. 1980. *The Global 2000 Report to the President*. Washington, D.C.: Government Printing Office.

Cox, Mike K., and William L. Franklin. 1989. Terrestrial Vertebrates of Scotts Bluff National Monument, Nebraska. *Great Basin Naturalist* 49 (1):597-613.

Cumming, Edid E. 1993. Birds of Treebeard Trail. In *Wolf Country*, Sask.: Prince Albert National Park.

Cuthbert, Calvin W., Jean I. Horton, Mamie W. McCowan, Barbara G. Robinson, and Norman G. Short. 1990. *Birder's Guide to Southwestern Manitoba*. Brandon, Manitoba: Brandon Natural History Society.

Dale, Edward E., Jr., and Michael R. Watts. 1980. Vegetation of Hot Springs National Park, Arkansas. Photocopied report to National Park Service.

Daniel, Glenda. 1984. *Dune Country: A Hiker's Guide to the Indiana Dunes*. Athens, Ohio: Swallow Press.

DeBenedictis, Paul A. 1993. The Thirty-ninth Supplement to the American

Ornithologists' Union Check-list of North American Birds. *American Birds* (Fall): 384-86.

De La Torre, Julio. 1990. *Owls: Their Life and Behavior.* New York: Crown Publishers.

Diamond, Antony W., Rudolf L. Scheiber, Walter Cronkite, and Roger Tory Peterson. 1989. *Save the Birds.* Boston: Houghton Mifflin.

Doolittle, Thomas C. J. 1992. Status of the Eastern Taiga Merlin *Falco c. columbianus.* Master's thesis, University of Wisconsin, Eau Claire.

Douglas, William O. 1967. *Farewell to Texas A Vanishing Wilderness.* New York: McGraw-Hill.

Duncan, Bob. 1990. Weather and Birding. *Birding* (Aug.): 173-75.

Dunne, Pete, David Sibley, and Clay Sutton. 1988. *Hawks in Flight.* Boston: Houghton Mifflin.

Ehrlich, Paul R., David S. Dobkin, and Darryl Wheye. 1988. *The Birder's Handbook.* New York: Simon & Schuster.

_____. 1992. *Birds in Jeopardy.* California: Stanford University Press.

Ellis, David H., James C. Bednarz, Dwight G. Smith, and Stephen P. Flemming. 1993. Social Foraging Classes in Raptorial Birds. *BioScience* 43:14-20.

Erskine, Anthony J. 1977. *Birds in Boreal Canada.* Ottawa: Canadian Wildlife Service.

Farb, Peter. 1963. *Face of North America.* New York: Harper & Row.

Fisher, Charles D. 1974. A Preliminary Survey of Avian Fauna of Big Thicket National Preserve. Photocopied report to National Park Service.

Flyr, David. (undated) A Preliminary Study of the Paleoecology of the Amistad Reservoir Area. Photocopied report to National Science Foundation.

Freeman, Judith. 1986. The Parks as Genetic Islands. *National Parks* (Jan./Feb.): 12-17.

Getty, Stephen R. 1993. Call-notes of North American Wood Warblers. *Birding* (June): 159-68.

Godfrey, W. Earl. 1966. *The Birds of Canada.* Ottawa: National Museums of Canada.

Graham, Frank, Jr. 1990. 2001: Birds That Won't Be with Us. *American Birds* (Winter): 1074-81 + 1194-99.

Graham, J. Robertson. (undated) *Where Canada Begins: A Visitor's Guide to Point Pelee National Park.* Leamington, Ont.: Friends of Point Pelee.

Griscom, Ludlow, and Alexander Sprunt, Jr. 1957. *The Warblers of America.* New York: Devin-Adair.

Grossman, Mary Louise, and John Hamlet. 1964. *Birds of Prey of the World.* New York: Clarkson N. Potter.

Gruson, Edward S. 1972. *Words for Birds: A Lexicon of North American Birds with Biographical Notes.* New York: Quadrangle Books.

Guggisberg, C.A.W. 1970. *Man and Wildlife.* New York: Arco Publishing.
Halle, Louis J. 1947. *Spring in Washington.* New York: Harper and Brothers.
Hauk, Joy Keve. 1969. *Badlands: Its Life and Landscape.* Interior, South Dakota: Badlands Natural History Association.
Headstrom, Richard. 1951. *Birds' Nests of the West: A Field Guide.* New York: Ives Washburn.
Henry, Suzanne. undated. *Bird-Watching in Prince Albert National Park.* Waskesui Lake, Sask.: Friends of Prince Albert National Park.
Howe, Steve. 1992. Raptor Redux. *National Parks* (July/Aug.): 28-33.
Hunt, W. Grainger, F. P. Word, B. S. Johnson, C. M. Anderson, and G. P. Vose. 1980. A Study of the Spring Passage of Peregrine Falcons at Padre Island, Texas, Using Radio Telemetry. Photocopied report.
Hutto, Richard L. 1988. Is Tropical Deforestation Responsible for the Reported Declines in Neotropical Migrant Populations? *American Birds* (Fall): 375-79.
Jackson, Jerome A. 1992. Red-capped Sap-tapper. *Birder's World* (Dec.): 24-27.
James, Douglas, Edward E. Dale, Jr., M. Joseph Lockerd, David Schick, and Charles R. Preston. 1979. Appraisal of the Avifauna, Mammalian Fauna, and Plant Communities at Developmental Sites Proposed for the Buffalo National River. Photocopied report to National Park Service.
James, Douglas A., and Joseph C. Neal. 1986. *Arkansas Birds Their Distribution and Abundance.* Fayetteville: University of Arkansas.
Johnsgard, Paul A. 1979. *Birds of the Great Plains.* Lincoln: University of Nebraska Press.
————————. 1986. *Birds of the Rocky Mountains.* Lincoln: University of Nebraska Press.
Johnson, Morris D. 1988. *Black and White Spy: The Magpie.* Dickinson, N.D.: Professional Printing.
Jones, Fred B. 1975. *Flora of the Texas Coastal Bend.* Sinton, Texas: Rob and Bessie Welder Wildlife Foundation.
Kastner, Joseph. 1986. *A World of Watchers.* San Francisco: Sierra Club Books.
Kaufman, Kenn. 1983. Yellow-rumped warbler. In *The Audubon Society Master Guide to Birding,* ed. John Farrand, Jr., 136: New York: Alfred A. Knopf.
————————. 1990. *Advanced Birding.* Boston: Houghton Mifflin.
Kenner, Brian C. 1992. Peregrine Falcon Re-Establishment Efforts. *Pictured Rocks Resource Report,* August, Pictured Rocks Lakeshore. Photocopied report to National Park Service.
Klein, Tom. 1989. *Loon Magic.* Minocqua, Wis.: NorthWord Press.
Knox, Margaret L. 1990. Beyond Park Boundaries. *Nature Conservancy* (July/Aug.): 16-23.
Lehman. Paul. 1983. Tennessee warbler. In *The Audubon Society Master*

Guide to Birding, ed. John Farrand, Jr., 114. New York: Alfred A. Knopf.
_____. 1993. Rufous-sided towhee. In *The Audubon Society Master Guide to Birding,* ed. John Farrand, Jr. 218. New York: Alfred A. Knopf.

Leopold, Aldo. 1966. *A Sand County Almanac.* New York: Oxford University Press.

Line, Les. 1993. Silence of the Songbirds. *National Geographic* (June): 68-91.

LoBello, Rick L. 1976. Vertebrates of the Lake Amistad Recreation Area, Texas. Dissertation at Sul Ross State University, Alpine, Texas.

Maechtle, Thomas L. 1988. Padre Island Peregrine Falcon Survey Report Concerning Field Data Collected During Spring and Autumn 1988. Photocopied report to National Park Service.

Marshall, Joe T., Jr. 1967. *Parallel Variation in North and Middle American Screech-Owls.* Monograph Western Foundation of Vertebrate Zoology. No. 1. Los Angeles: Western Foundation of Vertebrate Zoology.
_____. Roger B. Clapp, and Joseph A. Grzybowski. 1985. Status report: *Vireo atricapillus* Woodhouse black-capped vireo. Photcopied report to U.S. Fish and Wildlife Service.

Matthiessen, Peter, and Ralph S. Palmer. 1967. *The Shorebirds of North America.* New York: Viking Press.

National Audubon Society. 1974. The Seventy-fourth Christmas Bird Count. *American Birds* 28 (2). New York: National Audubon Society.
_____. 1980. The Eightieth Audubon Christmas Bird Count. *American Birds* 34 (4). New York: National Audubon Society.
_____. 1985. The Eighty-fifth Christmas Bird Count. *American Birds* 39 (4). New York: National Audubon Society.
_____. 1992. The Ninety-second Christmas Bird Count. *American Birds* 46 (4). New York: National Audubon Society.

National Fish and Wildlife Foundation. 1990. Proposal for a Neotropical Migratory Bird Conservation Program. Photocopied report.

National Geographic Society. 1987. *Field Guide to the Birds of North America* 2nd ed. Washington, D.C.: National Geographic Society.

Nice, Margaret Morse. 1964. *Studies in the Life History of the Song Sparrow.* New York: Dover Publications.

Oberholser, Harry C. 1974. *The Bird Life of Texas.* Austin: University of Texas Press.

Olson, Sigurd. 1987. *Songs of the North.* New York: Penguin Books.

Palmer, Ralph S. 1962. *Handbook of North American Birds. Vol. 1* New Haven: Yale University Press.
_____. 1988. *Handbook of North American Birds. Vol. 4.* New Haven: Yale Univ. Press.

Peterson, Richard A. 1993. *A Birdwatcher's Guide to the Black Hills and Adjacent Plains.* Vermillion, S.D.: PC Publishing.

Peterson, Roger Tory. 1961. *A Field Guide to Western Birds*. Boston: Houghton Mifflin.
_____. 1963. *A Field Guide to the Birds of Texas*. Boston: Houghton Mifflin.
_____. 1980. *A Field Guide to the Birds East of the Rockies*. Boston: Houghton Mifflin.
Peterson, Wayne R. 1983. Eastern Kingbird. In *The Audubon Society Master Guide to Birding Vol. 2*, ed. John Farrand, Jr., 288. New York: Alfred A. Knopf.
_____. 1983. Veery. In *The Audubon Society Master Guide to Birding Vol. 2*, ed. John Farrand, Jr., 52. New York: Alfred A. Knopf.
_____. 1983. Swainson's Thrush. In *The Audubon Society Master Guide to Birding Vol. 2*, ed. John Farrand, Jr., 52. New York: Alfred A. Knopf.
_____. 1983. House Wren. In *The Audubon Society Master Guide to Birding Vol. 2*, ed. John Farrand, Jr., 350. New York: Alfred A. Knopf.
_____. 1983. Winter Wren. In *The Audubon Society Master Guide to Birding Vol. 2*, ed. John Farrand, Jr. 352. New York: Alfred A. Knopf.
_____. 1983. Red-eyed Vireo. In *The Audubon Society Master Guide to Birding Vol. 3*, ed. John Farrand, Jr. 106. New York: Alfred A. Knopf.
_____. 1983. Blackburnian Warbler. In *The Audubon Society Master Guide to Birding Vol. 3*, ed. John Farrand, Jr. 144. New York: Alfred A. Knopf.
_____. 1983. Lincoln's Sparrow. In *The Audubon Society Master Guide to Birding Vol. 3*, ed. John Farrand, Jr. 264. New York: Alfred A. Knopf.
Petrides, George A. 1972. *A Field Guide to Trees and Shrubs*. Boston: Houghton Mifflin.
Pettingill, Olin Sewall, Jr. 1953. *A Guide to Bird Finding West of the Mississippi*. New York: Oxford University Press.
_____. 1977. *A Guide to Bird Finding East of the Mississippi*. New York: Oxford University Press.
Polson, James R. 1993. Weapons to Cradle. *American Birds* (Summer): 216-19.
Pough, Richard H. 1957. *Audubon Western Bird Guide: Land, Water, and Game Birds*. Garden City, New York: Doubleday.
Pratt, Paul. 1990. *Point Pelee National Park and Vicinity Season Status of Birds*. Leamington, Ont.: Friends of Point Pelee.
Pretzman, Chip. 1989. Birder's Guide to the Indiana Dunes. *WildBird* (Jan.): 36-41.
Read, Robert H. 1975. Vascular Plants of Pictured Rocks National Lakeshore, Alger County, Michigan. *Michigan Botanist* 14:3-43.

Reader's Digest. 1985. *Our National Parks*. New York: Reader's Digest Association.

Remsen, J. V., Jr. 1983. House Finch. In *The Audubon Society Master Guide to Birding Vol. 3*, ed. John Farrand, Jr., 332. New York: Alfred A. Knopf.

Rich, Terry. 1989. Forests, Fire and the Future. *Birder's World* (June): 10-14.

_____. 1993. Beacons in the Sage. *Birder's World* (Aug.): 12-17.

Ripley, S. Dillon. 1965. Surface-feeding Ducks and Tree Ducks. In *Water, Prey, and Game Birds of North America*, ed. Alexander Wetmore. Washington, D.C.: National Geographic Society.

Robbins, Chandler S., John R. Sauer, Russell S. Greenberg, and Sam Droege. 1989. Population Declines in North American Birds That Migrate to the Neotropics. *Population Biology* 86:7658-62.

Saunders, Aretas A. 1951. *A Guide to Bird Songs*. Garden City, New York: Doubleday.

Shafer, Craig L. 1990. *Nature Reserves Island Theory and Conservation Practice*. Washington, D.C.: Smithsonian Institution.

Shandruk, Len, and Rob Kaye. 1989. Elk Island National Park, Trumpeter Swan Reintroduction 1989/90. Photocopied report.

Shelton, Napier. 1975. *The Life of Isle Royale*. Washington, D.C.: National Park Service.

Sieg, Carolyn Hull. 1991. *Rocky Mountain Juniper Woodlands: Year-Round Avian Habitat*. U.S. Department of Agriculture Research Paper RM-296 Fort Collins, Colo: Rocky Mountain Forest and Range Experiment Station.

Simons, Ted, John Peine, and Richard Cunningham. 1989. Proposed Migratory Bird Watch to Encompass Research, Monitoring, and Interpretation. *Park Science* 9:8.

Skeel, M., and S. Bondrup-Nielsen. 1978. Avifauna Survey of Pukaskwa National Park. Photocopied report.

Stoltenburg, William. 1991. The Fragment Connection. *Nature Conservancy* (July/Aug.): 19-25.

Sutton, Ann and Myron Sutton. 1974. *Wilderness Areas of North America*. New York: Funk & Wagnalls.

Sykes, Paul W., Jr. 1983. Yellow-throated Warbler. In *The Audubon Society Master Guide to Birding Vol. 3*, ed. John Farrand, Jr., 146. New York: Alfred A. Knopf.

_____. 1983. Pine Warbler. In *The Audubon Society Master Guide to Birding Vol. 3*, ed. John Farrand, Jr., 148. New York: Alfred A. Knopf.

_____. 1983. Louisiana Waterthrush. In *The Audubon Society Master Guide to Birding Vol. 3*, ed. John Farrand, Jr., 168. New York: Alfred A. Knopf.

_____. 1983. Painted Bunting. In *The Audubon Society Master*

Guide to Birding Vol. 3, ed. John Farrand, Jr., 212. New York: Alfred A. Knopf.

Tainter, Fern R. 1993. Little Coal of Fire. *Birder's World* (June): 68-71.

Tanner, James. 1942. *The Ivory-billed Woodpecker.* New York: Dover Publications.

Teale, Edwin Way. 1971. Big Thicket: Crossroads of Nature. *Audubon* (May): 12-32.

Temple, Stanley A., and James T. Harris. 1985. *Birds of the Apostle Islands.* Hartland, Wis.: The Wisconsin Society for Ornithology.

Terborgh, John. 1989. *Where Have All the Birds Gone?* Oxford: Princeton University Press.

_____. 1992. Why American Songbirds Are Vanishing. *Scientific American* (May): 98-104.

Terres, John K. 1987. *The Audubon Society Encyclopedia of North American Birds.* New York: Alfred A. Knopf.

Udall, James R. 1991. Launching the Natural Ark. *Sierra* (Sept./Oct.): 80-89.

Van Bruggen, Theodore. 1992. *Wildflowers, Grasses & Other Plants of the Northern Plains and Black Hills.* Interior, N.D.: Badlands Natural History Association.

Van Stappen, Julia F., and Thomas C. J. Doolittle. 1991. 1990 Migratory Bird Survey, Apostle Islands National Lakeshore. Resource Management Report to National Park Service.

_____. 1992. 1992 Breeding Bird Survey, Apostle Islands National Lakeshore. Resource Management Report to National Park Service.

Vickery, Peter D. 1983. Marsh Wren. In *The Audubon Society Master Guide to Birding Vol. 2*, ed. John Farrand, Jr. 354. New York: Alfred A. Knopf.

_____. 1983. Yellow Warbler. In *The Audubon Society Master Guide to Birding Vol. 3*, ed. John Farrand, Jr., 126. New York: Alfred A. Knopf.

_____. 1983. Black-and-white Warbler. In *The Audubon Society Master Guide to Birding Vol. 3*, ed. John Farrand, Jr. 160. New York: Alfred A. Knopf.

_____. 1983. Indigo Bunting. In *The Audubon Society Master Guide to Birding Vol. 3*, ed. John Farrand, Jr., 210. New York: Alfred A.Knopf.

_____. 1983. Vesper Sparrow. In *The Audubon Society Master Guide to Birding Vol. 3*, ed. John Farrand, Jr., 240. New York: Alred A. Knopf.

Wauer, Roland H. 1992. *Naturalist's Mexico.* College Station: Texas A&M University Press.

_____. 1993. *The Visitor's Guide to the Birds of the Rocky Mountain National Parks United States and Canada.* Santa Fe, NM: John

Muir Publications.

_____, and Terrell Johnson. La Mesa Fire Effects on
Avifauna—Changes in Avian Populations and Biomass. In *La Mesa Fire
Symposium, Los Alamos, New Mexico, October 6 and 7, 1981*. Los Alamos,
NM: Los Alamos National Laboratory.

Weidensaul, Scott. 1991. *The Birder's Miscellany*. New York: Simon &
Schuster.

Welty, Joel Carl. 1963. *The Life of Birds*. New York: Alfred A. Knopf.

Wilcove, David. 1990. Empty Skies. *Nature Conservancy* (Jan./Feb.): 4-13.

Wilhelm, Gerould S. 1990. *Special Vegetation of the Indiana Dunes National
Lakeshore*. Lisle, Ill.: Morton Arboretum.

Wilkinson, Kathleen. *1990. Trees and Shrubs of Alberta*. Edmonton, Alberta:
Lone Pine Publishing.

Wolverton, Ruthe, and Walt Wolverton. 1988. *The National Seashores The
Complete Guide to America's Scenic Coastal Parks*. Kensington, Md.:
Woodbine House.

Youth, Howard. 1992. Birds Fast Disappearing. In *Vital Signs 1992*.
Worldwatch Institution. New York: W.W. Norton.

Zimmerman, Paul. 1993. Comeback Trail. *Birder's World* (Aug.): 18-22.

INDEX

Other Books from John Muir Publications

Travel Books by Rick Steves
Asia Through the Back Door, 4th
ed., 400 pp. $16.95
Europe 101: History and Art for the
Traveler, 4th ed., 372 pp. $15.95
Europe Through the Back Door,
12th ed., 434 pp. $17.95
Europe Through the Back Door
Phrase Book: French, 112 pp. $4.95
Europe Through the Back Door
Phrase Book: German, 112 pp.
$4.95
Europe Through the Back Door
Phrase Book: Italian, 112 pp. $4.95
Europe Through the Back Door
Phrase Book: Spanish &
Portuguese, 288 pp. $6.95
Mona Winks: Self-Guided Tours of
Europe's Top Museums, 2nd ed.,
456 pp. $16.95
*See the 2 to 22 Days series to follow
for other Rick Steves titles.*

A Natural Destination Series
Belize: A Natural Destination, 2nd
ed., 304 pp. $16.95
Costa Rica: A Natural Destination,
3rd ed., 320 pp. $16.95 (available
8/94)
Guatemala: A Natural Destination,
336 pp. $16.95

Undiscovered Islands Series
Undiscovered Islands of the
Caribbean, 3rd ed., 264 pp. $14.95
Undiscovered Islands of the
Mediterranean, 2nd ed., 256 pp.
$13.95
Undiscovered Islands of the U.S.
and Canadian West Coast, 288 pp.
$12.95

For Birding Enthusiasts
The Birder's Guide to Bed and
Breakfasts, U.S. and Canada, 288
pp. $15.95
The Visitor's Guide to the Birds of
the Central National Parks: U.S.
and Canada, 400 pp. $15.95 (avail-
able 8/94)
The Visitor's Guide to the Birds of
the Eastern National Parks: U.S.
and Canada, 400 pp. $15.95
The Visitor's Guide to the Birds of
the Rocky Mountain National
Parks, U.S. and Canada, 432 pp.
$15.95

Unique Travel Series
Each is 112 pages and $10.95 paper.
Unique Arizona (available 9/94)
Unique California (available 9/94)
Unique Colorado
Unique Florida
Unique New England
Unique New Mexico
Unique Texas

2 to 22 Days Series
Each title offers 22 flexible daily itiner-
aries useful for planning vacations of any
length. Included are "must see" attrac-
tions as well as hidden "jewels."
2 to 22 Days in the American
Southwest, 1994 ed., 192 pp. $10.95
2 to 22 Days in Asia, 1994 ed., 176 pp.
$10.95
2 to 22 Days in Australia, 1994 ed., 192
pp. $10.95
2 to 22 Days in California, 1994 ed.,
192 pp. $10.95
2 to 22 Days in Eastern Canada, 1994
ed., 192 pp. $12.95
2 to 22 Days in Europe, 1994 ed., 304
pp. $14.95
2 to 22 Days in Florida, 1994 ed., 192
pp. $10.95
2 to 22 Days in France, 1994 ed., 192
pp. $10.95
2 to 22 Days in Germany, Austria, and
Switzerland, 1994 ed., 240 pp. $12.95
2 to 22 Days in Great Britain, 1994 ed.,
208 pp. $10.95
2 to 22 Days Around the Great Lakes,
1994 ed., 192 pp. $10.95
2 to 22 Days in Hawaii, 1994 ed., 192
pp. $10.95
2 to 22 Days in Italy, 1994 ed., 208 pp.
$10.95
2 to 22 Days in New England, 1994
ed., 192 pp. $10.95
2 to 22 Days in New Zealand, 1994 ed.,
192 pp. $10.95
2 to 22 Days in Norway, Sweden, and
Denmark, 1994 ed., 192 pp. $10.95
2 to 22 Days in the Pacific Northwest,
1994 ed., 192 pp. $10.95
2 to 22 Days in the Rockies, 1994 ed.,
192 pp. $10.95
2 to 22 Days in Spain and Portugal,
1994 ed., 208 pp. $10.95
2 to 22 Days in Texas, 1994 ed., 192
pp. $10.95
2 to 22 Days in Thailand, 1994 ed.,
192 pp. $10.95

22 Days (or More) Around the World, 1994 ed., 264 pp. $13.95

Other Terrific Travel Titles
The 100 Best Small Art Towns in America, 256 pp. $12.95 (available 8/94)
Elderhostels: The Students' Choice, 2nd ed., 304 pp. $15.95
Environmental Vacations: Volunteer Projects to Save the Planet, 2nd ed., 248 pp. $16.95
A Foreign Visitor's Guide to America, 224 pp. $12.95
Great Cities of Eastern Europe, 256 pp. $16.95
Indian America: A Traveler's Companion, 3rd ed., 432 pp. $18.95
Interior Furnishings Southwest, 256 pp. $19.95
Opera! The Guide to Western Europe's Great Houses, 296 pp. $18.95
Paintbrushes and Pistols: How the Taos Artists Sold the West, 288 pp. $17.95
The People's Guide to Mexico, 9th ed., 608 pp. $18.95
Ranch Vacations: The Complete Guide to Guest and Resort, Fly-Fishing, and Cross-Country Skiing Ranches, 3rd ed., 512 pp. $19.95
The Shopper's Guide to Art and Crafts in the Hawaiian Islands, 272 pp. $13.95
The Shopper's Guide to Mexico, 224 pp. $9.95
Understanding Europeans, 272 pp. $14.95
A Viewer's Guide to Art: A Glossary of Gods, People, and Creatures, 144 pp. $10.95
Watch It Made in the U.S.A.: A Visitor's Guide to the Companies that Make Your Favorite Products, 272 pp. $16.95 (available 7/94)

Parenting Titles
Being a Father: Family, Work, and Self, 176 pp. $12.95
Preconception: A Woman's Guide to Preparing for Pregnancy and Parenthood, 232 pp. $14.95
Schooling at Home: Parents, Kids, and Learning, 264 pp., $14.95
Teens: A Fresh Look, 240 pp. $14.95

Automotive Titles
The Greaseless Guide to Car Care Confidence, 224 pp. $14.95

How to Keep Your Datsun/Nissan Alive, 544 pp. $21.95
How to Keep Your Subaru Alive, 480 pp. $21.95
How to Keep Your Toyota Pickup Alive, 392 pp. $21.95
How to Keep Your VW Alive, 15th ed., 464 pp. $21.95

TITLES FOR YOUNG READERS AGES 8 AND UP

American Origins Series
Each is 48 pages and $12.95 hardcover.
Tracing Our Chinese Roots
Tracing Our German Roots
Tracing Our Irish Roots
Tracing Our Italian Roots
Tracing Our Japanese Roots
Tracing Our Jewish Roots
Tracing Our Polish Roots

Bizarre & Beautiful Series
Each is 48 pages and $14.95 hardcover.
Bizarre & Beautiful Ears
Bizarre & Beautiful Eyes
Bizarre & Beautiful Feelers
Bizarre & Beautiful Noses
Bizarre & Beautiful Tongues

Environmental Titles
Habitats: Where the Wild Things Live, 48 pp. $9.95
The Indian Way: Learning to Communicate with Mother Earth, 114 pp. $9.95
Rads, Ergs, and Cheeseburgers: The Kids' Guide to Energy and the Environment, 108 pp. $13.95
The Kids' Environment Book: What's Awry and Why, 192 pp. $13.95

Extremely Weird Series
Each is 48 pages and $9.95 paper. $12.95 hardcover editions available 8/94.
Extremely Weird Bats
Extremely Weird Birds
Extremely Weird Endangered Species
Extremely Weird Fishes
Extremely Weird Frogs
Extremely Weird Insects
Extremely Weird Mammals
Extremely Weird Micro Monsters
Extremely Weird Primates
Extremely Weird Reptiles
Extremely Weird Sea Creatures
Extremely Weird Snakes
Extremely Weird Spiders

Kidding Around Travel Series

All are 64 pages and $9.95 paper, except for *Kidding Around Spain* and *Kidding Around the National Parks of the Southwest*, which are 108 pages and $12.95 paper.

Kidding Around Atlanta
Kidding Around Boston, 2nd ed.
Kidding Around Chicago, 2nd ed.
Kidding Around the Hawaiian Islands
Kidding Around London
Kidding Around Los Angeles
Kidding Around the National Parks of the Southwest
Kidding Around New York City, 2nd ed.
Kidding Around Paris
Kidding Around Philadelphia
Kidding Around San Diego
Kidding Around San Francisco
Kidding Around Santa Fe
Kidding Around Seattle
Kidding Around Spain
Kidding Around Washington, D.C., 2nd ed.

Kids Explore Series

Written by kids for kids, all are $9.95 paper.

Kids Explore America's African American Heritage, 128 pp.
Kids Explore the Gifts of Children with Special Needs, 128 pp.
Kids Explore America's Hispanic Heritage, 112 pp.
Kids Explore America's Japanese American Heritage, 144 pp.

Masters of Motion Series

Each is 48 pages and $9.95 paper.
How to Drive an Indy Race Car
How to Fly a 747
How to Fly the Space Shuttle

Rainbow Warrior Artists Series

Each is 48 pages and $14.95 hardcover.
Native Artists of Africa
Native Artists of Europe (available 8/94)
Native Artists of North America

Rough and Ready Series

Each is 48 pages and $12.95 hardcover.
Rough and Ready Cowboys
Rough and Ready Homesteaders
Rough and Ready Loggers (available 7/94)

Rough and Ready Outlaws and Lawmen (available 6/94)
Rough and Ready Prospectors
Rough and Ready Railroaders

X-ray Vision Series

Each is 48 pages and $9.95 paper.
Looking Inside the Brain
Looking Inside Cartoon Animation
Looking Inside Caves and Caverns
Looking Inside Sports Aerodynamics
Looking Inside Sunken Treasures
Looking Inside Telescopes and the Night Sky

Ordering Information

Please check your local bookstore for our books, or call **1-800-888-7504** to order direct. All orders are shipped via UPS; see chart below to calculate your shipping charge for U.S. destinations. **No post office boxes please; we must have a street address to ensure delivery.** If the book you request is not available, we will hold your check until we can ship it. Foreign orders will be shipped surface rate unless otherwise requested; please enclose $3 for the first item and $1 for each additional item.

For U.S. Orders Totaling	Add
Up to $15.00	$4.25
$15.01 to $45.00	$5.25
$45.01 to $75.00	$6.25
$75.01 or more	$7.25

Methods of Payment

Check, money order, American Express, MasterCard, or Visa. We cannot be responsible for cash sent through the mail. For credit card orders, include your card number, expiration date, and your signature, or call **1-800-888-7504**. American Express card orders can only be shipped to billing address of cardholder. Sorry, no C.O.D.'s. Residents of sunny New Mexico, add 6.2% tax to total.

Address all orders and inquiries to:
John Muir Publications
P.O. Box 613
Santa Fe, NM 87504
(505) 982-4078
(800) 888-7504